FAMILY LAW AND CUL

EUROPEAN FAMILY LAW SERIES

Published by the Organising Committee of the
Commission on European Family Law

Prof. Katharina Boele-Woelki (Utrecht)
Prof. Frederique Ferrand (Lyon)
Prof. Cristina Gonzalez Beilfuss (Barcelona)
Prof. Maarit Jantera-Jareborg (Uppsala)
Prof. Nigel Lowe (Cardiff)
Prof. Dieter Martiny (Frankfurt/Oder)
Prof. Walter Pintens (Leuven)

FAMILY LAW AND CULTURE IN EUROPE

Developments, Challenges and Opportunities

Edited by

Katharina BOELE-WOELKI
Nina DETHLOFF
Werner GEPHART

intersentia

Cambridge – Antwerp – Portland

Intersentia Publishing Ltd.
Sheraton House | Castle Park
Cambridge | CB3 0AX | United Kingdom
Tel.: +44 1223 370 170 | Email: mail@intersentia.co.uk

Distribution for the UK:
NBN International
Airport Business Centre, 10 Thornbury Road
Plymouth, PL6 7 PP
United Kingdom
Tel.: +44 1752 202 301 | Fax: +44 1752 202 331
Email: orders@nbninternational.com

Distribution for the USA and Canada:
International Specialized Book Services
920 NE 58th Ave. Suite 300
Portland, OR 97213
USA
Tel.: +1 800 944 6190 (toll free)
Email: info@isbs.com

Distribution for Austria:
Stämpfli Verlag AG
Wölflistrasse 1
Postfach 5662
3001 Bern
Switserland
Tel.: +41 31 300 66 77
Email: verlag@staempfli.com

Distribution for other countries:
Intersentia Publishing nv
Groenstraat 31
2640 Mortsel
Belgium
Tel.: +32 3 680 15 50
Email: mail@intersentia.be

Family Law and Culture in Europe. Developments, Challenges and
Opportunities
Katharina Boele-Woelki, Nina Dethloff and Werner Gephart (eds.)

© 2014 Intersentia
  Cambridge – Antwerp – Portland
  www.intersentia.com | www.intersentia.co.uk

ISBN 978-1-78068-159-7
D/2014/7849/99
NUR 822

British Library Cataloguing in Publication Data. A catalogue record for this book is
available from the British Library.

PREFACE

The fifth conference of the Commission on European Family Law (CEFL) on 'Family Law and Culture in Europe: Developments, Challenges and Opportunities' was held in Bonn in August 2013 in collaboration with the University of Bonn and the Käte Hamburger Center for Advanced Study in the Humanities 'Law as Culture', which aims to contribute to an understanding of the cultural dimension of law and the promotion of the research on law from the perspective of the humanities. The participation of more than 200 participants from around 33 countries made the conference a valuable experience and fostered a stimulating discussion during the three conference days.

The discussions were introduced by eminent conference speakers from all over Europe. Additionally, twelve young researchers from eight different countries were selected after a call for papers. They presented their research in four parallel working groups which addressed Cross-Border Family Relationships, Transnational Families, The (Un-)Wanted Child, and the Relationship Breakup. Their papers are also included in this volume.

The book consists of five parts. It starts with four presentations of the CEFL Principles on Property Relations between Spouses. Part 2 examines the breakup of (non-)formalized relationships with special reference to unmarried cohabitation and the current debate on its legislation. It also addresses alternative instruments of conflict resolution in family law like the Irish collaborative law approach. Part 3 analyses the interdependence between legal, social and biological parenthood. It also deals with the problems of cross-border surrogacy as well as mechanisms for the anonymous relinquishment of children and baby boxes. It ends with a contribution on legal issues concerning stepfamilies. Part 4 addresses the legal aspects on international family relationships and contains a critical view on the 2011 Proposal for a Regulation on jurisdiction, applicable law and the recognition and enforcement of decisions in matters of matrimonial property regimes. It also analyses the notion of 'habitual residence' in European family law and refers to the criteria of nationality and domicile as a connecting factor for private international law questions regarding same-sex relationships. Finally, Part 5 reveals interesting aspects of transnational families such as the EU citizenship. It also reports about recent research on the effects of the new Moroccan Family Code on Moroccan nationals living abroad. The last contribution on family sociology explores the question why and to what extent culture matters in family law either as a constraint or as a condition. Moreover, it critically investigates the concept of European universalism which might bridge the gap between different legal cultures as far as family law is concerned.

The conference organizers and editors of the book are very grateful to the German Federal Ministry of Education and Research, the Alexander von Humboldt Foundation and the Käte Hamburger Center for Advanced Study in the Humanities 'Law as Culture' who generously supported the conference. Thanks are also due to the University of Bonn for making it possible for international and comparative family lawyers in Europe and from abroad to meet again in order to exchange ideas and to discuss new developments. Cordial thanks are owed to Dr. Steffen Mehlich from the Alexander von Humboldt Stiftung and Ramona Pisal, president of the German Women Lawyers Association, who both addressed the participants during the conference. Finally, without the valuable support of the staff of both the Institute for German, European and International Family Law and the Käte Hamburger Center for the Advanced Study in the Humanities 'Law as Culture', the conference could not have taken place. Many thanks for all their dedication and enthusiasm!

Katharina Boele-Woelki, Nina Dethloff and Werner Gephart
Bonn and Utrecht, April 2014

CONTENTS

PART FOUR
INTERNATIONAL FAMILY RELATIONSHIPS

**The Proposal for a Regulation on Matrimonial Property: A Critique
of the Proposed Rule on the Immutability of the Applicable Law**

**'Habitual Residence' in European Family Law: The Diversity,
Coherence and Transparency of a Challenging Notion**

**New Approaches to Same-Sex Marriage: The End of Nationality as a
Connecting Factor?**

**Protection Orders across Europe: First Remarks on Regulation
No. 606/2013**

PART FIVE
TRANSNATIONAL FAMILIES: ACROSS NATIONS AND CULTURES

Family Life and EU Citizenship: The Discovery of the Substance
of the EU Citizen's Rights and its Genuine Enjoyment

Private and Family Life versus Morals and Tradition in the Case Law
of the ECtHR

Real-Life International Family Law: Belgian Empirical Research
on Cross-Border Family Law

LIST OF AUTHORS

Professor Anne Barlow
Professor of Family Law and Policy, University of Exeter

Professor Katharina Boele-Woelki
Professor for Private International Law and Comparative Law, University of Utrecht, Utrecht Centre for European Research into Family Law (UCERF); Chair of the Commission on European Family Law

Professor Andrea Bonomi
Professor for Comparative Law and Private International Law at the Faculty of Law and Criminal Justice, University of Lausanne; Center of Comparative, European and International Law (CDCEI)

Professor Gabriele Britz
Justice at the German Federal Constitutional Court; Professor for German Public Law and European Law, University of Gießen

Professor Christine Budzikiewicz
Professor of Civil Law and Private International Law, University of Marburg

Angela d'Angelo
Post-doctoral Researcher at the Sant'Anna School of Advanced Studies of Pisa

Stuart Davis
Solicitor; PhD Candidate at the University of Reading

Professor Nina Dethloff
Professor for Civil Law, Comparative Law, Private International Law and European Private Law, University of Bonn, Institute for German, European and International Family Law; Vice Director of the Käte Hamburger Center for Advanced Study in the Humanities 'Law as Culture'

Dr Eva de Götzen
Teaching Assistant at the University of Milan

Dr Martin Engel
Post-doctoral Researcher and Assistant Lecturer at the Ludwig Maximilians University, Munich

Dr Claire Fenton-Glynn
College Teaching Officer at Lucy Cavendish College, University of Cambridge

Professor Frédérique Ferrand
Professor at the Institute of Comparative Law Edouard Lambert, University Jean Moulin 3, Lyon

Professor Marie-Claire Foblets
Director of the Department of Law and Anthropology, Max Planck Institute for Social Anthropology, Halle/Saale; Professor of Law, University of Louvain

Professor Werner Gephart
Professor for Sociology at the Institute for Political Science and Sociology, University of Bonn; Director of the Käte Hamburger Center for Advanced Study in the Humanities 'Law as Culture'

Connie Healy
PhD Candidate at the National University of Ireland

Dr Katharina Hilbig-Lugani
Post-doctoral Researcher and Assistant Lecturer at the University of Göttingen

Katharina Kaesling
PhD Candidate and Academic Assistant at the University of Bonn

Professor Nigel Lowe
Professor of Law, Cardiff Law School

Professor emeritus Dieter Martiny
Professor Emeritus, Europe-University Viadrina in Frankfurt/Oder; Guest Researcher at the Max Planck Institute for Comparative and International Private Law, Hamburg

Françoise Monéger
Former Justice at the French Cour de Cassation

Marketa Rihova Batista
PhD Candidate at the Ludwig Maximilians University, Munich

Professor Anna Singer
Professor of Private Law, Uppsala University

Professor Tone Sverdrup
Professor at the Institute for Private Law, University of Oslo

Dr Jinske Verhellen
Post-doctoral Assistant at the University of Ghent

Kajsa Walleng
PhD Candidate at Uppsala University

Geoffrey Willems
PhD Candidate and Teaching Assistant at the Catholic University of Louvain

PART ONE

THE CEFL PRINCIPLES
ON PROPERTY RELATIONS
BETWEEN SPOUSES

GENERAL RIGHTS AND DUTIES IN THE CEFL PRINCIPLES ON PROPERTY RELATIONS BETWEEN SPOUSES

Katharina BOELE-WOELKI

Contents

1. A NEW SET OF PRINCIPLES OF EUROPEAN FAMILY LAW

In 2013, the CEFL finished its Principles Regarding Property Relations between Spouses after more than six years of intensive work.[1] The field of law which has been explored from a comparative perspective is commonly denoted as matrimonial property law. It is a complicated area of the law, which is regulated differently in the European jurisdictions that have been taken into account in CEFL's comparative survey. Moreover, the CEFL took the necessary time to consider every single detail at great length, since we were not under pressure from any organisation. A total of 17 meetings of the Organising Committee[2] and one expert meeting of CEFL experts who wrote a national report[3] were dedicated

---

[1]   See Boele-Woelki/Jänterä-Jareborg, *Initial Results of the Work of the CEFL in the Field of Property Relations between Spouses*, in: Boele-Woelki/Miles/Scherpe (eds), *The Future of Family Property in Europe*, European Family Law Series No. 29, 2011, pp. 47–62.

[2]   Consisting of Frédérique Ferrand, Cristina González Beilfuss, Maarit Jänterä-Jareborg, Nigel Lowe, Dieter Martiny, Walter Pintens and this author.

[3]   Consisting of the Organising Committee and Masha Antokolskaia, Anne Barlow, Bente Braat, Nina Dethloff, Ruth Farrugio, Miloš Hatapka, Milana Hrusaková, Achilles Koutsouradis, Kirsti Kurki-Suonio, Ingrid LundAndersen, Andrzej Mączyñski, Jane Mair, Miguel Martín-Casals, Filip Melzer, Valentinas Mikelenas, Guilherme De Oliveira, Salvatore

to the drafting of this new set of European Family Law Principles. The result is contained in the book[4] which all the participants in the 5th CEFL Conference[5] have received.

This contribution focuses on the rights and duties of the spouses. The relevant Principles are laid down in the first Chapter which can be considered as the general part of the whole set of Principles. Right from the outset it was clear that such a general part would be included and that it would naturally be placed at the beginning of the Principles. The two other Chapters and Sections are subsequently presented in this book by Nigel Lowe,[6] Dieter Martiny,[7] and Frédérique Ferrand.[8]

2. GENERAL AND SPECIFIC STRUCTURAL ISSUES

The structure of the Principles is clear. Three chapters address all the issues – as far as the CEFL was able to consider – that should be regulated in the field of property relations between spouses. Two matrimonial property regimes have been drafted: the participation in acquisitions and the community of acquisitions.

Table 1. Overview of the Chapters and Sections

Preamble	
Chapter I: General Rights and Duties of the Spouses	
Chapter II: Marital Property Agreements	
Chapter III: Matrimonial Property Regimes	
Section A: Participation in Acquisitions	Section B: Community of Acquisitions

The whole set entails 58 Principles. Each Principle consists of four elements: the text of the Principle in the English, French and German languages (*Principle*); an overview of the international and European instruments which regulate the issue addressed in the Principle (*international instruments*); extensive comparative overviews of the 26 European jurisdictions represented in the CEFL as regards the aspects addressed in each Principle (*comparative overview*) and

---

Patti, Marianne Roth, Ingeborg Schwenzer, Geoffrey Shannon, Tone Sverdrup, Orsolya Szeibert, Velina Todorova and Emilia Weiss.

[4] *Principles of European Family Law Regarding Property Relations between Spouses*, European Family Law Series No. 33, 2013.

[5] The conference took place in Bonn from 29–31 August 2013.

[6] *Marital Property Agreements*, in this volume, pp. 13–23.

[7] *The Participation in Acquisitions Regime*, in this volume, pp. 25–35.

[8] *The Community of Acquisitions Regime*, in this volume, pp. 37–61.

motivations, justifications and explanations of the content of each Principle (*comment*).

Chapter I contains nine Principles which address the following issues.

Table 2. General Rights and Duties of the Spouses

General application 4:1	
Equality of spouses 4:2	Legal capacity of spouses 4:3
Contribution to the needs of the family 4:4	Protection of the family home and the household goods 4:5
Protection of the leased family home 4:6	Representation 4:7
Duty to inform 4:8	Freedom to enter into marital property agreements 4:9

In the following each Principle of Chapter I will be briefly introduced. All information is derived from the publication of the Principles[9] that contains extensive references to national reports and international and European instruments. First, however, a concise introduction to the Preamble which precedes the three Chapters will be given.

3. CEFL'S AIMS AND OBJECTIVES

The specific underlying values and concepts, which have guided the CEFL in its search for a well-balanced and consistent set of Principles, are explained in the respective comments on each individual Principle. In addition, the Preamble provides explanations of the aims and objectives of this set of Principles. It also includes both generally acknowledged considerations and commonly felt desires with regard to the situation of family law in Europe as well as the European values regarding the equality of spouses which functioned as the main guideline in the drafting process.

The Preamble refers to the free movement of persons in Europe which is hindered by the existing differences in family law systems. It is generally acknowledged that, to date, in cross-border situations spouses cannot rely on the recognition of their matrimonial property regime when changing residence. The unification of private international law rules (jurisdiction, applicable law, recognition and enforcement) through a Regulation in matters of matrimonial

---

9   See note 4.

property regimes[10] is unable to completely eliminate the obstacles experienced by European citizens moving across jurisdictions.[11] As with the previous sets of Principles the CEFL's main objective in drafting the Principles regarding Property Relations between Spouses is that they can be used in the harmonisation process of family law in Europe. If the CEFL Principles play a role in this development the ultimate goal has been achieved. Harmonisation will lead to more certainty in cross-border cases and will contribute to the development of a truly European area of law and justice.[12]

Furthermore, the Preamble contains specific considerations which address issues regarding the property relations between spouses and the family.

First and foremost, the CEFL wishes to contribute to the equality of spouses which is a commonly acknowledged principle throughout Europe by introducing rules which better live up to the goal of equal rights and equal opportunities. This Principle is of paramount importance and is indisputable. In addition to equality between the spouses, the principles of sharing and fairness, solidarity, flexibility, legal certainty, protection of the weaker spouse, and the promotion of party autonomy are likewise of fundamental importance in this area of the law. The drafting of the Principles, on the other hand, was specifically guided by concerns that the proposed system should be relatively easy to understand and that the proposed rules should be such as to enable spouses to settle their conflicts on their own without needing to engage lawyers and the courts in the dispute.

Specific objectives expressed in the Preamble concern the protection of the family home and – as regards the dissolution of the matrimonial property regime – the fair participation of each spouse in the wealth (earnings, capital and assets) acquired during the marriage, irrespective of the nature of his or her contribution thereto (for example, paid employment, household work and/or child-rearing).

Chapter I on the rights and duties of the spouses transforms many of CEFL's considerations – others will be explained in the following contributions[13] – into mandatory rules.

---

[10]   Proposal of a Regulation regarding jurisdiction, applicable law and the recognition and enforcement of decisions in matters of matrimonial property regimes, COM(2011) 126/2.

[11]   See Gray/Quinzá Redondo, *Stress-Testing the EU Proposal on Matrimonial Property Regimes: Co-operation between EU private international law instruments on family matters and succession*, Familie & Recht 2013, available at www.familieenrecht.nl/tijdschrift/fenr/2013/11/ FENR-D-13-00008, (last accessed 26.02.2014).

[12]   See Boele-Woelki, *Why and How to Accommodate an Optional European Family Law*, in: Ellger/Mankowski/Merkt/Remien/Witzleb (eds), *Festschrift für Dieter Martiny*, 2014 (forthcoming).

[13]   See notes 6–8.

4. BRIEF COMMENTARY ON EACH PRINCIPLE OF CHAPTER I

> **Principle 4:1**
> *The Principles contained in this Chapter apply irrespective of the matrimonial property regime.*

The importance and relevance of the Principles contained in the first Chapter is clearly expressed in the very first Principle on the general application. All other eight Principles of Chapter I should be applied irrespective of the spouses' matrimonial property regime, be it a separation, participation or a community regime, be it either based on a marital property agreement or on a default system that applies in the absence of a marital property agreement. Besides, the term 'irrespective' implies that the rights and duties of Chapter I are intended to be mandatory. Consequently, the spouses may not set them aside by an agreement and this prohibition applies to all marriages. It goes without saying that marriages include same-sex and different-sex couples.

> **Principle 4:2**
> *Both spouses have equal rights and duties.*

Undoubtedly, the equality of spouses is of paramount importance. Moreover, it is so self-evident that initially we thought that it would not be necessary to stress this principle also in our Principles, since it is strongly embedded in binding international and European instruments. However, in our pluralistic societies different cultures and different value systems co-exist and therefore safeguarding the equality of spouses in a specific Principle has been considered indispensable. Equality justifies participation in property acquired by the other spouse; equality forms the foundation for protecting the spouse against the other spouse's transactions and equality justifies treating principal carers at home the same as breadwinners. Both kinds of contributions to the welfare of the family and to the acquisitions of property should carry the same weight.

> **Principle 4:3**
> *Subject to the following Principles, each spouse has full legal capacity and in particular is free to enter into legal transactions with the other spouse and with third persons.*

The next Principle regarding the legal capacity of the spouses has evidently been included for the same reason as Principle 4:2. In all jurisdictions that were surveyed in our research all restrictions on married women's capacity have been removed. For a long time, also under the influence of the Convention on the Elimination of All Forms of Discrimination against Women of 1979, marriage no longer incapacitates either spouse. However, in our multicultural societies in Europe some religious and cultural groups do not accept the full legal capacity of married women. Therefore it is essential that both spouses have full and equal legal capacity; that they are free to enter into transactions with each other and with a third person.

There are, however, some restrictions on this freedom regarding transactions concerning the family home and the household goods and regarding certain kinds of transactions between the spouses in order to protect third parties; think, for example, of guarantees and the loan agreements of sureties. These restrictions aim to protect the spouses themselves or to protect the interests of the family. These protection rules are contained in other Principles.

Principle 4:4
(1) *Each spouse should contribute to the needs of the family according to his or her ability.*
(2) *The contribution to the needs of the family encompasses contributions to the running of the household, the personal needs of the spouses and the maintenance, upbringing and education of the children.*
(3) *If a spouse does not fulfil his or her obligation to contribute to the needs of the family the other spouse may request the competent authority to determine the contribution.*

Principle 4:4 addresses three issues: first, the obligation to contribute to the needs of the family; second, a definition of the needs of the family and, third, the determination of the contribution by a competent authority if one of the spouses fails to fulfil his or her duty to contribute. It follows from the first section that the spouses' contribution is according to their respective ability and capabilities. This is the common core of the jurisdictions surveyed. Section two classifies what the needs of the family entail. Such a definition is needed since otherwise we do not know whether or not a spouse has fulfilled his or her duty to contribute. It is up to the competent authority to decide how and to what extent the spouse's contribution will be determined. From the national systems it can be derived that usually it is a maintenance claim.

Principle 4:5
(1) *Any act of disposal of rights to the family home or household goods requires the consent of both spouses.*
(2) *Any act of disposal by one spouse without the consent of the other is valid if the latter ratifies it.*
(3) *If a spouse refuses or is unable to give consent, the other spouse may request authorisation by the competent authority.*
(4) *Any act of disposal in breach of the preceding paragraphs may be annulled by the competent authority upon the application of the non-consenting spouse.*

One of the Principles which restricts the freedom of the spouses to enter into legal transactions with third persons as stated in Principle 4:3 is Principle 4:5. It protects the family home and the household goods. The majority of European legal systems compared in our study define the family home as the habitual dwelling place of the family, whereas household goods are often not defined or are defined differently. In some jurisdictions, for example, valuable paintings, cars or domestic animals are excluded from the concept of household goods. In our view, household goods should cover movables that are used within the family home. The most important message contained in Principle 4:5 is that any act of disposal of rights to the family home and the household goods requires the consent of both spouses, even if only one of them is the owner. The consent of the other spouse can also be provided at a later stage, but if it is unreasonably withheld then authorisation by the competent authority can be requested. As a result, acts of disposal in breach of Principle 4:5 are voidable.

Principle 4:6
(1) *Where the family home is leased to one spouse, the lease is deemed to belong to both spouses, even if it has been concluded before the marriage.*
(2) *One spouse may not terminate or modify the lease without the consent of the other.*
(3) *The landlord should notify both spouses to terminate the lease.*

The leased family home should also be protected in the same way as the matrimonial home that is owned by the spouses. The lease should be deemed to belong to both spouses even if only one of them actually entered into the contract. Principle 4:6 establishes that the other spouse holds the position of a legal tenant with the same rights and obligations as the contractual tenant. As a result the consent of both spouses is required if the leasehold is terminated or modified. This reflects the common core. In some jurisdictions the rules protecting the leased family home are part of tenancy law.

> **Principle 4:7**
> (1) *One spouse may authorise the other spouse to represent him or her in legal transactions.*
> (2) *When a spouse is unable to express his or her intentions, the competent authority may authorise the other spouse*
>   (a) *to act alone where the consent of his or her spouse would otherwise be required;*
>   (b) *to represent his or her spouse when the latter has the power to act alone.*

There is also a clear common core as regards spousal representation which in the majority of the jurisdictions surveyed is regulated by specific rules. What are the main considerations upon which Principe 4:7 is based? The starting point is that generally spouses trust each other and assume that they are authorised ex lege to act on behalf of the other due to their marital status. However, it follows from the right to self-determination that the represented spouse's consent should be required since his or her legal position is affected. This means that each spouse should have the freedom to decide whether or not the other spouse may act as a representative. Consent is required; however, whether this should explicitly be given or whether an implicit authorisation suffices has not been regulated by the CEFL Principle. Thus, the formal requirement has been left to national law. This means that once a national system adopts this Principle it should provide a rule which addresses this issue. In which situation the competent authority can decide and which decisions should be taken has been regulated in the second section.

> **Principle 4:8**
> *Each spouse has the duty to inform the other about his or her assets and debts and about significant acts of administration in so far as it is necessary to enable the other to exercise his or her rights.*

The objective of the duty to inform Principle is twofold. It encompasses information about assets and debts and about significant acts of administration. This duty to inform and the right to be informed applies during the marriage. It should be distinguished from the spouses' duty to disclose upon entering into a marital property contract. This is specifically regulated in Chapter II. Principle 4:8 is based on a common core Principle. The duty to inform is also supported by

Resolutions and Recommendations of the Council of Europe which were adopted in 1978 and 1989. Evidently, it belongs to the primary regime as a mandatory rule. Do spouses have to disclose everything? It depends. The answer is in the affirmative as regards assets and debts without any restriction and regarding significant acts of administration but only in so far as this is necessary to enable the other spouse to exercise his or her rights. Which acts fall under this restriction? The acquisition, alienation and encumbrance of immovable property, for example, but also loan agreements or significant gifts given by a spouse. The aim is to reduce the risk of the mismanagement of property by one spouse to the detriment of the other spouse.

> **Principle 4:9**
> *Spouses should be free to enter into agreements determining their marital property relationship.*

The last Principle of Chapter I is dedicated to the spouses' contractual freedom. This freedom concerns the choice of an appropriate matrimonial property regime, but also within the framework of a single regime modifications are possible. The ability to enter into a private arrangement creates a certain degree of legal certainty, in particular when the couple move to other jurisdictions. In the majority of jurisdictions which have been included in our comparative study spouses enjoy broad freedom to construct a system of their own choice.

However, here the civil law–common law divide is visible. Pre-nuptial and post-nuptial property agreements are allowed in civil law jurisdictions albeit with some restrictions, whereas in the common law jurisdictions, such as Ireland and England and Wales, the binding force of marital property agreements is not accepted. The starting point in these countries is a separation of property with the possibility of a distribution by the court at the end of the marriage. The court has wide discretion regarding the distribution of assets. However, due to recent case law the impact of marital property agreements is under discussion in England and Wales. In this discussion our Principles might be a source of inspiration.

Principle 4:9 should also be considered to be a mandatory rule; it constitutes the intermediary between Chapter I and Chapter II.

5. A COMPREHENSIVE PRIMARY REGIME

Following most of the 26 jurisdictions that have been included in CEFL's comparative survey – this is in fact the common core – the CEFL has opted for a set of rules which applies irrespective of whether a contractual or default matrimonial property regime governs the property relations of the spouses. Thus, the first Chapter reflects the personal or general legal effects of marriage in relation to property issues. In this context, the French term *régime primaire* is also known; however, it all means the same. In forming the first Chapter, the rights and duties are given a more prominent role than they currently have in many European jurisdictions. None of the European systems which the CEFL has studied contains such a comprehensive primary regime, nevertheless in one way or another they more or less adhere to the Principles contained in the CEFL's Principles. Based upon the common core they constitute European family law. Hence, there is nothing new under the sun. However, the existing national legal rules have not only been re-stated in CEFL's new set of Principles but have also been made clearer and more explicit.

MARITAL PROPERTY AGREEMENTS

Nigel LOWE

Contents

1. INTRODUCTION

Chapter II of the CEFL's *Principles of European Family Law Regarding Property Relations Between Spouses*[1] deals with what is entitled 'Marital Property Agreements' by which is broadly meant agreements made before or during the marriage determining the spouses' property relationship. Insofar as statistics are available,[2] the evidence is that the number of such agreements has become more frequent.

---

[1]   BOELE-WOELKI, FERRAND, GONZÁLEZ BEILFUSS, JÄNTERÄ-JAREBORG, LOWE, MARTINY, PINTENS, *Principles of European Family Law Regarding Property Relations Between Spouses* (2013, Intersentia).

[2]   See the Comparative Overview to Principle 4:10, pp. 102–104.

1.1. SOME BASIC DILEMMAS

In drawing up these Principles it was sought, on the one hand, to promote spousal autonomy and, on the other, to balance the freedom to make agreements with the need to give fair protection to each spouse and to third parties. Spousal autonomy has been a guiding philosophy underlying all the CEFL's Principles, as can be seen in its *Divorce Principles*, which essentially promoted divorce by consent with little or no State interference depending on whether there are children under the age of 16 and, more particularly, in its *Maintenance Principles*, according to Principle 2:10 of which, spouses are permitted to make maintenance agreements again subject to minimal State scrutiny.[3] But unbridled freedom to make marital property agreements could lead to injustice and the CEFL has sought to balance that freedom against the important general purpose of matrimonial property law to grant each spouse the right to obtain a fair share in the property of the other[4] and to give fair protection to third parties against fraudulent manoeuvres.

To achieve this balancing act, the *Property Principles* provide in the first instance for the basic freedom to make martial property agreements but nevertheless require such agreements to conform to certain conditions as to form and disclosure. The Principles also prescribe the obligations of notaries or other persons with comparable functions; set out the effects of such agreements against third parties and, consistently with other Principles on distribution (that is Principles 4:32 and 4:57) and Principle 2:6 of the *Maintenance Principles,* empower a competent authority to set aside or adjust the agreement in cases of exceptional hardship.

1.2. ACCOMMODATING THE DIVERSITY OF EXISTING APPROACHES

Of course, a fundamental difficulty bedevilling the formulation of the Principles is how best to accommodate the multiplicity and diversity of existing approaches. In the context of marital property agreements the common law jurisdictions presented the challenge that unlike civil law jurisdictions, they do not have matrimonial property *regimes* as such. Furthermore the courts' post-divorce distributive powers embrace both property and maintenance. Consequently in a very fundamental way the concept of marital property agreements differs from

---

[3]   See BOELE-WOELKI, FERRAND, GONZÁLEZ BEILFUSS, JÄNTERÄ-JAREBORG, LOWE, MARTINY, PINTENS, *Principles of European Family Law Regarding Divorce and Maintenance Between Former Spouses* (2004, Intersentia).

[4]   A principle enshrined, for instance, in the Council of Europe's Recommendation, R(89)1 on Contributions Following Divorce (January, 1989).

all the civil law systems. On the other hand, at any rate in the sense that such agreements in the common law context must of necessity be aimed at curbing or, at the very least, influencing the court's exercise of its redistributive powers, there is a very broad analogy with the Nordic systems of deferred community inasmuch as the function of marital property agreements is, to a large extent, aimed at modifying the rules on participation at the end of a matrimonial property regime.

The common law and Nordic jurisdictions arguably share another characteristic, namely that there is no choice of so-called regimes. Consequently the option of choosing one of several regimes does not exist.[5] A similar position obtained in Hungary before their November 2009 reforms.[6] In most civil law jurisdictions, however, spouses can choose between several existing regimes and, in some, different combinations are possible so that different matrimonial property regimes apply to different types of property or assets, as is the case in Lithuania and, by the technique of excluding certain assets from a particular regime, in Portugal.

In most civil law jurisdictions spouses can modify the statutory or chosen regime and in some, such as in Austria, Belgium, France, Hungary, Netherlands, Portugal and Russia, can create their own tailor-made regime. But this is not possible in Germany, Italy, Malta, Slovakia, Spain and Switzerland.[7]

Apart from the issue of choosing or modifying a particular regime, another issue upon which there is variation is whether or not a distinction is made between *pre-* and *post-*marital property agreements. Whilst many jurisdictions do not make any distinction at all, a number do. At the extremes, pre-marital property agreements are not permitted at all in Italy and Slovakia and post-marital agreements are not permitted in Portugal. Some jurisdictions such as France and Germany, impose some restrictions on making post-marital agreements.[8]

There are, of course, other important issues and differences, for example, those determining, where relevant, to which category of assets (or mass or pot) particular property belongs; the ability to modify the administration of assets; the ability to modify the distribution of assets; distinguishing the position according to whether the marriage ends upon the death of one of the spouses or upon divorce and, finally providing different rules for where it is sought to change as opposed to modifying the matrimonial property regime.[9]

It is not possible, of course, to reconcile all the differences and, in any event, the Principles take a broad brush approach and strive to avoid points of detail

---

5   Though this is not say that in the Nordic jurisdictions spouses cannot make considerable modifications to the application of the legal rules, see the Comparative Overview to Principle 4:9 at p. 95.

6   See the Comparative Overview to Principle 4:10, p. 100.

7   For more detail see the Comparative Overview to Principle 4:10, p. 105.

8   See the Comparative Overview to Principle 4:10, pp. 107–109.

9   For full comparative analysis of all these issues and approaches, see the Comparative Overview to Principle 4:10, pp. 110–116.

that inevitably arise in any given system. Wherever possible, however, the Principles seek to embrace what may be considered the common core, at any rate, in a functional sense. All that said, before looking at the Principles themselves, three general points may be made:

(1) Notwithstanding the common law position, the basic concept of a matrimonial property agreement contained in Principle 4:10 refers to matrimonial property *regimes*. The expectation is that the common law jurisdictions will be able to interpret this provision broadly and purposively and apply the Principles accordingly to their systems.
(2) No overall formal technical definition of a marital property agreement is provided as that might lead to sterile debate. Instead, the approach taken in Principle 4:10 is to describe the *concept* of such an agreement. Although the broad term 'agreement' is used, this is not to deny that such agreements have a contractual nature, though, in any event, they can ultimately be overridden by a competent authority as provided for in Principle 4:15.
(3) The Principles make no substantive distinction between pre-marital and post-marital property agreements.

2. THE SPECIFIC PRINCIPLES

2.1. THE GENERAL FREEDOM TO MAKE AGREEMENTS

As has been explained by Professor Boele-Woelki,[10] Principle 4:9 enshrines the basic principle that spouses should be free to enter into agreements determining their marital property relationship. This basic standpoint reflects the common core of all the jurisdictions surveyed.

Principle 4:9 is in effect made more specific by Principle 4:10, which provides:

'(1) In a marital property agreement made before the marriage the future spouses may choose their matrimonial property regime.
(2) During the marriage the spouse may modify their matrimonial property regime or change it for another regime.'

By permitting spouses or prospective spouses to make a matrimonial property agreement at any time, Principle 4:10 draws no fundamental distinction between pre-marital and post-marital property agreements.

Although Principle 4:10 entitles spouses to choose or change a property regime for *all* their property, this does not prevent them from restricting their

---

[10] See above at p. 11.

property regime to certain parts of their assets, for example, to their immovable property (in fact this can be done by expressly agreeing that specific assets be governed by the chosen regime or that specified assets are classed as 'non marital property'). It is similarly open to spouses or potential spouses to restrict their matrimonial property regime to a limited period of time.

Under the CEFL Principles, the regimes that can be chosen are either the participation in acquisitions or community of acquisitions regimes. But it is of course open to national law to determine whether other property regimes exist and can be chosen.

Principle 4:10 (2) permits changes from one regime to another or to modify a chosen or default regime. In each case, however, these changes can only be effected by 'a marital property agreement' made in accordance with Principles 4:11 and 4:12, which are discussed below.

Permitting modifications gives the spouses or potential spouses the freedom to shape the property regime according to their own particular situation and needs. If no choice or modifications have been made, the default system will apply.

2.2. FORMALITIES

In all the jurisdictions surveyed and which permit marital property agreements to made, certain formalities have to be observed for the agreements to have any effect, though for these purposes some jurisdictions make a distinction between pre-marital and post-marital property agreements.

Principle 4:11 takes a minimal approach by requiring that marital property agreements:

> 'should be drawn up by a notary or other legal professional with comparable functions, be dated and should be signed by both spouses.'

Requiring that such agreements have to be drawn up by a notary, or other legal professional with comparable functions, before they have effect, reflects the common core, at any rate, outside the Nordic jurisdictions. The rationale underlying this requirement is to ensure that in making such an important agreement the spouses or potential spouses have impartial legal advice before making them. This point is further underscored by Principle 4:13 which is concerned with the obligations of notaries etc. (see below).

To accommodate the fact that in many jurisdictions notaries as such are unknown, Principle 4:11 also refers to 'other legal professional with comparable functions' by which is meant legal practitioners involved in the drafting or in advising on the drafting of such agreements.

Apart from the involvement of notaries or other legal professional with comparable functions, Principle 4:11 stipulates that the agreement must be in writing, dated and signed by both spouses. This requirement reflects the common core. However, Principle 4:11 only sets out the minimum requirements and does not prevent national law from requiring more. It is a common requirement, for instance, that the spouses' signatures have to be witnessed. Some jurisdictions require, particularly for post-marital property agreements, that they be formally registered or that they be approved by a court.

2.3. DISCLOSURE

Principle 4:12 addresses the important issue of disclosure and provides:

> 'When entering into a marital property agreement the spouses should be under a mutual duty to disclose their assets and debts.'

In providing for a general duty of disclosure, Principle 4:12 does not follow the common core, at any rate among civil law jurisdictions (it is the common core among the common law jurisdictions), but the view was taken that it inevitably followed from Principle 4:8 by which spouses are under a general duty to inform each other about their debts and assets,[11] that there be a mutual duty of disclosure when making marital property agreements. Furthermore, given the increased incidence of cohabitation, it made no sense to distinguish pre-marital property agreements from those made during the marriage. This Principle is also in line with the general policy of making no distinction between pre-marital and post-marital property agreements.

However, because it does not reflect the common core, Principle 4:12 is silent on the effects of non-disclosure, leaving that to be determined by national law. The expectation must be, however, that at any rate where the non-disclosure is significant, the agreement may be set aside.[12]

2.4. OBLIGATIONS OF NOTARIES OR OTHER LEGAL PROFESSIONALS WITH COMPARABLE FUNCTIONS

As has been seen, to constitute a marital property agreement for the purposes of these Principles, such agreements have, in accordance with Principle 4:11, to be drawn up by a notary or other legal professional with comparable functions.

---

[11]   Discussed by BOELE-WOELKI, above, pp. 10–11.

[12]   In England and Wales, where full disclosure is normally required for martial property agreements to be taken into account, it will be noted that in the leading Supreme Court decision, *Granatino v Radmacher (formerly Granatino)* [2010] UKSC 42, [2011] 1 AC 424 in which the spouses were effectively held to their pre-marital agreement, there had not in fact been full disclosure.

Principle 4:13 sets out what the obligations of such professionals should be, namely, that they should:

'(a) give impartial advice to each spouse separately;
(b) ensure that each spouse understands the legal consequences of the marital property agreement, and
(c) ensure that both spouses freely consent to the agreement.'

The three requirements listed in (a) to (c) of this Principle reflect the clear common core. It will be noted that the duties are the same regardless of whether the agreement is made before or during the marriage.

Requirements (b) and (c) are straightforward and uncontroversial and call for no further comment, but the first requirement that impartial advice be given to each spouse separately does call for further discussion. Although it is acknowledged that there is a difference between impartial and independent advice, Principle 4:13 stops short of requiring that each spouse or potential spouse be given independent advice by different notaries of or other legal professionals on the grounds of practicality and costs. However, there is nothing in the Principle that prevents national law from requiring separate advice, which is effectively the position, for example, in England and Wales and Ireland.

Principle 4:13 is silent on the effects of any breach of duty by a notary or other legal professional, again leaving that to be determined by national law. Commonly, however, breaches render the notary to disciplinary action and a liability to pay compensatory damages, but the agreement itself is not thereby invalidated.[13] In England and Wales, it is less likely that an agreement made without full legal advice would carry much weight, unless the spouse or potential spouse was clearly aware of the consequences when making the agreement.

2.5. EFFECTS AGAINST THIRD PARTIES

An important aspect of marital property agreements is their effect on third parties. This is addressed by Principle 4:14, which provides:

'As against third parties marital property agreements are binding if at the time of making the transaction with a spouse

(a) such information is publicly documented; or
(b) they knew of the relevant parts of the agreement.'

---

[13] See the Comparative Overview to Principle 4:13, pp. 126–128, where it is also noted that in Lithuania and Malta a failure to inform the parties about the content and consequences of the agreement can lead to a nullification of the agreement.

In effect, what Principle 4:14 provides is that third parties will be bound by the terms of a marital property agreement if, *at the time of making the transaction*, with a spouse or spouses they either actually knew or are deemed to know (because the information is publicly available) of the relevant part(s) of the agreement. This Principle again adopts the clear common core, though in line with the general approach, no distinction is drawn, as it is in some jurisdictions,[14] between pre-marital and post-marital property agreements. Furthermore, no distinction is drawn, again as it is in some jurisdictions,[15] between the types of property included in the agreement.

Principle 4:14 does not attempt to prescribe how information may be publicly documented, again leaving that to be determined by national law. Although it is common to provide for some form of registration,[16] that is by no means a universal solution. Switzerland, for example, abolished the need for registration in 1998.[17] Principle 4:14 reflects these different standpoints by not insisting upon a registration scheme. Moreover, it preserves the position taken in some jurisdictions, for example, Poland and Slovakia, only to fix third party liability upon actual knowledge.

Principle 4:14 does not state at what point in time third parties will be bound by a marital property agreement, again leaving that to be determined by national law. In jurisdictions where liability is dependent upon the agreements' inclusion in a publicly available document, it usually dates from its formal registration or recording, but this is not a universally accepted position.

2.6. THE COMPETENT AUTHORITY'S POWERS

The extent to which a competent authority should be able to interfere with a marital property agreement is addressed by Principle 4:15, which provides:

> 'Having regard to the circumstances when the agreement was concluded or those subsequently arising, the competent authority may, in cases of exceptional hardship, set aside or adjust a marital property agreement.'

In so empowering competent authorities, Principle 4:15 does not follow the common core, for in many civil jurisdictions and the majority of those surveyed, marital property agreements are regarded as contracts which cannot therefore

---

[14]   For example, Belgium and France, see the Comparative Overview to Principle 4:14, p. 133.
[15]   For example, Catalonia, Norway and Spain, see the Comparative Overview to Principle 4:14, pp. 132–133.
[16]   This is the position taken in the Nordic jurisdictions, Germany, Greece, Lithuania, Malta, The Netherlands and Portugal, see the Comparative Overview to Principle 4:14, pp. 131–132.
[17]   In Hungary there are no special rules governing the enforceability of marital property agreements against third parties save that they must be countersigned by a lawyer.

be modified or set aside save upon well-established contractual grounds, such as misrepresentation, fraud, duress etc. In contrast, the common law jurisdictions do empower the courts to intervene, though interestingly, in England and Wales, following the Supreme Court's ruling in *Granatino v Radmacher (formerly Granatino)*,[18] the powers to do so have become more limited, in the sense that an agreement entered into by each party with full awareness of its implications will have effect unless it can be shown that in the circumstances prevailing it would not be fair to hold the parties to their agreement. Conversely, in some civil law jurisdictions, certain 'family law' powers of intervention have been introduced either by statute, as in Catalonia, Finland, Lithuania, Portugal and Switzerland, or by case law as in Germany.[19]

The view consistently taken in these Principles is that because of the special relationship between spouse or potential spouses there needs to be some broad judicial powers of intervention. Hence, similar powers are provided in relation to participation of acquisition regime and to community of acquisitions regime are provided for in Principles 4:32 and 4:57 respectively, as they are in Principle 2:6 of the *Maintenance Principles*.

This stance is taken inter alia because in the first place, as spouses or potential spouses are emotionally dependent upon each other and trust their relationship and its future they may be led to disregard negative aspect of the agreement. Secondly, the influence of other family members should neither be disregarded nor underestimated. Thirdly, agreements are meant to be long lasting and very often do not take into account changed circumstances, such as child rearing and unforeseen family illness, that may force one of the spouses, commonly still the wife, to give up her job for the benefit of the family.

Notwithstanding all that has just been said, the powers of intervention need to be limited lest the whole point of permitting marital property agreements to be made is lost. For this reason, Principle 4:15 only permits judicial intervention in cases of *exceptional* hardship which is intended to be interpreted strictly, though not to the extent of adding further gloss by requiring the exceptional cases themselves to be extreme. That said, the concept of 'exceptional hardship' is left open, though in making an assessment regard can be had to *all* the circumstances, be they those when the agreement is made, those subsequently arising or the overall circumstances. It may be, given the requirement of impartial advice before making the agreement, that in practice it will be harder to establish exceptional hardship solely on the basis of circumstances at the time of making the agreement, but it is not impossible. One can imagine, for example, cases where a potential spouse in particular feels pressurised to make the agreement.[20]

---

[18] Above at n. 12.

[19] See the Comparative Overview to Principle 4:15, pp. 135–137.

[20] For example, where the woman is pregnant and wants her baby to born within marriage but the father is only prepared to marry if she signs the pre-marital property agreement. This

Although Principle 4:15 permits a competent authority to set aside the whole agreement, the expectation is that that remedy would be one of last resort. Given that intervention should be kept to minimum so as not to undermine the generally binding nature of marital property agreements, the first remedy must be to set aside or adjust *part* of the agreement.

3. SOME FINAL REMARKS

Chapter 11 forms an important part of the CEFL's *Property Principles*. Like the general Principles contained in Chapter 1, Principles 4:10 to 4:15 have universal application and apply irrespective of what property regime might otherwise be applicable. The statistical evidence, such that it exists, points to the increasing number of marital property agreements being made across Europe so that these Principles are very much of contemporary relevance.

As the civil law jurisdictions have long recognised, it seems right in general (though subject to certain safeguards) that spouses and potential spouses should be able to determine their property relationship for themselves. The freedom to make marital property agreements is reflected in various international instruments, for example, the 1978 Hague Convention on the law applicable to matrimonial property regimes, the Council of Europe's Resolution (78) on Equality of Spouses in Civil Law, the Convention between Denmark, Finland, Iceland, Norway and Sweden on Issues of Private International Law concerning Marriage (revised in 2006), and the French-German Agreement on the Establishment of an Optional Matrimonial Property Regime 2010.

For the common law jurisdictions in general and England and Wales in particular, the recent journey has been to move from disregarding marital property agreements altogether to giving them some effect. For the civil law jurisdictions the question, recently addressed by some, is to what extent, if at all, the competent authority should have 'family law' powers to police the parties' marital property agreements. In other words, there is some evidence of a gradual merger between the civil and common law systems.[21]

By accepting the basic freedom of spouses and potential spouses to make binding matrimonial property agreements, subject to being fully informed as to their partner's assets and debts and after receiving impartial legal advice yet nevertheless empowering a competent authority to override the agreement in

---

alone would not be enough to establish duress. For an English example of this type of scenario, see *M v M (Prenuptial Agreement)* [2002] 1 FLR 654.

[21] For a further general overall survey, see SCHERPE, 'Marital Agreements and Private Autonomy in Comparative Perspective' in *Marital Agreements and Private Autonomy in a Comparative Persepctive* (2012, Hart), pp. 443–518.

cases of exceptional hardship, Principles 4:10 to 4:15 attempt to bridge the remaining gaps between the systems. By so doing, it is hoped to provide a common way forward for all European systems.

THE PARTICIPATION IN ACQUISITIONS REGIME

Dieter MARTINY

Contents

1. THE PARTICIPATION IN ACQUISITIONS APPROACH

Participation in acquisitions is one of the two matrimonial property regimes found in the CEFL Principles (4:16 to 4:32). It forms the first part of Chapter III: matrimonial property regimes.[1] The CEFL chose the label 'participation in acquisitions' because it expresses the two main features of the regime: establishing a participation which is, however, restricted to the acquisitions.

When comparing the existing participation regimes, the CEFL primarily looked at the existing regimes described in the national reports.[2] In Catalonia

---

[1]   See BOELE-WOELKI/FERRAND/GONZALEZ BEILFUSS/JÄNTERÄ-JAREBORG/LOWE/MARTINY/PIN-
      TENS, *Principles of European Family Law Regarding Property Relations Between Spouses*,
      Cambridge, Antwerp, Portland, Intersentia, 2013.
[2]   See the Comparative Overview concerning Principle 4:16, at pp. 140–141. See also PINTENS,
      "Matrimonial Property Law in Europe", in: BOELE-WOELKI/MILES/SCHERPE (ed.), *The Future*

the default regime is the separation of property,[3] with, however, a compensation claim in the case of divorce.[4] In Catalonia there is also an optional regime of participation in acquisitions.[5] Also under French law participation in acquisitions is only an optional regime.[6] Several jurisdictions have opted for a participation regime as a default matrimonial property regime. In Greece the default system is a participation in acquisitions.[7] Of particular interest was the Swiss system of participation in acquisitions (*Errungenschaftsbeteiligung*).[8] In Germany we find a comprehensive system entailing a so-called community of accrued gains (*Zugewinngemeinschaft*).[9]

At a later stage the solutions of the French-German Agreement of 2010 instituting an optional regime of participation in accrued gains were also taken into account.[10] This bilateral agreement is of interest as it combines a primary regime (*régime primaire*) similar to French law with a participation in accrued gains closely based on the German model.[11] The Nordic systems of deferred community and the redistribution of property in common law jurisdictions have also been taken into account.[12] However, because the national reports were restricted to the two national regimes most used in practice, the CEFL did not receive that many national reports dealing in detail with a participation regime.

of Family Property in Europe, Cambridge, Antwerp, Portland, Intersentia, 2011, pp. 23, 27–32.

3   Art. 232-1–232-12 Catalan Civil Code. Former Art. 37–47 Catalan Family Code. For the reform project see MARTÍN-CASALS/RIBOT, in: Boele-Woelki/Braat/Curry-Sumner (ed.), *European Family Law in Action IV: Property Relations Between Spouses*, Antwerp, Oxford, Intersentia, 2009, Catalan Report, Q 3, at pp. 81–82.

4   Art. 232-5 Catalan Civil Code. Former Art. 41 Catalan Family Code. See MARTÍN-CASALS/ RIBOT, Catalan Report, Q 2, 18 at pp. 52, 261.

5   Art. 232-13–232-34 Catalan Civil Code. Former Art. 48–60 Catalan Family Code. See MARTÍN-CASALS/RIBOT, Catalan Report, Q 18, 57 at pp. 261–262, 605.

6   Art. 1569–1581 French Civil Code.

7   See Art. 1400–1402 Greek Civil Code and KOUTSOURADIS/KOTRONIS/HATZANTONIS, Greek Report, Q 16, 18 at pp. 246, 274–275.

8   Art. 196–220 Swiss Civil Code and SCHWENZER/BOCK, Swiss Report, Q 16, 18 at pp. 248, 292.

9   §§1363–1390 German Civil Code and DETHLOFF/MARTINY, German Report, Q 16, 18 at pp. 246, 272–273.

10 *Accord entre la République fédérale d'Allemagne et la République Française instituant un régime matrimonial optionnel de la participation aux acquêts* of 4 February 2010, *Journal Officiel de la République Française* 2013, p. 9733 (*Abkommen zwischen der Bundesrepublik Deutschland und der Französischen Republik über den Güterstand der Wahl-Zugewinngemeinschaft*), Federal Law Gazette (*Bundesgesetzblatt*) 2012 II, p. 178.

11 See FÖTSCHL, "The Common Matrimonial Property Regime of Germany and France", *European Review of Private Law* 2010, pp. 881–889 = *Yearbook of Private International Law* 2009, pp. 395–404; MARTINY, "Der neue deutsch-französische Wahlgüterstand, *Zeitschrift für Europäisches Privatrecht* 2011, pp. 577–600; MEYER, "Der neue deutsch-französische Wahlgüterstand", *Zeitschrift für das gesamte Familienrecht* 2010, pp. 612–617; SIMLER, "Le nouveau régime matrimonial optionnel franco-allemand de participation aux acquêts", *Droit de la famille* 2010 No. 5, pp. 9–19.

12 See the Comparative Overview concerning Principle 4:16, at p. 140.

The issue of the best default regime was one of the points of discussion in earlier meetings of the CEFL experts.[13] Despite a certain tendency to choose the participation in acquisitions regime as the Principles' default regime – participation in acquisitions is applicable in 11 of the analysed jurisdictions – it is presented on an equal footing together with the community system.

The participation in acquisitions regime is the first matrimonial property regime dealt with in Chapter III of the Principles, but community property is nevertheless treated with the same intensity or even more accuracy. The structure of Chapter III Section A reflects the main issues of this matrimonial property regime. Section A consists of 16 Principles. A first provision deals with the applicability of the acquisitions regime (Principle 4:16). Then follow six parts with several Principles in the same order as for the community of participation regime. Hereinafter, the concept (the Concept of participation in acquisitions; Principle 4:17) and the different categories of assets (Acquisitions, Principle 4:18; Reserved property, Principle 4:19; the Presumption of joint ownership, Principle 4:20) are explained. Some provisions on debts follow (Personal debts, Principle 4:21; Recovery of personal debts, Principle 4:22). Administration is the subject of the next part (Administration of property, Principle 4:23). Then follow rules granting each spouse, upon the termination of the regime, a right to obtain a fair share in the property of the other spouse. For this purpose it is necessary to define the stages of dissolution and liquidation. The part on dissolution determines the grounds and the date (Grounds for dissolution, Principle 4:24; Date of dissolution, Principle 4:25). The next part on the participation regime deals with liquidation (Determination and valuation of acquisitions, Principle 4:26; Detrimental transactions, Principle 4:27; Compensation, Principle 4:28). Then the participation as such is defined and dealt with (Agreement on participation, Principle 4:29; Allocation of the family home and household goods, Principle 4:30; Equal participation in the net acquisitions, Principle 4:31; Adjustment by the competent authority, Principle 4:32). This reflects only the skeleton of the property regime. Many details are dealt with in the commentaries.

2. CONCEPT OF PARTICIPATION IN ACQUISITIONS

2.1. CONCEPT

The participation in acquisitions regime aims to promote self-sufficiency, gender equality and the autonomy of the spouses. This is achieved through a separation

---

13　See BOELE-WOELKI/JÄNTERÄ-JAREBORG, "Initial Results of the Work of the CEFL in the Field of Property Relations between Spouses", in: Boele-Woelki/Miles/Scherpe (ed.), *The Future of Family Property in Europe*, Cambridge, Antwerp, Portland, Intersentia, 2011, pp. 47, 56–57.

of ownership which prevails during the regime, giving each spouse considerable autonomy in respect of assets owned by him or her. The separation of ownership during the regime creates a need for both spouses to have assets of their own which, in turn, may require that both of them are gainfully active. This promotes gender equality, as the spouses are expected to assume equal responsibilities in ensuring the welfare of the family. It also protects each spouse against the consequences of economic losses by the other spouse, as their own assets and liabilities remain unaffected. These are fundamental differences in relation to a community of acquisitions regime.

Inter-spousal solidarity and fairness between the spouses play the main role in the dissolution of the regime in the form of a protected right of each spouse to take part in the acquisitions of the other spouse which were acquired during the regime. Compared to a pure separation regime and the common law system of the separation of property with distribution by the competent authority, the difference here is that the participation in acquisitions regime not only establishes an explicit right for both spouses to share in the acquisitions upon the dissolution of the regime, but also creates the model for facilitating this. In this manner, it recognises each spouse's direct or indirect contributions to these acquisitions, in addition to providing increased predictability in respect of the outcome. Equal participation in the net value of the acquisitions acquired during the regime secures a fairness of distribution.[14]

2.2. ACQUISITIONS

There are two kinds of assets. Each spouse's property comprises acquisitions and a separate category of personal or individual property (called reserved property). The existence of the latter category is an expression of the concept that matrimonial solidarity is not so far-reaching as particularly in the German community of accrued gains.[15] It is therefore necessary to determine what kind of assets fall under the two categories. No additional categories exist.

Upon the dissolution of the regime each spouse is given a claim to take part in the acquisitions of the other spouse acquired during the regime. The participation in acquisitions regime is only one of the patrimonial consequences of marriage. After a divorce maintenance obligations may also exist.

Under the participation in acquisitions regime the key concept is acquisitions (*Errungenschaft* in the Swiss system)[16]. All property acquired during the regime, with the exception of reserved property, qualifies as acquisitions. It is irrelevant

---

[14]   See in more detail Comment concerning Principle 4:17, at pp. 147–148.
[15]   See Comment 4 concerning Principle 4:18, at p. 155.
[16]   See the Comparative Overview concerning Principle 4:17, at p. 145 and Art. 197 Swiss Civil Code.

what kind of assets, for example movable or immovable property, is at stake. The acquisitions include in particular each spouse's income and gains, whether derived from earnings or from property, and assets acquired by means of either spouse's income or gains (Principle 4:18 (1)). It follows that all income and gains of each spouse realised during the regime are included irrespective of when – or how – the source of the income or gains was acquired.[17] To add simplicity to the system, it is stated that the assets of the spouses are presumed to be acquisitions unless proved to be reserved property (Principle 4:18 (2)).

2.3. RESERVED PROPERTY

Principle 4:19 defines the reserved property of either spouse: it is the property that is not included among the acquisitions. Reserved property qualifies by its very nature as property that is protected against claims of equalisation by the other spouse upon the dissolution of the regime. It can consist of any kind of assets, such as movable or immovable property, including stocks and shares. There is a list of five categories.[18]

The grounds for classifying the property as belonging to either spouse include the *timing* when the property was acquired, meaning that is before the commencement of the regime (Principle 4:19(a)).[19] The grounds also include the *manner* in which the property was acquired, meaning that it must have been acquired by either spouse without any remuneration as a gift, inheritance or bequest (by means of a will) (Principle 4:19(b)). This is in line with national laws.[20]

In addition, the rules on substitution apply, so that property acquired during the regime with the owner spouse's reserved property continues to be the owner's reserved property (Principle 4:19(c)).[21] Substitution may take place both directly, for example when an insurance company pays compensation for a destroyed object, or indirectly, when one object has been replaced by another. If an asset has been funded partly by acquisitions and partly by reserved property, the category to which the largest amount of the funding belonged should be determinative. In this respect the interpretation has been inspired, in particular, by the model provided by Switzerland.[22]

---

[17] See in more in detail Comment 2 concerning Principle 4:18, at p. 154.
[18] Cf. the list in Art. 198 Swiss Civil Code. In the German 'community' of acquisitions there is no separate category. However, a similar effect is attained by adding the value of certain transactions to the 'initial assets' (cf. §1374 para. 2 German Civil Code). The same is true for Art. 8 para. 2 French-German Agreement of 2010.
[19] See the Comparative Overview concerning Principle 4:19, at pp. 157 – 158.
[20] Cf. §1374 para. 2 German Civil Code, Art. 198 No. 2 Alt. 2 Swiss Civil Code.
[21] See Comment 4 concerning Principle 4:19, at p. 160.
[22] See SCHWENZER/BOCK, Swiss Report, Q 61.

In addition, assets that are personal in nature belong to each spouse's reserved property.[23] Such assets are for a spouse's personal use only, such as clothing and everyday jewellery, having regard to the spouse's standard of living, but also compensation claims for pain and suffering. Compensation to either spouse for the spouse's pain and suffering or for personal or moral injury caused to that spouse also qualifies as reserved property because of the special link with that spouse and its purpose of offering personal compensation.[24] The same applies to rights of a spouse that cannot be assigned to another person.

Assets exclusively acquired for a spouse's profession, such as necessary tools for his or her profession, belong to the category of reserved property (Principle 4:19(e)). The justification for this is that such assets are used exclusively by that spouse to enable him or her to carry on with his or her profession. On the other hand, all income and gains from the profession and the professional assets are ranked as acquisitions according to Principle 4:18.

If assets qualifying as acquisitions under Principle 4:18 have been used to acquire professional materials, then rights of compensation may arise. The definition of reserved property in Principle 4:19 essentially corresponds with the composition of personal property in the community of acquisitions (cf. 4:36).

According to Principle 4:19(f), reserved property also includes increases in the value of the property listed in (a) to (e). This is a logical consequence of the starting point that reserved property is a separate category which is not subject to participation claims.[25] Only income and gains are included. One has to admit, however, that this may have serious consequences if the wealth of the family is made up of personal property acquired before marriage. There may be a considerable increase in value not materialised in profits eligible for distribution. The definition of what constitutes income and gains and thus belongs to the acquisitions is very important. However, the Principles do not enter into the numerous details of this problematic field. A certain remedy may be a compensation claim against the reserved property.[26]

Principle 4:20 follows the common core and establishes a rebuttable presumption that property is owned jointly by both spouses.[27] This presumption of ownership is justified on grounds of practicality, since in many cases, particularly for movables, it will not be possible to prove who the actual owner of an item of property is.[28] The presumption is rebuttable by any means available under national law to prove ownership.

[23] According to Principle 4:19(d). Cf. Comparative Overview concerning Principle 4:19, at p. 157.
[24] Expressly mentioned in Art. 198 No. 3 Swiss Civil Code.
[25] See Comments 2–4 concerning Principle 4:18, at pp. 154–155 and Comment 7 concerning Principle 4:19, at p. 161.
[26] See Comment 3 concerning Principle 4:18, at pp. 154–155.
[27] See the Comparative Overview concerning Principle 4:18, at pp. 152–153.
[28] See the Comparative Overview concerning Principle 4:20, at pp. 162–164.

3. DEBTS AND THE ADMINISTRATION OF PROPERTY

Principle 4:21 on debts follows the common core.[29] In all matrimonial property regimes based on the separation of property during the marriage, debts incurred by one spouse are his or her personal debts and can only be recovered from his or her personal property.[30] This encompasses, according to the Principles, the acquisitions and the reserved property. However, debts have to be deducted for the calculation of the net acquisitions (Principle 4:31(2)). Debts may also become relevant for compensation claims. If spouses have incurred debts jointly and severally, such debts follow the general law of obligations and can be recovered from the property of either spouse.[31]

The basic rule for the administration of property is relatively simple. Principle 4:23 establishes that each spouse is in principle free to administer his or her property independently.[32] This means that a spouse does not, as a rule, need the consent of the other spouse for the administrative measures he or she takes in respect of his or her property. It would however be wrong to ignore the existence of marriage. There are limitations on the right of free administration. Principle 4:5 and Principle 4:6 on the family home and household goods are fully applicable. Any act of disposal of the rights to the family home or the household goods intended for the spouses' joint use requires the consent of both spouses, irrespective of whether the family home or the household goods are the acquisitions or reserved property of one spouse. The owner spouse should therefore not be able to administer these assets freely but must have the consent of the other spouse for purposes of disposal. Each spouse is under a general duty to administer his or her personal property in order to ensure that the right of each spouse to participate in the acquisitions of the other spouse is not infringed. This duty can be enforced upon the dissolution of the regime (cf. Principle 4:24(d)). Detrimental transactions can also be taken into account in calculating the acquisitions according to Principle 4:27.

4. DISSOLUTION AND LIQUIDATION

4.1. DISSOLUTION

The matrimonial property regime comes to an end with the four grounds for its dissolution listed in Principle 4:24. In the first place, the death of a spouse is

---

29   See the Comparative Overview concerning Principle 4:21, at pp. 165–166.
30   See the Comparative Overview concerning Principle 4:21, at pp. 165–166.
31   See Comment 2 concerning Principles 4:21 and 4:22, at pp. 166 and 168.
32   Cf. §1364 German Civil Code, Art. 201 para. 1 Swiss Civil Code.

referred to since the spouse's death immediately terminates the marriage. Another ground is divorce or legal separation. A factual separation between the spouses has no effect as such, not only due to the difficulties in determining the date of such an event but mainly due to the structure of a mere participation regime.[33] Additionally, an agreement to change to another matrimonial property regime brings the former regime to an end. Finally, the decision of a competent authority based upon serious grounds is also a ground for dissolution.

It is also necessary to determine the date of the dissolution of the regime. Principle 4:25 determines that the dissolution takes effect on the date of the death of a spouse. If a divorce or legal separation is granted, the decree takes effect retroactively from the date of the application. This approach, which is followed by only half of the jurisdictions surveyed,[34] promotes foreseeability in situations where inter-spousal solidarity has come to an end. A change to the matrimonial property regime and its replacement by another by agreement dissolves the previously existing regime as of the date of the agreement. The date of the change is the relevant date not only for its effectiveness between the spouses but also for its effectiveness in relation to third parties. If there is a dissolution of the regime by the decision of a competent authority, the date of the application constitutes, in line with the common core,[35] the decisive cut-off event.

4.2. LIQUIDATION

After the dissolution of the regime by death, by divorce or by a change of the matrimonial property regime, a liquidation takes place. Each spouse participates in the acquisitions acquired by the other during the regime. For the acquisitions to be taken into account in the liquidation of the regime there is also a cut-off date. This is the date of the dissolution of the regime, since the regime has come to an end. No subsequent acquisitions shall be taken into account (Principle 4:26).

However, there is often a lapse of time between the regime's dissolution and its liquidation, and therefore changes in the value of the assets may occur. Whereas in this respect the relevant date is in some systems the date of dissolution, others apply the date of liquidation.[36] The Principles follow an approach according to which both spouses equally share the risks relating to the changes in the value of the acquisitions after the date of the regime's dissolution. Therefore, the value of the acquisitions is to be determined at the

---

[33]   See the Comment concerning Principle 4:24, at p. 177.
[34]   See the Comparative Overview concerning Principle 4:25, at pp. 180–181.
[35]   See the Comparative Overview concerning Principle 4:25, at p. 182.
[36]   See the Comparative Overview concerning Principle 4:26, at pp. 186–188.

date of the liquidation of the regime. If the result would lead to exceptional hardship for a spouse, the outcome may be adjusted by a decision of the competent authority.

Protection against the detrimental transactions of a spouse is necessary. Certain transactions which can diminish the acquisitions are enumerated in Principle 4:27. Account shall be taken of any excessive gifts by a spouse, a dissipation of assets and other acts that have intentionally diminished the value of the acquisitions to the detriment of the other spouse. The notional amounts by which the acquisitions have been diminished qualify as acquisitions that have to be shared.[37]

Since there are different categories of assets of each of the spouses in the matrimonial property regime of participation in acquisitions, the relationship between them has to be clarified. In order to avoid unjust enrichment, in some cases compensation between the different categories of assets takes place according to Principle 4:28 (1). Such compensation claims also exist in national law.[38] Acquisitions of a spouse shall be compensated for any contribution profiting his or her reserved property, for example an inherited house. The same principle applies to the reserved property. It shall be compensated for any contribution profiting the spouse's acquisitions (Principle 4:28 (2)).

It is clarified that debts encumber the property in relation to which they were incurred, for example for an inherited immovable. In cases of doubt they are presumed to encumber the acquisitions since all assets are presumed to be acquisitions (Principle 4:28 (3)). A special rule deals with cases of investment for the acquisition and an improvement or preservation of an asset, for example a house. Here the calculation of the compensation should take into account any resulting increase or decrease in the market value of the asset on the date of the dissolution of the regime (Principle 4:28 (4)).[39] The compensation claim has a monetary character (Principle 4:28 (5)).

The Principles do not contain a specific rule for the unpaid work of one of the spouses for the other. It would be conceivable to allow a special claim by one spouse against the other. The Principles, however, do not take a position in this respect.[40]

---

[37] See the Comparative Overview concerning Principle 4:27, at pp. 192–194.

[38] See the Comparative Overview concerning Principle 4:28, at pp. 196–197 and Art. 209 Swiss Civil Code.

[39] See the example in Comment 5 concerning Principle 4:28, at pp. 198–199.

[40] Cf. for a participation in acquisitions regime Art. 206 Swiss Civil Code and SCHWENZER/BOCK, Swiss Report, Q 81, 83; for a separation of property regime Art. 232–5 Catalan Civil Code and the former Art. 41 Family Code and MARTÍN-CASALS/RIBOT, Catalan Report, Q 2, 150.

5. PARTICIPATION

Following the common core, agreements on participation are allowed.[41] Spouses are free to agree on participation in the acquisitions (Principle 4:29). This may concern the individual assets, their value or a participation in kind or in money and is another expression of the autonomy of the spouses (cf. Principle 4:10).

There is also a special rule on the allocation of the family home and household goods (Principle 4:30). The competent authority may, in the interest of the family and subject to the payment of compensation, allocate the family home and household goods to one of the spouses. Such an allocation requires a careful consideration of the interests of each spouse and the children. Amongst the factors to be considered will be the financial and personal situation of the spouses. A separate issue arises when the family home is also the place of business if, for example, one of the spouses has his or her practice in the family home. The competent authority should also give special consideration to the needs of the children of the family, particularly accommodation for them during their period of minority and the creation of a family environment.

The basic principle on equal participation in the acquisitions is provided for in Principle 4:31. This rule reflects the principle of equality between the spouses. Regardless of who is actually the title holder of the assets that have been accumulated during the regime and independently of the different roles the spouses might have played, both are deemed to have made equally valuable contributions. To the extent that one spouse's net acquisitions exceed the value of those of the other, the latter participates in the surplus to the amount of one half (Principle 4:31 (1)). Therefore a calculation is necessary.[42] At first the net acquisitions of each of the spouses have to be determined. These net acquisitions are the value of the acquisitions after deducting the debts (Principle 4:31 (2)). Joint debts have to be taken into account on a proportional basis. The value of the acquisitions is determined at the date of liquidation in accordance with Principle 4:26. However, the Principles do not enter into details regarding the methods for the calculation and determination of the value of the assets.

Losses incurred by one spouse exceeding his or her acquisitions should not be shared by the other spouse (Principle 4:31 (3)). This means that the participation claim always has a positive value. Deficits are to be disregarded. After this calculation the net acquisitions of the spouses can be compared and a participation claim can be determined. The participation claim is half the value of the surplus.

The participation claim is a monetary one. The ownership of the assets does not change. However, the spouses can reach an agreement that provides for payment in kind (Principle 4:31 (4)). Upon the request of the debtor spouse the

---

[41]   See the Comparative Overview concerning Principle 4:29, at pp. 201–203.
[42]   For examples see Comment 7 concerning Principle 4:31, at p. 213.

competent authority may, where there are serious grounds for doing so, authorise payments to be deferred or made payable in instalments (Principle 4:31 (5)).

One could accept the result of the calculation process as the final result, as in the French-German optional regime.[43] However, in other legal systems a modification of the final result is possible.[44] Also under the Principles, in cases of exceptional hardship an adjustment by the competent authority is allowed (Principle 4:32). This means that there can be a deviation from the principle of equal participation where there are compelling reasons. Examples could be a marriage of extremely short duration or patrimonial damage based on the extremely unfair behaviour of a spouse.[45] This is also possible where there is a spousal agreement. In cases of exceptional hardship the competent authority can set aside or modify such an agreement. A judicial review of the substance therefore takes place. However, any intervention should be kept to a minimum.

6. CONCLUSION

On the whole, the Principles provide manageable rules for a participation regime. During the existence of the matrimonial property regime there is autonomy between the parties. Restrictions are found mainly in the primary regime. After the dissolution the leading principles of equality and participation apply. The existence of the reserved property of each spouse guarantees, however, that there is no total participation. The process of participation requires the application of some rules for the classification of the different categories of property and a calculation to reach an appropriate result. The Principles, though limited to what is strictly necessary, try to give clear answers. Nevertheless, they avoid too much rigidity and allow for some flexibility.

---

[43]   Cf. SIMLER, *Droit de la famille* 2010 No. 5, pp. 9–19.

[44]   Cf. RIBOT, "The financial consequences of divorce across Europe", *ERA Forum* 12 (2011), pp. 71, 76–77. In Germany an objection based on gross unfairness may be made (§1381 Civil Code).

[45]   See Comment 2 concerning Principle 4:32, at p. 216.

THE COMMUNITY OF
ACQUISITIONS REGIME

Frédérique FERRAND

Contents

1.   INTRODUCTION

The CEFL eventually decided not to establish only one single matrimonial property regime but drafted two such regimes and refrained from giving one of them the function of a default regime and the other the status of an optional regime. Therefore, both the participation in acquisitions regime and the community of acquisitions regime are presented in the Principles of European Family Law Regarding Property Relations between Spouses[1] as equal default regimes. The second regime, called community of acquisitions, corresponds with the French terminology *communauté d'acquêts* and the German *Errungenschafts-gemeinschaft*. The CEFL held that the label 'community of acquisitions' is preferable to the terminology 'community of property' because it clearly expresses the main feature of the regime as a restricted community.[2]

Community of acquests or acquisitions is a matrimonial regime that several jurisdictions have opted for as a default regime. This is for example the case for Belgium (*communauté des acquêts, Gemeenschap van aanwinsten*),[3] Bulgaria,[4] Croatia, the Czech Republic, France (*communauté réduite aux acquêts*),[5] Hungary, Italy *(Comunione dei beni)*,[6] Lithuania, Malta (community of acquests),[7] Poland, Portugal (*regime da comunhão de adquiridos*),[8] Russia, Slovakia, Slovenia,

---

[1]   See BOELE-WOELKI/FERRAND/GONZÁLEZ-BEILFUSS/JÄNTERÄ-JAREBORG/MARTINY/LOWE/PIN-TENS, *Principles of European Family Law Regarding Property Relations Between Spouses*, Cambridge, Antwerp, Portland, Intersentia ed., 2013.

[2]   See BOELE-WOELKI/FERRAND/GONZÁLEZ-BEILFUSS/JÄNTERÄ-JAREBORG/MARTINY/LOWE/PIN-TENS, *Principles of European Family Law Regarding Property Relations Between Spouses*, Principle 4:33, Comment 2, p. 220.

[3]   Art. 1398 Belgian Civil Code.

[4]   Art. 19 семеен кодекс 1985. In Bulgaria, the new Family Law Code that came into force on 1 October 2009 allows the spouses to choose a regime out of three options: separation, common ownership and a matrimonial contract (Art. 18, para. 1 of the Family Code). Future spouses may choose between three matrimonial property regimes – two statutory and one contractual. The first statutory regime is the community of property, which was the regime in force until 2009 but with some modifications; it is not a full community but a combination between community and separation. This regime applies (as a default regime) if no other option has been selected by the spouses. The separation of property is the second statutory regime available for opting in. The third regime is contractual. The spouses can make such a choice before or during the marriage.

[5]   Art. 1401 French Civil Code.

[6]   Art. 177 Codice civile (Italian Civil Code).

[7]   Art. 1316 Maltese Civil Code.

[8]   Art. 1717 Código Civil Português (Portuguese Civil Code).

and Spain (*sociedad de ganaciales*).[9] It appears that in mostly the Romanic European jurisdictions and the Central and Eastern European legal systems the community of acquisitions constitutes the default matrimonial regime.[10]

Why did the CEFL decide to draft a set of Principles regarding the community of acquisitions regime?

First, because the comparative research-based drafting of the Principles revealed that the elements of all national systems surveyed cannot be merged into one single matrimonial property regime. There are two main systems with more or less important nuances and subcategories: a community system, on the one hand, and a participation system, on the other, while 'their basic starting points are diametrically opposed'.[11] A community of property regime between the spouses automatically takes effect at the moment of concluding the marriage, which is not the case in a participation system that treats the property of each spouse as the owner's separate property and only upon the dissolution of the marriage does it allow each spouse to partake in the assets of the other through a deferred community or a statutory compensation clause. Since both systems are represented in a large number of European jurisdictions, it appeared to be very difficult and erroneous to exclude one of the models from the European Principles.

Secondly, there are huge differences between the economic situations of married couples within Europe, especially with regard to the level of women's labour participation. Even though some sociological studies[12] carried out in Finland and in the Netherlands show that dual-earners is increasingly the rule, the picture varies from one country to another and is partly influenced by cultural, regional and educational factors.[13] Therefore, it can be appropriate to offer a matrimonial property regime that takes into account spouses' inequality in the financial situation and their access to employment.

Thirdly, the advantages of the community of acquisitions regime are especially important when one of the spouses is not involved with the labour

---

9   See Art. 1344 Código Civil español (Spanish Civil Code). However, in Spain the Código Civil only applies where the law of the autonomous communities does not make alternative provisions.

10   See also PINTENS, Matrimonial Property Law in Europe, in: BOELE-WOELKI/MILES/SCHERPE (ed.), *The Future of Family Property in Europe*, Cambridge, Antwerp, Portland, Intersentia ed., 2011, p. 23.

11   See BOELE-WOELKI/FERRAND/GONZÁLEZ-BEILFUSS/JÄNTERÄ-JAREBORG/MARTINY/LOWE/PINTENS, *Principles of European Family Law Regarding Property Relations Between Spouses*, p. 25.

12   See MALINEN/KINNUNEN/TOLVANEN/RONKA/WIERDA-BOER/GERRIS, Happy spouses, happy parents? Family relationships among Finnish and Dutch dual earners, *Journal of Marriage and Family* 2010, pp. 293–306.

13   See BOELE-WOELKI/FERRAND/GONZÁLEZ-BEILFUSS/JÄNTERÄ-JAREBORG/ MARTINY/LOWE/PINTENS, *Principles of European Family Law Regarding Property Relations Between Spouses*, pp. 23 et seq. See also MILES/SCHERPE, The Future of Family Property in Europe, in: BOELE-WOELKI/MILES/SCHERPE (ed.), *The Future of Family Property in Europe*, p. 425 about the shared social and legal policy challenges.

Frédérique Ferrand

market e.g. because he or she cares for the children: it promotes solidarity between the spouses not only upon the dissolution of the marriage but as soon as they enter into the marriage.[14] This regime is particularly suitable for a spouse who does not own property. The community of acquisitions regime gives the spouse a title to property if assets are to be divided at the end of the marriage, whereas the participation in acquisitions regime solely provides for a monetary claim. Therefore, the community of acquisitions appears to be best suited for couples whose earnings and property are very unequal and where one spouse – mostly the wife – has no or very few earnings since he or she has devoted his or her time to the care and upbringing of the children. Even if this is not necessarily a model that deserves to be promoted, this sociological reality must be taken into account and, in this respect, the community of acquisitions regime can function as a protection for the 'weaker' spouse. As Walter Pintens stated, 'a community system creates equality from the very start of the marriage'.[15] Community of acquisitions realises matrimonial solidarity already during the marriage by creating a special category of assets called common property. It does not prevent the spouses from being autonomous during the marriage since – as we will see in the framework of the CEFL community of acquisitions regime – there are different categories of assets and each spouse autonomously administers his or her personal property. The jurisdictions that have adopted the community of acquisitions regime (as a default or as an optional regime) do not all follow the same pattern; more or less assets are encompassed in the community property; the same applies to debts. The CEFL Principles have tried to reach the right balance between solidarity and the independence of the spouses;[16] therefore, they have opted for a restricted definition of common assets[17] in order 'to enhance self-sufficiency and independence of both spouses'.[18] The aim of the

---

[14] The community of acquisitions regime promotes solidarity and fairness between the spouses both during the regime and upon its dissolution, see BOELE-WOELKI/FERRAND/GONZÁLEZ-BEILFUSS/JÄNTERÄ-JAREBORG/MARTINY/LOWE/PINTENS, *Principles of European Family Law Regarding Property Relations Between Spouses*, Principle 4:33, Comment 3, p. 220.

[15] PINTENS, Matrimonial Property Law in Europe, in: BOELE-WOELKI/MILES/SCHERPE (ed.), *The Future of Family Property in Europe*, p. 42.

[16] As acknowledged by BOELE-WOELKI/JÄNTERÄ-JAREBORG (Initial Results of the Work of the CEFL in the Field of Property Relations between Spouse, in: BOELE-WOELKI/MILES/SCHERPE (ed.), *The Future of Family Property in Europe*, p. 48): 'Given their lack of enforceability, the Principles must convince on their own, as they are formulated'.

[17] For example, property acquired by one spouse before the marriage shall not be included in the division or distribution of property when the marriage comes to an end. And reciprocally, debts incurred by one spouse before the marriage remain his or her personal debts and shall not be supported by the community property.

[18] See BOELE-WOELKI/FERRAND/GONZÁLEZ-BEILFUSS/JÄNTERÄ-JAREBORG/MARTINY/LOWE/PINTENS, *Principles of European Family Law Regarding Property Relations Between Spouses*, p. 27 ('This reflects the modern tendency in the majority of jurisdictions surveyed. It is also in accordance with the standard set in Principle 2:2 of the Principles Regarding Divorce and Maintenance between Former Spouses').

European Principles on community of acquisitions drafted by the CEFL is to modernise this regime in order to guarantee a fair sharing of property upon the dissolution of the marriage and to give the competent authority the power to adjust the distribution in the case of exceptional hardship, so that a more flexible approach is possible,[19] but nevertheless without endangering too much the foreseeability of the outcome.

These balanced regulations are contained in Section B (Community of Acquisitions) of Chapter III (Matrimonial Property Regimes). Section B consists of 25 Principles: the first one (Principle 4:33) generally states, as does Principle 4:16 for participation in acquisitions, that the community of acquisitions regime will apply if the spouses have not agreed otherwise. The following are divided into six parts: (1) *Concepts* (Applicability of the community of acquisitions regime, Principle 4:33; Concept of the community of acquisitions, Principle 4:34; Community property, Principle 4:36; Personal property, Principle 4:36; Substitution, Principle 4:37; Investment or reinvestment, Principle 4:38; Presumption of community property, Principle 4:39); (2) *Debts* (Community debts, Principle 4:40; Personal debts, Principle 4:41; Recovery of community debts, Principle 4:42; Recovery of personal debts, Principle 4:43); (3) *Administration* (Administration of community property, Principle 4:44; Acts requiring joint administration, Principle 4:45; Annulment of acts of administration, Principle 4:46; Administration of personal property, Principle 4:47; Divestment of the right to administer community property, Principle 4:48); (4) *Dissolution* (Grounds for dissolution, Principle 4:49; Date of dissolution, Principle 4:50; Administration after dissolution, Principle 4:51); (5) *Liquidation* (Determination and valuation of the community property, Principle 4:52; Compensation, Principle 4:53; Ranking of community debts, Principle 4:54; and (6) *Distribution* (Agreement on distribution, Principle 4:55; Allocation of family home, household goods and professional assets, Principle 4:56; Equal sharing and adjustment, Principle 4:57; and Recovery of community debts after distribution of the community, Principle 4:58).

With regard to the community of acquisitions regime, three main issues arise: first, the determination and the contents of the different categories of property and debts; secondly, the rules governing the administration of the different categories of property; and thirdly, the grounds for the regime to be dissolved and the following liquidation and distribution.

---

19   See BOELE-WOELKI/FERRAND/GONZÁLEZ-BEILFUSS/JÄNTERÄ-JAREBORG/MARTINY/LOWE/PIN-TENS, *Principles of European Family Law Regarding Property Relations Between Spouses*, p. 27.

2. PERSONAL AND COMMUNITY PROPERTY, ASSETS AND DEBTS

2.1. MAIN FEATURES OF COMMUNITY OF ACQUISITIONS: THREE CATEGORIES OF PROPERTY

Typically a matrimonial regime called community of acquests or of acquisitions distinguishes between three categories of property: the wife's personal property, the husband's personal property and the common property (in Belgian and French law called '*la communauté*' or '*les biens communs*'). CEFL Principle 4:34 therefore states that the community of acquisitions regime comprises 'community property and personal property'.

In order to enhance solidarity and to facilitate the classification of assets, Principle 4:39 formulates a (rebuttable) presumption in favour of the category of community property: 'Assets are presumed to be community property unless they are proved to be personal property in accordance with Principles 4:35 to 4:38'.[20]

Community property is defined as 'property acquired during the community of acquisitions and which is not personal property', whereas personal property is 'each spouse's own property'. Therefore, it is necessary to take a deeper look at the assets encompassed in each category.

2.1.1. What Does the Personal Property of Each Spouse Comprise?

Even if the CEFL Principles first give a definition of community property (Principle 4:35), it is easier to start with personal property since its contents are precisely formulated in Principle 4:36 whereas community property is defined in contrast to personal property. Pursuant to Principle 4:36, personal property (one could also say 'separate property' but the CEFL opted for personal property in order to express the idea of a personal, exclusive right of a spouse to certain assets) encompasses five kinds of assets:

(a) *Assets acquired before entering into the community of acquisitions*: pursuant to the clear common core,[21] pre-marital assets do not fall within the community since there is no specific reason to impose an equal share in

---

[20] See the explanation in BOELE-WOELKI/FERRAND/GONZÁLEZ-BEILFUSS/JÄNTERÄ-JAREBORG/ MARTINY/LOWE/PINTENS, *Principles of European Family Law Regarding Property Relations Between Spouses*, Principle 4:39, Comment 1, p. 245: 'The presumption is justified on the grounds of practicality since in many cases, especially over a period of time and particularly with regard to movable property, it will not be possible to prove who the actual owner of an item or an asset is'.

[21] With the exception of the Netherlands that has established a universal community as a default regime. See also for some nuances Hungary and Malta.

property acquired by one spouse before entering into the community of acquisitions.

(b) *Gifts, inheritances and bequests acquired during the regime*: they are in most cases made by the donor or testator specifically to one spouse, which explains that the property acquired in this way should remain personal to the benefiting spouse, unless the donor/testator has expressly specified that the gift/bequest be assigned to the community. This also follows the common core.[22]

(c) *Assets acquired through substitution, investment or reinvestment in accordance with Principles 4:37 and 4:38*: this category of personal property follows the logic of initial personal property: if one asset that was the personal property of one spouse is replaced by another or is used for investment or reinvestment, it seems only fair that the new asset (with some nuances and exceptions)[23] remains the personal property of that spouse.

(d) *Assets which are personal in nature and are acquired during the regime*: such assets are, for example, clothing or other items of personal use. Some jurisdictions expressly exclude the qualification of personal property where the assets are luxury items. This category aims to preserve the autonomy of each spouse with regard to assets that are used personally by one of them due to their very nature.

(e) *Assets exclusively acquired for a spouse's profession*: this solution is based on the essential and indispensable character of such assets for the spouse who needs them for his or her profession.

Most of these categories reflect the common core within the jurisdictions surveyed. The assets falling outside the community are numerous, which shows the attempt by the CEFL Principles to strike a balance between the solidarity of the spouses and a certain independence.

2.1.2. Assets Belonging to Community Property

As a consequence of the comprehensive determination of the personal property of each spouse in Principle 4:36, community property is defined as that which is not personal property: 'Community property comprises any property movable or immovable acquired during the regime that is not the personal property of one of the spouses' (Principle 4:35 (1)).

---

[22]   However, see the slightly different solution in Austria: the gift/bequest is the personnel property of the benefiting spouse only if the donor/testator has specifically added a condition obliging the benefiting spouse to make an agreement with the other spouse that the asset will be separate property (*Vorbehaltsgut*), see ROTH, Austrian report, Q 27, available on the CEFL website http://ceflonline.net/wp-content/uploads/Austria-Property.pdf (last accessed 13.11.2013).

[23]   See under 2.1.3.

Still, three special kinds of assets are expressly mentioned as being included in community property:

(a) *The spouses' income and gains whether derived from earnings, community property or personal property*: this category is broad since it encompasses not only the earnings of both spouses – which in practice are a very important kind of property for the majority of spouses[24] – but also all income and gains derived not only from community property, but also from *personal property*,[25] which is not the general rule adopted by some jurisdictions that have established a community of acquisitions regime.[26]

(b) *Assets acquired either jointly or individually by the spouses during the community of acquisitions by means of the spouses' income and gains*: it is logical that assets acquired jointly by the spouses during the marriage belong to the community property. The latter should also encompass all assets acquired by one spouse during the marriage, except in the case of the substitution of a personal asset, or the investment or reinvestment of personal assets.[27]

(c) *Gifts and bequests to both spouses or to one spouse on condition that they belong to the community property*: if during the marriage one spouse or both receive gifts and bequests subject to such a condition, the will of the donor or testator shall be respected and the asset(s) classified as community property. This is an exception to the rule that gifts, inheritances and bequests acquired by one spouse during the regime remain his or her personal property.

Such solutions have been widely adopted in the jurisdictions surveyed by the CEFL. Some add other categories of assets to the community property, e.g. gains derived from lotteries or other games of chance (Malta, Slovakia, Spain).[28]

Principle 4:35 reflects the common core in Europe. It provides a definition of community property which is determined with regard to two criteria: the nature and source of the assets and the timing of their acquisition. The same criteria apply when defining what belongs to the personal property of each spouse.

---

[24]   In most of the jurisdictions surveyed by the CEFL, earnings belong to community property, except in Italy, where earnings are not treated as community property *per se*. They only become so in respect of 'gains' not used up at the moment of the community's dissolution.

[25]   For a comparative analysis of legal systems differentiating between income derived from employment and income derived from personal property such as Croatia, Serbia and Slovenia, see PINTENS, Matrimonial Property Law in Europe, in: BOELE-WOELKI/MILES/SCHERPE (ed.), *The Future of Family Property in Europe*, p. 23.

[26]   See BOELE-WOELKI/FERRAND/GONZÁLEZ-BEILFUSS/JÄNTERÄ-JAREBORG/MARTINY/LOWE/PINTENS, *Principles of European Family Law Regarding Property Relations Between Spouses*, Principle 4:35, p. 227.

[27]   See under 2.1.3.

[28]   See BOELE-WOELKI/FERRAND/GONZÁLEZ-BEILFUSS/JÄNTERÄ-JAREBORG/ MARTINY/LOWE/PINTENS, *Principles of European Family Law Regarding Property Relations Between Spouses*, Principle 4:35, Comparative Overview, p. 226.

2.1.3. Specific Situations

Two specific situations are dealt with in the CEFL Principles: the substitution of assets (section 2.1.3.1) and investment or reinvestment (section 2.1.3.2).

2.1.3.1. Substitution

Substitution encompasses cases where new movable or immovable property replaces the personal property of one spouse, for example when an asset has been destroyed and the spouses receive an insurance payment, or when an asset belonging personally to one spouse is sold and a new one is bought with the proceeds.

Principle 4:37 contains nuanced solutions: if an asset substitutes personal assets without extra payment, it should be regarded as the personal property of the spouse (para. 1). But if additional payment is required, a distinction has to be made: the new asset is personal property 'unless the payment provided by community property *equals*[29] or exceeds the value of the substituted asset' (para. 2). This formulation gives priority to the qualification as community property where 50 per cent or more of the value of the new asset has been paid by community property. If the payment provided by community property is less than 50 per cent, the substituted asset remains the personal property of the spouse but compensation is due to the community property (para. 3).[30]

Another possible solution could be, as in Malta,[31] to decide that the alienation of personal assets are subsumed into community property but the value of the personal asset ranks as a credit in favour of the property-owning spouse. However, the rule laid down in Principle 4:37 seems to be preferable since it more directly protects the spouse whose personal property has been substituted.

2.1.3.2. Investment or Reinvestment

Principle 4:38 is the counterpart of Principle 4:37 with regard to investment or reinvestment. The basic principle is the same: if the asset is acquired solely through the investment or reinvestment of personal assets, it should be regarded as personal property (para. 1). Similar to the principle of substitution, where the asset is acquired partly through the investment or reinvestment of personal

---

[29]   This means that when the funding is equal the community should be favoured, see BOELE-WOELKI/FERRAND/GONZÁLEZ-BEILFUSS/JÄNTERÄ-JAREBORG/MARTINY/ LOWE/PINTENS, *Principles of European Family Law Regarding Property Relations Between Spouses*, Principle 4:37, Comment 2, p. 239.

[30]   And vice versa, if an asset belonging to community property is substituted by another one with additional payment provided by personal property, compensation is due, see the formulation in Principle 4:37 (para. 3).

[31]   Art. 1320 sub. e Maltese Civil Code.

assets and partly through community assets (so-called mixed investments), the qualification of the new asset shall depend on the proportion of the investment, that is, if one fund provides the greater source of funding, it will belong to that fund but with compensation being payable (paras. 2 and 3). Again, the fact that community property is being slightly favoured is perceivable since the new asset becomes community property if the community has invested 50 per cent or more.

Principles 4:37 and 4:38 reflect the common core in Europe, although some jurisdictions do not have specific regulations concerning these issues[32] whereas others have established very detailed statutory regulations (Belgium, France). The purpose of the two Principles is to respect the initial composition of each spouse's personal property in the case of substitution or investment/ reinvestment, but also to give the community a slight advantage where an additional payment has been made.

2.2. DEBTS

With regard to debts in the community of acquisitions regime, two issues are dealt with in the CEFL Principles: first, the determination of what debts are community debts or personal debts (section 2.2.1); and secondly, from what property may those debts be recovered (section 2.2.2). The qualification as community or personal debts often mirrors the qualification of community or personal property.

2.2.1. Determination of Community Debts and Personal Debts

2.2.1.1. Community Debts

Principle 4:40 provides a long list of community debts that consists of not less than seven categories:

(a) *Debts incurred jointly by both spouses*: it is self-evident that that a debt incurred jointly by both spouses shall belong to community debts; the participation of both spouses in the transaction is deemed to prove their willingness to be bound by it. This reflects a broad common core.
(b) *Debts incurred by one spouse in order to meet the appropriate family needs*: this provision is in accordance with Principle 4:4 (see Chapter II on the general rights and duties of the spouses) that imposes a duty on each spouse

---

[32]   This is the case for Austria, Poland and Slovakia, see BOELE-WOELKI/FERRAND/GONZÁLEZ-BEILFUSS/JÄNTERÄ-JAREBORG/MARTINY/LOWE/PINTENS, *Principles of European Family Law Regarding Property Relations Between Spouses*, Principle 4:38, Comparative Overview, p. 241.

to contribute to the needs of the family according to his or her ability. Where a debt is incurred by one spouse only in order to meet the family needs, this debt should qualify as a community debt. These are, for example, debts incurred by one of the spouses for the benefit of the housekeeping and the education of the children.[33] Nevertheless, some safeguards should protect the other spouse from excessive expenses; this is the reason why only debts related to *appropriate* family needs are concerned. The appropriateness of the family needs depends on the financial and social situation of the family, which requires an assessment *in concreto*; in case of conflict between the spouses, the competent authority (often the court) shall decide whether the debt was really incurred to meet appropriate family needs.

(c) *Debts related to the maintenance of children*: the CEFL decided that such a debt should qualify as a community debt since it is closely linked with 'family needs' in a broad sense. This should apply regardless of whether the child is the child of only one spouse and lives in the family home or not.[34] The purpose is to favour the equal treatment of children.

(d) *Debts incurred by one spouse for the use or administration of community assets or in the interest of the community property*: logically, any expenses related to community assets or interests should be borne by the community property.

(e) *Debts related to a spouse's professional activities*: this category of community debts mirrors the qualification of each spouse's earnings as community property.

(f) *Debts related to gift s and bequests belonging to community property*: here again, where the community benefits from gifts/bequests, the relating debts should also be common to the spouses.

(g) *Debts that have not been proved to be personal debts*: This mirrors the presumption contained in Principle 4:39 (assets are presumed to be community property unless they are proved to be personal property).

2.2.1.2. Debts which are Personal to One Spouse

As already mentioned, where it is not proved that a debt is personal to one spouse, it shall be presumed that it is a community debt. The jurisdictions that stipulate which debts are personal to one spouse often make a distinction

---

[33] See e.g. Art. 1409 French Civil Code.

[34] However, if the child, who is the creditor of the maintenance, is the child of only one spouse, the maintenance should not be recovered from the personal property of the other spouse, see BOELE-WOELKI/FERRAND/GONZÁLEZ-BEILFUSS/JÄNTERÄ-JAREBORG/MARTINY/LOWE/PINTENS, *Principles of European Family Law Regarding Property Relations Between Spouses*, Principle 4:40, Comment 3. See also Principle 4:41.

between personal debts which are designated as such because of their origin, and those that are designated due to their nature or purpose.[35]

Principle 4:41 contains five categories of debts that are personal to one spouse:

(a) *Debts incurred before entering into the community of acquisitions*: this reflects the idea that what occurred before entering into the community of acquisitions should not be taken into account: if the assets acquired before the marriage remain the personal property of the spouse, the debts incurred before entering into the community should also remain personal.
(b) *Debts related to gifts, inheritances and bequests acquired by one spouse during the regime*: the same reason explains the qualification of debts related to gifts/bequests acquired by one spouse during the marriage as personal debts, except if the donor/testator expressly stated that they should become the common property of both spouses.
(c) *Debts related to personal property*: the same reasons apply as under (b).
(d) *Debts which are personal by nature*: this category of personal debts is not precisely defined and gives rise to various interpretations in the jurisdictions surveyed. Typical examples of debts that are personal by nature are damages to be paid by one spouse on the ground of tortious liability, a fine to be paid on the basis of a criminal conviction, or maintenance owed by one spouse to a parent or grandparent.
(e) *Debts incurred without the required consent of the other spouse*: some transactions are particularly significant and can have serious consequences for the wealth of the family. This is e.g. the case for loan agreements, guarantees or sureties. Therefore, for such transactions Principle 4:45 requires joint administration by both spouses. If only one spouse has incurred the debt, it remains personal to him/her. This does not necessarily mean that only the personal assets of that spouse can be seized by the creditor. Thus, it is important to present the Principles relating to the recovery of debts.

2.2.2. Recovery of Community Debts and Personal Debts

Two Principles are dedicated to the recovery of debts. Principle 4:42 deals with the recovery of community debts whereas Principle 4:42 states from what property personal debts can be recovered.

---

[35] See e.g. Belgium (see PINTENS/ALLAERTS/PIGNOLET/SEYNS, Belgian Report, Q 30, available under http://ceflonline.net/wp-content/uploads/Belgium-Property.pdf [last accessed 13.11.2013]) and France (see FERRAND/BRAAT, French Report, Q 30, available at http://ceflonline.net/wp-content/uploads/France-Property.pdf [last accessed 13.11.2013]).

2.2.2.1. Recovery of Community Debts

The comparative study carried out by the CEFL shows a clear common core that has been adopted by the Principles: all community debts can be recovered from the community property. Moreover, they can also be recovered from the personal property of the spouse who incurred the debt (Principle 4:42 (1)).

The majority of the jurisdictions surveyed[36] even admit that community debts can be recovered from the personal assets of *each* spouse. However, with regard to the aim of the CEFL to strike a balance between solidarity and the independence of the spouses, it appears preferable not to overly extend the categories of property from which community debts may be recovered. This is the reason why Principle 4:42 distinguishes between debts for which both spouses are jointly and severally liable and those without such joint liability. Only where the spouses are jointly and severally liable may the debt also be recovered from the personal property of either spouse (para. 2). This distinction does not follow the common core but a better law approach and reflects the concept of a 'community debt' as laid down in Principle 4:40. Joint and several liability exists mainly for debts incurred to meet the family needs that encompass, in most jurisdictions, the care and education of children as well as household expenses, sometimes with the restriction that those debts must be 'appropriate' or should not be 'manifestly excessive'.[37]

In this context the issue of a possible ranking can be mentioned. A few national laws lay down a specific order of ranking to be followed by the creditor. In Italy, Lithuania and Portugal for example, the creditor shall first claim against the community assets; only if they are not sufficient may the creditor discharge his or her claim from the personal property of the spouses. The CEFL Principles refrain from going this far and prefer to leave this issue to national law.

2.2.2.2. Recovery of Personal Debts

Principle 4:43 contains a general rule in para. 1 and a specific one in para. 2.

2.2.2.2.1. GENERAL RULE

The basic rule laid down in CEFL Principle 4:43 (1) is that the personal debts of one spouse can be recovered from three categories of property: the debtor

---

[36] This is the case in Austria, Belgium with some exceptions (see Art. 1414, para. 2 Belgian Civil Code), Bulgaria, the Czech Republic, Hungary, Italy, Lithuania, Malta, Portugal and Russia, see the national reports available on the CEFL website http://ceflonline.net/property-relations-reports-by-jurisdiction/ (last accessed 13.11.2013).
[37] See e.g. Art. 220, para. 2 French Code civil.

spouse's personal property, the debtor spouse's income and gains[38] and the community assets to the extent of their merger with the debtor spouse's personal property. This solution is slightly restrictive in comparison with most national laws which state that debts which are personal to one spouse can be recovered by the creditor not only from the property of that spouse but also from the community assets.[39] The position taken by the CEFL is to favour recovery from the personal property of the debtor spouse:[40] a debt which is personal to one spouse should primarily be recovered from the personal assets of that spouse.

Even if this solution is rational and fair, one should be aware of the fact that in many cases the major property of one spouse will consist of his or her income. Therefore, in order to prevent the personal creditor of one spouse from being disadvantaged, the income and profits of the debtor spouse should also satisfy the payment of the debt, even if these qualify as the spouses' community assets'.[41] Moreover, personal debts should also be recovered from community assets where a personal asset of the debtor spouse has been merged with community assets (for example, where the personal funds of one spouse have been placed in a private bank account and are then subsequently moved to the spouses' joint bank account).

2.2.2.2.2. SPECIFIC RULE

Principle 4:43 (2) lays down a specific rule for personal debts related to tort or crime. This second paragraph was suggested during the Expert meeting that took place in Sweden (Sigtuna) in September 2011. It aims to protect the victim that has a claim related to tort or crime against a spouse. The victim should not bear the consequences of insufficient amounts in the recovery of the debtor spouse's personal property, income and gains. Therefore, Principle 4:43 (2) states that such a debt can be recovered from half of the net value of the community property. The victim's interest is considered to prevail over the spouses' independence and over the logical connection of the debt with a category of property and/or with a spouse.

---

[38] In a broad sense, see Principle 4:43, Comment 2 ('not only salaries from employment, but also earnings from other activities such as intellectual property rights, lottery wins etc.').

[39] See BOELE-WOELKI/FERRAND/GONZÁLEZ-BEILFUSS/JÄNTERÄ-JAREBORG/MARTINY/LOWE/PINTENS, *Principles of European Family Law Regarding Property Relations Between Spouses*, Principle 4:43, Comparative Overview, p. 266.

[40] However, Principle 4:53 does not impose any order of ranking between the personal property of one spouse and common property.

[41] Principle 4:43, Comment 1, which explains that 'this choice reflects a better law approach and aims both to respect the balance between the spouses and to discharge the community property from debts with which it has no connection'.

This is the only situation where the CEFL Principles on community of acquisitions state an order of ranking[42] with regard to property to be seized by the creditor: the debt should primarily be recovered from the debtor's personal property, income and gains. Only subsequently, where this property is not sufficient, may a part of the value of the community property be seized.

3. ADMINISTRATION OF PROPERTY

Five Principles are dedicated to the issue of the administration of assets. A distinction shall be made between the administration of personal property (section 3.1) and the administration of community property (section 3.2). Under 'administration' is meant 'a wide range of different acts and situations. It includes all acts of disposal (alienation, transfer or title, encumbrance) and pure management of property, for example repair of a movable'.[43] Three models are available: concurrent, joint and exclusive administration.

3.1. ADMINISTRATION OF PERSONAL PROPERTY

Principle 4:47 deals with the *administration of personal property* and states that 'subject to Principles 4:6 and 4:7 each spouse is entitled to administer his or her personal property independently'. Principles 4:6 and 4:7 belong to the general rights and duties of the spouses (protection of the leased family home[44] and representation).[45]

This shows that even if personal property is generally subject to personal administration, exceptions must be provided in order to protect specific assets (especially the family home and household assets) or specific interests.

---

[42] Principle 4:43, para. 2: 'Personal debts related to tort or crime can also be recovered from half of the net value of the community property *where the debtor spouse's personal property, income and gains are insufficient for recovery*'.

[43] See Principle 4:44, Comment 2.

[44] Principle 4:6: '(1) Where the family home is leased to one spouse, the lease is deemed to belong to both spouses, even if it has been concluded before the marriage. (2) One spouse may not terminate or modify the lease without the consent of the other. (3) The landlord should notify both spouses to terminate the lease'.

[45] Principle 4:7: '(1) One spouse may authorise the other spouse to represent him or her in legal transactions. (2) When a spouse is unable to express his or her intentions, the competent authority may authorise the other spouse (a) to act alone where the consent of his or her spouse would otherwise be required; (b) to represent his or her spouse when the latter has the power to act alone'.

3.2. ADMINISTRATION OF COMMUNITY PROPERTY

With regard to the *administration of community property*, a basic rule is laid down (section 3.2.1) but an exception is made for important acts which may have serious consequences for the spouses and the family (section 3.2.2).

3.2.1. Basic Rule

Pursuant to Principle 4:44 (1), each spouse is entitled to administer community property. This means that community property is subject to *concurrent administration* by both spouses, so that each spouse is entitled to autonomously administer the community. This basic rule is the solution which has been adopted in many jurisdictions.[46] However, it has to be restricted in order to take into account the other spouse's or, more globally, the family interest. Therefore, it is common to differentiate between different acts of administration: a spouse can act alone concerning everyday transactions whereas joint administration is required for significant and/or risky transactions (in some jurisdictions,[47] the terminology used is an 'act of extraordinary administration'). Moreover, just as some jurisdictions[48] do, the CEFL Principles include specific provisions governing transactions in respect of the matrimonial or family home irrespective of the matrimonial property regime (see Principles 4:5 and 4:6). The protection of the family home limits the decision-making power of the spouse regardless of whether the family home is common property or the personal property of one spouse.

Not only with regard to the family home, but also in a more general way, the CEFL Principles require joint administration for important acts.

3.2.2. Exception: Acts Requiring Joint Administration

3.2.2.1. Important Acts

Principle 4:44 (1) requires joint administration for '*important acts*'. Principle 4:45 refers to Principles 4:4 to 4:8[49] and to 'the economic circumstances of the

---

[46]   See e.g. Belgium, France, Portugal and the national reports available at http://ceflonline.net/property-relations-reports-by-jurisdiction/ (last accessed 13.11.2013). In other jurisdictions, the administration of the common property is undertaken by both spouses jointly (Austria, Hungary, Lithuania, Russia, Spain) but there is sometimes a rebuttable presumption that there is spousal consent for transactions entered into between either of the spouses and a third party, at least where ordinary transactions are involved.

[47]   See BOELE-WOELKI/FERRAND/GONZÁLEZ-BEILFUSS/JÄNTERÄ-JAREBORG/MARTINY/LOWE/PINTENS, *Principles of European Family Law Regarding Property Relations Between Spouses*, Principle 4:45, Comparative Overview, p. 282 et seq.

[48]   Belgium (Art. 215 Belgian Civil Code), Bulgaria, France (Art. 215 French Civil Code).

[49]   Principles laying down the general rights and duties of the spouses irrespective of the matrimonial property regime chosen by them.

spouses'; it states that acts requiring joint administration include *in particular* the following:

(a) acquisition, alienation and encumbrance of immovable property;
(b) entering into significant loan agreements, guarantees and sureties;
(c) making significant gifts.

This list is not exhaustive. That means that other important acts can require joint administration. As stated in Comment 2 under Principle 4:45, 'although it might be helpful to have a precise definition of what may be considered to be significant, the great diversity of the single transactions and their intimate relationship with national contract and property law precludes giving an exhaustive list'.

3.2.2.2. Refusal of a Spouse to Give his or her Consent

It was necessary to determine the consequences of a spouse's refusal to consent to an act requiring joint administration. Principle 4:44 (2) states that in such a case the other spouse 'may apply to the competent authority for authorisation to act alone'. This provision aims to prevent the negative effects of the behaviour of one spouse who unreasonably withholds his or her consent to an act requiring joint administration. The competent authority (in most cases a court) will take the interest of the community into account. If the act that requires joint administration appears to be in that interest, the court authorisation given to a spouse to act alone shall be restricted to this specific act.

The authorisation of the competent authority can be helpful since it avoids a paralysis where one spouse objects to the planned act without any reasonable ground.[50]

3.2.2.3. Annulment of Acts

Where joint administration by both spouses is required because of the significance of the planned act, it must be determined how far a transaction entered into by only one spouse is legally effective. A sanction should be specified if one spouse acts alone. Pursuant to Principle 4:46, 'acts requiring joint administration may be annulled by the competent authority upon the application of the non-consenting spouse'.

---

[50] Cf. Art. 217 French Civil Code: 'Un époux peut être autorisé par justice à passer seul un acte pour lequel le concours ou le consentement de son conjoint serait nécessaire, si celui-ci est hors d'état de manifester sa volonté *ou si son refus n'est pas justifié par l'intérêt de la famille*'.

This solution is well balanced: no automatic nullity should apply[51] but only a relative invalidity so that the spouse who has not consented may give his or her consent retroactively and ratify the performed transaction. If he or she does not do this, an application may be made to the court to have the act annulled. Principle 4:46 aims to protect the spouse whose consent was required and was not given; it does not address the difficult issue of the consequences for the relationship with third parties. This question is closely linked with contract and property law. The CEFL Principles could not take a specific position and preferred to leave it to national law.

3.2.3. Divestment of the Right to Administer Community Property

In order to protect the interest of the community and of the spouses, Principle 4:48 lays down several grounds allowing the competent authority, upon an application by one spouse, to divest the other spouse of the right to administer, in whole or in part, the community property. The three grounds are of a different nature:[52]

(1) *Inability of the spouse to express his or her intentions*: this can be the case when the spouse is suffering from a mental disorder or where the spouse remains abroad for a long period of time and cannot administer the property[53] or is absent and there is uncertainty as to whether he or she is still alive.
(2) *Serious maladministration*: this covers situations of mismanagement that endanger community property or seriously diminishes its value. Mismanagement does not require voluntary behaviour. In some jurisdictions and pursuant to Principle 4:49(d), serious maladministration can even lead to the dissolution of the community of acquisitions regime.
(3) *Serious failure to comply with the duty to inform in accordance with Principle 4:8*: Pursuant to Principle 4:8, each spouse has the duty to inform the other about his or her assets and debts and about significant acts of administration in so far as this is necessary to enable the other spouse to exercise his or her rights. Only a serious failure to comply with this duty shall justify the partial or total divestment of the right to administer community property. This ground has been formulated by the CEFL in a better law approach in order to strengthen the duty to inform that belongs to the General Part of the

---

[51] See Principle 4:46, Comment 1: 'absolute invalidity may be an inappropriate sanction. It is sufficient that these acts may be annulled by the competent authority at the request of the other spouse'.
[52] The first two grounds can often be found in national law provisions, see the Comparative Overview concerning Principle 4:48.
[53] Cf. the formulation in Art. 1426, para. 1 French Civil Code: 'Si l'un des époux *se trouve, d'une manière durable, hors d'état de manifester sa volonté,* ou si sa gestion de la communauté atteste l'inaptitude ou la fraude, l'autre conjoint peut demander en justice à lui être substitué dans l'exercice de ses pouvoirs'.

Principles (Rights and Duties of the Spouses) since a duty deprived of any sanction might not be taken seriously by the spouses.

Consequently, the power to administer the community property then vests exclusively with the other spouse[54] (para. 2). However, upon an application by either spouse the competent authority may reinstate the divested spouse (para. 3).

In some jurisdictions, in the case of maladministration by a spouse, the other spouse may bring proceedings before the courts for the dissolution of the community or for the separation of property.[55] The CEFL Principles also allow the dissolution of the community of acquisitions regime by a decision of the competent authority based upon 'serious grounds ordering separation of property' (Principle 4:49).

4. DISSOLUTION, LIQUIDATION AND DISTRIBUTION

The CEFL Principles lay down four grounds for the dissolution of the community of acquisitions regime (section 4.1). The community shall then be liquidated (section 4.2) and the property will be distributed between the spouses (section 4.3).

4.1. GROUNDS FOR DISSOLUTION

Principle 4:49 contains four grounds for the dissolution of the community of acquisitions regime. Three of them are self-evident: (1) the death of a spouse;[56] (2) the annulment of the marriage, divorce or legal separation;[57] (3) a change to the matrimonial property regime by agreement between the spouses (e.g. the

---

[54] But only to the extent that one spouse has been divested of the right to administer the community property.

[55] France (Art. 1443 French Civil Code), Italy (Art. 193 Italian Civil Code), Portugal, Spain, see the national reports available at http://ceflonline.net/property-relations-reports-by-jurisdiction/ (last accessed 13.11.2013).

[56] The dissolution operates *ex lege;* the same applies for divorce and legal separation. Absence (meaning that the body of the spouse has not been found but that it is clear from the circumstances that death is certain) can be assimilated with death, as is done in many jurisdictions, see BOELE-WOELKI/FERRAND/GONZÁLEZ-BEILFUSS/JÄNTERÄ-JAREBORG/MART-INY/LOWE/PINTENS, *Principles of European Family Law Regarding Property Relations Between Spouses*, Principle 4:49, Comparative Overview, p. 306. However, the CEFL Principles leave this issue to national law since provisions on the effects of absence belong to the law of persons and not to the law of matrimonial property.

[57] By contrary, in most of the jurisdictions surveyed, factual separation is not a ground for the dissolution of the community of acquisitions, except in Hungary and Lithuania (see the national reports available on the CEFL website http://ceflonline.net/property-relations-

spouses had chosen a community of acquisitions but one of them changes his or her profession and commences a risky activity, for example setting up a self-employed enterprise; in order to protect the other spouse and the family, the spouses will agree on a change of matrimonial property regime and often opt for a separation of property. The amended regime logically requires the liquidation of the previous one). In all the jurisdictions surveyed these grounds lead to the dissolution of the community of acquisitions.

The fourth ground stated in Principle 4:49 is 'the decision of the competent authority *based upon serious grounds* ordering separation of property'. It also belongs to the common core in Europe since most jurisdictions surveyed allow a spouse to apply to the competent authority for the separation of property.[58] They mostly provide for the possibility to request a separation of property on the basis of a general clause;[59] however, some national laws lay down a list of specific grounds that the court will consider *in concreto* in each proceeding. Where a general clause exists, it is based on maladministration by one spouse that endangers the rights of the other spouse in the community.[60]

The CEFL Principles also opt for a broad general clause based on *'serious reasons'*. This formula allows the courts to scrutinise the facts and to order a separation of property, for example in cases of gross maladministration, a severe violation of matrimonial duties, factual separation, the absence or incapacity of a spouse. Also the bankruptcy or insolvency of a spouse could lead to such an order but, unlike a few jurisdictions, the CEFL decided not to make them an autonomous ground for the separation of property, so that the courts shall decide whether or not it can be considered as a serious ground in the pending case. The general clause based on 'serious grounds' appeared to the members of the CEFL Organising Committee to be more flexible and adaptable to all possible national contexts.

---

reports-by-jurisdiction/). Bulgaria and Spain also recognise under some circumstances that a factual separation may be a sufficiently serious reason for the judicial separation of property.

58   Belgium (Art. 1427 Belgian Civil Code), Bulgaria (Art. 26, para. 2 Bulgarian Family Code), France (Arts. 1441 and 1443 French Civil Code.), Hungary (§31, para. 1 Hungarian Family Act), Italy (Art. 193 Italian Civil Code), Lithuania (Art. 3.100 Lithuanian Civil Code), Malta (Art. 1332 Maltese Civil Code), the Netherlands (Art. 1:99, para. 1 Dutch Civil Code), Poland (Art. 52 Polish Family and Guardianship Code), Portugal (see DE OLIVEIRA/MARTINS/VÍTOR, Portuguese Report, Q 43), Russia (Art. 38, para. 2 Russian Family Code), Slovakia (See HAŤAPKA, Slovakian Report, Q 43) and Spain (Art. 1393 Spanish Civil Code).

59   As in Belgium, Bulgaria and France.

60   See e.g. Art. 1443, para. 1 French Civil Code: 'Si, *par le désordre des affaires d'un époux, sa mauvaise administration ou son inconduite*, il apparaît que le maintien de la communauté *met en péril les intérêts de l'autre conjoint*, celui-ci peut poursuivre la séparation de biens en justice'. See also Art. 1470 Belgian Civil Code: 'Un des époux ou son représentant légal peut poursuivre en justice la séparation de biens lorsqu'il apparaît que par le *désordre des affaires de son conjoint, sa mauvaise gestion ou la dissipation de ses revenus*, le maintien du régime existant *met en péril les intérêts de l'époux demandeur*'.

Principle 4:50 contains rules on the date of dissolution.[61] Principle 4:51 states that after the dissolution of the community of acquisitions the general rules of joint ownership apply to administration. This reflects the common core of the jurisdictions surveyed.[62]

4.2. LIQUIDATION OF THE COMMUNITY OF ACQUISITIONS

Three Principles deal with the liquidation of the community of acquisitions regime. Principle 4:52 contains a temporal criterion for the determination and valuation of community property: the determination should take place at the date of the dissolution of the community of acquisitions.[63] The community assets should be valued upon the date of their distribution.

This distinction between determination and valuation is common to most jurisdictions. The determination of the community property at the date of the dissolution of the community means that after this date, the composition of the community cannot be changed.[64] A valuation at the date of the distribution

---

[61]   Principle 4:50: 'The dissolution of the community of acquisitions regime takes effect (a) at the date of the death of a spouse; (b) in the case of annulment of the marriage, divorce or legal separation as between the spouses, either at the date of the application or, if the spouses separated earlier, at the date of their separation and as against third persons, at the date of the registration of the decision of the competent authority; (c) in the case of an agreement to change to another matrimonial property regime as between the spouses, at the date of the change and as against third persons, at the date of the publication of the agreement; (d) in the case of separation of property ordered by the competent authority as between the spouses, at the date of the application and against third persons, at the date of the publication of the application'. In some cases, it appears to be necessary to make a distinction, like most jurisdictions do, between the date of effect as to the spouses and as to third parties since the latter are only informed when publication has taken place. All the solutions stated in Principle 4:50 reflect the common core, except the date of the effect of the dissolution against third parties in the case of a judicial separation of property order (no common core could be asserted in this respect). The CEFL Principles have opted for a better law approach as explained in Comment 7 under Principle 4:50: 'The protection of the interests of the applicant spouse can only be effective when there is also retroactivity against third parties. The reason for the application is the disorder in the financial affairs and the outstanding debts of the other spouse. Without retroactivity against third parties there is a real danger that during the proceedings the situation will become increasingly detrimental for the applicant. But the interests of third parties also require protection. Retroactivity from the date of the application does not guarantee this protection. Principle 4:50(d) accordingly opts for retroactivity from the date of publication of the application'.

[62]   However, a few jurisdictions apply matrimonial property law until the community is liquidated and the assets are distributed (Russia, Slovakia, partially Hungary, see the national reports, Q 48, available on the website of the CEFL http://ceflonline.net/property-relations-reports-by-jurisdiction/ (last accessed 13.11.2013).

[63]   This date is determined pursuant to Principle 4:50.

[64]   See Principle 4:52, Comment 1.

allows possible fluctuations in the market value of the assets belonging to the community to be taken into account.

All jurisdictions are aware that the community and personal property of the spouses are not always kept separate. A spouse can use community funds to improve his or her personal property. In some cases, a creditor can recover the debt of one spouse from community property. The personal property of a spouse or the community property can be impoverished or enriched. Unjust enrichment will give rise to compensation (*récompenses* in French law) in proprietary rights or in value. In most legal systems,[65] proprietary rights in the assets are not modified but compensation is due to a spouse or to the community property.

Therefore, Principle 4:53 (1) states that the community property should be compensated for any contribution profiting the personal property of a spouse. And reciprocally, the personal property of a spouse should be compensated for any contribution profiting the community property (Principle 4:53 (2)).[66]

Some legal systems calculate the compensation due at the nominal value without having regard to an increase or decrease in value.[67] This is also the basic solution provided by Principle 4.53,[68] but para. 3 excludes this rule in the case of investment: 'In the case of investment for the acquisition, improvement or preservation of an asset, the calculation of the compensation should *take into account any resulting increase or decrease in the value of the asset'*. Two reasons justify this exception: (1) it reflects the common core of the jurisdictions surveyed; and (2) the profit that can be made by the beneficiary category of property should also benefit the category that made the investment: if community money has been invested to improve a dwelling which is the personal property of a spouse and if the value of this house has increased at the moment of the liquidation of the regime, it is fair to allow community property take part in the enrichment. The same applies in case of a decrease in the value of the asset.

Like the majority of the legal systems surveyed, the CEFL Principles state that *compensation should be paid in money,* unless the spouses agree otherwise (Principle 4:53 (4)). This reflects the common core but leaves room for possible spousal agreements in this respect, which provides for flexibility.

Principle 4:54 deals with the *ranking of community debts* and states that community debts and compensation rights rank equally. This solution is not self-evident since two patterns can be found in national legal systems: the first

---

[65]   However, in Hungary, Lithuania and Russia, a court decision may change proprietary rights in the assets and declare personal assets which have improved with community funds to be community assets, see the national reports, Q 45, available on the CEFL website http://ceflonline.net/property-relations-reports-by-jurisdiction/ (last accessed 13.11.2013).

[66]   An increase or decrease in the value of the asset should, however, be taken into account, see the example provided in Comment 1 to Principle 4:53.

[67]   See Bulgaria, Poland, Portugal and Slovakia, see the national reports, Q 45.

[68]   The basic rule can be deduced from Principle 4:53, para. 3 that lays down an exception as to reinvestment. It could for example apply where a debt which is personal to a spouse has been paid from community property.

one gives priority to community debts over compensation rights whereas the second give both equal ranking. As explained in Comment 1 to Principle 4:54, both systems have advantages and disadvantages. The first pattern strengthens the position of creditors of the community, which can facilitate transactions between the spouses and third parties; the position of the spouse having a compensation claim is weaker if there are many community debts to be paid. The second model puts the creditor in a weaker position since his or her claim has no priority over compensation due to a spouse. The CEFL has opted for a better law approach considering that no serious or imperative reason justifies a better position for the creditor.

4.3. DISTRIBUTION BETWEEN THE SPOUSES

The underlying principle of the community of acquisitions regime is that community property should be shared equally upon the dissolution of the regime (Principle 4:57 (1)). However, Principle 4:55 allows the spouses to agree on the distribution of community property. This is largely recognised by national legal systems, except in Poland and Portugal[69] where the rules on division in equal shares are mandatory and cannot be set aside by the will of the spouses. Since the CEFL Principles are aimed at favouring spousal autonomy and therefore marital property agreements,[70] it seemed useful to repeat this favour in a provision regarding the community of acquisitions regime.[71] The agreement can relate to all aspects of liquidation and distribution (the renouncement of compensation, evaluation of the assets, distribution in kind or in money etc.).[72] However, like in Principle 4:15[73] contained in Chapter II dedicated to Marital Property Agreements, the Principles dealing with the community of acquisitions give the competent authority, in case of 'exceptional hardship', the power to 'set aside or modify any spousal agreement made in accordance with Principle 4:55'.

Equal sharing can therefore be set aside not only by a spousal agreement, but also by the competent authority in cases of exceptional hardship. The competent

---

69   See the national reports, Q 55.
70   See Chapter II of the Principles of European Family Law Regarding Property Relations Between Spouses, Principles 4:10 to 4:15.
71   For the participation in acquisitions regime, see Principle 4:29.
72   The agreement on distribution applies as between the spouses and cannot affect the rights of third persons. Especially in the case of fraud, some legal systems give the creditor a special claim called an *action pauliana* (*action paulienne*, see e.g. Art. 1167, para. 1 French Civil Code: the creditors 'peuvent aussi, en leur nom personnel, attaquer les actes faits par leur débiteur en fraude de leurs droits'), which is a remedy for the creditor against fraudulent transfers by his debtor.
73   Principle 4:15 Exceptional hardship: 'Having regard to the circumstances when the agreement was concluded or those subsequently arising, the competent authority may, in cases of exceptional hardship, set aside or adjust a marital property agreement'.

authority can then 'adjust the distribution' (Principle 4:57 (2)(a)). This rule is based on a better law approach: in many jurisdictions[74] the competent authority has the power to set aside or to adjust the division of the community property because at least in divorce and legal separation cases maintenance or lump-sum compensation can be awarded to the financially weaker spouse. The CEFL Principles strive to strike a balance between foreseeability and predictability, on the one hand, and fairness, on the other. This is the reason why *exceptional* hardship may lead to an adjustment by the court of the division of community property. Admittedly, the concept of 'exceptional hardship' is a vague one and should give discretion to the national courts to scrutinise whether an unequal distribution is absolutely necessary to provide for the needs of a spouse who, for example, cannot rely on maintenance and/or social security benefits.

Fairness and interest of the family are also the underlying grounds of the provisions on the allocation of the family home, household goods and professional assets (Principle 4:56): in determining the distribution of community property a competent authority may, *in the interest of the family* and subject to the payment of compensation, allocate to one of the spouses (a) the family home and household goods; (b) professional assets.[75] This possibility only concerns the community property and not the personal assets of the spouses. The competent authority shall examine whether the interest of the family (in most cases after divorce when the children reside with only one parent) requires such an allocation of community property to one spouse.

In contrast to Principle 4:57, which gives the court the power to set aside equal sharing and to adjust the distribution on the ground of exceptional hardship, such exceptional hardship is not required for the allocation of the family home, household goods and professional assets. The spouse who benefits from the allocation therefore has to pay compensation. However, if the competent authority considers that there is a situation of exceptional hardship for one spouse, it can apply Principle 4:57 (2) and refrain from ordering compensation to be due.

---

[74] See Belgium, Portugal, Slovakia and also France but the court, when ordering a *prestation compensatoire* in the divorce decree, takes into account the property of the spouses after the liquidation of the community. See the national reports, Q 55. Some adjustments are possible in Bulgaria, Hungary, Poland and Russia and seem to be justified by the housing problems in these countries as well as by low maintenance amounts after divorce, see the national reports, Q 55 and BOELE-WOELKI/FERRAND/GONZÁLEZ-BEILFUSS/JÄNTERÄ-JAREBORG/MARTINY/LOWE/PINTENS, *Principles of European Family Law Regarding Property Relations Between Spouses*, Principle 4:57, Comparative Overview, p. 338.

[75] For this category of assets, which are normally the personal property of the spouse, see Comment 2 to Principle 4:56: 'Principle 4:56(b) only deals with assets that are not exclusively used for the professional activities of one spouse. This will be the case when the assets are used for the professional activities of both spouses or when those assets are also used for other purposes'.

The recovery of community debts after the distribution of the community is the subject dealt with in Principle 4:58. The basic rule is that community debts can be recovered, after the distribution of the community, from the share of the community of each spouse and from the personal property of the spouse who has incurred the debt (para. 1). This rule in Principle 4:58 concerns only debts that were not settled upon the liquidation of the community either because there were no assets available to recover them or because the debts were not yet due upon the liquidation. For debts to be settled during the regime and upon liquidation, Principle 4:42 applies.

If a spouse has paid a community debt after the distribution of the community property, he or she has recourse against the other spouse for half of this payment (Principle 4:58 (2)). This share has to be adjusted in two cases: (1) where the spouses have agreed to an unequal sharing; or (2) where the competent authority has adjusted the distribution of community property on the ground of exceptional hardship (Principle 4:58 (2)).

PART TWO
BREAKUP OF (NON-)FORMALISED RELATIONSHIPS

STATUTORY REGULATION OF COHABITING RELATIONSHIPS IN THE NORDIC COUNTRIES

Recent Developments and Future Challenges

Tone Sverdrup

Contents

1. THE REASON FOR SHARING ASSETS UPON A RELATIONSHIP BREAKDOWN

Whereas the marital property regimes are quite similar in the Nordic countries, the legal response to cohabiting relationships differs greatly among these countries. Sweden is the only country where assets can be divided equally upon termination. In the other countries, compensation or restitution may be granted according to different rules. This differing approach might come as a surprise, as socio-demographic characteristics are more or less the same in all five countries.

One characteristic of the Nordic countries' labour force is the high participation of women, while at the same time there is a high fertility rate. The institution of the lifelong housewife is definitely a thing of the past. However, complete gender equality has not been achieved in the Nordic countries, since about 40 per cent of employed women are working part time, while very few men work part time.[1] A large number of women in the Nordic countries continue to assume the main responsibility for childcare; they often earn less than their partners and, as a result, have little surplus income to invest. This fact – in my opinion – is the core of the rationale in favour of legislation pertaining to the termination of cohabiting relationships: many cohabitants – albeit far from all of them – live as financially interdependent entities, especially if the relationships have lasted for a period of several years and the couples have children. Together, they form a work unit, as well as a consumption and investment unit, and for these reasons the financial position of one party can hardly be unaffected by that of the other. The most typical example of this is when one cohabitant undertakes more than her (or his) share of the 'unprofitable' tasks in the family, such as childcare and the coverage of consumption expenses, and as a result ends up with no appreciable assets even after a longer cohabitating relationship. By taking on more than her share of the non-profitable tasks, she has enabled part of her partner's income to accrue, and if that income is used for investments she has contributed indirectly to the other's accumulation of capital.

One could argue, however, that the full-time breadwinner would have earned just as much even if she had not performed more than her share of the childcare duties; most likely, he would have paid for a nanny or placed the children in a childcare centre. Therefore, the cohabitant who takes care of the children has only freed a relatively smaller amount of the wage earner's capital.[2] The purpose of causal reasoning, however, is to trace the economic significance of domestic labour for the acquisition of assets, and not to predict the most likely outcome in the concrete case. If the father and mother had been two disassociated stakeholders in the market, the most obvious option would have been to find out what would most probably have occurred in the alternative instance. But this is about two equal parties who have joined forces to start a family and a situation in which neither is employed by the other. Therefore it seems foreign to measure childcare at the value of the amount it would have cost to purchase equivalent services on the market. From a legal standpoint, the party who undertakes the unprofitable part of the double task (domestic and outside work) is random in the sense that the parties do not normally base their division of labour on the consideration of which party will own items acquired during the relationship. The choice is usually based on other factors such as the

---

[1] Norway has the highest rate of about 42 per cent of women working part time, Sweden 39 per cent and Denmark 37 per cent. Finland stands out with a share of only 19 per cent of employed women in part-time work, cf. *Kvinder og mænd på arbejdsmarkedet 2012*, table 11.2.1 (Danish official report), available at http://bm.dk/upload/BEM/Files/Dokumenter/Publikationer/2013/Kvinder%20og%20maend%20p%C3%A5%20arbejdsmarkedet%202012.pdf (last accessed 03.12.2013).

[2] The Law Commission for England and Wales argues along these lines in its report, *Cohabitation: The Financial Consequences of Relationship Breakdown* 2007 Law. Com. No. 307, para. 4.48, cf. T. SVERDRUP, 'An ill-fitting garment: Why the logic of private law falls short between cohabitants', in B. VERSCHRAEGEN (ed.) *Family Finances* (2009), pp. 360.

wage level, gender roles, commitment, interests, etc. The person who undertakes the outside work should therefore not be the ultimate owner of the acquisitions merely on the basis of that rationale. In other words, the care undertaken by parents and third persons is not fully replaceable in this calculation. When one party is at home with small children (part time or full time) while the other is the full-time breadwinner, the parties have chosen a division of labour where the children are taken care of (partly) by the parents, as opposed to an outside party. The fact that the children are cared for by the parents should remain a constant factor in the causal reasoning, that is, as a premise in the assessment of how great a retained benefit her domestic contributions have conferred upon the breadwinner.[3]

From this perspective, losses sustained and contributions made during the relationship are two sides of the same coin. Childcare and homemaking has enabled the other party to pursue his own career and earn more money. The 'coin' is the childcare and household work, which constitutes, on the one side, an indirect contribution to the breadwinner's acquisitions and, on the other side, an obstacle to the (part-time) homemaker's being able to seek paid work, which results in a loss of income.[4]

A widespread argument *against* legal regulation is related to the fact that marriage is an option available to most cohabiting couples. It is claimed that there is no need to legislate at all for cohabitation, since the couple can decide to marry and thus acquire sufficient protection through the existing marriage legislation. However, one word in this argument – the word 'couple' – shrouds the reality. It takes two to marry; the reluctant party has the right of veto. Therefore, the question is not whether the couple can marry, but whether the cohabitants agree to marry. In the past, this difference (between a couple and two cohabitants) did not matter so much, because it was not socially acceptable for a cohabitant to suggest continuing cohabitation instead of marriage, especially if they were expecting children. But this is no longer the case – unmarried cohabitation, even lifelong, is now socially acceptable in all the Nordic countries. This acceptability has changed the entire nature of the legislative issue. Nowadays, a cohabitant can always decline marriage, or require a favourable pre-nuptial agreement as a condition for marrying. Thus, the

---

[3] This is also the position of the Norwegian Supreme Court. The Court speaks of the freeing of time and not of the freeing of capital when children are concerned, cf. Rt. 1975, p. 220; 1976, p. 694; 1980, p. 1403 and Rt. 1983, p. 1146.

[4] Even though losses and gains are two sides of the same coin, they do not always go equally far. For example, if the alternative income for the cohabitant that takes care of the children would have been lower than the breadwinner's income, one could argue that she has not lost as much as he has gained, and that her compensation should therefore be limited to her loss, cf. T. SVERDRUP, 'Compensating Gain and Loss in Marriage: A Scandinavian Comment on the ALI Principles', in R.F. WILSON (ed.), *Reconceiving the Family. Critique on the American Law Institute's Principles of the Law of Family Dissolution*, Cambridge University Press 2006, p. 472.

vulnerable party has lost the safety net that marriage represents. The argument that cohabitants can simply marry lacks any real impact in the Nordic countries.

Other arguments against legislation are still valid, for example that cohabitants are independent individuals having responsibility for their own financial future even if they move in with another person (see section 4 below). Statutory regulation in cohabitation requires solid justification even today.

With these considerations as a backdrop, I shall compare the different legal solutions in the Nordic countries and discuss the regulation that is deemed most suitable. In the end, I will ask whether it is realistic to imagine the harmonisation of the legal regulation in the Nordic countries.

2. THE LEGAL SITUATION IN THE NORDIC COUNTRIES

As mentioned, Sweden is the only Nordic country where assets can be divided equally upon the dissolution of the relationship. In the other countries, only limited possibilities to grant compensation exist.[5] Cohabitants own their property separately during the relationship in all countries, and they are not required to provide for each other during the relationship. If none of the special rules apply in a particular case, the cohabiting partners retain their property and debts upon a relationship breakdown. In other words, a settlement along property lines takes place. These property lines, however, are drawn differently in each country. In Norway, co-ownership can be established solely on the basis of indirect contributions in the form of childcare or the meeting of consumption expenses.[6] This is not possible in the other Nordic countries.

Cohabitants are free to enter into an agreement aimed at regulating the financial consequences upon the dissolution of their relationship in all countries. Such a contract can be fully or partially annulled if it affects one of the cohabitants unfairly.[7] However, such annulments only occur in exceptional cases. Not many cohabitants regulate the financial consequences by an agreement.[8]

---

[5] The Norwegian Household Community Act 1991 applies to cohabitants; however, this act only provides a limited opportunity for a household member to purchase the previously common residence at market value upon the termination of the relationship.

[6] Rt. 1978, p. 1352 and 1984, p. 497.

[7] See for example the Danish, Norwegian and Swedish Acts relating to the conclusion of agreements, s. 36.

[8] In 1997 about 20 per cent of Norwegian cohabiting couples had contracted an agreement, cf. NOU 1999: 25 Samboerne og samfunnnet, p. 71.

2.1. SWEDEN

In 1987, the Swedish government wanted to adopt a neutral stance towards the two family forms, marriage and cohabitation, and introduced the first Cohabitation Act that divided certain assets equally. The present Act from 2003 applies both to different-sex and same-sex couples. As a general rule, the value of the family home and household goods is divided equally upon termination, but only as long as these items are acquired for joint use.[9] Other items are not subject to an equal division. If an equal division of assets would lead to an unreasonable result for the cohabitant who owns most of the divisible assets, the settlement can be adjusted so that a smaller portion – or no assets at all – is divided.[10] Such an adjustment would typically take place in relationships of shorter duration where gifts, inheritance, etc. are invested in the home.[11] The objective of the Swedish Cohabitation Act is 'to provide a minimum level of protection for a financially vulnerable party, by sharing the value of a home that has been jointly built up'.[12]

One could argue that the Swedish Cohabitation Act has its pitfalls. Seen in the light of the cohabitants' contributions, the requirement that the family home must be 'acquired for joint use', aims both too low and too high. Substantial discrepancies may arise between the cohabitants' contributions, on the one hand, and what they are left with upon termination, on the other. A cohabitant who makes substantial contributions, for example to the down payments on the house of the other cohabitant will be left with nothing in cases where the dwelling was not acquired for joint use. On the other hand, as long as the house was acquired for joint use, the full value of the house is divided equally, even if the owner has financed the whole house with his or her inheritance or gifts. At first glance this might seem to be an unreasonable solution, because pre-relationship assets, gifts and inheritances are not part of the regular communion between cohabitants, and the other party is presumed not to have contributed to these acquisitions. But contributions made should not be the sole justification for the sharing of assets. If the cohabitants form a consumption and investment unit, the favourable financial position of one party at the beginning of the relationship is often an impediment to capital accumulation during the relationship.

An economic adaptation between the parties lies solely in the fact that most cohabitants must be content with one dwelling; it is in the nature of family life that both parties live in a single family home. If only one of the parties owned

---

9   Swedish Cohabitation Act 2003 section 3, cf. section 4.
10   Swedish Cohabitation Act 2003 section 15.
11   See for example NJA 2003, p.650.
12   M. BRATTSTRÖM, 'The protection of a Vulnerable Party when a Cohabitee Relationship Ends – An Evaluation of the Swedish Cohabitees Act', in B. VERSCHRAEGEN (ed.) *Family Finances*, Sramek 2009, p. 350.

the house before they started to cohabit, the other will not make future investments (savings) in a house in most cases. If one of the cohabitants brings a house into the relationship, the basic investments are already available to the family. In this situation, it is natural for the parties to apply most of their disposable income to current expenses during the union. The party without property will benefit from the other party's housing investment while they live together, but will sustain considerable losses if nothing is saved when the cohabitants part company after many years. In order to preclude the non-owning party's emergence from a dissolved union empty-handed, the said party must set aside part of his or her income during the relationship in the event of a possible break-up. But how many cohabitants would do such a thing in practice? Court cases indicate that non-owning cohabitants do not make these provisions. Cohabitants (and spouses) live in a shared living relationship, one of the consequences of which is that they form a joint consumption unit. They adjust the level of consumption to each other and to the fact that basic investments such as a family home are already available. Due to the fact that women generally have less income and property than men and tend to marry men who are older than themselves, this is primarily a problem for women.

The Swedish Cohabitation Act protects the non-owning cohabitant in this situation, but only as long as the house is acquired for joint use. In a market relationship it would be unthinkable to claim compensation on the ground that one had been living in the owner's home and therefore had been impeded from investing in a house oneself. In intimate relationships, however, the logic is quite different, cf. above. The family home holds a unique position and cannot be compared with any other item of property. As long as most couples must be content with one dwelling, the non-owning party should at least share in the price rise (and fall) in the real estate market, otherwise he or she will be 'trapped', and be disproportionately equipped to acquire a new dwelling on the dissolution of a long-lasting relationship (and conversely, in the event of a price decline).

2.2. DENMARK AND NORWAY

In the 1980s, non-statutory rules to avert unjust enrichment developed through Supreme Court practice both in Denmark and in Norway. In Denmark, compensation may be granted if the cohabitant enables, to a significant degree, the other party to create or preserve a considerable fortune. The amount shall be determined with regard to, among other things, the duration of the relationship and the financial position of the parties.[13] In Norway, two conditions must be met in order to grant compensation.[14] First, the cohabitant must have provided

---

[13]   U 1980.480 H, U 1984.166 H, U 1985.607 H.
[14]   Rt. 2011, p. 1168.

the other party with a significant financial benefit in order to receive any compensation. Secondly, the granting of compensation must be reasonable. Compensation shall only be granted in exceptional cases.[15]

These case-law rules have proved to be ill-suited to correct imbalances in the settlements after cohabitation. In Denmark, this is partly due to the fact that contributions in the form of childcare and housework are only acknowledged to a limited degree.[16] In Norway, it is in part due to the fact that compensation is rarely granted.[17]

Norway is the only Nordic country where cohabitants may inherit from one another. These rules were enacted in 2008 and apply only to cohabitants who have children together.[18] Surviving cohabitants with children can either inherit a total of approximately €40,000, or choose to postpone the settlement and keep part of the deceased's estate undivided. This so-called *right of undistributed estate* applies to the family home and household goods, to holiday homes and vehicles as long as they are for joint use.[19] The Norwegian inheritance rules for cohabitants have gained significant acceptance in Norwegian society. However, some settlements have proved difficult to carry out in practice, and we might experience some amendments to the law in the future.

2.3. FINLAND

So far, Finland is the only Nordic country to codify special family law rules to avert unjust enrichment. The Finnish Act on the Dissolution of the Household of Cohabiting Partners from 2011 applies to couples who have lived in a shared household for at least five years or have children together.[20] According to the Act compensation is granted if a cohabitant has assisted the other in accumulating his or her property, and a separation of property solely on the basis of ownership would result in enrichment at the expense of the other.[21] Compensation is not granted if this enrichment is insignificant. Not only

---

15   Rt. 1984, p. 497, Rt. 2000, p. 1089 and Rt. 2011, p. 1168.
16   I. LUND-ANDERSEN, 'The division of property between unmarried cohabitees on the termination of cohabitation – a Scandinavian perspective', in A. BÜCHLER and M. MÜLLER-CHEN (eds.), *Private Law – national – global – comparative Festschrift fur Ingeborg Schwenzer zum 60. Geburtstag*, Stämpfli Verlag 2011, p. 1129 and I. LUND-ANDERSEN, *Familieøkonomien: Samlevendes Retsforhold, Ægtefællers Retsforhold, Retspolitik*, Jurist- og Økonomforbundets Forlag 2011, pp. 380–381 and p. 424.
17   T. SVERDRUP, 'Vederlagskrav og lemping i samboerforhold – to nye høyesterettsdommer', *Tidsskrift for Familierett, arverett og barnevernsrettslige spørsmål*, (FAB) 4/ 2011, pp. 323.
18   Norwegian Inheritance Act 1972 ch. III A, cf. J. ASLAND and P. HAMBROS, 'New Developments and Expansion of Relationships Covered by Norwegian Law', in B. ATKINS (ed.), *The International Survey of Family Law. 2009 Edition*, Jordan Publishing 2009, pp. 378–384.
19   Norwegian Inheritance Act 1972 section 28 c.
20   Finnish Cohabitation Act 2011 section 3.
21   Finnish Cohabitation Act 2011 section 8.

financial contributions, but also domestic work and long-term care work at home can establish grounds for compensation.

It is not yet clear whether the Finnish provisions function any better than the Danish and Norwegian rules, because the Act has not been in force for very long. However, information tends to indicate that compensation is granted more regularly in Finland than in Denmark and Norway. The legal procedure is simpler in Finland, as an estate distributor may decide on compensation instead of the district court.[22]

3. FIXED RULES AND THE LOGIC OF COHABITATION

Each couple's relationship is unique, and since a fixed rule for the division of assets cannot meet the needs in each individual case, one would think that a tailor-made approach to making restitution aimed at averting unjust enrichment is the best solution. I do not share this view, however.

In my opinion, Sweden's fixed rules have proved to be the best way of regulating cohabiting relationships, despite its pitfalls, as mentioned above. Fixed rules, like the Swedish Cohabitation Act, have the potential to equalise economic differences in many cohabiting relationships, whereas restitution rules have failed to protect the vulnerable party, at least in Denmark and Norway. This should come as no surprise. In my view, legislation based on the restitution of unjust enrichment (or enrichment without any basis) is unsuited to correct financial imbalances after the break-up of cohabitating relationships for several reasons.

Most importantly, the principle of unjust enrichment and similar principles fundamentally contradict the financial and emotional mechanisms that prevail in cohabitations. These legal principles have developed with a view to market relationships, where most benefits have a legitimate contractual basis. The principle of unjust enrichment applies to the atypical incidents where a mistake has been made or another unusual event has occurred. The entire principle is aimed at extraordinary situations. In cohabitation, however, enrichments stemming from indirect contributions are neither atypical nor extraordinary. On the contrary, they are embedded as an inevitable part of many cohabiting relationships. Indirect contributions arise, as mentioned, when one cohabitant undertakes more than his or her share of the unprofitable consumption tasks in the family and thus enables the other party to invest more. The two cohabitants' work efforts may be equal at any given moment, yet inequality is generated over time because the work performance of one is consumed and that of the other is

---

[22] Finnish Cohabitation Act 2011 sections 7 and 9.

invested. Because these contributions occur indirectly and gradually, it is nearly impossible for a cohabitant to ensure a reciprocal service by means of a contract.

Secondly, the whole idea that a person should regain what he or she has contributed to the other in a loving relationship is – in a way – wrong. Transfers of goods and services are normally not mutually conditioned in a joint living relationship. Rather than being conditioned, in a number of cases a service would lose its value if it were conditionally dependent on a reciprocal service. Thus, compensating disadvantages or making restitution *on a regular basis* contradicts what should be the norm in a cohabiting relationship.

Even though a single service is normally not conditional upon a reciprocal service, there is reason to believe that the concept of reciprocity or an overall balance exists in many cohabitating relationships, for example, an ideal balance between contributions rendered during the relationship and returns after the relationship. And it could be argued that the restitution of *indirect* contributions does not contradict the social norm that a cohabitant should not regain what has been given, because indirect contributions are not 'given' at all. They are, per definition, not transferred directly to the other party. Indirect contributions are not intended at all; they arise as a side-effect of an unequal division of labour and expenses, cf. above.

However, the norm that a cohabitant should regain what he/she has been given only in exceptional cases could easily 'rub off on' indirect contributions. In my view, making restitution or compensating disadvantages due to indirect contributions is not possible on a regular basis. It contradicts the 'logic of cohabitation' as well as the law of restitution.

Thus, principles of unjust enrichment and similar principles where the actual contributions, gains or losses are measured in each individual case are only applicable in exceptional cases. And because indirect contributions are embedded as an inherent part of many relationships, such legal provisions will not be effective. Principles of unjust enrichment may correct mistakes and misunderstandings in individual cases, but are not suited to correct the overall system error stemming from an unequal division of labour and expenditure. This system error can only be corrected by fixed rules that ensure equal sharing on a regular basis.

Furthermore, the applications of restitution rules involve the exercise of discretion and the result will often be difficult to predict. Cohabitants will often find it too costly to claim their rights through the legal system. And if they instigate a claim, they might very well find that a whole range of facts and incidents are subject to dispute. Fact finding is predominant in cases involving restitution or compensation. These rules can easily create conflicts that could harm the future relationship between the cohabitants and therefore also harm their children.

4. CLOSING REMARKS

As individualisation increases in the Nordic societies, novel arguments against regulation have emerged from both the liberal and conservative sides of the political spectrum.

Social democrats could argue that statutory regulation will impede gender equality, as an equal division of assets upon termination would favour women who work only part time, thereby cementing gender roles. Others will object and maintain that statutory regulation in cohabiting relationships plays a subordinate role in women's choice between full-time or part-time work. In any event, one could question whether it is ethically justifiable to let such political considerations determine the content of settlements upon a relationship breakdown.

Among conservatives, resistance to any kind of legislation lies in the genes, and some would argue that the problems could be solved along contractual lines. But market mechanisms do not operate between two cohabitants. Cohabitants have already established a relationship; they are not replaceable market actors. A cohabitant cannot deselect the other party just because the conditions in a cohabitation contract are unfavourable. Furthermore, in the market, both parties expect to gain from a transaction. A cohabitation contract, on the other hand, determines the division of their future assets. The termination of such a contract is like a cake that is divided, it is a zero-sum game where one will lose and one will win. Therefore, it comes as no surprise that few enter into cohabitation contracts.

Even though several arguments can be made against these individualistic approaches, the above arguments from both the left and the right share a basic commonality which, in my view, should be the basis for legislation in this area: As a starting point, cohabitants should be viewed as autonomous legal entities with the right to their own property and with a responsibility for their own financial future. The question of equal sharing occurs only when they form a unit, in labour, consumption or investment, so that the financial position of one party can hardly avoid being affected by the other.

Is it realistic to imagine the harmonisation of the legal regulation in the Nordic countries? I believe that Denmark, Norway and Iceland will introduce statutory regulations in the foreseeable future. However, I fear that these countries will not follow Sweden's example and enact fixed division rules, but instead enact regulations where gains are measured on a case-by-case basis, as is already done in Finland. Such rules serve as an ideal compromise for politicians who do not want to alienate any of their voters. Supporters of legislative action get a cohabitation act, and the opponents get what they want as well, namely an act that is ineffective because restitution will be granted only in exceptional cases, cf. above under section 3. Besides being ineffective, restitution and compensation rules stand in contrast to the precisely worded statutes with predictable outcomes found in Nordic marriage laws. Restitution rules contain a degree of ambiguity and discretion alien to Nordic legal culture, and therefore they tend to be especially costly to enforce.

In my view, the conflict between autonomy and community could be solved by a more realistic and functional compromise: fixed rules should divide at least some assets equally to ensure an effective application, but the law could be confined to relationships where the division of labour and expenditure typically leads to an unequal accumulation of assets. The most striking example of this is relationships where the cohabitants have children together.

LEGISLATING FOR COHABITATION IN COMMON LAW JURISDICTIONS IN EUROPE
Two Steps Forward and One Step Back?

Anne Barlow

Contents

1. ABSTRACT

Within Europe, the common law jurisdictions of England and Wales, Scotland and the Republic of Ireland have not taken a unified approach in their legal response to the increasingly common social phenomenon of unmarried cohabitation. Whereas both Scotland and Ireland have recently legislated to provide financial provision remedies as between cohabiting partners on relationship breakdown, in England and Wales (and in Northern Ireland), there are still no family law remedies for financial provision when such relationships break down. This is despite the Law Commission for England and Wales recommending reform in 2007 (see *Cohabitation: the financial consequences of relationship breakdown*, Law Com No 307, CM 7182, (2007) London: TSO). Interestingly, in the recent Supreme Court decision of the Scottish case of *Gow v Grant* (Scotland) [2012] UKSC 29, the Supreme Court Justices expressed their frustration at this state of affairs, calling loudly for English law to be changed in line with that of Scotland. Yet so far these calls have fallen on deaf ears. Thus whilst England and Wales has now embraced legal recognition of same-sex marriage, heterosexual cohabitation continues to be regarded by government as a social problem and a threat to formal marriage, with both the Scottish approach to compensating economic disadvantage within cohabitation relationships and an extension of civil partnerships to different-sex couples having been recently rejected once again by government.

Drawing on socio-legal research evidence and discussion (including the continued existence of the 'common law marriage myth'), this paper will explore these legal and policy developments in all three jurisdictions against the background of the changing socio-demographic nature of family structures within these societies. It will consider whether the piecemeal legal response to cohabitation in England and Wales provides adequate remedies, given policy objectives, or alternatively whether the Irish and/or Scottish solutions could be appropriately adopted within England and Wales (and Northern Ireland) or indeed, whether a different approach is called for.

2. INTRODUCTION

At the beginning of the 19th century, Napoleon reportedly said, 'Cohabitants ignore the law, so the law ignores them'. Love and marriage, according to the received wisdom embedded in popular culture in the mid 20th century, were still felt to go together 'like a horse and carriage'.[1] Certainly, in most jurisdictions within Europe this hierarchy of relationship recognition, with marriage firmly at the top, remains in place, with jurisdictions increasingly now extending this gold standard to same-sex couples. Yet, arguably, the key question for family law within today's Europe is whether, in the light of clearly changed cultural shifts and social trends surrounding modern partnering and parenting practices, such a strategy is in need of radical revision to make family law fit for purpose in the 21st century. For if family law principally regulates those who marry, yet increasingly fewer (heterosexual) people choose to marry, whilst growing numbers choose to cohabit, surely there comes a point when family law is completely missing its target and it consequently stands accused of failing to fulfil the function expected of it; namely to regulate fairly family life within contemporary society.

In many parts of the common law world, this is exactly the conclusion that has been arrived at and we see a pragmatic legal response being made to such changing social trends. Thus common law jurisdictions such as Australia and New Zealand have taken an inclusive and presumptive approach to regulating cohabitation, by extending the rights and responsibilities of married couples presumptively (that is, without any need to 'opt-in' or formally register a

---

[1]   So says the famous popular Frank Sinatra song, dating back to 1955 (released by Capitol Records).

partnership or civil union) to those who cohabit, unless they actively choose to 'opt-out'. In these jurisdictions, there is no material difference between the rights and responsibilities and legal remedies available on the death of a partner or on relationship breakdown between those who marry and those who cohabit.[2]

One might therefore expect this same approach to have been adopted within what might be termed 'common law Europe'; that is the three United Kingdom (UK) jurisdictions of England and Wales, Scotland, Northern Ireland plus the Republic of Ireland, which often draws on experience in these other common law jurisdictions to resolve common problems. These are, after all, societies which share histories, culture, social problems and social trends, as well as language. However this has not been the case with regard to the phenomenon of cohabitation, despite broadly similar demographic patterns.

Drawing on empirical research findings within the UK, this author and others have long argued that family law needs to formally acknowledge and adapt to social change and shifting social norms around marriage decline and increased cohabitation. Ideally, it has been suggested, this should be done through legislation in a cohesive way, creating a clear legal status for the increasingly large numbers of couples who cohabit and form families outside marriage. Indeed, the four Law Commissions within the UK and Ireland have each independently drawn the same conclusion. However, the reaction to these changing trends within these four jurisdictions of the British Isles[3] has been far from cohesive, with different states choosing different regulatory approaches to a common changing social landscape. Thus, whilst reforms have occurred, we have not witnessed a unified response. Rather, there have been differential legal responses which, when judged against the social trends, are not what might have been predicted and do not copy the marriage-mirror solutions favoured in Australia and New Zealand. Neither, however, have solutions found elsewhere in Europe (most often an 'opt-in' registered partnership approach), been adopted in the context of heterosexual cohabitants, although civil partnerships providing marriage-like rights, status and remedies, are available to same-sex couples within all four jurisdictions.[4]

---

2 Both jurisdictions do require cohabitants to show they are eligible to be treated as married. In New Zealand, eligibility for equal sharing of assets arises after three years cohabitation (or marriage or same-sex civil union) under the 2002 and 2005 amendments to the Property (Relationships) Act 1976; Australia requires two years of cohabitation or birth of a child under the Family Law Amendment (De Facto Financial Matters and Other Measures) Act 2008 to apply the same remedies as married couples.

3 The British Isles is a geographical term for the whole of the United Kingdom plus the Republic of Ireland.

4 All parts of the UK adopted the Civil Partnership Act 2004 which provides same-sex couples with the same rights as those extended to married couples, with very minor differences. The Irish legislation is contained in the Civil Partnership and Certain Rights and Obligations of Cohabitants Act 2010 and also provides for same-sex civil partnership.

The aim of this chapter is therefore to compare and contrast the differential legal and policy developments towards the legal status of (heterosexual) cohabitants in the different 'common law' jurisdictions of England and Wales, Scotland and the Republic of Ireland[5] and to assess the relative merits of these different 'common law' responses. It will go on to consider the calls for reform in England and Wales in the context of demographic trends, socio-legal research and the unpacking of the role of family law in the modern western world.

3. CHANGING SOCIAL TRENDS IN THE BRITISH ISLES

The incidence of heterosexual cohabitation in the constituent parts of the UK and Ireland has broadly followed the same upward trajectory, with people delaying or rejecting marriage. Across the different parts of the UK, the numbers marrying have declined whereas those choosing to cohabit have increased. The 2012 data from the Office for National Statistics (ONS) indicate the number of couples who cohabit has doubled since 1996 and has reached 2.9 million. This makes couples living together without being married the fastest-growing type of family in the UK and there are no significant differences between the trends as experienced in England and Wales as compared to Scotland.[6] Added to this, over the same period the number of dependent children living in opposite sex cohabiting couple families doubled from 0.9 million to 1.8 million and in 2012, 30 per cent of all births were to cohabiting couples. Thus although marriage is still the most popular family form in the UK where there are a total of 12.2 million married couples, this represents a decrease of 457,000 over the same period. These figures indicate that cohabiting couples now represent some 20 per cent of all couples who share a household. Research has also revealed that many characteristics of cohabitants overlap with those of married couples in the UK, although cohabitants are on average younger, and less likely to be religious than

---

[5]   It is not proposed to discuss Northern Ireland as despite recommendations made by the Law Reform Advisory Committee for Northern Ireland in *Matrimonial Property* Report No 10 (Belfast: TSO, 2000), the law is currently the same as in England and Wales and in contrast to Scotland and the Republic of Ireland, there have been no recent reforms or proposals for reform.

[6]   UK Labour Force Survey, Families and Households, 2012, ONS; see also BBC news report 01.11.2012, available at www.bbc.co.uk/news/uk-20174078 (last accessed 19.11.2013). Northern Ireland, not specifically under discussion in this chapter, experiences increasing yet significantly lower levels of heterosexual cohabitation, thought mainly to be due to the very specific divided religious context within that jurisdiction, with religious the likelihood of marriage increasing with the levels of religious adherence (see A. BARLOW, C. BURGOYNE, E. CLERY and J. SMITHSON, 'Cohabitation and the Law: Myths, Money and the Media' in A. PARK, J. CURTICE, K. THOMPSON, M. PHILLIPS and E. CLERY (eds) *British Social Attitudes – The 24th Report*, London: Sage, 2008, pp. 29–51).

married couples and are a more diverse group.[7] However, the average length of cohabitation is steadily increasing, particularly where there are children of the relationship.[8] Although they are on the face of it statistically more likely to break down than married relationships and are seen as less committed, with any commitment made being private rather than public, recent research by the Institute of Fiscal Studies show that when you control for other factors (such as age, education, socio-economic group), there is no statistically significant difference between the likelihood of cohabitation breakdown and marriage breakdown for those with children.[9]

Despite no legal recognition of cohabitation whatsoever in the Republic of Ireland prior to implementation of the Civil Partnership and Certain Rights and Obligations of Cohabitants Act 2010, Ireland saw a four-fold increase in cohabitation between 1996 and 2006 and according to the 2006 census, cohabitants represented 11.6 per cent of family units.[10] This on its own shows that family law does not have the power to directly constrain changing social norms when greater social forces (such as decline in religious adherence and increased financial independence of women) are at work. In Ireland, these trends seem to show that most cohabiting couples ultimately go on to marry, but are marrying later than in previous generations. Whereas in the UK it is quite common for couples to have children and continue cohabiting for some years before marrying, in Ireland, by contrast, parents of children born within cohabitation tend to marry quite soon after birth, with a smaller minority seeing cohabitation as an alternative to marriage. One shared feature of cohabitation in Ireland and the UK is that whilst the majority of cohabitants are young never-

---

[7]   See A. BARLOW et al, 2008, above n. 6. One typology of cohabitants in Britain classifies them in the overlapping categories of 'ideologues, romantics, pragmatists and uneven couples', a more nuanced analysis of Smart and Steven's spectrum ranging from the mutually committed to the contingently committed in C. SMART and P. STEVENS, *Cohabitation Breakdown*, London and York: Family Policy Studies Centre/Joseph Rowntree Foundation, 2000. See further A. BARLOW and J. SMITHSON, 'Legal assumptions, cohabitants' talk and the rocky road to reform' (2010) 22 (3) *CFLQ*, pp. 328–338.

[8]   A. BARLOW et al, 2008, above n. 6.

[9]   A. GOODMAN and E. GREAVES, *Cohabitation, Marriage and Relationship Stability*, London: Institute of Fiscal Studies, 2010. Thus although parents who are cohabiting when their child is born in the UK are three times more likely to split up by the time their child is five than married parents (27% compared to 9%), they are also typically younger, less well off, less likely to own their own homes, have fewer educational qualifications and are less likely to plan their pregnancies than married people. Institute of Fiscal Studies (IFS) analysis of such parents within the Millennium Cohort Study shows that once these differences between the two groups are accounted for, the difference in the likelihood of separation almost disappears (falling to 2 percentage points). The IFS analysis concludes that relationship stability is mainly determined not by marriage but by other factors such as age, education, occupation and income, and delaying and planning pregnancy. These factors are also influential in whether people choose to marry or not. So while married couples have more stable relationships than couples who cohabit, this is not because they are married, but because of the other characteristics they have that lead to marriage.

[10] CENTRAL STATISTICS OFFICE, *Census 2006 Principal Demographic Results*, TSO, 2007, p. 21.

---

married couples, in quite a high proportion of such couples – one quarter in Ireland and 30 per cent in the UK – one or both partners have been in a married relationship prior to their current relationship. However, it is clear that most longer-term cohabitation in Ireland is childless. Whereas over half of all couples without children in Ireland cohabit rather than marry, the vast majority of those with children marry, with cohabitants representing just 10 per cent of such parents (half the proportion of the UK).

4. THE LEGAL LANDSCAPE

As noted above, each of the Law Commissions of the jurisdictions within the British Isles have considered and recommended reform of cohabitation law in the light of social trends, yet England and Wales (and Northern Ireland), whilst having previously responded piecemeal to some issues affecting cohabitants, have explicitly rejected comprehensive reform for the time being. In contrast, reforming legislation following similar recommendations has now been enacted in both Scotland and the Republic of Ireland. Interestingly, whilst rejecting the Antipodean approach of marriage-equivalence, neither have they adopted the 'opt-in' model adopted by some of their European neighbours such as France and the Netherlands. Instead, they have each chosen a 'presumptive' or 'opt-out' approach to regulation which gives cohabitants rights inferior to those available to married couples, treating them as a similar but different style of family to married couples; so 'opt-out' but *without* equivalence.

4.1. LEGAL RESPONSE: SCOTLAND

Whereas Scotland has virtually identical social trends to England and Wales in recent years, it has always had a separate legal system and in family law it has consistently chosen its own path. In contrast to England and Wales, prior to 2006 Scotland did not amend its legislation piecemeal to accommodate cohabitation, although it did retain a form of informal 'common law marriage' – marriage by cohabitation, habit and repute, which permitted legal recognition as a marriage of established cohabitation relationships where a couple had held themselves out as married and were recognised as such within the community.[11]

Although the Scottish Law Commission recommended reform as long ago as 1992,[12] it was only in 2005 that the devolved Scottish Executive recommended

---

[11] See further A. BARLOW and A. BISSETT-JOHNSON 'Cohabitation and the Reform of Scots Law' (2003) (2) *Juridical Review*, pp. 105–28.
[12] SCOTTISH LAW COMMISSION, *The Effects of Cohabitation in Private Law*, Discussion Paper No 86, 1990; *Report on Family Law*, Scot Law Com No 135, 1992.

further consideration of reform. This resulted in the Family Law (Scotland) Act 2006 which implemented the Scottish Law Commission recommendations and also abolished the last remaining form of common law marriage for the future. Whereas in England and Wales, cohabitation reform was seen politically as something which might undermine marriage and family life and was thus to be avoided, in Scotland a positive view was taken by the Scottish Minister for Justice in 2004, who was happy to defend the extension of rights to unmarried couples, saying,

> 'Some will see any change in the law in this area as a "defeat" for traditional values. They should not – for the reforms published today are based around a principle that is central to everything we stand for as a country and as a society – the best interests of children. That must be the pillar around which we build strong family law in Scotland.'[13]

However, the model finally chosen ensured that in Scotland, cohabitants have different (and fewer) rights to married couples and civil partners on relationship breakdown. There is no possibility of periodical maintenance payments and different, less generous principles apply on relationship breakdown and on the death of a partner. Instead, the Family Law (Scotland) Act 2006 is based on redressing economic disadvantage suffered by a cohabitant, rather than any principle of entitlement to relationship property. After some consideration, it was agreed that there would be no time qualification period before a cohabitant was eligible to apply for redress, recognising that economic disadvantage could occur early in a relationship (section 25)). The key provisions are set out in section 28 which states:

> '(3) The court may make an order for payment of a capital sum by one cohabitant to the other, having regard to:
>
> a) whether (and if so to what extent) the defender[14] has derived economic advantage from contributions made by the applicant; and
> b) whether (and if so to what extent) the applicant has suffered economic disadvantage in the interests of (i) the defender or (ii) any child...'

The court must also have regard under ss 28(5) and (6) to:

> '(5) the extent to which any economic advantage derived by the defender from contributions by the applicant is offset by any economic disadvantage suffered by the defender in the interests of the applicant or any child; and
> (6) the extent to which any economic disadvantage suffered by the applicant in the interests of the defender or any child is offset by any economic advantage the applicant has derived from contributions made by the defender.'

---

13   Launch of the consultation on *Improving Scottish Family Law,* 5 April 2004.
14   This is the Scots law term for 'the respondent'.

The Act did not trigger a mass of litigation between cohabitants in the Scottish courts. Indeed a review of the workings of the Act based on research into practitioner experience by Miles, Wasoff and Mourant concluded that the Act was working relatively well.[15] However, exactly how generous the law should or could be in interpreting economic disadvantage in the Scottish context under section 28 became an issue in 2012 before the UK Supreme Court, which is the final appellate court for all the UK jurisdictions. Thus clarification was sought in the case of *Gow v Grant*.[16]

The facts of this case involved an older couple, Mrs Gow (aged 64) and Mr Grant (aged 58). At the outset of their relationship they each owned their own home. Mr Grant was keen that they should cohabit but Mrs Gow only agreed to move in, selling her own flat to do so, on condition that they became engaged to be married, which they did in 2003. Although Mr Grant encouraged her to sell the flat at a value of £50,000 (leaving her with £36,000 net after mortgage repayment), there was no duress. The couple lived together for five years in Mr Grant's property (valued at £200,000 in 2003), during which time Mr Grant also encouraged Mrs Gow to give up her part-time job as a typist. Whilst she applied the sale monies from her flat partly for her own use, paying off other debts, lending £4,000 to her son, investing £5,000 in an investment bond, she also invested £7,000 in a timeshare arrangement and then paid £1,000 on a holiday, both jointly with Mr Gow, and used the balance of her money to contribute to joint living expenses. When the relationship broke down, Mr Grant continued living in his home, whereas Mrs Gow had to find rented accommodation. Her previous flat, it was found, would have been worth £88,000 meaning she had potentially lost a maximum of £38,000. She therefore brought a claim against Mr Grant. At first instance, the Sherriff, employing a restrictive interpretation of section 28, found that there was no evidence she had suffered any economic disadvantage. On appeal to the Second Division, the court found that although there had been 'encouragement' by Mr Grant to sell the flat, there was not enough to show that this was disadvantage Mrs Gow had suffered 'in his interests' pursuant to section 28(2) and that any disadvantage suffered by Mrs Gow was offset by Mr Grant's contributions to their joint living expenses. Mrs Gow therefore appealed again to the Supreme Court. In particular, the questions before the court were whether an intention to benefit the other cohabitant was

15   F. WASOFF, J. MILES and E. MORDAUNT, *Legal Practitioners Perspectives on the Cohabitation Provisions of the Family Law (Scotland) Act 2006*, October 2010, available at www.crfr.ac.uk/assets/Cohabitation-final-report.pdf (last accessed 10.11.2013), p. 125. The authors suggest that the decision not to include a minimum cohabitation requirement in the Scottish legislation may be regarded as a success because of 'limited evidence of "nuisance claims", in so far as these might be manifested by claims brought after only short relationships'. See further, F. WASOFF, J. MILES and E. MORDAUNT, 'Cohabitation: lessons from research north of the border?' (2011) 23 (3) *CFLQ*, pp. 302–322.

16   *Gow v Grant (Scotland)* [2012] UKSC 29.

required by section 28(3)(b) and (6); whether disadvantage suffered must benefit the defender alone or whether it could be to provide a joint benefit; and lastly, if relevant economic disadvantage was established, what was the extent of the court's discretion as to the award to be made.

In hearing the case, Lord Hope in confirming that different principles to the divorce and civil partnership context applied to cohabitants' claims under the Act, imported a 'fairness' principle into the calculation, drawing on the original Scottish Law Commission report and Ministerial statements in which it had been stated that through these provisions they sought to establish a 'fair' remedy and confirmed:

> 'the statutory purpose does no more than reflect the reality that cohabitation is a less formal, less structured and more flexible form of relationship than either marriage or civil partnership. I think therefore, contrary to the views expressed by the Second Division in para 3, that it would be wrong to approach section 28 on the basis that it was intended simply to enable the court to correct any clear and quantifiable economic imbalance that may have resulted from the cohabitation. That is too narrow an approach.'[17]

Fairness is a principle which has been developed by the courts under provisions for financial relief on divorce in English and Welsh family law to avoid discrimination between financial and non-financial contributions to a marriage or civil partnership or to redress 'relationship-generated disadvantage' on relationship breakdown. This does not apply in Scots law but the Supreme Court were ready to find the need for a broader approach than had been used up until that point in order to achieve a fair remedy (perhaps influenced by English jurisprudential thinking) in favour of Mrs Gow. They accepted she had suffered economic disadvantage for Mr Grant's benefit and not withstanding their joint benefit and used their discretion to award her £39,500 which they adjudged to be the extent of her overall disadvantage.

Thus the Scottish legislation, whilst based on economic disadvantage, arguably since this decision provides a more generous remedy to situations where cohabitation does cause financial loss suffered for the benefit of the relationship, rather than solely for the other partner. Whilst it does not adopt the same approach as the divorce legislation in Scotland, it nonetheless allows the financial consequences of the relationship to be addressed in a more global way than had previously been the case. This therefore seems to provide some family law protection from less than legally rational financial decisions taken for the benefit of a relationship at a moment in time and from which one partner alone would otherwise suffer the consequences.

---

[17]   *Gow v Grant (Scotland)* [2012] UKSC 29, para. 58.

4.2. LEGAL RESPONSE: IRELAND

The Republic of Ireland is a traditionally Catholic country where marriage is constitutionally protected[18] and which has only recently considered its response to changing social trends. As noted above, whilst these do not exactly mirror British patterns and affect fewer children, growing numbers of cohabitants is an observed social phenomenon, although unlike the UK, Ireland has at the same time witnessed an upsurge in the numbers marrying since 1997.[19] Following an earlier consultation paper, the Ireland Law Reform Commission reported on the rights and duties of cohabitants in 2006, recommending reform.[20] It cited changing demographic trends, the lack of cohesion in the piecemeal reforms which had taken account of cohabitants' legal situation and the fact that cohabitation was likely to 'continue at some level' and was functioning as 'a route into marriage'.[21] It took the view that 'the current legal framework does not reflect this social reality'.[22]

Legislation, which also addressed the rights of same-sex couples, was enacted in 2010 in the Civil Partnership and Certain Rights and Obligations of Cohabitants Act. Cohabitants are defined in section 172 as two adults (whether of the same or opposite sex) who live together as a couple in an intimate relationship and who are not related, married or civil partnered to each other. The legislative scheme gives 'qualifying cohabitants' (where there has either been five years' cohabitation or two years' where there is a dependent child of the relationship) the right to apply for redress on relationship breakdown or intestacy which is within the discretion of the court. It also in section 202 sanctions the making of 'cohabitants' agreements' by all cohabitants (traditionally considered void for immoral consideration (purpose) in common law jurisdictions).

The main principles of the Irish scheme include a right for qualifying cohabitants on relationship breakdown to apply for 'redress' in the form of a property adjustment order and/or in contrast to Scotland, where no claim for maintenance is possible, a compensatory maintenance order. In addition, applications can also be made for a pension adjustment order or for an order for

---

18 Article 41, Irish Constitution.
19 The results of the Irish *Census 2002 Principal Demographic Results* (Central Statistics Office 2003) is available at www.cso.ie/en/census/2002censusreports/census2002principaldemo-graphicresults/ (last accessed 16.02.2014); data between 1997 and 2000 show that the number of marriages increased dramatically, from 15,631 in 1997 to 19,168 in 2000, with the marriage rate increasing correspondingly from 4.5 to 5.1. CSO data shows that the marriage rate has been maintained, averaging 5.1 between 2000 and 2005. The data reveals that cohabitation increased by 250% between 1994 and 2002.
20 IRELAND LAW REFORM COMMISSION, *Report: Rights and Duties of Cohabitants* (LRC 82–2006), Dublin: ILRC, 2006.
21 Above n. 20 p. 9.
22 Above n. 20, p. 11.

provision from the estate of the other cohabitant on their death.[23] The Act, as in Scotland, quite deliberately gives different (and fewer) rights to cohabitants than married couples and civil partners. Section 173 sets out the circumstances in which a 'qualifying cohabitant' may obtain a property adjustment order under section 174 of the Act, a compensatory maintenance order under section 175 or a pension adjustment order under section 187.

However, the 2010 Act has attracted some serious criticism in Ireland. One key limitation on the scheme is that the claimant must establish 'financial dependency' as a prerequisite of a remedy. The financial dependence must be caused by the relationship or its breakdown, but the statute is not clear on what exactly 'financial dependency' means. Professor John Mee in his analysis of the legislation[24] argues this requirement significantly limits the scope of the scheme and is likely to generate anomalous results, whereby a remedy will be denied to claimants who have suffered serious loss as a result of a relationship but who have not become 'financially dependent'. An example might be if one cohabitant transfers their home into the joint names of themselves and their partner but can support themselves at the end of the relationship. Whereas under the Scottish scheme this would be likely to represent economic disadvantage which could be compensated, under the Irish scheme, the claim would not be successful. Thus if Ms Gow's case had been brought under Irish law, she may not have succeeded in bringing a claim, as that sort of financial interdependence would seem likely to be insufficient in the Irish context. The Irish court must also go on to find that it is 'just and equitable' to make the order according to a statutory checklist, even where financial dependence is established. If it does, it has a large discretion as to the award that can be made, with no specific protection for the defendant's own position such as exists in the Scottish scheme. The Act is of course very recent and is yet to be tested in the higher courts in Ireland. However, Mee goes so far as to suggest in light of the scheme's limited nature and the various potential problems with its provisions, that it is questionable whether its enactment represents a positive development. He is pessimistic about the impact the Act is likely to have, promising more than it can deliver and is also concerned at the complexity of the cohabitation contract provisions. He states:

'Given the tendency of the public to misunderstand the law in respect of the property rights of cohabitants, the introduction of limited statutory reform risks misleading cohabitants into believing that it is safe for them to rely on their relationship rather than seeking to protect their separate property rights. Moreover, the measures in the Act in relation to cohabitation contracts, which impose onerous formal requirements for such contracts to be valid, do not appear justifiable in light of the limited rights

---

[23]   See further ss 173, 175, 187 Civil Partnership and Certain Rights and Obligations of Cohabitants Act 2010.

[24]   See J. MEE, 'Cohabitation law reform in Ireland' (2011) 23 (3) *CFLQ*, pp. 323–343.

afforded by the Act and may serve to thwart some attempts by cohabitants to regulate their entitlements by agreement.'[25]

4.3. LEGAL RESPONSE: ENGLAND AND WALES

Yet the fact that any law reform relating to cohabitants' rights was enacted in Ireland is a matter to be marvelled at in England and Wales, where there has been stout political refusal to act, despite the recommendations of the Law Commission for England and Wales. The current position in this jurisdiction is that cohabitants have no specific legal status and cannot 'opt in' to civil partnerships, which are limited to same-sex couples exclusively. Although legislation enabling same-sex marriage has been passed, it has only just been implemented.[26] As for the legal rights of cohabitants (whether same- or opposite-sex), piecemeal reforms since the 1970s see cohabitants treated as married in some situations, as inferior to married couples in others, and as separate unrelated individuals in yet others. Thus, on relationship breakdown, some family law remedies exist under the Schedule 1 Children Act 1989 to provide financial provision for the benefit of the child as between parents of children under 18, but there is no maintenance or asset redistribution for cohabitants on relationship breakdown. Rented tenancies can be transferred between cohabitants but general property and trusts law must be used to litigate property disputes (including family home) between couples as if there were no personal relationship. This is complex, lengthy and very expensive and has been heavily criticised by the Law Commission, which recommended reform in 2007 on remedies available on relationship breakdown and made further recommendations in 2011 regarding inheritance rules as they affect cohabitants on death of a partner who dies without making a will.[27]

Leading up to and after the Law Commission's recommendations for reform, there has been much socio-legal research conducted around attitudes to marriage, cohabitation and the law and also to experiences of using existing piecemeal remedies. For example, the British Social Attitudes Surveys in 2001 and 2008 show the continued existence of a 'common law marriage myth' whereby people falsely believe that those cohabiting do have the same rights as if they were formally married. This is coupled with great support for cohabitation law reform and the public are even in favour of extending marriage equivalence to cohabitants where there are children or long relationships in England and

---

[25]   J. Mee, above n. 24, p.343.
[26]   The Marriage (Same Sex Couples) Act 2013 was implemented on 29 March 2014.
[27]   See Law Commission, *Cohabitation: The Financial Consequences of Cohabitation Report*, Law Com No 307, Cm 7182, London: TSO, 2007; and Law Commission, *Intestacy and Family Provision Claims on Death*, Law Com No 331, London: TSO, 2011.

Wales.[28] Thus many studies confirm the public confusion, difficulties and dissatisfaction with the current law in England and Wales.[29] Miles, Wasoff and Mordaunt in their 2011 study of the Scottish system concluded that the introduction of broadly similar provisions in England and Wales would not place significant additional demands on court and other justice system resources, were it made available for such claims.[30] The demographer Kiernan, has shown that introduction of cohabitant rights is not a statistically significant factor in decline in marriage rates in Australia or indeed in Europe.[31] Yet the government has twice declined to implement the Law Commission recommendations for England and Wales.

The approach proposed by the Law Commission was more similar to the Scottish scheme based on economic advantage and disadvantage during the relationship than the Irish scheme based on meeting need at the discretion of the court at the point of breakdown. Its 2007 report strongly criticised current law and accepted the need for reform. However, it rejected the idea that cohabitation should be placed on a par with marriage.[32] Rather, it put forward a radical new presumptive scheme which did not mirror marriage but which proposed the acceptance of cohabitation contracts (as in Scotland and Ireland) plus redress for relationship-generated economic disadvantage or retained benefit from which people could opt-out. So this was to be a presumptive scheme with the ability for people to opt-out and draw up their own cohabitation agreements. The Law Commission recommended that its scheme should apply to all cohabitants with children and other childless cohabitants (whether same or different sex) who have lived together for a qualifying period, which they suggested should be between two and five years. Couples should be able to opt out of the scheme in order to protect individual autonomy providing certain conditions were satisfied, notably that the agreement was in writing, signed by both parties and made clear the parties' intention to disapply the scheme.[33] In the case of manifest unfairness a court would have power to set aside an opt-out agreement,[34] an approach ultimately rejected by the Irish 2010 Act, despite a similar recommendation by its Law Reform Commission.

---

[28]   A. BARLOW et al, 2008, above n. 6.

[29]   See for example G. DOUGLAS, J. PEARCE and H. WOODWARD, 'Cohabitants, property and the law: a study of injustice' (2009) 72 (1) *Modern Law Review*, pp. 24–47; A. BARLOW et al, 2008, above n. 6.

[30]   F. WASOFF, J. MILES and E. MORDAUNT, 'Cohabitation: lessons from research north of the border?' (2011) 23 (3) *CFLQ*, pp. 302–322.

[31]   K. KIERNAN, A. BARLOW and R. MERLO, 'Cohabitation Law Reform and its impact on Marriage: Evidence from Australia and Europe International' (2007) 63 *International Family Law*, pp. 71–74.

[32]   See LAW COMMISSION, *Cohabitation: The Financial Consequences of Relationship Breakdown*, Law Com No 307, CM 7182, London: TSO, 2007.

[33]   Above n. 32, para. 5.56.

[34]   Above n. 32, para. 5.61.

The idea of the England and Wales scheme was to base a former cohabitant's claim upon the 'economic impact' of cohabitation. On separation, an eligible applicant in making a claim against their partner would have to prove that either the respondent has a retained benefit, or the applicant has an economic disadvantage as a result of qualifying contributions the applicant made. It recommended that the same style of orders would be available for financial provision as is currently the case on divorce or civil partnership dissolution with the exception of periodical maintenance payments, although the grounds for making the orders were to be quite different.

Only those who had made qualifying contributions – defined as any contribution to the shared lives or welfare of members of the family and could be non-financial – were eligible to apply under the scheme. An economic disadvantage was stated to be a present or future loss. It could include a diminution in current savings as a result of expenditure or of earnings lost during the relationship, lost future earnings or the future cost of paid child care. A retained benefit, on the other hand, could take the form of capital, income or earning capacity that has been acquired, retained or enhanced.

The proposed remedy in respect of retained benefit was straightforward. The court would be able to order the reversal of any retained benefit 'in so far as it is reasonable and practical and having regard to the discretionary factors' which were similar to those applying on divorce. With regard to a finding of economic disadvantage, however, how exactly this would be calculated in practice was cause for concern among commentators, with a crystal ball being seen as a useful piece of equipment in the calculation of lost future earnings.[35] In any event, only one half of any economic disadvantage would be paid over according to the principle that any loss should be shared equally, and in making any order, the court 'shall not place the applicant for the foreseeable future in a stronger economic position than the respondent'. The proposals were not needs-based and did not create an equal sharing principle and so were accepted as a distinct (yet presumptive) remedy to those available on divorce or civil partnership dissolution. They also respected the autonomy of the parties by permitting couples to opt out through contract, at a time when pre-nuptial agreements had no binding force in English law.

Notwithstanding this, the government response to the proposals has been to ignore them. Parliament (under the New Labour government) wished to see the effects of the Scottish legislation before committing to reform in 2008. In 2009, the same government also opposed Lord Lester's Private Member's Cohabitation Bill proposing a needs-based reform for cohabitants. Despite the research discussed above by Miles et al published in 2011, the coalition government again rejected legislating on the Law Commission proposals 'during this Parliament', meaning any reform will not be considered again before 2015. Furthermore, in

---

35   R. PROBERT, 'Cohabitation: contributions and sacrifices' (2006) *Family Law*, p. 1060.

March 2013, it also announced it rejected the proposed intestacy reforms for cohabitants in the Law Commission's Draft Inheritance (Cohabitants) Bill contained in their 2011 Report.

5. CONCLUSION

Within common law Europe, it can be seen that Scotland and Ireland have legislated to give cohabitants a legal status and presumptive rights and remedies on relationship breakdown and death of a partner. Arguably this represents two steps forward, although we cannot yet assess the impact of the Irish reforms. Yet in England and Wales, it seems that although the Law Commission is completely convinced that presumptive reform is the way forward, reforming cohabitation law is an impossible political hurdle. No government wants to be seen to undermine marriage, and indeed the Prime Minister has reacted to the current pro-marriage political atmosphere by agreeing to the symbolic re-introduction of (minimal) tax relief for married couples, under pressure from members of his party who contested his initial decision to delay any such tax reform.[36] Some consider this to be a step backwards, when tax relief or credits had been reformed in the 1990s to focus on families with children rather than just those who marry. What is more, it is clear from research that the public in general and thus the electorate are very tolerant of those who cohabit, considering it a matter of private choice, a view which aligns with the 'right to private and family life' contained in Article 8 of the European Convention on Human Rights (ECHR). In addition, perhaps surprisingly, heterosexual civil partnership (unlike same-sex marriage) was fiercely resisted by government during the passage of the Marriage (Same-Sex Couples) Act 2013 and this is subject to a claim before the ECHR.[37]

Meanwhile the flexible approach of the common law courts in property law plus piecemeal, inconsistent legislation developed since the 1970s remains the reality for the growing number of cohabitants in England and Wales, whilst the 'common law marriage' myth thrives amid shifted social norms, with research showing that over half the population still believe they have general rather than patchwork 'marriage-equivalence'.[38]

However, although Parliament is happy for matters to remain as they are, the senior judiciary are not and perhaps judicial activism may help to rescue the

---

[36] A married couples transferable tax allowance benefiting eligible couples by up to £200 per year was announced in the Autumn Statement by the Chancellor of the Exchequer on 5 December 2013. Further details are available at https://www.gov.uk/government/news/autumn-statement-2013-key-announcements (last accessed 16.02.2014).

[37] *Ferguson & others v UK*, File No 8254/11.

[38] See A. BARLOW et al, 2008, above n. 6.

situation. In *Gow v Grant*,[39] the Supreme Court Justices expressed their frustration at this state of affairs, calling loudly for English and Welsh law to be changed in line with that of Scotland, citing socio-legal research in support of the case for reform.[40] They have also attempted to reduce the strictures of trusts law to build in a more family law approach to disputes, which has divided trusts lawyers and family lawyers.[41]

Another possible source pressure for reform may come through the ECHR. The application made to the ECHR in *Ferguson and others v UK* was initially challenging the lack of same-sex marriage in the jurisdiction on the grounds that it was discriminatory under Articles 12 and 14 to offer civil partnership that gave all the same substantive rights as marriage but could not be called marriage. However, although this has been addressed by the Marriage (Same-Sex Couples) Act 2013, the other argument advanced under Articles 8 and 14 was that heterosexual couples were being discriminated against as they were forbidden from entering into civil partnerships. Given that the 2013 Act will keep civil partnership for same-sex couples who will then have the choice of either marriage or civil partnership, whereas heterosexual couples must either marry or cohabit, this claim seems strong given the Marriage (Same-Sex Couples) Act 2013 was indeed implemented without repeal of the Civil Partnership Act 2004, although this will be subject to review.

Thus in England and Wales as elsewhere in Europe, the social trends away from marriage into cohabitation speak for themselves and demand a response. In reality, we cannot turn the clock back through law and surely the Napoleonic approach has had its day and needs to be revisited. Whilst there are arguments against reforms adopting 'presumptive' marriage equivalence, to fail to legislate for cohabitants is surely to bury the governmental head in the sand. To open civil partnership to different-sex couples would be a European-style 'opt-in' solution which would assist but not protect those who believe in the common law marriage myth in England and Wales, unless it triggered a culture change. Nonetheless, this would be a choice welcomed by some groups of cohabitants, according to research.[42] The Scottish and Irish reforms (and the English Law Commission proposals) do address some gaps in the law and are worthy of further consideration, although to compensate economic disadvantage without addressing need or vice versa is arguably an unprincipled way to ensure a distinction between remedies for cohabitants and those divorcing or dissolving civil partnerships. They do however try to combine autonomy through permitting enforceable cohabitation contracts with presumptive protection from

---

[39] *Gow v Grant* (Scotland) [2012] UKSC 29.
[40] A. BARLOW, S. DUNCAN, G. JAMES and A. PARK, *Cohabitation, Marriage and the Law: Social Change and Legal Reform in the 21st Century*, Oxford: Hart, 2005, and F. WASOFF et al, 2011, above n. 30.
[41] See for example dicta in *Jones. v Kernott* [2011] UKSC 53.
[42] A. BARLOW and J. SMITHSON, 2012, above n. 7.

at least some aspects of relationship-generated disadvantage, which undoubtedly can be suffered by cohabitants who should have some redress. As Lady Hale observed in her judgment in *Gow v Grant*, '[t]he [Scottish] Act has undoubtedly achieved a lot for Scottish cohabitants and their children, English and Welsh cohabitants deserve no less'.

Perhaps the real problem is that we have not to date been clear about what we want family law to achieve for cohabitants. Do we want to make them marry? If so, a Napoleonic approach is understandable, although recent history would indicate that it does not work. Are we trying to ensure the law protects the economically vulnerable within families (including children)? In which case presumptive marriage equivalence, or a compensation or needs-based approach, are all possibilities which address the problem and provide differently incentivised risks for partners as between themselves. Or do we feel that partners within cohabiting relationships are now equal and family life does not provide sufficient relationship-generated disadvantage for the law to undermine a couple's autonomy to decide these matters at the outset of a relationship? If so, we can use family law to promote autonomy and encourage a contractual or opt-in approach to cohabitation contracts. This sounds ideal, yet research shows that it is more ideal for some cohabiting couples than for others and the balance of power within any relationship may make this an appealing yet quite often a substantively unfair remedy in practice, where the ability to change agreements as circumstances change is often illusory rather than real. Cohabitants are a diverse group and reasons for cohabiting are wide-ranging and so perhaps one thing we should agree on, as different jurisdictions grapple with the same problem, is that we need a pluralistic approach which gives people choice where there is real agreement and roughly equal power, but which protects in other circumstances. To agree this would indeed be a step in the right direction for Europe as a whole.

THE SWEDISH COHABITEES ACT IN TODAY'S SOCIETY

Kajsa WALLENG

Contents

1.   INTRODUCTION

Unmarried cohabitation (hereinafter, 'cohabitation') has increased considerably in Sweden during the last decades as in many other European countries. The question of if and how this increasing number of cohabiting couples should be dealt with from a legal point of view has been discussed in several European countries, resulting in a variety of legal solutions. Sweden was the first country in Europe where cohabitation was regulated in a specific statute. Cohabitation was first regulated in statutory law in 1973.[1] The law gave an opportunity for a cohabitee with the greatest need to stay in the joint home after separation – against payment – even if the other cohabitee was the owner of the dwelling. The law was mainly protective legislation for women and children in their care, and was only applied to apartments for rent and condominiums, which at that time had no major economic value. The first rules on the division of property were introduced in 1987; the law was called the Cohabitees Joint Homes Act.[2] The current law – the Cohabitees Act – was introduced in 2003.[3] The legal consequences, however, are the same as in the Act from 1987. What happened in 2003 was that the law was retitled, some unclear rules were clarified, and the law became directly applicable to homosexual cohabitees.[4]

Even though the Cohabitees Act[5] is no more than 25 years old, society has changed quite a lot during this time in terms of our family-forming habits. The question is to what extent the Cohabitees Act functions for cohabitees in today's Swedish society? This is the overarching question I am trying to answer in an ongoing PhD project at Uppsala University. To answer this question I have carried out an empirical study that was made in 2010 in cooperation with Statistics Sweden. In the study unmarried men and women answered questions relating to the Cohabitees Act.[6] The respondents who at the time of the survey lived in cohabitation also had to answer questions relating to their own relationship.[7]

2. UNMARRIED COHABITATION: A SOCIAL NORM

In many countries marriage is seen as the only socially acceptable form for living together with another person. This was also true in Sweden, but the statistics indicate that things have changed: see figure 1. When Sweden introduced a regulation for cohabitees in 1973 about 6 per cent of all couples living together were cohabitees.[8] In 1987, when the Cohabitees Act came into force, the proportion

---

[1] Lag 5 juni 1973 om ogifta samboendes gemensamma bostad (nr 651).

[2] Lag (1987:232) om sambors gemensamma hem.

[3] Sambolag (2003:376).

[4] Previously same-sex cohabitees had been dealt with separately in the 'Homosexual Cohabitees Act' – Lag (1987:813) om homosexuella sambor – that stipulated that the Act from 1987 was equally applicable to homosexual cohabitees.

[5] In the rest of this contribution I will use the term 'Cohabitees Act' as a generic term for the laws from the years 1987 and 2003.

[6] Some results will be presented in this article. All the results will be included in my thesis that will be completed in the autumn of 2014.

[7] Since there is no register for cohabitation, it was not possible to find and only pose questions to this group. In order to catch as many cohabitees as possible the sample group was chosen to include unmarried men and women between the ages of 20–70. The results of the study have been adjusted to population levels. Statistics Sweden has been in charge of all statistical data.

[8] Prop. 1973:32 Förslag till lag om ändring i giftermålsbalken m.m., p. 43.

of cohabitees was around 20 per cent.[9] Some 15 years later the proportion had risen to 33 per cent.[10] Nowadays, my study shows that 41 per cent of all couples living together are cohabitees, which in numbers is almost two million people.

Figure 1. The proportion of cohabitees in relation to all couples living together (spouses and cohabitees)

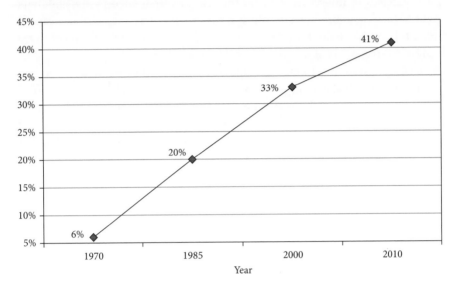

I would claim that we no longer just have one social norm for living together with another person, but rather two – marriage and cohabitation. Since Sweden has a regulation for cohabitees and since it is almost as common to be a cohabitee as to be married, many people think that the legal rules between the two different family forms are more or less equal. However, the legal rules regarding marriage and cohabitation differ substantially. The differences will shortly be accounted for below, in order to provide a background to the questions asked in the empirical study.

3. LEGAL RULES: MARRIAGE *VERSUS* UNMARRIED COHABITATION

Both the Cohabitees Act and the Marriage Code have rules on the division of property when the relationship ends. The Marriage Code gives the spouses a legal right to an equal share of the value of all property upon the termination of the marriage, if there is no prenuptial agreement. In contrast, when a cohabitation is terminated, the Cohabitees Act gives the cohabitees a legal right

---

9   Prop. 1986/87:1 Äktenskapsbalk m.m., p. 40.
10   Prop. 2002/03:80 Ny sambolag, p. 24.

only to an equal share of the value of the joint dwelling and household goods that have been obtained for the joint home during the cohabitation. This right can be excluded by a cohabitee agreement.

Married couples inherit from each other according to the law,[11] while cohabitees have to make a will in order to inherit from each other. The possibility for cohabitees to inherit from each other is however limited by the children's right to their statutory portion, which means that a surviving cohabitee cannot inherit more than half of the deceased partner's estate if the deceased cohabitee had heirs – regardless of whether the child is his or hers.[12]

One can start by asking why the regulations differ so widely between marriage and cohabitation. Very simply, this can be explained by political positions, but also by the prevailing conditions during the mid-1980s. Most cohabitees at that time were young people – who usually lived in rented accommodation, without much money being spent on the home. Cohabitation was seen as a stage before marriage, instead of being seen as a long-term relationship. Cohabitees were more or less seen as a homogeneous group of people. The purpose of the Cohabitees Act has never been to provide comprehensive protection for the weaker party in cohabitation, but only to give minimum protection. Instead cohabitees have been encouraged, by the lawmaker in the preparatory works, to consider what extra economic protection they might need for either separation or in the case of the death of one of them and to arrange this through different agreements or through marriage.

4. RESULTS OF THE EMPIRICAL STUDY

4.1. INTRODUCTION

Today, there are almost two million cohabitees in Sweden. Today's cohabitees are not made up of one kind of couple, but rather of a variety of couples with different protective needs and different views of their relationship. Minimum protection is no longer enough to protect the diversity of cohabitees. The lawmaker has pointed at the importance for cohabitees to consider what extra protection they might require and to achieve this through agreements. However, this requires both

---

[11]   There is one exception to this rule: if a deceased spouse had a child from a previous marriage, that child is entitled to receive his/her inheritance immediately when the parent dies. The child can however refrain from receiving his/her inheritance for the benefit of the surviving spouse. In order to prevent a child from a previous relationship inheriting all of the deceased´s estate, the spouse (that is the parent) needs to make a will for the benefit of his/her spouse. The child will then only have the right to receive its statutory portion.

[12]   The only possibility to inherit all of the property is if the child renounces his/her heritage for the benefit of the surviving cohabitee. However, this is not possible in the case of a minor child, whose rights are to be safeguarded by a legal guardian.

knowledge of the law and action by the cohabitees themselves. What I am trying to discover in my research is whether the Cohabitees Act meets the needs of cohabitees – considering factors like knowledge of the law, what people think about the law, how cohabitees themselves live their lives and what extra protection they establish of their own accord. Below, some results from the empirical study will be presented. The results provide a starting point for the discussion of to what extent the law fulfils its purpose of protecting cohabitees in today's society.

4.2. BACKGROUND QUESTIONS

4.2.1. The Proportion of Cohabitees by Age

As mentioned above, the lawmaker assumes in the preparatory works that it is mainly young people who cohabit. Cohabitation is certainly most common among younger people, but, as is shown in figure 2, nowadays cohabitation is common among all age groups. This is of importance in many ways; previous relationships or marriages and/or children from a previous relationship are more likely if the cohabitees are older, as well as the likelihood that the cohabitation is terminated by the death of one of the cohabitees. In general young people also have less money to spend on the home in comparison with older people (at least middle-aged people). If a large amount of money is spent on objects for the home, it makes the shared economy between cohabitees more extensive, which has to be taken into account when evaluating the Cohabitees Act.

Figure 2. The proportion of cohabitees by age

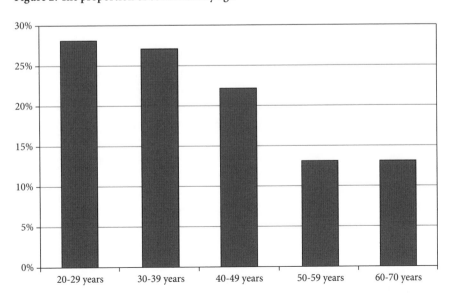

4.2.2. Duration of (Ongoing) Cohabitation

Cohabitation is no longer just a preliminary stage before marriage. Instead there is a tendency for cohabitation to last for many years: see figure 3. Many cohabitees never marry, or they marry after many years of cohabitation and often after they have had children.

Figure 3. The duration of ongoing cohabitation

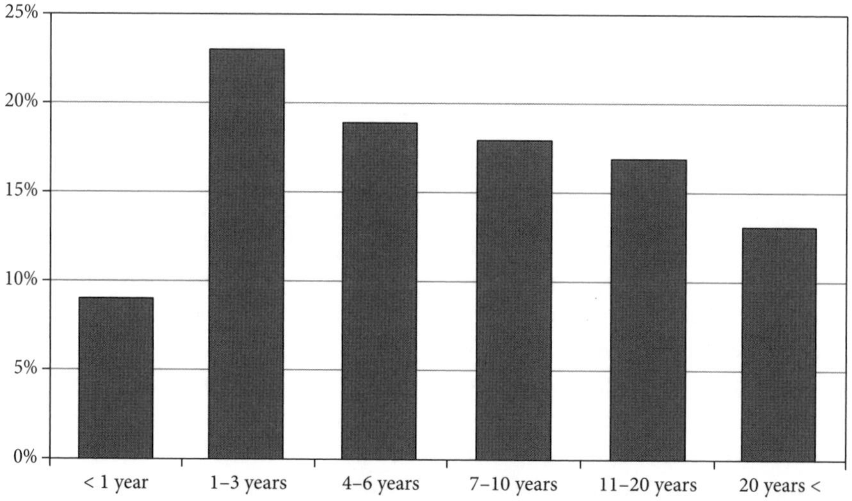

The duration of cohabitation affects the extent of the parties' shared economy, which has an effect on how much assets will be divided upon the termination of the cohabitation. However, the longer a cohabitation has lasted, the more likely it is that the cohabitees' shared economy extends beyond the joint dwelling and household goods; cohabitees might, for example, purchase a car or a holiday residence together, without really considering the ownership conditions or how much each of them has to pay for the assets. With a longer period of cohabitation, there will also be a greater part that will be dissolved by death, which can affect the need for economic protection compared to when the cohabitation is terminated by separation.

4.2.3. Presence of Children among Cohabitees

The shared economy between cohabitees – as well as cooperation concerning unpaid work in the home – is affected if the cohabitees have common children or live with the children of one cohabitee. As mentioned above, a child also affects the possibility for cohabitees to inherit all property from each other, since the child of a cohabitee always has the right to receive his/her statutory portion if the parent dies; this applies even if the child is a joint child, and even if the deceased had made a will for the benefit of his/her cohabitee.

Figure 4. Do you live together with children?

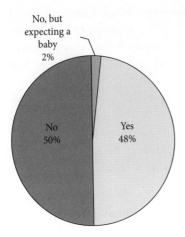

Almost half of all cohabitees live with children in their household – see figure 4 – and 81 per cent of those have one or more common children with their cohabitee (74 per cent have common children and 7 per cent have common and previous children), see figure 5.

Figure 5. Whose child is it?

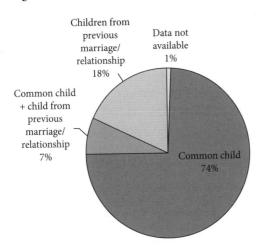

4.3. LEGAL RULES

4.3.1. Rules on the Division of Property

All men and women who took part in the study were asked what legal effects they thought cohabitation would bring. Overall, the result shows that a majority want the economic legal consequences to be more extensive than they are today, both when it comes to the division of property rules, as well as to inheritance rules.

The next diagram, figure 6, shows that 65 per cent of all people in the sample group want all property acquired for joint use to be shared equally, in comparison to today's legislation, where only a joint home and household goods are to be shared. In practice such a regulation would mean that, for example, the value of a car or a holiday residence bought during a cohabitation would be shared equally.

Figure 6. What property should be shared between cohabitees who separate?

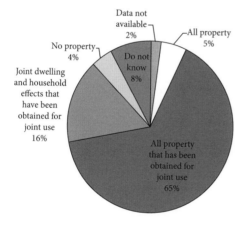

4.3.2. Inheritance

Cohabitees do not inherit from each other. A majority[13] however think that cohabitees should inherit from each other; 19 per cent think that cohabitees should inherit *all* property, as married couples do, and 43 per cent think that they should inherit at least to some extent; see figure 7.

---

13   A majority of all men and women in the sample group.

Figure 7. Should cohabitees inherit from each other?

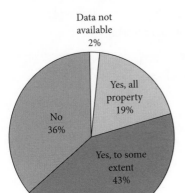

Despite the fact that a majority of all people in the sample group want cohabitees to inherit from each other, only 18 per cent of all cohabitees have made a will for the benefit of his/her cohabitee; see figure 8.

Figure 8. Have you drawn up a will for the benefit of your cohabitee?

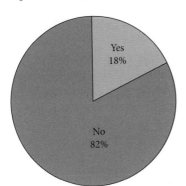

4.4. SHARED ECONOMY BETWEEN COHABITEES

One factor of great importance when discussing the legal effects for cohabitees is the shared economy between the parties. One thing that affects the extent of this shared economy is what kind of dwelling the parties live in. In 1987 when Sweden enacted its first Cohabitees Act, most cohabitees lived in rented accommodation. Nowadays, the study shows that 65 per cent of all cohabitees live in a dwelling that is owned – either a house (48 per cent) or an apartment (17 per cent); see figure 9. A dwelling which is owned generates expenses for renovation and maintenance – expenses that need to be allocated between the cohabitees, expenses not incurred in the same way if one lives in rented accommodation.

Figure 9. What kind of dwelling do you and your cohabitee live in?

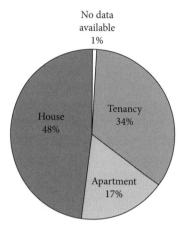

A majority (62 per cent) of those who live in a dwelling which is owned (not shown in the figure) also own the dwelling jointly. This result, as well as the results in figure 9 shows that many cohabitees have a very close and extensive shared economy. This is also supported by the result of another question where all cohabitees were asked if they in any way had a joint economy with their cohabitee – 74 per cent answered yes to this question; see figure 10.

Figure 10. Do you and your cohabitee have a common economy in any way?

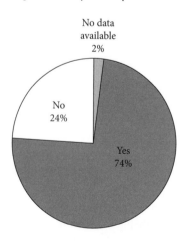

4.5. SUMMARY

As can be seen from the above results the conditions in today's society seem quite different compared to the mid-1980s in terms of family-forming habits. Today, cohabitation is common among all age groups, not only young people. Cohabitation is no longer just a preliminary stage before marriage; people tend to stay in cohabitation for many years – some for the rest of their lives. Cohabitation is seen as a family form which is equal to marriage and this is evident from the fact that many cohabitees live together with children, many of these being their common children. When it comes to the legal rules regarding cohabitation, a majority of all people in the sample group want rules that give the weaker cohabitee better economic protection than is present today when cohabitation is terminated. However, cohabitees themselves do not take action in order to protect one another, for example by drawing up wills for the benefit of their cohabitee. Many cohabitees also have an extensive shared economy, for example a majority of the cohabitees live in a dwelling which is owned and this is often owned by both cohabitees jointly.

5. A LAW NOT KEEPING PACE WITH TIME

5.1. INTRODUCTION

Even though Sweden has one of the most extensive regulations concerning cohabitees, the results above show that the legal rules regarding cohabitees do not reflect the reality of today's society to an extent that would be desirable. This results in a risk that the intention concerning the law cannot be fulfilled, which in the end will affect both society as well as individuals (cohabitees) in a negative way. If the intention concerning the law is to be fulfilled, there needs to be what I would like to call an 'interplay' between the law/the legislator (or society at large) and the people affected by the legislation, meaning that both sides need to consider each other to a certain extent. The first question to be asked is why is the law not keeping pace with time? And the second question is how can the 'interplay' be improved in order to make the law keep more in pace with time?

5.2. HOW CAN THE LACK OF 'INTERPLAY' BE EXPLAINED?

As the results from the empirical study show, questions concerning cohabitees are complex, which provides the overall answer to why the Cohabitees Act is not keeping pace with time. The meaning of cohabitation has changed from being a cohabitation form for young people before marriage, to today when cohabitees consist of a variety of couples – at different stages in their relationship and in their lives. In my opinion it is however possible to point to three different factors that explain, in more concrete terms, why the 'interplay' between the law and today's cohabitees has failed.

The first factor that can be identified is *knowledge* of the law. People's knowledge about the legal situation for cohabitees is inadequate.[14] Even though the law has had the same legal consequences for 25 years, people's knowledge of the Cohabitees Act and other regulations that affect cohabitees, for example the inheritance law, is still not satisfactory. Many cohabitees are in need of extensive economic protection in the case of the termination of cohabitation and they think that they already have that protection under the law – but in fact they do not. The importance of information has been pointed out several times by the legislature – already in the mid-1980s – and private actors have also engaged in different campaigns in order to inform cohabitees about the legal consequences of cohabitation. In my opinion, however, the dissemination of information has more or less failed.

The second factor is the *lack of action* by cohabitees themselves. Wills, and also different forms of contracts, do exist but there is a very small range thereof. To some extent this can be explained by a lack of knowledge about the law. There is often a reluctance to talk about sensitive subjects like separation and one's death, circumstances that can also explain the lack of action on the part of cohabitees.

The third factor is *legal restrictions*. As said above, cohabitees function poorly when it comes to drawing up wills and contracts to protect one another, but if they are unlikely to establish increased protection, there are also legal limitations when it comes to the possibility to draw up both wills and contracts. As mentioned above, children's right to their statutory portion limits the possibility for some cohabitees to inherit all property from each other. Cohabitees also cannot contract about everything. How far the possibility to contract extends is unclear, which in itself is a problem.

5.3. WHAT CAN BE DONE TO MAKE THE COHABITEES ACT FUNCTION IN TODAY'S SOCIETY?

What is there to be done – and who should be responsible – to remedy the gap between the law and the needs of cohabitees when it comes to this very private area – our family formation and economic family dilemmas? Is the legislator (or society at large) to be responsible, or is it fairer to lay the responsibility on the individuals themselves? A lack of 'interplay' affects both sides negatively in the end, but in different ways. The individuals, and then more specifically the weaker

---

14 No results about people's knowledge are included in this contribution, but will be presented in my thesis.

parties in cohabitations, are directly negatively affected in an economic way when a cohabitation is dissolved by separation or death. Society is affected in a more long-term view; if the weaker parties in cohabitations are not sufficiently protected by the law, society will be the one that has to take care of those individuals who, after a dissolved cohabitation, cannot manage economically by themselves. The question is then what each side can do to improve the 'interplay' between them.

The lawmaker/society can disperse information about the legal consequences of cohabitation. As mentioned above, knowledge of the law is inadequate, which means that those who would need to act to protect one another do not know or understand that they need to act. Better knowledge of the law might also, for some cohabitees, affect how they would share costs and also unpaid work in the home, for example parental leave and part-time work. If information is to have a widespread effect, it is important both to inform those who live in cohabitation as well as those who might become a cohabitee in the future. Information in high school, together with directed information to all cohabitees, could be one idea.[15]

The lawmaker could also change the legislation, which is what a majority of unmarried men and women want. To change the legislation is however a big challenge due to the fact that cohabitation comprises a diversity of couples and individuals. If the 'interplay' between law and society is to be improved in a legislative way, it is not possible only to extend the rules by, for example, giving cohabitation the same legal consequences as marriage – that would not be suitable for all the different kinds of cohabitees. Instead the legislator has to look at several legal solutions. One solution could be that more extensive rules than currently exist today are to be combined with different prerequisites like registration, a time limit for the duration of the cohabitation, or common children. However, if different legal solutions are to function in reality, information about different legal consequences, depending on different prerequisites, will be a very important factor.

Individuals/cohabitees also have some different steps that they can take to improve the interplay between themselves and the law. First of all, it is possible for all cohabitees to marry and receive more extended protection in the event that the relationship is dissolved.[16] However, a marriage requires the consent of both parties, which is a problem if just one of them wants to marry. Another obstacle when it comes to marriage is that many cohabitees want to marry, but

---

[15] Information directed towards cohabitees assumes some kind of register of cohabitees. There is no such register in Sweden. However, recently an apartment register has been completed, which in the future will make it possible to find cohabitees through data in public registers.

[16] Entering into a marriage is possible for all cohabitees over the age of 18 years old. A marriage with one of the parties under 18 years of age requires a dispensation from the authorities. Cohabitation can exist from 15 years of age, see Betänkande 2002/03:LU 19 – Ny Sambolag, pp. 10–11.

they postpone the event due to various reasons like their economic situation, a lack of time, children, etc.[17]

Individuals can also search for information themselves. Information is now easily accessible over the internet, at least to an extent that can give individuals an idea of whether or not they should contact a lawyer to discuss and perhaps establish economic protection which is tailored to their specific needs. It can also be better for individuals to take positive action, both when it comes to informing themselves, discussing these kinds of questions in their relationships and establishing additional protection.

It is obvious that both sides – the lawmaker/society and individuals – can do certain things to improve the interplay between them, things that would make the law keep more in pace with time. It is also necessary that something is done, and I would say that this is quite urgent. Of course the best thing would be if both sides could cooperate in this improvement of the 'interplay' between them. The prerequisite for finding legislation that suits the full range of cohabitees would then be greater, which in the end would be positive for both sides.

---

[17]   Results from my empirical study.

MAINTENANCE BETWEEN FORMER SPOUSES AND GENDER EQUALITY

Marketa Rihova Batista

Contents

1. INTRODUCTION

Maintenance as a claim between former spouses has a connection to many gender aspects, above all in opposite-sex marriages. These gender aspects have not yet been well researched in many European countries, and as a result we can see, for example, that amendment bills contain prejudiced argumentation or argumentation with general clichés.[1]

---

[1] An example would be the draft bill by the German Federal Government to amend maintenance laws, Bundestags-Drucksache 16/1830, 15.06.2006, especially the argumentation on p. 12 relating to changes to gender roles or women's desire to be independent after divorce.

In my research, based especially on German and Czech law, I seek to show that the background of many maintenance regulations is incompatible with gender equality.

I understand gender equality as a real type of equality that goes beyond formal equality *de jure*. A regulation is only equal when it does not reproduce traditional gender roles but respects the real differences between the sexes in society to avoid indirect discrimination. I will also draft some principles that would make maintenance more equitable.

2. NECESSITY TO JUSTIFY MAINTENANCE

Divorce should end every legal bond between spouses. According to German law, there is a basic principle that every person should be responsible for him/herself after divorce; it means that he or she should provide for his or her own support. In Czech law, there is no explicit basic principle of maintenance between former spouses in the law, but the interpretation of the law generally recognises the duty of the divorced spouse to provide for his own support, too.[2] Even in the CEFL Principles there is a basic principle of self-sufficiency.[3] It means that maintenance claims are an exception to this basic rule. Therefore a justification for this exception appears to be necessary.

However, there are also other reasons for the justification of maintenance claims. The social acceptance of maintenance between former spouses in the Czech Republic and in Germany is low.[4] A well-researched and structured justification supports the parties – the decision of one of the spouses to ask for maintenance and the other spouse to accept the claim and provide maintenance.

---

[2] M. Hrušáková, *Zákon o rodině. Zákon o registrovaném partnerství*, p. 441 (Praha: C.H. Beck, 2009).

[3] Principle 2:2. *CEFL Principles* in this article means *Principles of European Family Law Regarding Divorce and Maintenance between Former Spouses*, for more information see K. Boele-Woelki (ed.), *Principles of European Family Law Regarding Divorce and Maintenance between Former Spouses* (Antwerp: Intersentia, 2004).

[4] For Germany see: H.-J. Andress, B. Borgloh, M. Güllner, K. Wilking, *Wenn aus Liebe rote Zahlen werden. Über die wirtschaftlichen Folgen von Trennung und Scheidung*, p. 203 (Wiesbaden: Westdeutscher Verlag, 2003). According to the German data, two thirds of entitled women and about 90 per cent of entitled men do not receive maintenance at all or do not receive it regularly. For the Czech Republic see: M. Hrušáková, *Grounds for Divorce and Maintenance between Former Spouses. Czech Republic*, p. 27, available at http://ceflonline.net/wp-content/uploads/Czech-Divorce.pdf (last accessed 18.11.2013). The data show that the number of decisions of the Czech courts concerning maintenance between former spouses is extremely low – in 2000, there were 29,704 divorces and in 984 cases the courts granted maintenance to the former wife, in 86 cases to the former husband.

The justification of the maintenance claim also explains the sense and purpose of the law, which is important for its interpretation and application.[5]

Finally, a well-structured and researched justification for maintenance between former spouses appears to be necessary because of the gender dimension of maintenance between former spouses. This justification must not be gender-biased and must not be based on or refer to traditional gender roles. This would violate gender equality.

3. JUSTIFICATION FOR MAINTENANCE

3.1. POST-MARITAL SOLIDARITY

The theory that has affected German and Czech law is the theory of post-marital solidarity. Under this theory, a marriage, even if it has ended in divorce, still has some effects, so that the spouses remain responsible for each other after divorce because of the basic solidarity that remains between them after divorce.[6] The divorced spouse can request maintenance at any time after divorce if he or she is in need, even, for example, if he or she loses the ability to provide for himself or herself because of illness that has occurred after the divorce. The concept of post-marital solidarity has been discussed in Germany at least since the end of the 19th century, when the current Civil Code was elaborated. Critics have argued that the concept of post-marital solidarity does not provide a solid reason as to why there should be any solidarity between divorced spouses at all, above all in a situation after divorce when their interests contrast.[7] The lack of any rationale for this solidarity has been recognised since the creation of the German Civil Code. The authors of the Civil Code argued for equity because if there was no maintenance claim, the innocent spouse would either have had to continue in the marriage or be left without any means. Their other argument was that the absence of a maintenance claim would be at the public expense.[8]

Other critics of the theory of post-marital solidarity claim that it is based on the Christian idea of a lifelong marriage.[9]

---

5   U. DIEDERICHSEN, Geschiedenenunterhalt – Überförderung nachehelicher Solidarität?, *Neue Juristische Wochenschrift*, 1993, p. 2265.

6   See H.-J. DOSE, Ehe und nacheheliche Solidarität, *Zeitschrift für das gesamte Familienrecht*, 2011, pp. 1342, 1347.

7   H. SCHÜRMANN, Generelle Befristung des nachehelichen Unterhalts – eine überfällige Reform?, *Familie, Partnerschaft, Recht*, 2005, p. 494.

8   S. MEDER, Grundprinzipien des Geschiedenenunterhalts – "clean break" oder fortwirkende nacheheliche Solidarität?, in: K. SCHEIWE, *Soziale Sicherungsmodelle revisited. Existenzsicherung durch Sozial- und Familienrecht und ihre Geschlechterdimensionen*, p. 176 (Baden-Baden: Nomos, 2007).

9   S. FLÜGGE, Die ungelöste Frauenfrage: Was wird aus dem Familienernährer?, in: K. SCHEIWE, *Soziale Sicherungsmodelle revisited*, supra n. 8, p. 192.

3.2. COMPENSATION FOR DISADVANTAGES ARISING FROM THE MARRIAGE

Another justification for maintenance that influences Czech and German law is maintenance as compensation for disadvantages arising from the marriage. This concept has been established during the last few decades.[10] This kind of compensation is independent from the situation where the creditor spouse is in need. It concentrates on the losses occasioned by the marriage and by the divorce. The critics of this theory state that the concept of disadvantages arising from the marriage is very vague. It is difficult to define when a disadvantage arises from the marriage; in the end there is normally only one connection between the marriage and the disadvantage: that the period when the disadvantage occurred was within the marriage.[11] Furthermore, it is also necessary to define what kind of disadvantage or loss can be compensated. Is it only possible to compensate the loss of earning capacity or can the loss of a particular standard of living also be included, for example?

4. CZECH LAW

Since 2014, there is now a new Civil Code in the Czech Republic. Until 2013, maintenance was regulated by the Family Code, Act no. 94/1963. In order to be granted maintenance, the creditor spouse had to be unable to provide for himself or herself. On the other side, the debtor spouse had to provide support according to his or her abilities, possibilities and assets (§92 (1) Family Code). Thus, the crucial requirements of the old law were the needs of one spouse and the ability of the other spouse to provide maintenance. Although a theory of maintenance or a justification for maintenance has not developed in Czech law, it is possible to view the old law as being based on post-marital solidarity.

In the new Civil Code, Act no. 89/2012, the regulation of maintenance has notably changed. According to §760 (1) of the Civil Code, the divorced spouse can request maintenance if he or she is not able to provide for himself or herself and if this inability has its origin in the marriage or is related to the marriage. Furthermore, providing maintenance has to be equitable for the debtor spouse. This new regulation completely removes the idea of post-marital solidarity. The claim consistently depends on the needs of one of the divorced spouses, but the needs themselves are only relevant when they are related to the marriage. This

---

10   For example, the theory of alimony by Ira Mark Ellman, see: I.M. ELLMAN, The Theory of Alimony, *California Law Review*, 1989, pp. 1–81, or the American Law Institute Principles of the law of family dissolution, §5.02 – §5.05, see: *Principles of the Law of Family Dissolution. Analysis and Recommendations* (St. Paul: American Law Inst. Publ., 2008).

11   H. SCHÜRMANN, Generelle Befristung des nachehelichen Unterhalts – eine überfällige Reform?, *supra* n. 7, p. 494.

leads to a system of compensating an inability to provide for oneself that arises from the marriage. This new regulation cannot be viewed as a direct implementation of the principle of compensation for disadvantages arising from the marriage. However, the step back from the longstanding principle of solidarity after marriage towards maintenance as compensation for marital disadvantages is very obvious.

5. GERMAN LAW

The German Civil Code (BGB) regulates a few specific maintenance claims. The general requirements for all of them are the inability of the creditor spouse to provide for himself or herself (§1577 BGB) and the ability of the debtor spouse to provide maintenance for the other spouse (§1581 BGB). The grounds for maintenance claims are child care (§1570 BGB), maintenance for an aged spouse (§1571 BGB), the illness or infirmity of the creditor spouse (§1572 BGB), unemployment and an insufficient income for the creditor spouse (§1573 BGB), education, further education and retraining by the creditor spouse (§1575 BGB) and maintenance for reasons of equity (§1576 BGB).[12] The grounds for maintenance do not necessarily have to be a consequence of the marriage or to have occurred during the marriage.[13] There are some timeframes indicated by the law regarding when the grounds have to occur in order to be able to make a maintenance claim. For example, in the case of maintenance for reasons of illness or infirmity, an illness that has occurred after the divorce is relevant if the creditor spouse had a maintenance claim for reasons of unemployment and an insufficient income beforehand.

The whole system of maintenance claims in Germany is very strongly influenced by the theory of post-marital solidarity – mainly because claims are needs-based and because of the very long period of time during which the debtor spouse can have a claim as the various grounds for claiming follow each other – such as, for example, maintenance for reasons of retraining, followed by maintenance for reasons of unemployment, illness and, finally, maintenance for an aged spouse.

However, in the last few years there have been changes that have introduced some features of compensation for disadvantages arising from the marriage into the law of maintenance. The maintenance reform that occurred in 2008[14] made the criteria of the division of child care and paid work within the marriage

---

12   For further information in English see: D. Schwab, D. Martiny, *Grounds for Divorce and Maintenance between Former Spouses. Germany*, available at: http://ceflonline.net/wp-content/uploads/Germany-Divorce.pdf (last accessed 18.11.2013).

13   O. Palandt, G. Brudermüller, *Bürgerliches Gesetzbuch*, §1572, Rn. 3, p. 1843 (Munich: C.H. Beck, 2013).

14   By Act 'Gesetz zur Änderung des Unterhaltsrechts', effective from 01.01.2008.

relevant for the duration of maintenance for reasons of child care (§1570 (2) BGB). Since the reform, a loss of earning capacity during the marriage, caused mainly by the duration of child care or the division of housework and paid work within the marriage (§1578 b (1) BGB), has also been relevant for a reduction in maintenance payments by a court order – in those cases where the creditor spouse has suffered such a loss of earning capacity, the maintenance is normally not reduced by the court with the exception of the sound financial circumstances of the creditor spouse.[15]

6. CEFL PRINCIPLES

According to Principle 2:2 of the *Principles of European Family Law Regarding Divorce and Maintenance between Former Spouses* there is a basic rule for maintenance, which is the self-sufficiency of the spouses after divorce. As in the Czech and German provisions, the maintenance claim depends on the needs of the creditor spouse and the ability of the debtor spouse to satisfy those needs (Principle 2:3). The criteria in Principle 2:4 that should be taken into account when deciding on maintenance claims are also related to the justification by post-marital solidarity – for example, the employment ability of the spouses, their age or health. Only the criterion of *the division of duties during the marriage* and partly the criterion of *the care of children* can be considered as provisions to compensate the disadvantages arising from the marriage. Even if the claim is based on the needs of the creditor spouse, there is a provision in Principle 2:8 that maintenance should only be granted for a limited period of time.

7. GENDER ASPECTS OF MAINTENANCE

Maintenance between former spouses and its justification have many aspects regarding gender that are not compatible with gender equality.

7.1. A REFLECTION OF TRADITIONAL GENDER ROLES

The theory of post-marital solidarity reflects traditional gender roles. This theory is used to justify maintenance claims with a very long duration or maintenance for reasons not related to the marriage if the creditor spouse is in need. This situation appears to be the most likely in the lives of women who have chosen to follow the traditional division of roles – i.e. caring for the children and doing the

---

[15] H.-U. MAURER, Die Begrenzung des nachehelichen Alters- und Krankheitsunterhalt, *Familie, Partnerschaft, Recht*, 2013, p. 148.

housework. Furthermore, the theory of post-marital solidarity also presupposes that those women do not have the obligation to be self-sufficient after divorce. According to traditional patterns, women could rely on (almost) lifelong support after marrying. Independent of divorce, the former husband was responsible for his former wife when she was in need after the divorce.

Thus, the theory of post-marital solidarity is incompatible with gender equality. Therefore, it should not be possible to justify maintenance claims by means of this theory. Also the maintenance provisions that only rely on this theory are incompatible with gender equality. This objection concerns, above all, German law, which has a structure of maintenance claims with a long duration following each other. Also the provisions in the CEFL Principles completely relate to post-marital solidarity.

7.2. NO MOTIVATION FOR SELF-SUFFICIENCY

Maintenance claims with a long duration do not motivate the spouse who is the primary care provider – mostly the woman – to be self-sufficient during the marriage. Instead of agreeing with their husbands that the support they receive is used to increase their own earning capacity in the long term, maintenance claims with a long duration rather motivate wives to depend on their husbands. The result is that in cases of divorce, wives depend on their former husbands even in the situation where the former spouses have opposing interests.

7.3. TERMINATION OF THE MAINTENANCE OBLIGATION DUE TO HAVING ENTERED INTO A NEW RELATIONSHIP

According to German law and the CEFL Principles, the maintenance obligation of the debtor spouse is influenced by a new relationship of the other spouse. According to the CEFL Principles (Principle 2:9 (1)), the maintenance obligation of the debtor spouse terminates when the other spouse enters into a new relationship. Under German law (§1579, No. 2 BGB), the maintenance claim can be refused, reduced or restricted in time for reasons of serious inequity for the debtor spouse when the creditor spouse lives in a stable relationship with another person.

Thus, the law does not provide for a maintenance claim against the new partner of the creditor spouse. Even if the creditor spouse – mostly the entitled woman – is in need – for example, she is caring for young children from her marriage with the debtor spouse – she may lose the maintenance claim without having another claim instead. Established German legal practice assumes that there is a stable relationship when it has lasted for about two or three years, but it may take even less time for a relationship to be viewed as a stable one[16] – for example, only one year when the new partners have purchased or rented a flat together and have the intention to live in a stable relationship.[17] This means that post-marital solidarity comes to an end with a new, long-term and stable relationship, even if the creditor spouse is not self-sufficient.

However, these provisions reproduce a very traditional pattern of gender role expectations. According to this pattern, the maintenance obligation of the divorced husband ends when the divorced wife establishes a sexual relationship with another man. In such a situation she is no longer worthy of being supported even if she is in need. In spite of the common basic principle of maintenance between former spouses, which is the self-sufficiency of the former spouses, these provisions oblige a divorced woman to depend on a man who does not have any maintenance obligation towards her, rather than retaining the maintenance obligation from the terminated marriage until the creditor spouse is self-sufficient. The ability of the new partner to support the creditor spouse is of no importance in this case. Furthermore, a creditor spouse who is not self-sufficient is not able to freely decide on her own personal relationships. If she maintains a stable relationship, there is always a risk of losing her economic base. This can be a motivation for the divorced wife not to establish other relationships while the divorced husband has no limitations on establishing new relationships. These provisions are therefore also not compatible with gender equality.

In the Czech Republic, there are no legal provisions on the termination of the maintenance obligation because of a new relationship by the creditor spouse. However, opinions have been expressed in the literature to the effect that awarding maintenance in the situation of a long-term relationship by the creditor spouse might be inequitable.[18]

7.4. LAW IN CONTRAST WITH REAL DATA

Despite maintenance regulations within the law, maintenance between former spouses has been received by only a minority of those entitled, mostly women. In most cases, maintenance is not even claimed and, if it is claimed, actual payments are rather rare. According to German data, only about one third of entitled women and ten per cent of entitled men received maintenance in 2000.[19] This data shows that the acceptance of the maintenance claim by the (mostly

---

[16]   O. PALANDT, G. BRUDERMÜLLER, *Bürgerliches Gesetzbuch*, §1579, Rn. 12a, p. 1875 (Munich: C.H. Beck, 2013).

[17]   OLG Frankfurt am Main, 19.11.2010, 7 UF 91/09, in: *Neue Juristische Wochenschrift Rechtsprechungs – Report Zivilrecht*, 2011, p. 1156.

[18]   P. VRCHA, Výživné rozvedeného manžela, *Poradce*, 2006, Vol. 12, p. 255.

[19]   H.-J. ANDRESS, B. BORGLOH, M. GÜLLNER, K. WILKING, *Wenn aus Liebe rote Zahlen werden*, *supra* n. 4, p. 203.

male) debtors is very low. In addition, many German female creditors resist making a maintenance claim in order to avoid being dependent on their former husband.[20] There are no Czech data on this specific point but we know that in 2000 there were 29,704 divorces but only 984 court decisions on maintenance for the divorced wife[21] – in other words, the courts granted maintenance to women in only 3.3 per cent of cases. This is an extremely low number when we consider other aspects that negatively influence earning capacity – for example, child care: only about 0.5 per cent of Czech men were on parental leave in 2002.[22]

These data suggest that the acceptance of post-marital solidarity and maintenance claims based on post-marital solidarity is low. This means that maintenance based on post-marital solidarity does not fulfil its function of ensuring support for divorced spouses in need. Since these spouses are mostly women, the law leads to less gender equality.

8. A MORE EQUITABLE MAINTENANCE SYSTEM

Especially because of its incompatibility with gender equality, the system of maintenance claims based on post-marital solidarity should come to an end. The new system should follow the system of compensation for disadvantages arising from the marriage. This would be especially true for maintenance claims for reasons of child care that would be limited by the age of the youngest child, for example until the age of three.

Furthermore, there should be another claim that compensates the decline in the earning capacity of one spouse arising from the marriage. In deciding on this claim, the following should be taken into consideration: the division and duration of child care, the division of housework during the marriage and the agreements and declarations between the spouses during the marriage that influenced their future earning capacity – for example, if they agreed on a traditional role model or one of them compelled the other to accept such a role model.

In addition, the advantages arising from the marriage, such as an improvement in the earning capacity of one of the spouses that would not have been possible without a decline in the earning capacity of the other spouse, should also be considered. Compensation should be determined in one fixed amount in order to prevent feelings of long-term dependency and conflicts

---

20   H.-J. ANDRESS, B. BORGLOH, M. GÜLLNER, K. WILKING, *Wenn aus Liebe rote Zahlen werden*, *supra* n. 4, pp. 196, 203.

21   M. HRUŠÁKOVÁ, *Grounds for Divorce and Maintenance between Former Spouses. Czech Republic, supra* n. 4, p. 27.

22   H. MAŘÍKOVÁ, Caregiving Fathers: Theoretical and Empirical Analysis, in: L. SOKAČOVÁ (ed.), *Family Policy: Parental and Maternity Leave in the Context of Work-Life Balance and Equal Opportunities for Women and Men*, p. 35 (Praha: Gender Studies, 2010).

between former spouses and should preferably be paid as a lump sum. A decision on maintenance when deciding about the division of marital property should be made possible in order to prevent problems with the enforcement of maintenance.

Finally, the principles of self-sufficiency during marriage and the equal division of duties during marriage should be laid down by law. The purpose of this would be declaratory, in order to motivate men and women to break free from traditional gender roles.

These provisions would encourage women to ensure their own financial independence during the marriage and would protect them in the case of a lower earning capacity arising from the marriage. Women who have adopted the traditional role in a marriage of long duration would be sufficiently protected. The regulations would not grant maintenance only because of the poor financial situation of divorced women and there would be no solidarity between two people only because they had been married in the past. The whole system would also support the acceptance of maintenance claims by debtor spouses who would rather see a direct connection between marriage and maintenance and who would rather understand the reasons why they have the obligation to compensate losses of creditor spouses arising from marriage. All in all, such a maintenance system would be more in line with the principles of gender equality.

Finally, these maintenance claims should not only be available for former spouses but also for former partners in long-term relationships. Nowadays, in long-term relationships there are often the same dependency patterns connected to the same decline and improvement in earning capacity as in a marriage. There is no reason to leave people living in long-term relationships without protection.

COLLABORATIVE PRACTICE

An Interdisciplinary Approach to the Resolution of Conflict in Family Law Matters

Connie HEALY

Contents

1. INTRODUCTION

Divorce has been described as:

> '[D]reams unfilled, or dreams that have run their course. It may be profound grief and it may be bittersweet freedom. It is about families restructuring: financially,

emotionally and practically. It is both conflict and resolution. It is pain and it is relief.'[1]

This paper examines a new method of alternative dispute resolution in family law which purports to provide an interdisciplinary framework within which to explore and resolve the legal, financial and emotional aspects of relationship breakdown. This process, known as collaborative practice or collaborative divorce, originated in the US in the early 1990s and is now used worldwide in the resolution of conflict in family law matters.

Menkel-Meadow notes that '[d]isputing … will (often) reflect the culture's values, and it may not be wise to attempt to transplant a form of disputing that is not indigenous to, or compatible with, a different culture.'[2] This chapter will therefore explore the extent to which the collaborative model is compatible with the Irish family law system and will examine the changes that have been made to the process to adapt it to meet the relevant cultural needs of Irish society.

While research has been carried out into the process in the US,[3] Canada[4] and England and Wales,[5] this chapter will present the preliminary findings of the first known empirical research into collaborative practice in Ireland, contextualising the Irish position within the international framework. Specifically, the paper will present the results of one aspect of a larger multi-layered research project into the development of collaborative practice in Ireland: the views of separating parties who have used the process in the resolution of their family law disputes.

2. THE IRISH DIVORCE LANDSCAPE

The right to marry and found a family was enshrined in the Irish Constitution in 1937.[6] The family is described therein as:

---

[1]   N. CAMERON, *Collaborative Practice: Deepening the Dialogue,* The Continuing Legal Education Society of British Columbia 2004, p. 9.

[2]   C. MENKEL-MEADOW, "Mothers and Fathers of Invention: The Intellectual Founders of ADR", *Ohio Journal on Dispute Resolution* 2000 16 (1), pp. 1–37 (11).

[3]   International Academy of Collaborative Professionals, see www.collaborativepractice.com (last accessed 06.11.2013).

[4]   J. MACFARLANE, "The Emerging Phenomenon of Collaborative Family Law (CFL): A Qualitative Case Study", Department of Justice Canada 2005, available at www.justice.gc.ca (last accessed 06.11.2013).

[5]   M. SEFTON, "Collaborative Family Law, A Report for Resolution", February 2009. Report available by request from Resolution, UK.

[6]   Bunreacht na hÉireann, available at www.irishstatutebook.ie/constitution.html (last accessed 06.11.2013).

'the natural primary and fundamental unit group of Society, and as a moral institution possessing inalienable and imprescriptible rights, antecedent and superior to all positive law.'[7]

The State also pledged 'itself to guard with special care the institution of Marriage, on which the Family is founded, and to protect it against attack.'[8]

The first attempt to amend the Constitution to allow for divorce in 1986 was defeated by a majority of two to one by the Irish electorate. As a country which was, at that time, strongly influenced by the teachings and pronouncements of the Catholic Church, the introduction of divorce to Ireland was much debated. Duncan comments however, that the defeat was not solely related to religious concerns but also to fears about the social consequences 'underpinning the stability of marriage' and the possible 'hardship to dependent family members.'[9] A second referendum was held in 1996 and after another long and divisive debate the referendum was passed by a small majority (50.3 per cent in favour, 49.7 per cent against). The accompanying legislation, the Family Law (Divorce) Act 1996 came into effect on 27 February 1997.

Subsequent to the referendum, the Constitution was amended. Article 41.3.2 now provides:

'2° A *Court* designated by law may grant a dissolution of marriage where, but only where, it is satisfied that

i.   at the date of the institution of the proceedings, the spouses have lived apart from one another for a period of, or periods amounting to, at least four years during the five years,
ii. there is no reasonable prospect of a reconciliation between the spouses,
iii. such provision as the Court considers proper having regard to the circumstances exists or will be made for the spouses, any children of either or both of them and any other person prescribed by law, and
iv. any further conditions prescribed by law are complied with.'[10]

Enshrining these specific provisions in the Constitution rather than providing more general powers to legislate for divorce was seen as an attempt to ensure that the Court would remain the arbiter in divorce proceedings and that so-called 'administrative divorce' (undefended divorce through the post) as is available in England would not be permitted.[11] Thus, compared to England where recent research has shown that up to 62 per cent of those divorcing had

---

[7]   Art. 41.
[8]   Ibid 41.3.
[9]   W. DUNCAN, "The Divorce Referendum in Ireland: Resisting the Tide", *International Journal of Law and the Family* 1988 vol. 2, pp. 62–75 (69).
[10] Emphasis added.
[11] W. DUNCAN, "The Divorce Referendum in Ireland: Resisting the Tide", *International Journal of Law and the Family* 1988 vol. 2, pp. 62–75 (69).

not sought legal advice at all,[12] divorce in Ireland is very much centred around the courts' system. This is also in contrast with the position in certain civil law jurisdictions. Boele-Woelki refers, for example, to research in Sweden which has shown that '75% of couples who carry out a property division after their divorce, divide their assets by themselves without the "interference" of lawyers'.[13]

Under the Family Law (Divorce) Act 1996, solicitors are required to advise separating parties about the availability and potential benefits of mediation as a means of resolving issues in a more amicable fashion.[14] If terms are agreed within the mediation process, however, these family law mediated agreements are not legally binding. An additional step is required to either have lawyers draw up a Deed of Separation or to rule agreed terms as part of a consent order for Judicial Separation[15] or Divorce.[16]

3. 'ORDINARY LAWYER NEGOTIATION'[17]

Research has shown that most cases commenced within the adversarial system will settle.[18] A full hearing before a judge is therefore only required in a small percentage of cases.[19] My research has demonstrated, however, that the final terms of these settlements may not be agreed in many cases (over 54 per cent) until the day the case is actually listed for hearing.[20] Settlement negotiated in this way is often referred to as 'ordinary lawyer negotiation', and will frequently occur without the separating parties having had adequate time to reflect on the proposals being made. Collaborative practice aims to provide an alternative to 'ordinary lawyer negotiation', one that is more client-focused.

---

[12]   A. BARLOW et al, "Mapping Paths to Family Justice: a national picture of findings on out of court family dispute resolution", *Family Law* March 2013, pp. 306–309 (307).

[13]   K. BOELE-WOELKI/F. FERRAND/C. GONZÁLEZ BEILFUSS/M. JÄNTERÄ-JAREBORG/N. LOWE/ D. MARTINY/W. PINTENS, *Principles of European Family Law Regarding Property Relations Between Spouses*, Intersentia 2013, p. 33.

[14]   Sections 6 and 7 of the Family Law (Divorce) Act 1996.

[15]   A judicial separation under the Judicial Separation and Family Law Reform Act 1989 is a court ordered legal separation but does not permit the parties to remarry.

[16]   Section 5 of the Family Law (Divorce) Act 1996.

[17]   J. LANDE, "Teaching Students to Negotiate Like a Lawyer", *Washington University Journal of Law and Policy* 2012 vol. 39, pp. 109–144 (118).

[18]   C. COULTER, "Family Law Reporting, Pilot Project", *Report to the Board of the Court Service* 2007, pp. 1–80(3), available at www.courts.ie/Courts.ie/library3.nsf/(WebFiles)/C4FA6C02C7 B13A428025738400521CE9/$FILE/Report%20to%20the%20Board%20of%20the%20Courts% 20Service.pdf (last accessed 06.11.2013). Up to 90 per cent of cases settle.

[19]   Ibid.

[20]   A survey amongst solicitors revealed that up to 54 per cent of cases settle on the day of hearing.

4. WHAT IS COLLABORATIVE PRACTICE?

Collaborative practice is defined in the US as a 'voluntary, contractually based alternative dispute resolution process for parties who seek to negotiate a resolution of their matter rather than to have a ruling imposed upon them by a court or arbitrator.'[21] Under Irish law, this equates to using a structured negotiation process, where parties can actively participate in the decisions being made, supported by, and under the supervision of, their lawyers. Once an amicable agreement is reached, one that meets the needs of the separating parties and their children, this agreement can then be taken before a judge for his or her final seal of approval in accordance with the provisions of the Constitution.

When parties opt to use the collaborative law process they sign a contract called a 'participation agreement'. Under the terms of the 'participation agreement' the parties agree not to take the matter before the court while these negotiations are on-going. All negotiations take place at scheduled, face-to-face, four-way meetings, where the parties set the agenda for each meeting and each party has their own collaborative solicitor present.[22] Within the terms of the participation agreement, there is also an assurance given by both parties that they will be honest in their dealings with each other and that they will negotiate in good faith. They agree to provide full details of their up-to-date financial position and to focus on the interests of the family as a whole, rather than adopting an adversarial stance.

Under the terms of the signed participation agreement, all negotiations that take place within the process are confidential and may not be referred to in any future court proceedings. The solicitors continue to support and advocate for their own client, but in contrast to 'ordinary lawyer negotiation', as noted above, the clients are directly involved in the negotiations.

If full agreement is reached, the solicitors may either draw up a legal separation agreement or issue proceedings, by consent, solely to obtain a decree of judicial separation or divorce from the courts and, if necessary, have any ancillary matters ruled upon by the court.[23]

What makes the collaborative process unique is the disqualification clause. This provides that, in the event that settlement cannot be reached, the clients'

---

[21]   Prefatory Note to the United States – Uniform Collaborative Law Act, p. 1, available at www.law.upenn.edu/bll/archives/ulc/ucla/2010_final.htm (last accessed 06.11.2013).

[22]   See generally P. TESLER, *Collaborative Law, Achieving Effective Resolution in Divorce without Litigation*, 2nd ed. American Bar Association 2008; S. WEBB, *The Collaborative Way to Divorce, The Revolutionary Method That Results in Less Stress, Lower Costs and Happier Kids Without Going to Court*, Penguin 2007.

[23]   Orders may be required in relation to maintenance, property adjustment orders or orders in respect of a pension adjustment. While the parties may agree how to vary the terms of a pension, this will not be legally binding unless an order is obtained from the court and served on the trustees of a pension fund.

solicitors are disqualified from acting for them in any subsequent legal proceedings arising out of this issue or any related matter. Why is there a need for such a clause?

The process was structured in this way to help ensure the commitment of the separating parties and their solicitors to the negotiation process. Both the clients and the solicitors have a vested interest in reaching settlement. For the client, s/he may have built up a relationship with a solicitor and will be acutely aware that failure of the process means starting afresh with new legal representation and incurring additional legal costs. Solicitors, likewise, are aware that unless they make every effort possible to assist their clients to reach agreement, they may lose their client. This ensures that they, too, are settlement-focused from the outset and cases are therefore less likely to be settled at the door of the court. It is important to note that solicitors may also terminate the process if they believe that their client is not being forthcoming with information or co-operating with the ethos of the process. This is referred to as 'imputed disqualification'.

The disqualification provision is heralded by Stuart Webb, who developed the process, as essential in providing a 'safe and effective environment for settlement'.[24] Separating parties, in his view, feel free to negotiate in the knowledge that they will not be facing their ex-partner's solicitor in the event that the matter goes before the court. However, the need for such a clause has been the subject of much debate. Lawyers in the US and elsewhere have argued that it puts too much pressure on clients to settle within the process such that they may agree to terms they are unhappy with rather than incur the additional costs of having to instruct a new solicitor to take their case to court.[25] However, this fear does not appear to be borne out in research.[26]

The collaborative law model spread quickly throughout the US, Canada and indeed worldwide. As it developed it evolved into an interdisciplinary model where mental health and other experts are frequently retained to assist parties with the emotional or financial issues surrounding the breakdown of a relationship.[27] In the US the interdisciplinary model of collaborative practice is used more widely as clients seek help from 'mental health experts' or 'divorce coaches'. While there are benefits to such assistance, there has been some resistance to such intervention in Ireland. Collaborative solicitors interviewed for this research have indicated that, within the 'Irish psyche', there is still a stigma attached to seeking counselling. Culturally, Irish people are less likely to seek

---

24   S. WEBB/R. OUSKY, *The Collaborative Way to Divorce: The Revolutionary Method that Results in Less Stress, Lower Costs, and Happier Kids – Without Going to Court*, Penguin 2007, p. 12.

25   J. LANDE, "The Promise and Perils of Collaborative Law", *Dispute Resolution Magazine* 2005–2006 vol. 12, pp. 29–31 (29).

26   See section 6.3. of this paper.

27   In addition, parties may jointly instruct a financial professional to prepare an independent report on their financial position, investments and to assist with restructuring their finances. By doing this, the parties save themselves the expense of each party having to engage their own experts and the associated costs involved in these experts giving evidence and being cross-examined in court.

assistance outside of the 'family'. The Association of Collaborative Practitioners in Ireland[28] refer to 'mental health experts' as 'Personal and Family Consultants' in an effort to show the benefits that these professionals can provide in a 'whole family' context. However, the use of these experts in Ireland remains low.

The parties to a participation agreement may agree at the outset on the additional experts (mental health experts, financial experts or child specialists) they require and then proceed on a 'team' basis with the assistance of these experts at every stage of the process. Alternatively, the parties may proceed on a 'referral' basis, liaising with any additional experts as the need arises throughout the collaboration.

5. METHODOLOGY

The results being presented in this chapter are based on one element of a larger multi-layered mixed method empirical study which aims to provide a picture of the development of collaborative practice in Ireland in 2011/2012.[29] This article focuses on the views of the clients that used the collaborative process to resolve their marital issues. In order to get a broad based sample of clients, the author addressed the Association of Collaborative Practitioners'[30] Annual General Meeting, explained the aims of the research and requested that these solicitors ask their clients if they wished to participate. As a result, five collaborative solicitors made contact with the author and furnished details of ten clients who were willing to contribute.

The limitations involved in recruiting a sample in this way have to be acknowledged. The collaborative solicitors, arguably, acted as gate-keepers in that direct access to a list of clients was not possible for reasons of confidentiality. Thus, it was not possible for the author to select a random sample. The results, therefore, are not being presented as being representative of all clients that used the process but merely as reflecting the views of these particular participants. However, it is notable that eight out of the ten participants interviewed settled their cases through the process and this settlement rate is consistent with the results of research carried out into the process internationally.[31]

---

28   The Association of Collaborative Practitioners is the umbrella group for collaborative law solicitors in Ireland.

29   Quantitative research was undertaken by sending self-completing questionnaires to all trained collaborative lawyers in Ireland. Qualitative research, in the format of semi-structured interviews was also undertaken for a more in-depth perspective. These interviews were held with ten clients who used the process to resolve their family law issues, eight collaborative lawyers and eight litigators – defined as solicitors and barristers who operate within the adversarial courts' system and who do not engage in alternative methods of dispute resolution.

30   This is the umbrella body for collaborative solicitors in Ireland.

31   See J. MACFARLANE, n. 4; M. SEFTON, n. 5; L. WRAY, n. 42.

6. RESEARCH FINDINGS

6.1. DEMOGRAPHICS

Examining the demographics of those interviewed, it is evident that the process was used by those who were middle aged (eight were aged between the ages of 40–59) and that the majority had been in long marriages (nine of those interviewed had been married for over ten years). All of the participants interviewed had children, with seven participants having children who were under the age of 18 at the time they used the process. The majority of participants indicated that their household income was in excess of €50,000.[32] Seven had received tertiary level education.

6.2. SETTLEMENT RATES

Eight of those interviewed settled their cases through the collaborative process, with another one indicating that the agreement reached during the process was the 'foundation of what we took into court two years later.'[33]

6.3. IMPACT OF THE DISQUALIFICATION CLAUSE

As noted earlier, one of the main concerns expressed by the legal profession was the impact that the disqualification clause may have on clients' decisions to engage in or remain in the process. Interestingly, therefore, four of those interviewed said that the disqualification provision had no bearing whatsoever on their decision to use the process. A further three participants qualified this by noting that they were committed to reaching settlement within the process from the outset and that therefore it had no bearing. In fact, two of those interviewed perceived the disqualification provision as a positive element to the process with one commenting that 'it makes you grasp the nettle and move on'.[34] Another expressed this as follows:

> 'I would love to have got up and ran out screaming 25 times, but the fact that the solicitors were in a position as well to walk away and not just us, you kind of have more respect for each other … you think more. It wasn't an effect of keeping me

---

[32]   80 per cent of participants' household income was over €50,000, with 20 per cent indicating that their household income was over €100,000.

[33]   This settlement rate accords with the data established through the quantitative research undertaken. The quantitative research indicated that 81 per cent settled their cases, 19 per cent of cases terminated without settlement and in one case the parties reconciled. This is also consistent with the findings of research carried out in Canada and England and Wales.

[34]   Interview with CC 4, May 2011.

there, as in blocked me by keeping me there. It kept me there out of respect for the other three people involved in it.'

However, one participant did indicate that the disqualification provision kept her in the process longer than she would have stayed otherwise because she did not want to lose her lawyer.

6.4. COSTS

One of the arguments often used against the collaborative process, particularly the interdisciplinary model, is that it is prohibitively expensive. This question of costs was raised with all of the participants. Two participants indicated that they did not know whether the process was more or less expensive because they were unaware of how much it would have cost them to have taken their case to court. Six of those interviewed, however, were of the opinion that it was a much cheaper option.[35] Two participants, those for whom the process was not successful, thought that it was not a cheaper option.

6.5. CASES THAT TERMINATED

As noted above, two of the participants interviewed did not reach settlement during the process and had to go to court. One of these participants expressed regret at the failure:

'I was satisfied but sorry it failed … what was achieved in the collaboration was the foundation of what we took into court two years later so it is an awful shame to think it could not have been decided upon back then. Really, I suppose, nobody wants to go into court to decide how you are going to live the rest of your life so if there is an alternative it is better to go that route.'

For the other participant, however, they felt that the process had not met their needs and that they needed the formality and structure of the court process to ensure that matters were progressed to their satisfaction and that orders were complied with. They commented that they:

'loved the idea of it – being part of the arrangement … [but that] it allows parties who don't want to negotiate to get away with murder.'

---

[35]   These participants had used the lawyer-only model. Only two participants in the study used the interdisciplinary model. Of those, one considered it expensive and one said that they did not know how it would compare with the costs of going to court.

6.6. SATISFACTION WITH THE PROCESS

While the majority of participants were satisfied with the overall outcome, this did not always equate with getting a larger share of the family's assets. Satisfaction is obviously very subjective and was a very personal issue for many of the participants in that they reached a conclusion that suited their particular needs. Only one participant indicated that they were sure that they would have received a better settlement through the adversarial courts' system. However, their motivation in using the collaborative process was to maintain 'a working relationship' with the other party. Therefore, they were happy with the outcome because they have a good relationship now:

> 'I can ring X at any minute of the day if I wanted to and I can talk to him. I wouldn't rush to do it but I know I can. If he drops the kids back, he comes in and has a cup of coffee around the table which we wouldn't be doing if I had gone the other way.'[36]

One participant, though happy with the overall settlement, in that:

> 'mentally it worked out better for me. We are still talking and the kids are happy,' (but felt that at times they were) 'very unsure whether I was doing the right thing as regards the house and the estate ... I didn't know if that was the right amount, I was never really sure if I was giving too much or too little or whether [the other party] was giving nothing at all'.

This participant said that they felt that the solicitors 'came up with the figure and I just said that's fine if that's what you think the law says but they never said, ... the last two cases that went to court, this is how it worked out and this is what we have decided would be the best thing.' One of those three who were unsure as to where they stood commented that they 'didn't clearly know my rights', qualifying this by saying 'this does not mean that it wasn't explained to me, but you need things on paper'. At the time the research was concluded, this participant's case had progressed into the court system. However, the court system did not appear to have allayed their fears in that they felt that their entitlements were 'still not very clear – depends on the judge on the day and this creates a lot of fear as you are unsure about where you are going'.[37]

Some collaborative solicitors are of the view that it is better not to focus too much on rights or entitlements but to let the parties reach their own agreement. While this approach may have advantages, it is also extremely important that clients know where they stand legally so that agreements

---

[36] Interview CC 1, April 2011.
[37] Interview CC 10, August 2011.

reached are based on fully informed consent. Most participants interviewed felt that they were aware of their legal entitlements and that they felt supported by their lawyers.

6.7. RECOMMEND IT TO A FRIEND

The measure, in many respects, of a new process lies in the extent to which someone who has availed of it would recommend it to a friend in a similar situation. One hundred per cent of those interviewed said that they would recommend the process to a friend. However, half of the participants qualified this commenting that parties would need to be able to communicate with each other and demonstrate a willingness to resolve issues. One participant would only recommend it to the 'long term separated'.

Overall, nine of those interviewed were happy with the outcome achieved during the process. For many, this equated to what Wright refers to as the 'relationship objective',[38] commenting that they have a good relationship with their ex-spouse now and can call each other, when necessary, to discuss issues regarding their children or arrangements that need to be made for access, etc.

7. RESEARCH INTERNATIONALLY

Research into the collaborative process has been carried out in Canada, the US and in England and Wales. Examining the results globally, settlement rates within the process have been consistently high.[39] Parties choose the process mainly to avoid the acrimony involved in the court process and because they perceive it as a means of achieving better outcomes for their children.

Significantly, while Macfarlane, at the conclusion of her research, remained sceptical as to the need for the disqualification provision, she acknowledged that:

'data gathered by this study, where every case had a DA [disqualification agreement] suggest the collaborative process fosters a spirit of openness, cooperation and commitment to finding a solution that is qualitatively different, at least in many

---

[38]   K. WRIGHT, "The Role of Solicitors in divorce: A note of caution", *Child and Family Law Quarterly* 2007 19(4), pp. 481–495 (489).

[39]   In the US 90 per cent of cases settled in the collaborative process and 10 per cent terminated prior to settlement of all issues. No clients reconciled with their spouse during the collaborative process in the US. In the UK 83 per cent of cases settled, with 2 per cent reconciling. In Ireland the picture was much the same with 86 per cent of cases having settled by agreement and the parties having reconciled in 2 per cent of the cases.

cases, from the atmosphere created by conventional lawyer-to-lawyer negotiations – even those undertaken with a cooperative spirit.'[40]

Importantly, she concluded that there was no evidence that weaker parties do less well.[41]

8. MEDIATION *VERSUS* COLLABORATIVE PRACTICE

Macfarlane noted that participants in her research expressed a preference for collaborative practice over mediation. She questioned whether it was because collaborative lawyers may be dismissing mediation and promoting collaborative practice as an option. However, if one examines this across all studies, participants consistently chose collaborative practice over mediation because they felt that they needed the support of their lawyers through the process. In an extensive study to assess national awareness of alternative dispute resolution processes in England, mediation was the most commonly recognised method outside of the courts' system. However, '[w]hile solicitor negotiation and collaborative law were less well recognised as processes … than mediation, they both achieved higher satisfaction rates than mediation' both in terms of the process and the outcome.[42]

Participants in the US research commented that they '[n]eeded legal representation'[43] and:

'The benefit [of collaborative practice] is that it is less costly, faster, and definitely more fair in that you have the professional support (financially, legally and mental health-wise) not provided in mediation. I felt my needs and concerns were heard and fought for, and that I came out of the process feeling more whole and positive than a typical adversarial divorce would have been.'[44]

---

[40]   J. MACFARLANE, "The Emerging Phenomenon of Collaborative Family Law (CFL): A Qualitative Case Study", Department of Justice Canada 2005, p. 78, available at www.justice. gc.ca (last accessed 06.11.2013).

[41]   Ibid p. 57.

[42]   A. BARLOW et al, "Mapping Paths to Family Justice: a national picture of findings on out of court family dispute resolution", *Family Law* March 2013, pp. 306–309 (308). This result is being tested in ongoing research being carried out in the UK, the results of which will not be known for some time.

[43]   L. WRAY, "The International Academy of Collaborative Professionals Research Regarding Client Experience", presented by L. Wray at the IACP 11th Annual Forum, Washington October 2010, p. 8.

[44]   Ibid p. 16.

And in England and Wales, comments made by participants included:

> 'I didn't fancy it [mediation] at all because I felt as though I needed someone on my side. If it had just been one person who was like mediating between us, I knew that ... I wouldn't stand a chance.'[45]

In the research undertaken in Ireland, six of the collaborative clients interviewed had actually attended some form of mediation before engaging in the collaborative process. However, there still appears to be a misconception that mediation is akin to counselling or is a means of trying to assist the parties to reconcile. One participant commented that for mediation, there has to be 'some glimmer of hope of reviving the marriage' and another, that 'going to the mediation makes you feel like you did everything you can to stay, to make it work out, this is the only reason I would say it is good'.

Collaborative practice was chosen over mediation by one Irish participant because as she put it, 'at the end of the day I would still have to do it legally anyway' (referring to the fact that, as mentioned earlier, a family law mediated agreement is not legally binding in Ireland) and another participant commented:

> 'I didn't find the mediation process helpful at all. I would be reluctant to go down the mediation route a second time. I think a lot depends on the skill of the mediator ... They need to have a protective role, maintain neutrality and yet be fair. Having the support of my solicitor in the collaborative process made a great difference.'[46]

9.   CRITICS OF THE PROCESS IN IRELAND

The collaborative process has received some criticism in Ireland. Critics raise concerns regarding the 'efficiency' of collaborative practice. Davy, for example, commented that:

> '[c]ollaborative practice cases are likely to be far more expensive and far more time consuming (*and also less profitable for solicitors*) than those cases which can be settled amicably and at an early stage in the context of the traditional approach.'[47]

From a solicitor's point of view, taking a traditional approach to negotiations, the facts can be summarised quite quickly and a settlement reached once a case is listed for hearing. This, does not generally involve a large time commitment

---

45   M. SEFTON, "Collaborative Family Law, A Report for Resolution", February 2009, p. 30. Available on request from Resolution, UK.
46   Interview with CC 5, May 2011.
47   E. DAVY, "Problems Associated with Collaborative Practice", *Judicial Studies Institute Journal* 1 2009, pp. 14–18 (16) (emphasis added).

from solicitors or structured, client-centred negotiations such as are necessary within the collaborative process.

Solicitors and barristers who practice within the courts' process refer to the fact that it is the break-up of the relationship and not the method used to resolve it that causes the conflict.[48] Similarly, they argue that if separating parties have a sufficiently good relationship where they can sit down and work things out, then mediation would be a more suitable option than collaborative practice. This, they assert would also be less expensive for clients.[49] In an effort to test the veracity of these assertions, that in essence these were the type of clients that would have settled their cases anyway, a review was carried out of the participants who took part in this research. The focus was to determine the level of acrimony present at the time they entered the process and the effectiveness of collaborative practice as a method of dispute resolution.

It was noted that two of the participants were communicating relatively well with their ex-spouse at the time that they entered into the process.[50] However, for the other eight participants the situation was not as straightforward. For two participants a significant amount of time had elapsed since the initial break-up.[51] This had both advantages and disadvantages. For one participant, things that used to annoy them immediately after the break-up seemed less significant. However, against this, another participant, who had not been on speaking terms with her ex-husband since they separated, commented on how difficult it was to go into a situation where they are back sitting in a room together many years later. For the majority of the participants there was in fact quite a level of conflict and apprehension before engaging in the process. Participants commented:

- 'It [the relationship] was just good enough to get through it. Before the collaborative process we were at each other's throats.'[52]
- 'I was driving it and at that point in time X didn't want it at all, so he was very angry and very negative, so the first meeting was quite nerve wrecking.'[53]
- '[H]e was very antagonistic about the whole thing but I think he was much more favourable to that than going to a court, the pressure of lawyers, solicitors and stuff is very cold faced.'[54]

---

[48]   "Marital breakdown is acrimonious – it's an acrimonious place to be and I think the acrimony comes from that into the legal process rather than the legal process creating it", Interview with LI 1, January 2012.

[49]   Three barristers expressed this view.

[50]   Both of these parties had, in fact, tried mediation some time earlier. One party had managed to agree access arrangements within the mediation process but the remaining issues were not resolved. The other party did not find the mediation process helpful.

[51]   Four years in one case and eight in another.

[52]   Interview CC 5, May 2011.

[53]   Interview CC 1, April 2011.

[54]   Interview CC 2, May 2011.

Another indicated that they were 'absolutely terrified'[55] and that the first meeting did not go particularly well. They advised that their ex-spouse is quick to lose their temper but that by negotiating through the collaborative process that 'each meeting was slightly better' and that 'the meetings were helping them to communicate'.[56] One commented that they would say that their solicitors saw it as 'one of the most difficult collaborations' that they had undertaken.[57]

Therefore, it would not appear to be an accurate assessment to assert that these cases could be 'settled anyway'. From the clients interviewed as part of this research, it is evident that the separating parties had a number of issues to work through as part of the process.

10. IS COOPERATIVE LAW AN ALTERNATIVE?

Lawyers in the US, struggling with the restrictions imposed by the disqualification clause developed a new process which is referred to as cooperative law. Cooperative law purports to follow many of the principles of collaborative practice, without the disqualification requirement. Lawyers and their clients make a commitment to settlement. Cooperative lawyers described their approach as a 'reflection of dissatisfaction with certain aspects of both litigation-oriented and Collaborative Practice.'[58] However, it appears that the same efforts have not been made by the cooperative law movement to develop procedural frameworks or to ensure consistency of practice.[59] Research carried out into cooperative law in Wisconsin[60] shows that while there is a similarly high settlement rate to collaborative practice, the lawyers are less focused on structure and have a tendency to revert to what may be described as 'polite ordinary lawyer negotiation'.

While any process that results in positive outcomes for clients should be considered, it is submitted that there are dangers in either clients misunderstanding which process they are in, or more worryingly, clients requesting the collaborative process and their solicitors continuing to run the case in a manner which is at best 'cooperative', but more likely 'ordinary lawyer negotiation'.

---

55   Interview CC 8, June 2011.
56   Interview CC 8, June 2011.
57   Interview CC 7, June 2011.
58   J. LANDE, "Practical Insights from an Empirical Study of Cooperative Lawyers in Wisconsin", *Journal of Dispute Resolution* 2008, pp. 203–266 (206).
59   The International Academy of Collaborative Professionals has been active in developing ethical guidelines and standards for collaborative lawyers.
60   See J. LANDE, *supra* n. 58 p. 203.

11. CONCLUSION

The results of my research indicate that for these participants engaging in the collaborative process was a less acrimonious way to resolve the issues between them and resulted in them having better relationships afterwards. There was no evidence that the participants did not understand the process and the level of satisfaction overall was high. Two concerns were raised. Firstly, the need for the process to progress at a sufficient pace and secondly, the need for parties to be clearly advised in relation to their legal rights. Significantly, these results are in accordance with the results of similar research carried out internationally.

Therefore, though originating in the US, collaborative practice appears to bridge cultural boundaries in providing an additional, non-court based method of dispute resolution leading to, as evidenced by international research, better results for those who choose to avail themselves of the process.

PART THREE
NEW CONCEPTS OF PARENTAGE

THE RIGHT OF THE CHILD
TO PARENTS

Anna SINGER

Contents

1.   INTRODUCTION

What is a parent? And who is it? For ages, the law concerning the establishment of legal parenthood has been built on the postulate that a child's genetic parents *are* the parents of that child and, thus, the law should only confirm this. This notion that legislation is and ought to be a mere reflection of a biological fact has long characterised the legal discourse on parenthood. At the same time, however, it is obvious that parenthood, from a legal point of view, is not an unambiguous concept. Behind a uniform façade is a more complicated structure. Different ideologies and adjustments to reality have resulted in regulation that does not have one but rather several possible answers to the question of 'who is the parent?'

In recent decades, the view of what and who a parent is has rapidly changed. Several factors have led to this development. The family as a societal phenomenon has transformed over the years. The nuclear family, based on the married heterosexual couple, is no longer the only socially or legally accepted model. There has been a dramatic increase in the number of reconstituted families, single-parent families, and rainbow families. Children can have many 'parents' during a lifetime, in particular during childhood. The picture of parenthood becomes even more complex through the use of different methods for assisted reproduction that are easily accessible on a global market, helping many people become genetic and biological parents when this was previously impossible. At the same time as the concept of parent has been widened to also include non-genetic parents, legal ties between family members can now be questioned and revoked on scientific grounds, as DNA analysis is used more frequently in order to clarify genetic kinship.

In the midst of these developments stands the child, whose best interests should be the primary consideration when legal matters affecting the child are at stake. A need to re-evaluate the fundamentals of the regulation concerning legal parenthood emerges if it is the child's interests that are to be protected. Nature can no longer be used as the sole normative source for rules concerning the establishment of legal parenthood in the post-modern society. Genetics is obviously not sufficient as a basis for the legal status as parents, clearly demonstrated by the use of different methods for assisted reproduction. But neither is the interest of an individual to become a parent, notwithstanding his or her perceived right or freedom to become a parent, which has come into focus in recent general discussions, legislation and practice.

If a child is considered to be an individual with rights, rather than merely the object of discussions on the rights of parents, a more profound question might be whether the right of the child to parents should be the starting point for legal parentage. But do children have a *right* to parents? This is a question which is seldom asked and consequently not addressed. Traditionally, parenthood has not been perceived first and foremost as a question of rights, but instead as a fact of nature. And yet, parenthood can no longer be seen, or even portrayed, exclusively as such. Parenthood in our time is increasingly seen as a role that can be created, varied, negotiated, and defined in each specific case. And so it should be in order for the best interest of the child to be served. In other words, establishing legal parenthood should be seen as a way of protecting the interests of a child – a right of the child.

2. A 'RIGHT' TO PARENTS?

During the past several decades, protecting a child's interests has been the lodestar for law-making and law enforcement in almost all matters concerning children. One way of doing this is through the concept of rights. This is amply illustrated by a number of international instruments on human rights.

Early in the development of the notion of human rights, it was recognised that children have special needs and interests that require special protection through the recognition of rights.[1] The protection of children's specific

---

[1] See G. VAN BUEREN, *The International Law on the Rights of the Child*, Kluwer Academic Publishers 1995.

interests through human rights has been acknowledged in the UN Convention on the Rights of the Child (CRC).

Society's ability to provide the care that, at least, young children require is very limited. If a child's needs and interests are to be protected, it is imperative that someone is given the responsibility to protect these interests. This someone is a parent. It is, therefore, possible to characterise a child's right to legal parents as a human right. But how is this recognised in human rights instruments?

In the central instrument concerning children's rights, the CRC, the child's right to parents is expressly mentioned in Article 7. It states, *inter alia*, that 'the child shall have ..., as far as possible, the right to know and be cared for by his or her parents'.

The right to know one's parents is interpreted as a right to have knowledge of who the natural, i.e. genetic, parents are. This view of parenthood and kinship is further underscored by Article 8 of the CRC, which states that the child has a right to preserve his or her identity, including family relations as recognised by law. Identity is more than knowing one's genetic parents; identity also presupposes knowledge of others in the biological family. Genetics is seemingly considered fundamental for the concept of parents and family.

Article 7 of the CRC also gives the child a right to be taken care of by the natural parents, as far as this is possible. This declaration probably reflects the parental situation for a majority of children in the world. However, if the natural (genetic) parents cannot be found or do not wish or intend to fulfil the function of a parent, someone else will have to step in, *in loco parentis*. But are they parents?

Article 8 of the European Convention on Human Rights (ECHR), through the case law of the European Court of Human Rights (ECtHR), recognises that the concept of a parent must also include those who function as parents to a child, even if there is no genetic link.[2] This interpretation of the meaning of 'parent' makes sense if a parent's primary responsibility is to protect the interests of the child. However, the case law on parentage from the ECtHR almost exclusively deals with the question of the right to become a legally recognised parent, not the child's right to have parents. The child's perspective – indeed, the child's right to parents – is only present as the other, silent side of the parental claim. The parent has a right, but does the child?

If we are to take rights seriously, the child must also be considered to have the same rights as parents. In this context, rights are used to describe a mechanism to protect certain interests of an individual through duties for others to protect those interests. Central to the concept of rights is the idea that a claim from the holder of a right should activate a duty of another. If we say that children have a

---

2   See e.g. ECtHR rulings in *Yousef v. The Netherlands* (judgment 05.11.2002); *Kroon and others v. the Netherlands* (judgment 27.10.1994), *Nylund v. Finland* (decision 29.06.1999), *Różański v. Polen* (judgment 18.08.2006).

right to parents, then there should be a corresponding duty to make sure that a child is given parents. The fulfilment of such a duty should not be dependent on whether it is possible to identify the genetic parent nor on the mere desire of someone to become the legal parent. If so, we are not talking about a real right. A claim that others can define and satisfy cannot be called a right; it could at best be called welfarism.[3]

3. ESTABLISHMENT OF PARENTHOOD

In order to clarify and analyse the rights of the child to parents, it is necessary to turn to national regulation. Children are assigned legal parents according to the laws of the jurisdiction in which they are born or reside, through rules for the establishment of paternity and maternity, adoption or acknowledgement, or other mechanisms following assisted reproductive treatment. It is through the application of these rules that the child's right to parents is realised, if at all.

Since a right can be seen as protecting interests that the individual has, a key issue in this context is how we define the child's interests that are to be protected by a right to legal parents. Is the determination of legal parenthood at all considered a question that concerns the child's interest and, if so, to what extent?

The interest of the child to have legal parentage established has seldom been explicitly stated in the legislative process. However, it is possible to identify various interests depending on the rule in focus and individual circumstances. Depending on how the child's interests have been defined, the purpose of establishing legal parenthood varies.

Legal parentage encompasses several potential interests, each serving different purposes. One purpose is to give the child legal affiliation, to satisfy the child's interest to be someone's child in a legal sense. Another purpose is to make it possible to give someone the legal responsibility to satisfy the child's different needs, such as physical and psychological care and support, which is normally included in parental responsibility. The duty to provide economically for a child has also been a strong motive to have paternity established. Further still, establishing parenthood may give the child knowledge of his or her genetic origin. This is an interest that has been identified only in recent decades, as a consequence of the possibility to actually identify genetic kinship. Last but not least, the law may recognise the emotional bond between parents and child, to ensure that the persons whom the child considers parents have that legal status.

The question is how well these interests are met by the establishment of legal parenthood. If the child's natural (genetic) parents are given legal status as parents, it is generally thought that all of the child's interests are met. Hence the

---

3   J. EEKELAAR, The Importance of Thinking that Children Have Rights, *International Journal of Law and the Family*, (1992) 6, pp. 221–234.

establishment of legal parenthood is still often seen as a question of identifying the child's genetic parents. The rights and responsibilities that the law confers on parents follow automatically, as a fact of nature, rather than a legal concept that can be modelled as we want it. This view on parenthood is also reflected in the CRC.

However, with the use of different techniques for assisted reproduction with donated gametes, genetics as a basis for legal parenthood may not give the desired results for the parents-to-be concerned. The intention of becoming a parent has, therefore, gained in importance. But nature still plays a role, not only for the establishment of legal parenthood, but also as the model for parenthood established on other grounds.

By holding on to natural parenthood as a model, there is a risk that the interests of the child to be protected by parents are not served in an optimal way.[4] For example, children with parents of the same sex cannot always have their family legally recognised because the concept of natural parents presupposes a mother and a father. And the fact that children in reality can have more than two parents cannot be recognised either, since natural parents are two persons. What interests are protected by adhering to nature as a normative source?

In the following sections different ways of establishing legal parenthood are examined. What interests of the child are protected by the legislative solutions and how well do they work? Is it possible to say that a child has a right to legal parents, regardless of nature?

4. A RIGHT TO A MOTHER

'*Mater semper certa est*': 'we know who the mother is'. Maternity is still in most European legal systems established by birth alone, and no further action is necessary in order to establish legal parentage. Such a rule protects the child's right to at least one parent – a mother. With the development of health services in society, the number of mothers giving birth unaided by medical staff has decreased during the last century. When children are born in hospitals, there are witnesses as to who the mother is. However, French and French-inspired legislation sometimes require a confirmation of maternity and also gives a mother the choice to give birth anonymously.[5] In these cases the child's right to know and to be cared for by his or her parents is obviously violated. It is,

---

4   See, e.g. I. SCHWENZER (ed.), *Tensions Between Legal, Biological and Social Conceptions of Parentage*, Intersentia 2007. See also M. VONK, *Children and their parents. A comparative study of the legal position of children with regard to their intentional and biological parents in English and Dutch law*, Intersentia 2007.

5   I. SCHWENZER (ed.), *Tensions Between Legal, Biological and Social Conceptions of Parentage*, Intersentia 2007, p. 3. See also F. FERRAND, Streit um die Abstammung in Frankreich, in

therefore, surprising to notice that there has recently been an increase in the possibilities to give birth anonymously, e.g. through the use of 'baby-boxes' or 'baby hatches' as they are sometimes called.[6] The child's right to a legal mother is in this way undermined for reasons that are not always well founded.

But anonymous births are not the only occurrence that can limit the child's right to a legal mother. The *mater semper* rule is based on the assumption that the birth mother is the genetic mother of the child. When egg donation became possible, many jurisdictions introduced a statutory rule explicitly stating that the birth mother is the legal mother, regardless of genetics. A new maxim was invented, *mater est quam gestatio demonstrat*.[7]

Surrogacy arrangements have, in turn, challenged this rule. There is by now an abundance of stories about children born in jurisdictions lacking rules for the establishment of legal parenthood where maternity is not always determined by birth, but also when contracts transferring legal parenthood are not considered valid in the countries where the intended parents live. In many cases, the result has been that children are left in a legal vacuum until legal parenthood can be decided through adoption, if at all.[8]

There is an urgent need for clear rules for the establishment of legal parenthood following surrogacy arrangements in order to protect the child's right to a legal mother, i.e. a parent at birth.[9] Currently, establishing legal motherhood in these cases all too often becomes an unproductive battle between intended mothers and legal authorities. When a woman gives birth following implantation of an egg from another woman, legal motherhood cannot be established on grounds of nature since surrogacy may separate two traits – genetics and gestation – associated with natural motherhood. Nature as a source of law thus provides no clear answers that acknowledge the child's *de facto* situation in order to protect the child's right. It is something of a paradox that maternity, which was once one of the most given truths, is now unclear, while paternity, for a long time beyond full knowledge, is now easier to establish following surrogacy arrangements.

SPICKHOFF/SCHWAB/HENRICH/GOTTWALD (eds.) *Streit um die Abstammung – ein europäischer Vergleich*, Gieseking 2007, p. 112.

6   See C. FENTON-GLYNN, 'Anonymous Relinquishment and Baby-Boxes: Life-Saving Mechanisms or a Violation of Human Rights', *infra* pp. 185–197 in this book.

7   C. L. BALDASSI, 'Mater Est Quam Gestatio Demonstrat: A Cautionary Tale'. Cit. from J. STOLL, *Surrogacy Arrangements and Legal Parenthood. Swedish Law in a Comparative Context*, (diss.) Uppsala University 2013, p. 118.

8   For a comprehensive description of the legal situation in an international perspective for children following surrogacy arrangements see K. TRIMMINGS and P. BEAUMONT, *International Surrogacy Arrangements. Legal Regulation*, Hart Publishing 2013.

9   J. STOLL, *Surrogacy Arrangements and Legal Parenthood. Swedish Law in a Comparative Context*, (diss.) Uppsala University 2013.

5.   A RIGHT TO A FATHER

While biology and genetics have been the source of law concerning maternity, legal paternity has, by necessity, been a more flexible concept. Intent – or, rather, presumed intent based on marriage – has for a long time been enough as a basis for a legal status as a parent. Marriage is still used as proof of paternity, but now with the underlying assumption that it is also an acceptable proof of genetic kinship, reflecting a traditional view, perhaps, that the husband of the mother ought to be the genetic father of her children. This presumption, the *pater est* rule, has had several advantages. A child born to a married woman has, from birth, a second legal parent, a social family, and, in most cases, knowledge of his or her genetic origin.

The unmarried father's paternity has been considered more difficult to establish. In the absence of marriage as an indication of intent or genetic kinship, proof of intercourse and, later, DNA analysis has often been necessary.

In most European jurisdictions, paternity for a child born to an unmarried mother can be established by voluntary acknowledgement or adjudication.[10] Acknowledgement makes the child's right to a legal father effectively dependent on the will of a putative father. Furthermore, an acknowledgement of paternity in many countries requires the consent of the child or the child's mother, which also could impede the child's right to a second parent. Where there is no man willing to acknowledge paternity, or where the mother refuses to consent to his acknowledgement, paternity can be established in court, provided someone initiates proceedings.

In the Nordic countries, a legal presumption of paternity for the unmarried man living with the mother has been discussed, but not accepted. Such a rule would guarantee the child's right to a legal father. However, few legal systems presume that the unmarried man living with the mother is the father of the child.[11]

With the development of DNA analysis of genetic kinship, marriage and intent have lost importance relative to genetics as a basis for paternity. This is clearly illustrated by regulations concerning paternity challenges. It is now possible in most countries for the legal father to have his paternity revoked with reference to a lack of a genetic relationship. The child's right to a legal father, whether by marriage or acknowledgement, has in some countries been protected by limiting the possibilities to challenge legal paternity, through time limits and the number of persons entitled to instigate a case. In some jurisdictions,

---

[10]   I. SCHWENZER (ed.), *Tensions Between Legal, Biological and Social Conceptions of Parentage*, Intersentia 2007, p. 7.

[11]   Iceland is a notable exception. According to the Icelandic Children's Act a man who is registered in the population register as the cohabitee of the woman giving birth is automatically considered to be the child's father.

paternity can be challenged by anyone with sufficient interest.[12] Often, however, it is just the legal father and the child – and sometimes also the child's mother – who can challenge paternity based on marriage.[13]

The child's right to a legal father has increasingly been seen as a right to the 'correct' father, the genetic one, and not as a right to a social father. Having no legal father is thus often seen as better than having the 'wrong' one. There is, however, one exception to this point of view. With the advancement of methods for assisted procreation with donor sperm, the grounds for paternity have required much reconsideration. The intention of becoming the child's father after donor insemination is enough in many instances. For heterosexual couples, a man consenting to the insemination of a woman steps into the place of the genetic father.

If a man can prove genetic kinship to a child, his paternity is usually beyond question. The result is that paternity, in contrast to maternity, following surrogacy arrangements can be established in many European legal systems according to the general rules for the establishment of paternity. There is now a noticeable difference regarding the foundation of legal parenthood, depending on which one of the child's parents is questioned. Genetics is all for fathers, nothing for mothers. The child can thus be said to have a 'limping' right to parents.

6.   A RIGHT TO PARENTS UNRESTRICTED BY GENDER

Genetics as the foundation for legal parentage and, consequently, the presumption of two parents of different sexes, has been successfully challenged during recent years by same-sex couples seeking legal recognition of their parenthood. Expressed in a different way, one could also say that children with parents of the same sex have seen a rapid improvement in their possibilities to receive legal recognition of their *de facto* parents.[14]

In some jurisdictions, it is possible for lesbian couples to access assisted reproduction.[15] However, there are not in all cases mechanisms in place to

---

[12]   I.a. England and Wales, N. LOWE, Issues of Decent – The Position in English Law, in SPICKHOFF/SCHWAB/HENRICH/GOTTWALD (eds.), *Streit um die Abstammung – ein europäischer Vergleich*, Gieseking 2007, p. 330; Switzerland, A. BÜCHLER, Parentage in Swiss Law, in I. SCHWENZER (ed.), *Tensions Between Legal, Biological and Social Conceptions of Parentage*, Intersentia 2007, pp. 348–349.

[13]   Switzerland and Sweden are notable exceptions to this rule.

[14]   See K. BOELE-WOELKI and A. FUCHS, *Legal Recognition of Same-Sex Relationships in Europe. National, Cross-Border and European Perspectives*, Intersentia 2012.

[15]   See i.a. Belgium, Denmark, Finland, Iceland, the Netherlands, Norway, Spain, Sweden and the U.K., *Discrimination on grounds of sexual orientation and gender identity in Europe*,

guarantee that the child will be given two legal parents. Second-parent adoption is in most cases the way to achieve this, but is typically dependent on the agreement of all parties involved.[16] The child's right to two parents is, therefore, vulnerable. Swedish legislation makes it possible to declare a woman consenting to the insemination of her spouse or cohabitee to be the child's parent along with the birth mother.[17] However, this rule is only applicable when the child is conceived through treatment given at a Swedish hospital. For children conceived through treatment abroad or privately, paternity should be established, if possible, before adoption can take place. In Denmark new legislation in the Children's Act was introduced in December 2013 enabling the female spouse or partner of the birth mother to become the legal parent (co-mother) of the child under the same conditions as a male spouse or partner.[18]

It is not uncommon for children to be born to a surrogate mother and grow up with two male parents. If one of the men is the child's genetic father, he can become the legal father through acknowledgement or a court decision where this option exists. But the child's right to the second parent can only be met through adoption, a procedure dependent on a variety of factors for its success.

Thus, even if it is possible in many jurisdictions to give a child two legal parents of the same sex, the mechanisms to guarantee this are not well developed. It is remarkable that even if a method for assisted reproduction is made available, the right of the child to legal parents is not fully protected. It is still to a large extent the joint will of the parents-to-be, if they are not married, that determines whether the child will have two legal parents.

7. ADOPTION

Adoption is another way of protecting a child's right to parents. Historically a way to give a childless person an heir, adoption was described during the last century more as a child protection measure. It is a way to give children parents when the natural parents cannot be found or when it has been deemed better for the child to be transferred to other parents. In that sense, one could see it as a

---

Council of Europe 2011, p. 99, available at www.coe.int/t/Commissioner/Source/LGBT/report/Part6.pdf (last accessed 03.12.2013).

[16] In the Netherlands there seems to be a possibility for the female spouse of the birth mother to acquire legal status *ex lege* if sperm from an unknown donor has been used. If sperm from a known donor is used the partner of the birthmother can register her parenthood with the consent of the birthmother. See I. CURRY-SUMNER and M. VONK, 'Something old, something new, something international and something askew', in B. ATKIN (ed.), *The International Survey of Family Law 2012 Edition*, Family Law Jordan Publishing Ltd 2012, pp. 239–240.

[17] The Swedish Parent and Children Code, ch. 1 s. 9.

[18] Lov nr. 652 of 12/06/2013.

way of giving children parents.[19] In reality, however, adoption is often used to give childless parents a child.

The institution of adoption is modelled on the biological or genetic nuclear family, something that can be seen in the requirements placed on adoptive parents. In many legal systems, it is possible for single persons to adopt but the majority of adoptions are joint adoptions by a married, heterosexual couple. Most European legal systems allow second-parent adoption if the adopting parent is married to the parent of the child. In some jurisdictions it is also possible for cohabiting couples to adopt one another's child.[20]

Second-parent adoption is, in most legal systems, the only way for children born to same-sex couples through assisted reproductive methods to receive two legal parents. This is possible in many European countries.[21] In some countries it is also possible for same-sex couples to adopt a child jointly.[22] It can be noted, however, that in quite a few European countries it is still not possible for same-sex couples to adopt, either jointly or through second-parent adoption.[23]

Not to allow second-parent adoption in cases where the child has been brought up with two parents of the same sex – with no other basis for legal recognition of the second parent – can be considered an infringement of the child's right to parents or respect for family life. But it is not only children growing up with parents of the same sex who cannot have their right to parents met. Any child growing up with a 'parent' who is not a legal parent does not have a right to be adopted. The right to become parents through adoption is always dependent on the adoptive parent first fulfilling certain legal requirements, then the consent to the adoption of the child's legal parents, and, finally, a court finding that the adoption is in the best interests of the child. In short, it is possible to conclude that a child does not have a right to have his or her *de facto* parent legally recognised – a right to be adopted.

One reason to restrict the use of adoption is that adoption in most legal systems severs all legal ties between the natural parent and the child. Consent from the child's legal parents is, therefore, a requirement as a general rule. However, the consent of a parent with no parental responsibility can often be

---

[19] See e.g. ECtHR judgment *Pini and others v Romania* (judgment 22.06.2004).

[20] Iceland (five-year cohabitation), the Netherlands (three-year cohabitation, if the couple can marry), Belgium (three-year cohabitation, same or different sex), the UK (same or different sex). Swedish government committee report Modernare adoptionsregler (*More modern adoption regulation*) SOU 2009:61, pp. 112.

[21] Belgium, Denmark, Finland, Germany, Iceland, the Netherlands, Norway, Spain, Sweden and the UK. Not possible in France and Austria but possible to give joint parental responsibility to registered partners. *Discrimination on grounds of sexual orientation and gender identity in Europe*, Council of Europe 2011, p. 97–98, available at www.coe.int/t/Commissioner/Source/ LGBT/report/Part6.pdf (last accessed 03.12.2013).

[22] The same as the above except Germany and Finland.

[23] *Discrimination on grounds of sexual orientation and gender identity in Europe*, Council of Europe 2011, p. 97–98, available at www.coe.int/t/Commissioner/Source/LGBT/report/Part6. pdf (last accessed 03.12.2013).

dispensed with if an adoption is considered to be in the best interests of the child.[24] In some jurisdictions, it is also possible in exceptional cases to allow adoption against the will of a parent with parental responsibility.[25]

One way of facilitating adoption and, thereby, possibly protecting the child's right to parents to a greater extent could be to promote simple as opposed to full adoptions. In some jurisdictions, the child can retain some legal ties with the natural parents or relatives. This can include the right of contact or inheritance rights.[26] Such a solution could make it possible to give the child a right to all of his or her parents. It is also possible to give parental responsibility to an additional parent. This is an option used in some legal systems,[27] and it might lessen the need for adoption.

Even if adoption is an efficient way of transferring legal parenthood for a child in order for the legal situation to correspond to the child's *de facto* family life, from the child's perspective it in no way guarantees the child's right to parents. Not only is there a hesitation towards granting adoption as such, but the adoption procedure is also contingent on the consent of all the parties involved. This makes adoption an uncertain means of protecting the child's right to parents.

8. ENFORCING THE RIGHT TO PARENTS

If we are to take children's right to parents seriously, there is not only a need for a review of the foundations of legal parenthood, but also a need for a mechanism to ensure that legal parenthood for a child is established. Currently, the establishment of legal parenthood, to a large extent, lies in the hands of the ones wanting or not wanting to become parents. The situation following surrogacy

---

[24]   In the ECtHR ruling in *Söderbäck v Sweden* (judgment 28.10.1998) the court found that the child's right to have her de facto family ties legally recognised could outweigh the interests of the legal father with no parental responsibility to remain a legal parent. See also I. SCHWENZER (ed.), *Tensions Between Legal, Biological and Social Conceptions of Parentage*, Intersentia 2007, p. 23.

[25]   See I. SCHWENZER (ed.), *Tensions Between Legal, Biological and Social Conceptions of Parentage*, Intersentia 2007, e.g. the Netherlands, p. 301; Germany, p. 206; Belgium, p. 86. Denmark, I. LUND-ANDERSEN and I. NØRGAARD, *Familieret*, 2nd ed. Jurist- og økonomforbundets forlag 2012, p. 38; Norway, P. LØDRUPand L. SMITH, *Barn og foreldre*, 7th ed. 2006, pp. 234–237.

[26]   See I. SCHWENZER (ed.), *Tensions Between Legal, Biological and Social Conceptions of Parentage*, Intersentia 2007, e.g. England and Wales, p. 166; Germany, pp. 208–209. In Sweden contact can be determined according to the Parent and Children Code ch. 6 s. 15a in favour of the natural parents; however, this is seldom done.

[27]   See e.g. France, Centre de droit de la famille (Université Jean Moulin), A Chronicle of Family Law in 2011, in B. ATKIN (ed.) *The International Survey of Family Law 2012 Edition*, pp. 101–102. In England and Wales and the Netherlands it is also possible to give a step-parent parental responsibility, M. VONK, *Children and their parents. A comparative study of the legal position of children with regard to their intentional and biological parents in English and Dutch law*, pp. 118–124.

arrangements is especially in need of urgent regulation.[28] A child has a right to legal parents, regardless of how the child was conceived and regardless of the actions of the parties involved.

In this context it can be noted that we talk about the right of children to parents in the plural. The underlying assumption has been that a child has two parents and thus should have two legal parents. This might be a position which is about to be abandoned. Assisted reproductive treatment is, seemingly without discussion, also available to single women in many jurisdictions. This step is usually motivated by a desire not to discriminate against women depending on whether or not they have found someone to share parenthood with. If the interests of the child are considered to be sufficiently protected by one parent, there are reasons to review the regulation concerning legal parenthood for all children.

9. BEHIND THE UNEQUIVOCAL PARENTAL FAÇADE

Children have interests that can be protected if they are given parents. These include the interest of being someone's child – affiliation, the interest of receiving good care, and the interest to have knowledge of their genetic origin. The protection of these interests is so important that children should have a right to a parent. But which parent? Is it the one intending to be the parent, the one who wants to be a parent? Or is it the genetic parent, intended or otherwise?

From the child's perspective, intent as the foundation for the legal consequences tied to parenthood might in many cases be considered a better option than genetics. Intent is not a new criterion for legal parenthood. Historically, intent has been present in most legal systems but is often perceived, or described, as a sign of a genetic link and vice versa. Legal parenthood as intrinsically connected to genetic kinship has, however, been decisive for the construction of our legal regulation of parenthood, while genetics has gained importance with the increasing possibilities to actually establish genetic links.

Today it is obvious that it is no longer sufficient to define a parent by genetics. Intent must be included. But we should not exchange genetics for intent. Parenthood is not only a question of intent. If we take children's right to parents seriously, a more holistic look at the legal concept of parenthood is necessary. The protection of the child's interests calls for a more multifaceted view of parenthood, perhaps also including emotional bonds between a child and the one the child sees as a parent.

---

[28] Examples of such a mechanism are found e.g. in Israel, Greece and the UK, K. TRIMMINGS and P. BEAUMONT, *International Surrogacy Arrangements. Legal Regulation*, chapter 28, pp. 439–454.

Legal affiliation should be established, and intent would probably be a suitable basis for it, in most cases, still coinciding with genetic kinship. This is a parenthood that lasts during a lifetime and it cannot be substituted with parental responsibility.

But the child's right to good care can mean that different persons are given parental responsibilities during the child's upbringing. Legal solutions are already in existence in many jurisdictions and there are suggestions as to how this could be done.[29]

The third interest mentioned here is the child's right to knowledge of his or her origin. This is an interest that can be satisfied without affecting parental status and legal affiliation. Several legal systems recognise this but by no means all. The protection of the intended parents may be used to justify denying the child access to information about origin, even when this is available. This is clearly an infringement of the child's moral right, but is also in contradiction to the CRC.

It is clear that if it is the protection of the child's rights that is the main objective of the regulation of parenthood, there is a need to let go of genetics as a model for legislation, but not substituting genetics solely with intent. Both are important for the child. What is needed is a more flexible view of parenthood and its meaning if we are to give the child a real right to parents.

---

[29] A possible regulation of parental responsibilities for persons other that legal parents can also be found in the Model Family Code. I. SCHWENZER, *Model Family Code – From a Global Perspective*, Intersentia 2006, pp. 143–144. See also K. BOELE-WOELKI ET AL., *Principles of European Family Law Regarding Parental Responsibilities*, Intersentia 2007.

CONTRACTING ON PARENTAGE

Christine Budzikiewicz

Contents

1. INTRODUCTION

Since ancient times, the establishment of legal parentage has followed the child's
genetic and biological origins[1] based on the idea that the natural parents are

---

[1] K.J. Saarloos, *European private international law on legal parentage?*, Maastricht, 2010,
p. 15; M. Quantius, *Die Elternschaftsanfechtung durch das künstlich gezeugte Kind*, FamRZ
(*Zeitschrift für das gesamte Familienrecht*) (1998), p. 1145, 1146; A. Spickhoff, *Der Streit um
die Abstammung*, in A. Spickhoff, D. Schwab, D. Henrich and P. Gottwald (eds), *Streit
um die Abstammung*, Gieseking, Bielefeld, 2007, p. 13, 18; Y. Margalit, O. Levy and J. Loike,
*The New Frontier of Advanced Reproductive Technology: Reevaluating Modern Legal
Parenthood*, 37 Harv. J. L. & Gender (*Harvard Journal of Law & Gender*) (2014), p. 107, 110.

both willing and obliged to take care of the child.[2] However, until recently it was impossible to scientifically prove the genetic relationship between a child and his or her presumptive parents. Therefore, legally assigning a child to parents – especially to a father – could only be executed through fictions or legal presumptions. The Roman law principle of *pater is est quem nuptiae demonstrant*[3] (the father is he whom the marriage points out) is well known. The possibility that legal and genetic paternity might not coincide could obviously not be excluded.

As for the mother, for a long time the maxim *mater semper certa* (the mother is always certain) was considered valid. The woman who had given birth to the child was regarded as the child's mother. She was also without doubt the child's genetic mother.

Now, times have changed. Today it is possible to establish genetic relationships beyond doubt. However, medical progress and social change in recent decades have begun to question the concept of parentage based on genetic descent.[4] Not only has modern reproductive medicine increased the number of children who are not genetically related to one or to both of their legal parents (such as in the case of heterologous insemination or surrogacy), it is also no longer a matter of course that children are raised by their married, genetic parents.[5] Children frequently live in step-families where the new partner of one of the parents shares custody of the child.

Due to the developments outlined above, doctrine has called for social parenthood to be given more weight.[6] In practice, more and more people are attempting to establish parentage through contractual agreements.[7] Such agreements accompany medically-assisted forms of reproduction in particular. However, the legality and desirability of agreements which pertain to key aspects of parentage is even being discussed outside the realm of modern reproductive

---

[2]   Cf. BVerfG (Bundesverfassungsgericht, German Federal Constitutional Court), 29.07.1968, *BVerfGE (Entscheidungen des Bundesverfassungsgerichts)* 24, p. 119, 150.

[3]   PAULUS, Digest 2, 4, 5 ('Quia semper certa est, etiam si volgo conceperit: pater vero is est, quem nuptiae demonstrant').

[4]   Cf. A. SPICKHOFF, in A. SPICKHOFF et al. (eds), *Streit um die Abstammung*, p. 13, 20, 23; Y. MARGALIT, O. LEVY and J. LOIKE, *The New Frontier of Advanced Reproductive Technology: Reevaluating Modern Legal Parenthood*, 37 Harv. J. L. & Gender (2014), p. 107, 111.

[5]   Cf. E. STEINER, *The Tensions Between Legal, Biological and Social Conceptions of Parenthood in English Law*, EJCL *(Electronic Journal of Comparative Law)*, vol. 10.3 (December 2006), available at www.ejcl.org, p. 1 (last accessed 24.02.2014).

[6]   T. CALLUS, *A new parenthood paradigm for twenty-first century family law in England and Wales?*, 32 Legal Studies (2012), p. 347, 359 et seq.; U. WANITZEK, *Rechtliche Elternschaft bei medizinisch unterstützter Fortpflanzung*, Gieseking, Bielefeld, 2002, pp. 142 et seq., pp. 290 et seq.; cf. also European Court of Human Rights (ECtHR), 28.06.2007, Case 76240/01, *Wagner and J.M.W.L. v Luxembourg*.

[7]   Cf. Y. MARGALIT, *Artificial Insemination from Donor (AID) – From Status to Contract and Back Again*, 20 B.U. J. Sci. & Tech. L. *(Boston University Journal of Science and Technology Law)* (2014), No. 2, available at SSRN: http://ssrn.com/abstract=2342785, p. 2 (pdf) (last accessed 24.02.2014).

medicine, not only in areas such as maintenance agreements[8] but also in the field of the derivative acquisition of parental custody.[9]

A development could emerge in the law of filiation which in other areas has been dubbed 'from status to contract'.[10] This article will investigate to what extent the descent of a child could be open to contractual agreements or at least to private autonomy. I will begin with a comparative survey regarding private autonomy in the law of descent and develop guidelines to test the sustainability potential of agreements regarding the filiation of a child.

2. PRIVATE AUTONOMY IN THE LAW OF DESCENT: A COMPARATIVE SURVEY

2.1. THE NATURAL DESCENT OF THE CHILD AS A MODEL OF LEGAL PARENTAGE

So far, contractual agreements have only played a secondary role in creating legal parentage.[11] The law of descent still focuses mainly on genetic relationships. It provides a determined and limited number of elements to be considered for the assignment of parentage. The intention of the involved persons is important only insofar as the constitution of parentage requires the submission of specific declarations (e.g. the recognition of paternity, consent to recognition, etc.). A free disposition on the status by agreement is in any case excluded by European legal systems.

---

[8] Cf. M. JONKER, *Het recht van kinderen op levensonderhoud: een gedeelde zorg*, Boom Juridische uitgevers, 2011, pp. 130 et seq. (Dutch Law), pp. 160 et seq. (Norwegian law), pp. 189 et seq. (Swedish law), pp. 208 et seq., pp. 334 et seq.

[9] For agreements on parental responsibilities see K. BOELE-WOELKI, B. BRAAT and I. CURRY-SUMNER (eds), *European Family Law in Action, Vol. III: Parental Responsibilities*, Intersentia, Antwerp – Oxford, 2005, Question 17 (Agreement on attribution); S. HAMMER, *Elternvereinbarungen im Sorge- und Umgangsrecht*, Gieseking, Bielefeld, 2004.

[10] See H. MAINE, *Ancient Law – Its Connection With the Early History of Society, and Its Relation to Modern Ideas*, John Murray, London, 1981, ch. 5; Y. MARGALIT, *Artificial Insemination from Donor (AID) – From Status to Contract and Back Again*, 20 B.U. J. Sci. & Tech. L. (2014), No. 2; S. HOFER, D. SCHWAB and D. HENRICH (eds), *From Status to Contract? – Die Bedeutung des Vertrages im europäischen Familienrecht*, Gieseking, Bielefeld, 2005; I. SCHWENZER, *The Evolution of Family Law: From Status to Contract and Relation*, 3 EJLR (European Journal of Law Reform) (2001), p. 199; G. KACHROO, *Mapping Alimony: From Status to Contract and Beyond*, 5 Pierce L Rev. (Pierce Law Review) (2007), p. 163.

[11] For a different view in respect of heterologous insemination, see Y. MARGALIT, *Artificial Insemination from Donor (AID) – From Status to Contract and Back Again*, 20 B.U. J. Sci. & Tech. L., (2014), No. 2, available at SSRN: http://ssrn.com/abstract=2342785, pp. 5 et seq., pp. 14 et seq. (pdf) (last accessed 24.02.2014).

In many cases the rule is still valid that the mother of the child is the woman who gave birth to the child.[12] Yet there are exceptions. In French law, for example, maternity is established, as a rule, by the denotation on the child's birth certificate.[13] Without such an entry maternity may be acknowledged[14] or, in certain circumstances, can be based on the actual parent-child relationship (*possession d'état*).[15] Unlike those legal systems whose descent system follows the *mater certa* rule, in French law there is an autonomy-based component to establishing maternity.

As for establishing paternity, it is still common practice to assign the child to the husband of the child's mother.[16] Provided that the requirements for a presumption of paternity indicated by matrimony are met, the assignment of the child to the husband of the mother occurs *qua lege*; the intentions of the parties are of no importance. If the presumed paternity and the genetic paternity do not coincide, only a paternity contest remains as a means of rectification. In the event that the husband of the mother is not assigned as the father of the child, legal paternity can mostly be established by voluntary acknowledgment (provided that the mother and/or the child agree).[17] In this case, genetic descent is generally irrelevant for the acknowledgment of paternity to be valid. Legal parentage is attributed solely on the basis of the will of the parties. Here again paternity may be contested in the event that genetic and legal paternity differ.

The third classic way to establish paternity is by a court order, based on the proof of a genetic relationship.[18] As for the question of in which cases the establishment of paternity can be enforced by the courts, the answers vary. This is especially true for the question of whether, under what conditions the genetic

---

[12] Cf. I. SCHWENZER, *Tensions between Legal, Biological and Social Conceptions of Parentage*, in I. SCHWENZER (ed), *Tensions between Legal, Biological and Social Conceptions of Parentage*, Intersentia, Antwerp – Oxford, 2007, pp. 1, 3, 10; V. TODOROVA, *Recognition of parental responsibility: biological parenthood v. legal parenthood, i.e. mutual recognition of surrogacy agreements: What is the current situation in the MS? Need for EU action?*, note requested by the European Parliament's Committee on Legal Affairs, Brussels, 2010, available at www.europarl.europa.eu/studies, p. 16 (last accessed 24.02.2014).

[13] Article 311–25 French Civil Code (*Code Civil*).

[14] Article 316 French Civil Code.

[15] Articles 310–1 para. 1 and 311–1 et seq. French Civil Code. For further details, see V. MORGAND-CANTEGRIT, *La possession d'état d'enfant*, Thèse, Université de Lille II, 1993; cf. also C. FORDER and K. SAARLOOS, *The establishment of parenthood: a story of successful convergence?*, Maastricht Faculty of Law Working Paper 2007/1, pp. 9 et seq.

[16] Cf. I. SCHWENZER, in I. SCHWENZER (ed), *Tensions between Legal, Biological and Social Conceptions of Parentage*, Intersentia, Antwerp – Oxford, 2007, pp. 1, 5.

[17] Cf. I. SCHWENZER, in I. SCHWENZER (ed), *Tensions between Legal, Biological and Social Conceptions of Parentage*, Intersentia, Antwerp – Oxford, 2007, pp. 1, 7 et seq.; C. FORDER and K. SAARLOOS, Maastricht Faculty of Law Working Paper 2007/1, pp. 29 et seq., with reference to the fact that in English law the acknowledgment of paternity does not exist. For an overview of the establishment of paternity under English law, see also N. LOWE, *The Establishment of Paternity Under English Law*, available at http://ciec1.org/Etudes/ColloqueCIEC/PageAccueilColloqAngl.htm; E. STEINER, *EJCL*, vol. 10.3 (December 2006), available at www.ejcl.org, pp. 3 et seq., (last accessed 24.02.2014).

[18] See e.g. sec. 1592 and 1600d German Civil Code (*Bürgerliches Gesetzbuch – BGB*).

relationship can prevail over the autonomy-based acknowledgment of paternity. I will come back to this point later on.

2.2. THE AUTONOMY-BASED ESTABLISHMENT OF LEGAL PARENTAGE THROUGH ADOPTION

In addition to the assignment of the child to his or her parents based on the presumption of genetic and biological descent (as well as through court orders), most legal systems also provide for adoption as a means of establishing parentage in an autonomy-based manner regardless of genetic descent.[19] In this context, it is necessary to differentiate between (straight) adoption by contract and adoption by decree. While in the case of adoption by contract the relationship resulting from the adoption is created by a private legal act (the contract), adoption by decree requires a decision by a court or an administrative agency. By now most European States have changed to the decree system.[20] In those States which ratified the 1967 European Convention on the Adoption of Children (ECAC), the adoption process requires certain minimum standards: in addition to meeting certain agreement requirements, the adoption must be granted by a court or an administrative authority in order to be valid. This should prevent a child from being adopted by private contract without State participation and ensure that the adoption is in the child's interest.[21]

The adoption of a minor can be a full adoption or a simple adoption.[22] With a full adoption the adoptee acquires the legal status of a natural child of the adoptive parent. The child's legal relationship with his or her family of origin is completely terminated. With a simple adoption the connection with the natural parents survives in principle. In Europe the adoption of minors is most often arranged as a full adoption. Only a small number of legal systems provide a choice between a full and a simple adoption.[23] However, in recent years a discussion has begun concerning full adoption.[24] The child's right to know his

---

[19] For a comparative overview, see D. HENRICH, in *J. von Staudingers Kommentar zum Bürgerlichen Gesetzbuch: Staudinger BGB: EGBGB/IPR*, Sellier – de Gruyter, Berlin, 2008, preliminary note to Article 22 EGBGB (*Einführungsgesetz zum Bürgerlichen Gesetzbuche*, Introductory Act to the Civil Code), Mn 5 et seq.

[20] Except Austria (cf. sec. 192 Austrian Civil Code [*Allgemeines Bürgerliches Gesetzbuch – ABGB*]).

[21] Explanatory Report, Mn 16 (*re* Article 4), available at http://conventions.coe.int/Treaty/en/Reports/Html/058.htm (last accessed 24.02.2014).

[22] Cf. K. O'HALLORAN, *The Politics of Adoption: International Perspectives on Law, Policy & Practice*, Springer, 2009, p. 130.

[23] For example, France, Japan and Belgium, see D. HENRICH, in *J. von Staudingers Kommentar zum Bürgerlichen Gesetzbuch: Staudinger BGB: EGBGB/IPR*, Sellier – de Gruyter, Berlin, 2008, preliminary note to Article 22 EGBGB, Mn 5.

[24] See H.-U. MAURER, in F.J. SÄCKER and R. RIXECKER (eds), *Münchener Kommentar zum Bürgerlichen Gesetzbuch*, C.H. Beck, Munich, 2012, preliminary notes to sec. 1741 et seq.

or her own ancestry and to safeguard his or her cultural identity puts the decision to completely sever all connections with the family of origin into question.[25]

It should be mentioned here that in principle there is no provision for the termination of an adoption. Only a few legal systems allow the revocation of an adoption when the adopted child reaches the age of legal majority.[26]

2.3. PARTICULARITIES IN THE CONTEXT OF MEDICALLY-ASSISTED FORMS OF REPRODUCTION

It goes without saying that the needs of the persons involved are not always fulfilled by establishing legal parentage based on genetic and biological descent. Thus *in praxi* attempts are increasingly made to determine the child's assignment through contractual agreements, regardless of genetic descent. This is especially true in the context of medically-assisted forms of reproduction. Here a discrepancy between genetic and legal parentage is expressly intended. A comparative survey shows, however, that in this domain the desire for an autonomy-based arrangement is accounted for in rather different ways.

2.3.1. Heterologous Insemination

The problem starts with heterologous insemination: generally, the sperm donor is not expected to become the legal father of the child. If the mother lives in a relationship it is intended that the partner assumes the role of the second legal parent. Some legal systems take this into account in a rather comprehensive way: in some States the legal paternity of the sperm donor is excluded by the fact that his anonymity is guaranteed.[27] Other States explicitly exclude the legal paternity

---

BGB, Mn 43 et seq.; cf. also M. VONK, *Parent-child relationships in Dutch family law*, in I. SCHWENZER (ed), *Tensions between Legal, Biological and Social Conceptions of Parentage*, Intersentia, Antwerp – Oxford, 2007, pp. 279, 305.

[25] Cf. also E. JAYME, *Der deutsche Richter und das Common Law*, in J. BASEDOW et al. (eds), *Aufbruch nach Europa: 25 Jahre Max-Planck-Institut für Privatrecht*, Mohr Siebeck, Tübingen, pp. 447, 451.

[26] See sec. 201 para. 1 n. 4 Austrian Civil Code; sec. 18 para. 1 Danish Adoption (Consolidation) Act; Article 1573 para. 1 Greek Civil Code; cf. also Article 1:231 Dutch Civil Code (*Burgerlijk Wetboek*) and on this M. VONK, in I. SCHWENZER (ed), *Tensions between Legal, Biological and Social Conceptions of Parentage*, Intersentia, Antwerp – Oxford, 2007, p. 279, 306.

[27] See Belgium: Article 57 Belgian Law on Medically Assisted Procreation (*Loi relative à la procréation médicalement assistée (PMA) de 2007*); Spain: Article 5 para. 5 of the Spanish Assisted Reproductive Technology Act (*Ley 14/2006, de 26 de mayo, sobre técnicas de reproducción humana asistida*); Greece: Article 1460 Greek Civil Code and France: Article 16–8 French Civil Code and Articles L 1211–5, 1244–6 French Code of Public Health (*Code de la Santé Publique*). Recently, the French Council of State (Conseil d'État) confirmed the conformity of this regulation with Articles 8 and 14 European Convention on Human Rights (ECHR), Conseil d'État, Avis contentieux, 13.06.2013, M. M., Req. n° 362981. On Canadian law

of the biological sperm donor.[28] In exchange, the declaration given by the male partner of the mother that he intends to assume the legal parentage of the child in question is considered to have legal effect. Thus in Austria, Belgium and Switzerland, a husband who has agreed to the insemination cannot successfully contest the paternity, which is based on his marriage with the child's mother.[29] In addition, Austrian, Dutch and French laws also provide that the paternity of a man who is not married to the mother and who had agreed to the insemination may be established by law.[30] According to Portuguese law, the consenting husband or a consenting man living with the mother in a stable partnership becomes the legal father with the birth of the child.[31] Some legal systems go a step further in that they also provide legal parentage to the natural mother's homosexual partner, provided that she had agreed to the insemination.[32] Lastly, according to the new Family Law Act of British Columbia, the sperm donor can also become a legal parent in addition to the birth mother and her partner provided that there is a written agreement to that effect;[33] thus the child can have three legal parents.[34]

Yet not all legal systems show such a positive attitude towards autonomy-based agreements; in Italy, for example, heterologous insemination is illegal *per*

---

see A. CAMERON, V. GRUBEN and F. KELLY, De-Anonymising Sperm Donors in Canada: Some Doubts and Directions, 26 *Can. J. Fam. L. (Canadian Journal of Family Law)* (2010), p. 95.

[28] See Austria: sec. 148 para. 4 Austrian Civil Code; France: Article 311–19 French Civil Code; Spain: Article 8 para. 3 of the Spanish Assisted Reproductive Technology Act; Portugal: Article 21 Law No. 32/2006 of 26 July on medically assisted procreation (*Lei no. 32/2006 de procriação medicamente assistada de 26 de Joelho*); Greece: Article 1479 Greek Civil Code; cf. also Switzerland: According to Article 3 para. 3 Reproductive Medicine Act (*Fortpflanzungs-medizingesetz – FMedG*) heterologous insemination is reserved to married couples; the paternity of the husband may neither be contested by himself (Article 256 para. 3 Swiss Civil Code [*Zivilgesetzbuch – ZGB*]) nor by the child (Article 23 Reproductive Medicine Act).

[29] Austria: sec. 152 Austrian Civil Code; Switzerland: Article 256 para. 3 Swiss Civil Code; Belgium: Article 318 sec. 4 Belgian Civil Code (*Code Civil*).

[30] Austria: sec. 148 para. 3 Austrian Civil Code; the Netherlands: Article 1:207 para. 1 Dutch Civil Code; France: Article 311–20 French Civil Code.

[31] Article 20 para. 1 Law No 32/2006 of 26 July on medically assisted procreation.

[32] See South Africa: sec. 40 Children's Act; Sweden: sec. 9 Children and Parents Code; Canada (Quebec): Articles 538.1 and 539.1 Civil Code; for corresponding tendencies in the Unites States, see D. MEYER, 'Parenthood in a Time of Transition: Tensions Between Legal, Biological, and Social Conceptions of Parenthood', 54 *Am. J. Comp. Law (American Journal of Comparative Law)* (2006), pp. 2101, 2111 et seq.

[33] Sec. 30 Family Code of British Columbia.

[34] For a similar result under Delaware law, see N. POLIKOFF, *More thoughts on the Delaware de facto parent law – a child can have three parents*, Beyond (Straight and Gay) Marriage, 15 August 2009, available at http://beyondstraightandgaymarriage.blogspot.de/2009/08/more-thoughts-on-delaware-de-facto.html (last accessed 24.02.2014); W. DUNCAN, *The Legal Fiction of De Facto Parenthood*, 36 *Journal of Legislation* (2010), pp. 263, 264; cf. also N. POLIKOFF, *Where can a child have three parents?*, Beyond (Straight and Gay) Marriage, 14 July 2012 available at http://beyondstraightandgaymarriage.blogspot.de/2012/07/where-can-child-have-three-parents.html (last accessed 24.02.2014); also N. POLIKOFF, *Three parents (or more) okay in California – by adoption or otherwise*, Beyond (Straight and Gay) Marriage, 5 October 2013, available at http://beyondstraightandgaymarriage.blogspot.de/2013/10/three-parents-or-more-okay-in.html (last accessed 24.02.2014).

se.[35] German law allows heterologous insemination, but in some cases it concedes priority for legal paternity to the sperm donor. Neither the legal father nor the mother can challenge the paternity if the child was conceived through sperm donation as agreed by the man concerned and the mother,[36] but this is not true for the child, who after challenging the paternity of the man to whom he/she is not genetically related may have the legal paternity of the sperm donor established.[37] According to a recent decision by the German Federal Court of Justice, the sperm donor will also have the right to contest the paternity of the legal father if the legal paternity is based on acknowledgment, provided the legal father had not agreed to the insemination.[38]

2.3.2. Surrogacy

There are also discussions as to whether or not agreements regarding parentage are permissible in areas other than heterologous insemination. The question is more urgent in relation to surrogate motherhood,[39] where the woman giving birth to the child is not intended to be a legal parent; rather, the commissioning parents who are willing to take over the legal parentage are. As many legal systems have a general ban on surrogacy, taking such agreements into account is impossible.[40] Other systems allow it, but only within rather narrow margins. The reasons for rejecting this practice will not be discussed in detail in this paper.[41]

---

[35]   See Article 4 para. 3 Law No. 40 of February 19, 2004 'Norme in materia di procreazione medicalmente assistita' and on this P. HANAFIN, *Conceiving Life: Reproductive Politics and the Law in Contemporary Italy*, Ashgate Publishing, Hampshire – Burlington, 2007, p. 63.

[36]   Sec. 1600 para. 5 German Civil Code.

[37]   See G. BRUDERMÜLLER, *Palandt – Bürgerliches Gesetzbuch*, C.H. Beck, Munich, 2014, sec. 1600 BGB, Mn 13; T. HELMS, *Die Stellung des potenziellen biologischen Vaters im Abstammungsrecht*, FamRZ (2010), pp. 1, 4; T. HELMS, *Die künstliche Befruchtung aus familienrechtlicher Sicht: Probleme und Perspektiven*, in A. RÖTHEL, M. LÖHNIG and T. HELMS (eds), *Ehe, Familie, Abstammung – Blicke in die Zukunft*, Wolfgang Metzner Verlag, Frankfurt/Main, 2010, p. 49, 58. For a critical discussion of this issue that suggests an amendment of this regulation, see M. WELLENHOFER, *Die Samenspende und ihre (späten) Rechtsfolgen*, FamRZ (2013), pp. 825, 829; T. HELMS, *Die Stellung des potenziellen biologischen Vaters im Abstammungsrecht*, FamRZ (2010), pp. 1, 4; U. WANITZEK, *Ergänzungen des Abstammungsrechts durch das Kinderrechteverbesserungsgesetz*, FamRZ (2003), pp. 730, 734.

[38]   BGH (Bundesgerichtshof, Federal Court of Justice), 15.05.2013, *NJW (Neue Juristische Wochenschrift)* (2013), pp. 2589–2592; the decision is discussed by M. LÖHNIG and M. PREISNER, *Anfechtung der Vaterschaft durch den Samenspender*, *FamFR (Familienrecht und Familienverfahrensrecht)* (2013), p. 340.

[39]   Cf. Y. MARGALIT, O. LEVY and J. LOIKE, *The New Frontier of Advanced Reproductive Technology: Reevaluating Modern Legal Parenthood*, 37 *Harv. J. L. & Gender* (2014), pp. 107, 110.

[40]   See e.g. on French law the 13 September 2013 (12–18.315) decision by the French Court of cassation, available at www.courdecassation.fr/jurisprudence_2/premiere_chambre_civile_568/1092_13_27172.html (last accessed 24.02.2014).

[41]   For an overview of the discussion, see L. BRUNET, J. CARRUTHERS, K. DAVAKI, D. KING, C. MARZO and J. McCANDLESS, *A Comparative Study on the Regime of Surrogacy in EU Member States*, Study requested by the European Parliament's Committee on Legal Affairs, 2013, available at www.europarl.europa.eu/studies, p. 22 et seq. (last accessed 24.02.2014).

Here it is only of interest to demonstrate the level of importance attached to agreements concerning parentage by legal systems that permit surrogate motherhood in principle. The results vary. In England and Wales and the Netherlands, for example, a contractual agreement for the surrogate mother to surrender the child is not enforceable.[42] Even if the surrogate mother is willing to surrender the child to the commissioning parents, they will not become legal parents on the basis of the agreement with the surrogate mother; rather, they must adopt the child.[43] By law, initially only the surrogate mother is the legal mother of the child.[44]

A wider provision exists in Greek law. If the contract is approved by a court, legal parentage is awarded not to the surrogate mother, but directly to the commissioning parents.[45] South African law is similar:[46] here as well the

---

42   England: sec. 1A Surrogacy Arrangements Act 1985; cf. also (for Australia) J. MILLBANK, *The New Surrogacy Parentage Laws in Australia: Cautious Regulation or 25 Brick Walls?*, 35 *Melb. U. L. Rev.* (*Melbourne University Law Review*) (2011), p. 165. For the Netherlands see M. VONK, *Maternity for Another: A Double Dutch Approach*, 14(3) *EJCL* (December 2010), available at www.ejcl.org, p. 3 et seq. (last accessed 24.02.2014); K. BOELE-WOELKI, I. CURRY-SUMNER, W. SCHRAMA and M. VONK, *Commercieel draagmoederschap en illegale opneming van kinderen*, Boom Juridische uitgevers, The Hague, 2012, pp. 45 et seq.; L. BRUNET, J. CARRUTHERS, K. DAVAKI, D. KING, C. MARZO and J. McCANDLESS, *A Comparative Study on the Regime of Surrogacy in EU Member States*, Study requested by the European Parliament's Committee on Legal Affairs, 2013, available at www.europarl.europa.eu/studies, p. 304 (last accessed 24.02.2014).

43   For the Netherlands see M. VONK, *Maternity for Another: A Double Dutch Approach*, 14(3) *EJCL* (December 2010), available at www.ejcl.org, pp. 5 et seq. (last accessed 24.02.2014); L. BRUNET, J. CARRUTHERS, K. DAVAKI, D. KING, C. MARZO and J. McCANDLESS, *A Comparative Study on the Regime of Surrogacy in EU Member States*, Study requested by the European Parliament's Committee on Legal Affairs, 2013, available at www.europarl.europa.eu/studies, p. 305 (last accessed 24.02.2014); for England and Wales cf. sec. 54 Human Fertilisation and Embryology Act 2008 ('parental order') and K. BOELE-WOELKI, I. CURRY-SUMNER, W. SCHRAMA and M. VONK, *Commercieel draagmoederschap en illegale opneming van kinderen*, Boom Juridische uitgevers, The Hague, 2012, pp. 243 et seq.

44   England and Wales: sec. 33 Human Fertilisation and Embryology Act 2008; the Netherlands: Art. 1:198 Dutch Civil Code and M. VONK, *Maternity for Another: A Double Dutch Approach*, 14(3) *EJCL* (December 2010), available at www.ejcl.org, p. 4, (last accessed 24.02.2014); L. BRUNET, J. CARRUTHERS, K. DAVAKI, D. KING, C. MARZO and J. McCANDLESS, *A Comparative Study on the Regime of Surrogacy in EU Member States*, Study, requested by the European Parliament's Committee on Legal Affairs, 2013, available at www.europarl.europa.eu/studies, p. 305 (last accessed 24.02.2014).

45   Cf. Article 1464 Greek Civil Code and L. BRUNET, J. CARRUTHERS, K. DAVAKI, D. KING, C. MARZO and J. McCANDLESS, *A Comparative Study on the Regime of Surrogacy in EU Member States*, Study requested by the European Parliament's Committee on Legal Affairs, 2013, available at www.europarl.europa.eu/studies, pp. 281 et seq. (last accessed 24.02.2014); K. ROKAS, in K. TRIMMINGS and P. BEAUMONT (eds), *International Surrogacy Arrangements*, Hart Publishing, Oxford, 2013, pp. 143, 148 et seq.

46   Cf. sec. 297 Children's Act, 2005; L. BRUNET, J. CARRUTHERS, K. DAVAKI, D. KING, C. MARZO and J. McCANDLESS, *A Comparative Study on the Regime of Surrogacy in EU Member States*, Study requested by the European Parliament's Committee on Legal Affairs, 2013, available at www.europarl.europa.eu/studies, pp. 40 et seq., 339 et seq. (last accessed 24.02.2014); M. SLABBERT and C. ROODT, in K. TRIMMINGS and P. BEAUMONT (eds), *International*

commissioning parents become legal parents of the child immediately after his/
her birth on the basis of a court-approved contract with the surrogate mother;
however, the surrogate mother, provided she is also a genetic parent of the child,
can terminate the surrogate motherhood agreement within 60 days after its
birth.[47] In this case the surrogate mother and her husband or partner, if any –
or the commissioning father if none – become legal parents of the child. Finally,
it is the surrogate mother alone who can decide (within the limits of the valid
regulations) to terminate the pregnancy.[48]

The acquisition of legal parentage by the commissioning parents solely on the
basis of a written agreement between the surrogate mother and the intended
parents (and hence without adoption) is also provided for under the new Family
Law Act of British Columbia.[49] Here, however, the surrogate mother has to give
her written consent to surrender the child after birth.[50] With the appropriate
agreement of the parties, the surrogate mother may also become a legal parent in
addition to the commissioning parents; thus the child may have three legal
parents.[51]

2.4. CREATION OF CUSTODY IN FAVOUR OF THIRD PARTIES

In recent decades, however, parentage by intention in connection with medically-
assisted forms of reproduction is not the only topic to have come into focus.
Agreements where key aspects of parentage are involved are also discussed
outside the realm of modern reproductive medicine. The derivative acquisition
of parental custody is one particular example. There is an increased interest in
reflecting the social parentage of a mother or father's new partner in the law,
especially in blended families.

Surrogacy Arrangements, Hart Publishing, Oxford, 2013, pp. 325, 327 et seq.; M. SLABBERT,
Legal issues relating to the use of surrogate mothers in the practice of assisted conception, 5(1)
S. Afr. J. BL (South African Journal of Bioethics and Law) (2012), pp. 27–32; M. SLABBERT,
Medical Law in South Africa, Wolters Kluwer, Alphen aan den Rijn, 2011, p. 137.

[47] Sec. 298 Children's Act, 2005.
[48] Sec. 300 Children's Act, 2005.
[49] Cf. B. FINDLAY and Z. SULEMAN, *Baby Steps: Assisted Reproductive Technology and the B.C.
Family Law Act, The Family Law Act: Everything You Always Wanted to Know Paper 6.1,*
Vancouver: Continuing Legal Education Society of British Columbia, 2013, p. 32.
[50] Sec. 29 Family Code of British Columbia. A comparable provision exists in Russian Law, see
L. BRUNET, J. CARRUTHERS, K. DAVAKI, D. KING, C. MARZO and J. McCANDLESS, *A
Comparative Study on the Regime of Surrogacy in EU Member States*, Study requested by the
European Parliament's Committee on Legal Affairs, 2013, available at www.europarl.europa.
eu/studies, p. 337 (last accessed 24.02.2014); O. KHAZOVA, in K. TRIMMINGS and P. BEAUMONT
(eds), *International Surrogacy Arrangements*, Hart Publishing, Oxford, 2013, pp. 311, 317 et
seq.
[51] Sec. 30 Family Code of British Columbia.

A comparative survey shows that this need has been addressed in very different ways. German law only concedes the right to make joint decisions in matters of daily life to the new spouse of a parent with custody.[52] Other systems allow full custody to be given to a step-parent who is married to the parent with custody (or to the partner in a homosexual partnership),[53] and occasionally also to a third party.[54] In most cases the assignment of parental custody requires a court decision based on a joint application by the social parent and the parent with custody,[55] or an official endorsement of an appropriate agreement.[56] English law allows the assignment of parental custody based on an autonomy-based agreement, but requires specific standards of form.[57] Lastly, answers to the question whether, should the occasion arise, more than two persons can be entitled to custody vary.[58]

3. PERSPECTIVES OF AN AUTONOMY-BASED EXERTION OF INFLUENCE ON THE LAW OF PARENTAGE

3.1. NO FREEDOM TO DISPOSE

Even though a review of comparative law has shown that the level of importance given to private autonomy in the law of descent varies widely, I shall try to find common ground regarding the role of contractual agreements on parentage.

The most radical approach would be to also grant general contractual freedom in the law of filiation. Within such a model the legal provisions governing parentage based on biological descent would become non-mandatory law, and would hold good providing there was no differing contractual assignment of parentage.

---

52 Sec. 1687 German Civil Code.
53 See England and Wales: sec. 4a Children Act 1989; Iceland: Article 29a Act in Respect of Children no. 76/2003; cf. also Article 1:253sa Dutch Civil Code.
54 See Denmark: sec. 13 para. 2, Act on Parental Responsibility, Act no. 499 of 6 June 2007; the Netherlands: Article 1:253t Dutch Civil Code; Iceland: Article 32 para. 3 sentence 1 Act in Respect of Children no. 76/2003; South Africa: sec. 22 Children's Act, 2005.
55 See the Netherlands: Article 1:253t Dutch Civil Code.
56 See Denmark: sec. 13 para. 2, Act on Parental Responsibility, Act no. 499 of 6 June 2007; South Africa: sec. 22 Children's Act; Iceland: Articles 29a para. 2, 32 para. 5 Act in Respect of Children no. 76/2003.
57 See sec. 4a(1)(a), (2) in combination with sec. 4(2) Children Act 1989.
58 See, on the one side, Dutch law (not more than two persons) and, on the other side, English law (more than two persons), cf. M. VONK, *Children and their parents: a comparative study of the legal position of children with regard to their intentional and biological parents in English and Dutch law*, Intersentia, Antwerp – Oxford, 2007, p. 118.

The concept of free contractual arrangements regarding the child's descent must, however, be dismissed. Contractual freedom is a key characteristic of the right to self-determination, guaranteed in particular by Article 8 of the European Convention on Human Rights (ECHR). This also pertains in principle to family law, as has recently been shown for marriage contracts.[59] Yet there are limits to contractual freedom in the law of parentage because this is not only a matter of the arrangement of the parents' own affairs; rather, it is also – and to an even greater degree – a matter of the child's welfare. The interests of the child have to be taken into due account. In any case the child must not become an object of free disposition.[60]

At the other end of the spectrum lies a concept based solely on the genetic descent of the child, completely excluding any autonomy-based influence; it also goes against the child's best interests. There is no reason to deny legal parentage to biological parents who want to accept responsibility. However, in cases where the biological parents are not willing to assume parental responsibility, it is more in the child's interests to allocate parentage to persons who are willing (and qualified) to accept parental custody rather than to adhere to genetic parentage. In this context the admission of autonomy-based elements into the law of descent can also be understood as a means of ensuring the child's welfare.[61]

Despite the particular importance of the child's best interests, in individual cases other aspects may also influence the scope of contractual freedom in the law of descent. This is especially true for the interests of the biological parents involved. In many countries surrogacy agreements are not allowed, as we have

---

[59]   See N. DETHLOFF, *Contracting in Family Law: A European Perspective*, in K. BOELE-WOELKI, J. MILES and J. SCHERPE (eds), *The Future of Family Property in Europe*, Intersentia, Antwerp – Oxford, 2011, p. 65, 85.

[60]   That legal parentage is not a matter of free disposition for the parents is demonstrated by the fact that parents cannot give up their legal parentage without replacement; there is no provision for the child's abandonment, see for German law M. WELLENHOFER, in F.J. SÄCKER and R. RIXECKER (eds), *Münchener Kommentar zum BGB*, C.H. Beck, Munich, 2012, sec. 1591 BGB, Mn 41; C. KATZENMEIER, *Rechtsfragen der "Babyklappe" und der medizinisch assistierten "anonymen Geburt"*, FamRZ (2005), p. 1134, 1136; A. WOLF, *Über Konsequenzen aus den gescheiterten Versuchen, Babyklappen und "anonyme" Geburten durch Gesetz zu legalisieren*, FPR (Familie, Partnerschaft, Recht) (2003), pp. 112, 116. On the discussion of baby-boxes, cf. also C. FENTON-GLYNN, *Anonymous Relinquishment and Baby-boxes – Life-saving Mechanisms or a Violation of Human Rights?*, in this book. See, however, on the possibility of an anonymous birth in France ('*accouchement sous X*') W. PINTENS, *Filitation et Vérité*, in J. BERNREUTHER et al. (eds), *Festschrift für Ulrich Spellenberg zum 70. Geburtstag*, sellier, Munich, 2010, p. 631, 633 et seq.; M. FREEMAN and A. MARGARIA, *Who and What is a Mother? Maternity, Responsibility and Liberty*, 13 TIL (*Theoretical Inquiries in Law*) (2012), pp. 153, 155 (giving a comparative overview); and recently on the possibility of a confidential birth in Germany, T. HELMS, *Die Einführung der sog. vertraulichen Geburt*, FamRZ (2014), p. 609.

[61]   Cf. also BVerfG, 19.2.2013, *NJW* (2013), p. 847, 848 (on successive adoption), English version available at https://www.bundesverfassungsgericht.de/entscheidungen/ls20130219_1bvl000111en.html (last accessed 24.02.2014).

seen, because the birth mother's decision to surrender or keep the child can result in fierce conflicts.[62]

This leads us to the question of in what circumstances an autonomy-based influence on descent should be permissible. A clarification of this issue is essential. As important legal consequences are connected to the awarding of legal parentage (e.g. custody, liability to support, inheritance, etc.), requirements for the establishment, modification, or termination of status must be clearly defined.

3.2. PERMISSIBLE LEGAL ACTS

In Europe, the transfer of legal parentage through adoption for a child who has already been born falls under the generally accepted forms of autonomy-based influence on descent. The fact that adoption in Europe is most often organised as an adoption by decree[63] raises no objections from a perspective concerned with the child's welfare. A return to the concept of adoption by contract alone is not advisable for the child's best interests nor for those of the parents.

There is also a general consensus that in the case of heterologous insemination, autonomy-based influence on paternity should be possible in principle. In any case, this applies to those instances where instead of the sperm donor, the (male or female) partner of the prospective mother is willing to accept legal parentage. Here, intended parentage has priority over natural descent. This decision is justified in view of the expectation that it is far more likely for a social and familial relationship – which is essential for the child's well-being – to develop in relation to the intended parent than it is to the sperm donor.[64]

The question as to whether the sperm donor can also effectively renounce legal paternity in cases where there is no intended parent has a less clear answer.[65] Objections against renouncing parentage without a replacement exist in particular because the child is deliberately deprived of a legal parent and thus of

---

62 See on this argument the overview by L. BRUNET, J. CARRUTHERS, K. DAVAKI, D. KING, C. MARZO and J. MCCANDLESS, *A Comparative Study on the Regime of Surrogacy in EU Member States*, Study requested by the European Parliament's Committee on Legal Affairs, 2013, available at www.europarl.europa.eu/studies, pp. 23 et seq. (last accessed 24.02.2014); cf. for the discussion in Germany also S. GÖSSL, in K. TRIMMINGS and P. BEAUMONT (eds), *International Surrogacy Arrangements*, Hart Publishing, Oxford, 2013, pp. 131, 132 (with further references).

63 See above sub 2.2.

64 Cf. T. HELMS, *Die künstliche Befruchtung aus familienrechtlicher Sicht: Probleme und Perspektiven*, in A. RÖTHEL, M. LÖHNIG and T. HELMS (eds), *Ehe, Familie, Abstammung – Blicke in die Zukunft*, Wolfgang Metzner Verlag, Frankfurt/Main, 2010, p. 49, 55.

65 For a comparative overview, see T. HELMS, *Die künstliche Befruchtung aus familienrechtlicher Sicht: Probleme und Perspektiven*, in A. RÖTHEL, M. LÖHNIG and T. HELMS (eds), *Ehe, Familie, Abstammung – Blicke in die Zukunft*, Wolfgang Metzner Verlag, Frankfurt/Main, 2010, pp. 49, 54 et seq, 59 et seq.

---

a family line. This has consequences for the child not only as regards maintenance claims and inheritance, but also regarding the child's disadvantageous situation in the event that his/her mother dies prematurely. Due to similar considerations, there is considerable reluctance towards adoptions by single persons.[66] A Europe-wide consensus that in cases of heterologous insemination the desire of a woman to have children should take priority over the child's interests in having two legal parents is not yet in sight.

The legal position regarding surrogate motherhood is equally inconsistent. While it is still forbidden in a number of European States, others allow it in certain circumstances.[67] In view of this ambiguous situation, the admissibility of agreements regarding legal maternity does not yet belong to the accepted principles of European family law. In the face of this controversial discussion, which cannot be outlined here, it is impossible to develop a universally accepted regulatory proposal. Yet I will outline the main questions regarding the legalisation of surrogate motherhood.

It is crucial to have clarity on legal parentage at the moment of a child's birth. Since the commissioning parents are primarily responsible for the child's conception, they should be obliged to accept the obligation of parenthood. This applies in any case if the surrogate mother is willing to surrender the child and has no interest in legal parentage. However, to avoid thrusting the mother into a moral dilemma, she should be given the opportunity to decide to keep the child after the birth. Which legal construction can ensure this will not be discussed here. For examples, one can look to the South African and Canadian laws mentioned above.[68]

Finally, the question as to whether legal parentage should be assigned to more than two persons remains. The need for such an arrangement could arise in instances where, in addition to the commissioning parents, the sperm donor or surrogate mother also wants to accept legal parentage.[69] It is also conceivable that a step-parent might want to accept legal parentage while leaving the legal

---

[66] Cf. R. FRANK, in *J. von Staudinger – Kommentar zum Bürgerlichen Gesetzbuch*, Sellier – de Gruyter, Berlin, 2007, sec. 1741 BGB, Mn 50; H.-U. MAURER, in F.J. SÄCKER and R. RIXECKER (eds), *Münchener Kommentar zum Bürgerlichen Gesetzbuch*, C.H. Beck, Munich, 2012, sec. 1741 BGB, Mn 46; J. GERNHUBER and D. COESTER-WALTJEN, *Familienrecht*, C.H. Beck, Munich, 2010, p. 875 Mn 20. For a comparative overview of legal systems in which single adoptions are not allowed, see the study by the UNITED NATIONS, DEPARTMENT OF ECONOMIC AND SOCIAL AFFAIRS (POPULATION DIVISION), *Child Adoption: Trends and Policies*, New York, 2009, pp. 167 et seq.

[67] For an overview, see the country reports by L. BRUNET, J. CARRUTHERS, K. DAVAKI, D. KING, C. MARZO and J. MCCANDLESS, *A Comparative Study on the Regime of Surrogacy in EU Member States*, Study requested by the European Parliament's Committee on Legal Affairs, 2013, available at www.europarl.europa.eu/studies, pp. 200 et seq. (last accessed 24.02.2014) and in K. TRIMMINGS and P. BEAUMONT (eds), *International Surrogacy Arrangements*, Hart Publishing, Oxford, 2013.

[68] See above sub 2.3.2.

[69] For further examples, see Y. MARGALIT, O. LEVY and J. LOIKE, *The New Frontier of Advanced Reproductive Technology: Reevaluating Modern Legal Parenthood*, 37 *Harv. J. L. & Gender* (2014), pp. 107, 129 et seq.

relationship with the existing parents intact. However, considerable objections exist against a multiplicity of legal parentage.[70] After all, there is reason to fear that as the number of legal parents increases, so does the potential for conflict. As the German Federal Constitutional Court explained, if more than two parents with identical parental responsibility for the child exist, role conflicts and disputes regarding competence between the parents can take place. This could have a negative influence on the development of the child.[71] Furthermore, legal parentage does not only create rights and duties of the parents with respect to the child, but it also obliges the child with respect to his or her parents. When grown up, parents may bring claims for alimony against their child which, especially in case of three or more parents, may well exceed a child's financial means.[72]

In light of the above, one should consider whether a consolidation of social parentage could not be achieved in a different way. One possibility would be to transfer custody to a third party. The legal positions in Europe are inconsistent in this respect.[73] However, the increasing number of children who grow up in stepfamilies after the separation of their natural parents allows us to discern a growing need for the autonomy-based transfer of custody to those persons who have accepted social responsibility for the child. In many cases, transferring custody to a step-parent seems preferable to adopting the stepchild. Not only does the legal link with the original parents remain, but also in the event that the new family breaks up, custody can be revoked more easily than legal parentage, if necessary.

---

[70]   See in particular the debate following the Ontario Court of Appeal's 2 January 2007 decision in *A.A. v B.B.* recognising that a child can legally have three parents (in this particular case: two mothers and a father), 83 *O.R. (Ontario Reports)* (3d) (2007), p. 561 (C.A.); the decision is discussed by N. LaVIOLETTE, *Dad, Mom – and Mom: The Ontario Court of Appeal's Decision in A.A. v. B.B.*, 86 *The Canadian Bar Review* (2007), p. 665; R. LECKEY, *Lawmakers should create intermediate parenting category*, The Lawyers Weekly, 9 November 2007, p. 11; cf. also Y. MARGALIT, O. LEVY and J. LOIKE, *The New Frontier of Advanced Reproductive Technology: Reevaluating Modern Legal Parenthood*, 37 *Harv. J. L. & Gender* (2014), pp. 107, 133 et seq.; S. FRELICH APPLETON, *Parents by the Numbers*, 37 *HLR (Hofstra Law Review)* (2008), p. 11 (with further references). See in this context also the remark by the judge who heard (and rejected) the original application in *A.A. v B.B.*, Justice D. Aston: 'Furthermore, the court must also be concerned about the best interests of other children not before the court. For example, if this application is granted, it seems to me that the door is wide open to stepparents, extended family and others to claim parental status in less harmonious circumstances. If a child can have three parents, why not four or six or a dozen? What about all the adults in a commune or a religious organization or sect? Quite apart from social policy implications, the potential to create or exacerbate custody and access litigation should not be ignored.' *A.A. v B.B.*, (2003) 2139 (ON S.C.) at para. 41.

[71]   See BVerfG, 9.4.2003, *NJW* (2003), p. 2151, 2153; cf. also BVerfG, 19.2.2013, *NJW* (2013), p. 847, 849.

[72]   See on parental maintenance the 12 February 2014 decision by the German Federal Court of Justice, granting maintenance to a father who broke off the connection with his son in adulthood, BGH, 12.2.2014, Case XII ZB 607/12, available at www.bundesgerichtshof.de (last accessed 12.03.2014).

[73]   See above sub 2.4.

3.3. STATE CONTROL OF AUTONOMY-BASED AGREEMENTS ON PARENTAGE

As mentioned previously, the well-being of the child limits contractual freedom in the law of parentage.[74] Administrative institutions must determine whether the respective agreement is compatible with the child's interests. Most of the legal systems that were considered justifiably provide for the participation of a court or an administrative agency for both autonomy-based agreements concerning the status of the child and the transfer of custody to third parties.

However, agreements in connection with heterologous insemination are the exception. Pertinent declarations must (in general) be submitted in a specific way,[75] but they are not subject to administrative supervision. The absence of administrative participation when the commissioning father accepts parentage corresponds to the legal situation for the acknowledgment of paternity, where administrative certification is also unnecessary.[76] However, the need to follow a specific form should admittedly be maintained: it seems to be necessary in order to protect against haste.[77]

3.4. CONTRACTING ON PARENTAGE?

To conclude this article, it must be determined to what extent the autonomy-based impact on parentage should occur *de facto* in the form of an agreement. In cases of medically-assisted reproduction, this problem does not often arise for practical reasons. Thus, for heterologous insemination, there is usually no contact between the commissioning parents and the sperm donor, who wishes to remain anonymous. The influence on the status is based on the unilateral waiver

---

[74] See above sub 3.1.

[75] See e.g. sec. 148 para. 3 and sec. 152 Austrian Civil Code (the consent of the intended father requires a declaration before a notary); Article 311–20 para. 1 French Civil Code (a declaration before a judge or a notary); Article 51 para. 4 Family Code of the Russian Federation (written consent); for Greek law, see I. ANDROULIDAKIS-DIMITRIADIS, *Family Law in Greece*, Wolters Kluwer, Alphen aan den Rijn, 2010, p. 96 Mn 183. However, under German law the consent of the intended parents (sec. 1600 para. 5 Geman Civil Code) requires no specific form, see T. RAUSCHER, in *J. von Staudinger – Kommentar zum Bürgerlichen Gesetzbuch*, Sellier – de Gruyter, Berlin, 2011, sec. 1600 BGB, Mn 78; M. WELLENHOFER, in F.J. SÄCKER and R. RIXECKER (eds), *Münchener Kommentar zum Bürgerlichen Gesetzbuch*, C.H. Beck, Munich, 2012, sec. 1600 BGB, Mn 35.

[76] See e.g. sec. 1597 para. 1 German Civil Code: acknowledgment of paternity must be notarially recorded.

[77] Cf. T. RAUSCHER, in *J. von Staudinger – Kommentar zum Bürgerlichen Gesetzbuch*, Sellier – de Gruyter, Berlin, 2011, sec. 1600 BGB, Mn 78; P. ECKERSBERGER, *Auswirkungen des Kinderrechteverbesserungsgesetzes auf Vereinbarungen über eine heterologe Insemination*, MittBayNot (*Mitteilungen des Bayerischen Notarvereins, der Notarkasse und der Landesnotarkammer Bayern*) (2002), pp. 261, 263.

of the sperm donor and the equally unilateral acceptance of parentage by the (male or female) partner of the mother.

In the remaining cases of an autonomy-based influence on parentage, a contract does not seem advisable for reasons of the certainty of the status. The clearest example of this is adoption. If we understand adoption to be an agreement between parties that just needs official approval, the invalidity or possible termination of the agreement would question the validity of the transfer of parentage.[78] If, however, adoption takes place by means of an administrative act that requires only the autonomy-based intent of the parties to that effect, similar problems will not arise. Not least for this reason does adoption by decree prevail in Europe.[79]

For the same reasons in cases of surrogate motherhood – as far as it is permitted – the transfer of parentage for the sake of status should certainly not be based on an agreement between the parties, but rather on an administrative act.

Lastly, an administrative act seems to be preferable even for the transfer of custody to a third party. In this case, a direct influence on status is not evident. However, allowing the transfer of custody by means of an agreement between the parties that merely requires official approval could result in the subsequent contestation of the third party's custody due to the invalidity of the agreement. In addition, the question would have to be settled whether the invalidity of the custody transfer also resulted in voiding legal transactions made by the third party entitled to custody in the child's name.

To sum up, one can say the following: while there is room for the influence of private autonomy in the law of descent, this does not mean that the type of contractual agreements known in the law of obligations should serve as a model.

4. CONCLUSION: INTENTIONAL AND BIOLOGICAL PARENTAGE SIDE BY SIDE

To conclude: the law of descent does not exclude autonomy-based agreements at all. The break-up of traditional family structures gives rise to a cautious expansion of flexibility in this area. Limits are set mainly by the interests of the child. The child must not become an object of free disposition.

Under the adoption law, this is taken into account by a strictly regulated procedure. Here, an autonomy-based 'transfer' of parentage by a simple agreement is justifiably impossible. Furthermore, contractual agreements are

---

[78] Cf. R. FRANK, in *J. von Staudinger – Kommentar zum Bürgerlichen Gesetzbuch*, Sellier – de Gruyter, Berlin, 2007, sec. 1752 BGB, Mn 3.

[79] For the legislative change from adoption by contract to adoption by decree in German law, see P. MANKOWSKI, *Beseitigungsrechte: Anfechtung, Widerruf und verwandte Institute*, J.C.B. Mohr (Paul Siebeck), Tübingen, 2003, pp. 489 et seq.

thus far also the exception in the law of parentage. They can be found in the context of surrogate motherhood and the transfer of custody to third parties. In both cases, the need for detailed and particular regulations is especially great. In most cases such agreements will only gain legal force, and for good reason, after having been examined by the State.

In cases of heterologous insemination, an agreement between the commissioning parents and the sperm donor frequently cannot be achieved because contact is not wanted. Here, private autonomy can play a role only in the form of unilateral declarations.

However, autonomy-based agreements cannot replace genetic parentage as a connecting factor. A legal assignment of the child to his/her genetic parents is mandatory in those cases where other persons are not willing to accept legal and social responsibility. As a result, it is clear that a genetic and biological relationship as an expression of natural parentage and party autonomy as an expression of intended social parentage can exist side by side.[80] A functioning law of descent cannot dispense with either connection.

---

[80] Cf. also D. HENRICH, *Streit um die Abstammung – Europäische Perspektiven*, in A. SPICKHOFF, D. SCHWAB, D. HENRICH and P. GOTTWALD (eds), *Streit um die Abstammung*, Gieseking, Bielefeld, 2007, pp. 395, 412.

BIOLOGICAL AND SOCIAL PARENTHOOD

Gabriele Britz

Contents

Questions of biological and social parenthood are posing great challenges to German constitutional law. In the field of parenthood two decisions of the German Constitutional Court can be highlighted. The first one is a judgment from 2003 on the rights of biological fathers which addresses biological parenthood as well as social parenthood.[1] This ruling was a first step in strengthening the position of biological fathers. The other judgment was rendered in February 2013 when the Court held that the non-admission of successive adoption by registered civil (same-sex) partners is unconstitutional, and furthermore stated that same-sex parents can be considered to be parents in the sense of the Basic Law, and are thus protected by constitutional law, if the formal status of parenthood has been assigned to them by private law.[2]

---

[1]   BVerfGE 108, 82.
[2]   BVerfG, 1 BvL 1/11 Judgment of 19 February 2013, available at www.bverfg.de/
      entscheidungen/ls20130219_1bvl000111.html (last accessed 10.10.2013); also available in
      English.

1. SUPREMACY OF LEGAL PARENTHOOD

The Federal Constitutional Court largely follows the decisions taken by the parliamentary legislator: German constitutional law mainly focuses on legal parenthood as assigned by private law rules on descent. It is important to note that German private law rules on descent implicitly assume a close correlation between legal and biological parenthood.[3]

In German constitutional law the fundamental right to family relations (Article 6 of the German Basic Law) includes a specific fundamental right of parenthood. Under Article 6 paragraph 2 of the German Basic Law the 'care and upbringing of children is the natural right of parents and a duty primarily incumbent upon them'. Calling this right a 'natural' right seems to imply that the main criterion for parenthood is biological parenthood. However, this would be a false conclusion, even though in the majority of cases biological parents are indeed the holders of parental rights.

Under constitutional law the status of parenthood is closely tied to subconstitutional rules, notably the provisions of the BGB – the German Civil Code. The Federal Constitutional Court generally considers the very same person who is a parent by subconstitutional family law to be the holder of the fundamental right of parenthood under Article 6 paragraph 2 of the Basic Law.[4] Whether parenthood is rather a biological concept or a social one therefore depends on German private law. Thus – according to the German Civil Code – the mother is the woman who has given birth to the child (§1591 BGB); the father is the man who is married to this woman at the time of the child's birth (§1592 No. 1 BGB) or who has acknowledged paternity (§1592 No. 2 BGB) or whose paternity has been confirmed before a court (§1592 No. 3 BGB). Furthermore, parenthood can be assigned to men and women by adoption (§1741 BGB).

In three cases these subconstitutional assignments of parental rights are not based on biological parentage – and, therefore, parenthood under constitutional law is not necessarily accompanied by a biological bond either: the case of adoption, the case of paternity being automatically assigned to the mother's husband and the case of a man's acknowledgement of paternity. However, the latter two rules on paternity (husband; acknowledgement) follow the assumption that in a large number of cases the legal father will also be the biological father. Still – because in both cases biological paternity is not required for legal paternity – biological and legal paternity may diverge from each other. This possible divergence is the reason why subconstitutional law offers the option to challenge (mere) legal paternity (§1600 BGB). By such a challenge legal and biological paternity can be brought into line. And again, constitutional law follows subconstitutional law: if a man loses his legal paternity as a result of such a challenge, he also loses the constitutional right of parenthood.

---

[3]   BVerfGE 108, 82 <100>.
[4]   BVerfG, 1 BvL 1/11 Judgment of 19 February 2013, para. 48.

Summing up, the constitutional paternity status follows the subconstitutional right of parenthood.

2. CONSTITUTIONAL GUIDELINES

However, the Basic Law would not be a constitution if it did not set some limits and guidelines concerning access to parenthood that have to be observed by the legislator. The fundamental right of parenthood is considered – following the interpretation of the Federal Constitutional Court – to be a third-party interest fundamental right – serving the child.[5] Therefore, the guidelines provided by the Basic Law concerning access to parenthood are oriented towards the best interest of the child. These constitutional guidelines leave a great deal of discretion to the legislator.

2.1. ASPECTS WHICH ARE NOT NEGATIVELY OR POSITIVELY DETERMINED BY THE CONSTITUTION

First, one can identify several items which are not negatively determined by the constitution. The Federal Constitutional Court has been generous with regard to the question of who is generally able to be a legal parent under the Basic Law. Article 6 paragraph 2 does not exclude, for example, persons from parenthood because they are not also biological parents;[6] not because they are same-sex parents;[7] not because they are not married.[8]

On the other hand, the Basic Law does not positively define extensive requirements concerning who inevitably has to be a legal parent:

Article 6 paragraph 2 of the Basic Law does not compel the legislator to make the subconstitutional parental status accessible to (mere) social parents (for example, by adoption or the acknowledgement of parenthood).[9] Social parenthood is of great importance in constitutional law, though. It is a criterion for allocating paternity between a social father and a legal father competing for parental rights;[10] moreover, the broader fundamental right of family relations (Article 6 paragraph 1 of the Basic Law) may guarantee social parents a legal position to claim rights similar to those contained in the legal status of

---

5   BVerfGE 108, 82 <102>.
6   Legal Parenthood of non-biological but social fathers: BVerfGE 108, 82 <100 f.>.
7   BVerfG, 1 BvL 1/11 Judgment of 19 February 2013, para. 48.
8   Legal Parenthood of the biological father who is not married to the child's mother: BVerfGE 92, 158 <178>.
9   BVerfG, 1 BvL 1/11 Judgment of 19 February 2013, para. 59.
10 BVerfG, 1 BvL 1/11 Judgment of 19 February 2013, para. 59.

parenthood.[11] Still, taken by itself, mere social parenthood has not yet led to constitutionally granting the full legal status of parenthood.

Neither is the assignment of legal parenthood to the biological father compulsory under Article 6 paragraph 2 of the German Basic Law, as long as there is another – a legal – father. However, the Federal Constitutional Court has developed a procedural right for the benefit of the biological father on the basis of Article 6 paragraph 2. Therefore, the legislator has to provide a procedure which offers a possibility for the biological father to gain legal parenthood[12] – it is important to say that the biological father will gain legal parenthood only in the absence of a special necessity to protect the social relations between the child and its legal parents – this is one situation in which social parenthood matters.

2.2. CONSTITUTIONAL CONSTRAINTS RESULTING FROM THE 'TWO PARENTS ONLY' DOGMA

In a nutshell: in unclear situations the legislator enjoys discretion as to whom it chooses to assign legal parenthood. However, this discretion is limited by constitutional guidelines in case of a conflict between two or more persons willing to gain legal parenthood. In such a conflict a decision (as to whom to assign legal parenthood) is inevitable only because of the dogma of the two-person parenthood. The Federal Constitutional Court – mainly due to pragmatic considerations – assumes that having at most two legal parents is in the best interest of the child: the more persons who are sharing parental rights, the more complicated it becomes to make use of those rights in the best interest of the child, mainly because these situations might be particularly riddled with conflicts. Therefore, the Federal Constitutional Court considers a limit of at most two legal parents to be required in the best interest of the child.[13] Hence, in the case of an 'oversupply' a decision has to be taken.

2.3. CONSTITUTIONAL RULES ON THE ALLOCATION OF LEGAL PARENTHOOD BETWEEN CONCURRING ASPIRANTS FOR FATHERHOOD

In a few words one can identify constitutional rules on the allocation of legal parenthood according to the Constitutional Court's decision of 2003 on biological fathers:

---

[11]   BVerfGE 108, 82 <113>; see also BVerfG, 1 BvL 1/11 Judgment of 19 February 2013, paras. 60–70.
[12]   BVerfGE 108, 82 <104>.
[13]   BVerfGE 108, 82 <103>.

(1) It is almost impossible to deprive a person who is a biological and a legal parent of parenthood without his or her consent, even in the case where another person is fulfilling the function of a social parent, e.g. the child is his or her stepchild. Mere social parenthood is very weak.

(2) However, neither can a man who is both the legal and social father be deprived of his status by a claim challenging his paternity brought by the biological father. This holds true even if the biological father also has a social relationship with the child. Under these special circumstances, biological parentage appears to be weak as well.

(3) In the case where the biological father has already established familial bonds with the child, the mere biological father has a right to contact and access, though resulting from the fundamental right of family relations and not from the fundamental right of parenthood.

(4) Moreover, the Strasbourg Court has extended this right to those biological fathers who have not yet established such a relationship but wish to do so. These judgments have recently been implemented by the German legislator.[14] The German Federal Constitutional Court would have probably denied the legal obligation to extend the right to those fathers, because it might have accepted the reasoning of the former legal situation, which reflected the special need for absolute protection to be given to the social family against any intrusion by the biological father demanding contact and access. In contrast, the Strasbourg Court did not accept such a generalisation made by the legislator.

(5) If there exists no social familial bond between the legal father and the child, there is no reason to refuse the biological father legal parenthood. Where there is a lack of social relations, the biological father prevails over the legal father.

3. FUTURE QUESTIONS

While constitutional requirements for settling disputes between a biological and a legal father are now quite clear, the Federal Constitutional Court is facing new fundamental challenges in the field of the assignment of parenthood. First, the question of foreign surrogate motherhood is becoming pressing. Second, it is also not clear how to deal with parenthood in cases of sperm donation. In both fields the Federal Constitutional Court has not taken a decision yet.

---

[14]   Gesetz zur Stärkung der Rechte des leiblichen, nicht rechtlichen Vaters, 4 July 2013 BGBl. I, p. 2176.

FRANCE: BIOLOGICAL AND SOCIAL PARENTAGE

Françoise MONÉGER

Contents

Everybody has heard of the very difficult vote in France on the law on same-sex marriage. After weeks of demonstrations, the law was finally adopted on 17 May 2013. The title of the law, 'opening marriage to same-sex couples', does not really describe its full contents. As a matter of fact, the law makes marriage and adoption available to same-sex couples. A new provision in the Civil Code (Article 6-1) provides: *'Le mariage et la filiation adoptive emportent les mêmes effets, droits et obligations reconnus par les lois, à l'exclusion de ceux prévus au titre VII du livre 1er du présent code, que les époux ou les parents soient de sexe différents ou de même sexe.'*

This means that same-sex marriages and different-sex marriages do not have identical effects when it comes to parentage. Only adoption and not, at the moment, biological filiation is possible in same-sex marriages. Placing such a provision at the beginning of the Code together with other general principles was vigorously criticised[1] as this was not considered to be its rightful place.

---

[1]   J. HAUSER, Loi ouvrant le mariage aux couples de personnes de même sexe (et autre sujets), *JCP*, N, 2013, p. 31.

It has also been said that it is not 'a marriage for everybody' since there are two categories of marriages: on the one hand, the different-sex marriage with effects on filiation and the presumption of paternity, and on the other, the same-sex marriage with effects on adoption only.[2] However, this has nevertheless been a great victory for homosexual couples in that they have been given the rights to marry and to adopt.

Before presenting the contents of the new law as regards adoption (section 2), it might be interesting to briefly summarise the previous situation under French law (section 1), and then to look at what the next step will be (section 3).

1. THE PAST

The position of the Court of Cassation was very well exposed by the ECtHR in the case of *Gas and Dubois v France* (15 March 2012).[3]

1.1. *COUR DE CASSATION* 24 FEBRUARY 2006

The *Cour de cassation* accepted a delegation of parental responsibility provided by Article 377 of the Civil Code on 24 February 2006 in a case where a same-sex couple were involved.[4] Under Article 377 of the Civil Code, where the circumstances so require, one or both parents may apply to the family judge to have the exercise of parental responsibility delegated to a third party (an individual, an approved institution or the child welfare organisation concerned). This delegation of responsibility is not permanent and does not encompass the right to consent to adoption. In this context, parental responsibility may be transferred in whole or in part: parental responsibility continues to be vested in the parents, but its exercise is handed over to a third party.

In that case, the biological mother and her partner, who were united by a *pacte civil de solidarité*, obtained the delegation of parental responsibility. The court ruled that Article 377 of the Civil Code '[did] not prevent a mother with sole parental responsibility from delegating the exercise of that responsibility in whole or in part to the woman with whom she live[d] in a stable and lasting relationship, where the circumstances so required and the measure [was] compatible with the child's best interests'.

However, this possibility was quite narrow since the *Cour de cassation* required the applicants to demonstrate that the measure would improve the life

---

2   J.B. BINET, Article 6–1 du Code civil: deux mariages et un enferrement!, *Dr. famille*, 2013, p. 1.
3   On this decision, see J.P. MARGUENAUD, *RTD civ.*, 2012, p. 275; C. NEIRINCK, *Dr. famille*, 2012, comment No. 82.
4   Cass. 1ère civ., 24 février 2006, n° 04–17090, *Bull*, I, 2006, n° 101.

of the child, due to, for instance, the mother (or the father) working far from home.[5] Furthermore, as this is a question of fact, the case law of the courts of appeal is far from uniform. Some courts have considered that cohabitation between the parent and her or his partner is enough to prove the interest of the delegation, while others have not.

1.2. *COUR DE CASSATION* 27 FEBRUARY 2007

On 23 February 2007 the *Cour de cassation* refused an application for the simple adoption of a minor child of an individual's civil partner.[6] Later, several judgments followed suit.[7] The rationale was that, because of the terms of Article 365 of the Civil Code, an adoption in such a case would transfer the rights of parental authority to the adoptive parent, which would effectively deprive the biological mother of her rights. If the adoption had been allowed, the biological mother would have had to request a delegation of parental responsibility under Article 377 of the Code, as explained above.

For the court 'the adoption resulted in parental responsibility for the child being transferred, and the biological mother, who planned to continue raising the child, being deprived of her rights. Accordingly, although Ms Y has consented to the adoption, the Court of Appeal, in granting the application, acted in breach of the above-mentioned provisions'.

Article 365 of the Civil Code contains an exception when the adoption of the child is requested by the spouse of the father or mother. In others words, second-parent adoption is reserved for married couples, and under French law (at that time) only different-sex couples could be married.[8]

Since 1 March 2010, every citizen has had the right to contest the constitutionality of a law which helps to uphold the rights and liberties guaranteed by the Constitution. A same-sex couple, united by a pact of solidarity, and whose application to adopt had been refused under Article 365 of the Civil Code, decided to submit a *question prioritaire de constitutionalité* (QPC) to the *Cour de cassation* concerning this article. This court agreed to

---

5 Cass. 1ère civ., 8 juillet 2010, n° 09–12623, *JCP*, G, 2010, p. 994; note A. GOUTTENOIRE, *RTD civ.* 2010, p. 547, commented by J. HAUSER.
6 Cass. 1ère civ. 20 février 2007, n° 06–15647, *Dr. famille*, 2007, comment No. 80; B. BEIGNIER, *JCP*, G, 2007, para. 10068, annotated by C. NEIRINCK.
7 For example: Cass. 1ère civ. 19 décembre 2007, n° 06–21369.
8 Article 365: 'All rights associated with parental responsibility shall be vested in the adoptive parent alone, including the right to consent to the marriage of the adoptee, unless the adoptive parent is married to the adoptee's mother or father. In this case, the adoptive parent and his or her spouse shall have joint parental responsibility, but the spouse shall continue to exercise it alone unless the couple make a joint declaration before the senior register of the *tribunal de grande instance* to the effect that parental responsibility is to be exercised jointly', text as translated in *Gas and Dubois v. France* (§19).

transmit the question to the Constitutional Council. It was considered that the question was of sufficient importance because of the principle of equality, Article 365 of the Civil Code thereby making a distinction with regard to parental authority between children adopted by the spouse or the partner of the biological parent.

On 6 October 2012 the Constitutional Council determined that 'the difference in the situation of married and unmarried couples, justifies in the interest of the child, the differences of treatment in the adoption process'.[9] As was mentioned in the case of *Gas and Dubois v France*,[10] the Constitutional Council began by pointing out that the provision of Article 365 of the Civil Code did not hinder couples from cohabiting or entering into a civil partnership, nor did it prevent the biological parent from involving his or her partner or cohabitant in the child's upbringing. The Council determined that the right to family life as guaranteed by the Constitution did not confer the right to establish a legal adoptive relationship between the child and her or his parent's partner. Above all, it considered that it is up to the legislature to reconsider the issue of whether same-sex couples can adopt.

Finally, Article 365 of the Civil Code was also examined by the ECHR in *Gas and Dubois v France*. The Court 'found that there was no difference of treatment based on sexual orientation between an un-married different-sex couple and a same sex couple as, under French law, second-parent adoption was not open to either of them'.[11] In that case on Austrian law, the Court found that there had been a violation of Article 14 of the Convention in conjunction with Article 8 when the applicant's situation was compared with that of an unmarried different-sex couple in which one partner wishes to adopt the other partner's child.[12]

In a concurring opinion in *Gas and Dubois v France*, Judge Spielmann (joined by Judge Berro-Lefèvre), said in his conclusion: 'I echo judge Costa's call for the legislature to revisit the issue by bringing the wording of Article 365 of the Civil Code into line with contemporary social reality.'

The new French law of May 2013 has not amended Article 365 of the Civil Code, but marriage is now open to same-sex couples. So the application of Article 365 has now changed.

---

[9] Conseil constitutionnel, décision du 6 octobre 2010, n° 2010–39, QPC: JO 7 octobre 2010, p. 18154, *Rec. Cons. const.,* 2010, p. 264.
[10] N° 25951/07, 15 March 2012, §31.
[11] §131, Case of *X and others v Austria*, 19 February 2013.
[12] §153.

2. THE PRESENT: THE LAW OF 17 MAY 2013

We will only look at the new law with regard to the question of adoption which has been opened up to married same-sex couples, and concerning the situation of step-parents and social parentage which has been very slightly modified.[13]

2.1. ADOPTION BY A MARRIED COUPLE OR BY ONE PERSON ONLY

There are two types of adoption in French law: a full adoption and a simple adoption. A full adoption order can only be made while the child is still a minor under the age of 15 and it may be requested by a married couple or by one person only. It creates a legal parent–child relationship which takes the place of the original relationship (if this in fact existed). The child takes on the adoptive parent's/parents' surname. A new birth certificate is issued and the adoption is irrevocable.[14]

A simple adoption order does not sever the ties between the child and his or her original family, but creates an additional legal parent–child relationship (Articles 360 et seq.). The order can be made irrespective of the age of the adoptee, including when he or she has reached the age of majority. A simple adoption gives rise to reciprocal obligations between the adopter and the adoptee, in particular concerning maintenance requirements.

Article 343 of the Civil Code determines: 'Adoption may be applied for by a married couple who have not been judicially separated and have been married more than two years or are both over twenty-eight years of age' whereas Article 343-1 of the Civil Code provides that adoption may also be applied for by any person over twenty-eight years of age. If the adoptive parent is married and not judicially separated, the consent of his or her spouse is necessary, unless he or she is unable to provide such consent.

These two articles, which apply to either full adoption or simple adoption, have not been modified by the new law. The change concerns only the possibility for same-sex couples to marry and so to adopt a child jointly, or for one spouse to adopt a child with the consent of the other spouse. It must be emphasised that non-married couples cannot, under French law, adopt a child together. This provision applies to both different-sex and same-sex couples.

Furthermore, under French law, the adoption of children in State care or children from abroad oblige the adopter(s) to obtain an authorisation by the

---

[13]   On this point, see for example: P. MURAT, L'ouverture de l'adoption aux couples de même sexe … ou l'art de se mettre au milieu du gué, *Dr. famille*, juillet/août 2013, p. 30, H. FULCHIRON, Le mariage pour tous. Un enfant pour qui?, *JCP*, G, 2013, p. 1123.

[14]   Articles 355 et seq. of the Civil Code.

president of the council for the relevant *département*. The question whether a homosexual person may obtain such an authorisation has been very much debated by the Courts. In the case of *Fretté v France* on 26 February 2002, the ECtHR had considered that a refusal based on the applicant's 'choice of life' was possible in respect of the best interests of the child. Six years later in the case of *E.B. v France* on 22 January 2008, the Court modified its decision: 'French law allows persons to adopt a child, thereby opening up the possibility of adoption by a single homosexual'.[15]

It is now certain that with the new law, which has been approved in its entirety by the Constitutional Council,[16] it will no longer be possible to refuse an authorisation for adoption based on the applicant's sexual preferences.

Very few children are available for adoption in France. Just as in other European countries, adoptees come from abroad and it is more difficult and a longer process to adopt a child. Moreover, most foreign countries will prefer a child to be adopted by a couple consisting of parents of the opposite sex. This is the reason why adoption is very often a second-parent adoption.

2.2. SECOND-PARENT ADOPTIONS

Here we have to distinguish between full adoption and simple adoption.

Concerning full adoption, Article 345-1 of the Civil Code provides that the adoption of the birth child of one spouse is only permitted in three cases:

- the child has an established filiation with that parent only;
- the other parent has been deprived of rights concerning the child;
- the other parent is deceased and there are no family members to take care of the child.

The Law of 17 May 2013 adds an additional case in its Article 7: when one spouse has obtained an order for the full adoption of a child who has no other established filiation. That means that in such a case the child would be fully adopted twice, which is an exception to the rule of Article 346 of the Civil Code.

Concerning simple adoption, as we said above, Article 365, which has been very much discussed, has not been modified by the new law. A second-parent adoption is only possible for a married couple. As marriage has now been opened up to same-sex couples, there is no longer any discrimination on that ground.

---

15   ECtHR 22 January 2008 *E.B. v. France*, §94.
16   N° 2013–669 DC 17 May 2013.

Under Article 365 of the Civil Code an adoption will only be refused when the adopter is not married to the birth parent.

With regard to adoption, the new law enforces the obligation that only married couples can jointly adopt a child.

2.3. THE NEW LAW HAS NOT CREATED ANY SPECIFIC STATUS FOR A STEP-PARENT

Several proposed bills on this status have been prepared but never voted upon. This will be a matter for the next family law reform.[17]

During cohabitation, the only way to grant some rights to a step-parent is by the delegation of parental responsibility under Articles 377 and 377-1 of the Civil Code, as laid down by the Law of 4 March 2002, and explained above under section 1. The consent of the other parent is compulsory for such a delegation, which can be difficult to obtain.

The Law of 17 May 2013 modifies two articles from the Civil Code in order to grant certain rights to a step-parent, but only after a separation with the other parent.

Article 371-4 of the Civil Code lays down the child's right to form a relationship with third parties. A sentence has been added specifically addressing the situation where that third party has cohabited with the parent ('*en particulier lorsque ce tiers a résidé de manière stable avec l'enfant et l'un de ses parents, a pourvu à son éducation, à son entretien, ou à son installation et a noué avec lui des liens affectifs durables*'). This third party is obviously a step-parent.

Article 353-2 of the Civil Code has also been modified. This article provides the possibility to oppose a decision on adoption in the case of fraud by the adoptive parents. A new paragraph prescribes that '*constitue un dol la dissimulation au tribunal du maintien des liens de l'adopté et un tiers décidé par le juge aux affaires familiales sur le fondement de l'article 371-4*'.

3. THE FUTURE

First, it is quite obvious that the *jurisprudence* of the *Cour de cassation* on marriage and adoption as far as same-sex couples are concerned is no longer relevant. Second, opening up adoption to same-sex married couples has no real meaning as there are no children to be adopted.

---

[17] For example: S. TETARD, Quelle place juridique pour le beau-parent?, *Dr. famille*, 2013, p. 44.

3.1. WHAT IS A MARRIAGE?

The definition of marriage provided by the Court of Cassation on 13 March 2007 ('according to French law, marriage is the union between a man and a woman') no longer holds true.

Moreover, in two judgments on 7 June 2012 the *Cour de cassation* refused to recognise a full adoption pronounced abroad, one in Canada one in the UK, in favour of non-married male couples. These adoptions were said to be contrary to an essential principle in the French law of filiation, i.e. that a child cannot be born to two same-sex parents.[18] As full adoption has now been opened up to same-sex married couples, this is no longer an essential principle of French law.[19]

In these two judgments, the court also considered that Article 346 of the Civil Code, which reserves adoption to married couples, is not an essential principle of French law. This means that it would be possible to recognise adoptions pronounced abroad under a foreign law which accepts adoption by non-married couples.

As has been explained above, marriage remains essential for adoption, so the formula of the *Cour de cassation* can now be questioned.

3.2. SAME-SEX COUPLES AND CHILDREN

Adoption is now available to same-sex couples, but as we have said, there are no children to adopt, so the only way of doing so is by intra-familial adoption: adopting the partner's child.

Under French law artificial reproduction techniques are only available to different-sex couples, either married or cohabiting for more than two years, in the case of infertility or a risk of illness. This assistance is therefore obviously not available for a single woman or a same-sex couple. Many women have made use of such services abroad, e.g. in Belgium and in Spain, and have had babies. Even if the birth of these babies is the result of an illegal practice according to French law, the courts have nevertheless accepted, as we have said in section 1, the parental delegation of responsibility given to the partner according to Article 377 of the Civil Code. Now, if the birth mother and her partner decide to marry, the spouse will adopt the child (Article 365).

In the case of a male couple, the only way to a have a child is by surrogacy, which is strictly forbidden under French law according to Article 16-7 of the Civil Code. Some couples, however, have tried to bypass the French prohibition

---

[18]   Cass. 1ère civ. 7 juin 2012, n° 11–30261, et n° 11–30262, *JCP*, G, 2012, p. 857; note F. Chenede, *D.* 2012, p. 1992; annotated by D. Vigneau.

[19]   See P. Salvage-Gerest, Les incidences de la loi du 17 mai 2013 sur l'adoption internationale, *Dr. famille*, juillet/août 2013, p. 60.

on surrogacy by entering into a surrogacy agreement in a foreign State where they are recognised as the legal parents, and then returning to France hoping to have the parentage recognised.

In three judgments on 6 April 2011 the *Cour de cassation* refused to recognise surrogacy and, as a consequence, refused to register the birth of the children concerned in France. These three cases involved a different-sex couple, a married couple and an unmarried couple.[20] Recently the *Cour de cassation* has decided on two cases involving men having children in India with a surrogate mother. The men who gave their sperm recognised the children under French law and the Indian women were the mothers.

These cases were very delicate because the biological parents were mentioned on the birth certificate. So it was not possible to use the argument from 2011 based on the fact that the mother on the birth certificate was not the woman who had given birth to the child, but the legal mother. Here, the only possibility was to invoke fraud as the 'father' who gave his sperm had gone abroad and paid a woman to have a child, which is strictly forbidden in France and is considered to be a criminal offence.

In two judgments of 13 September 2013, the *Cour de cassation* refused to recognise the birth certificates of the children and annulled the recognition by the fathers.[21]

Is the legislature going to change the law on assisted human reproduction so as to make it available to single women? This question is currently under debate.

In addition, the acceptance of surrogacy will be extremely difficult, as all the Reports on the subject, except for one, are opposed to this.[22]

---

[20]   Cass. 1ère civ. 6 avril 2011, n° 09–17130, 09–66486, 010–19053, *Bull*, I, 2011, n° 70, 71, 72: Rapport de la Cour de cassation 2011, p. 400.

[21]   Cass. 1ère civ. 13 septembre 2013, n°12–30138 et 12–18315, *JCP*, G, 2013, p. 1731, annotated by A. Mirkovic.

[22]   F. Chenede, Et demain, la gestation pour autrui?, *Dr. famille*, 2013, p. 40; see International Academy of Comparative Law, XVIIIth Congress, Washington DC 25–31 July 2010, *Gestation pour autrui: Surrogate Motherhood*.

ANONYMOUS RELINQUISHMENT AND BABY-BOXES

Life-Saving Mechanisms or a Violation of Human Rights?

Claire FENTON-GLYNN

Contents

In the past 15 years in Europe, there has been an increasing trend towards the provision of mechanisms for the anonymous relinquishment of children to the care of the state. Anonymous birth or 'baby-boxes' are now available in many European countries, raising important questions concerning the right of children to life, to family and to identity.

This chapter will analyse the practice of anonymous relinquishment throughout Europe, and propose a solution to this difficult social and legal dilemma that will protect the children involved, without placing unnecessary and potentially harmful burdens on mothers. It will show that a balance is needed, placing the best interests of the child as the primary consideration, but also respecting the balance that must be achieved between children, their parents, and the state.

1. ANONYMOUS RELINQUISHMENT OF CHILDREN: WHAT IS IT, AND WHERE IS IT PRACTISED?

Anonymous birth is traditionally the practice by which mothers can give birth in a hospital without stating their identity, and the child is then placed for adoption. While France is the most prominent exponent of this practice,[1] it is also legal in Luxembourg and Austria.[2] Other European countries also incorporate secrecy not simply as a facet of the adoption process, when files are sealed, but at the time of birth. In Italy there is no requirement that the mother be entered onto the birth certificate of the child,[3] and in the Czech Republic[4] and Greece,[5] although the mother's identity is recorded, the birth records can be kept secret.

In addition to anonymous birth, in recent years there has been an increasing trend towards the creation of 'baby-boxes' throughout Central and Eastern Europe, which allow parents to leave children in the care of the state anonymously. This practice dates back to the 12th century in Italy, where Pope Innocent II installed foundling wheels in orphanages to prevent the more common practice of women drowning their unwanted children in the River Tiber. In modern times, baby-boxes more commonly take the form of an incubated crib in a hospital or child welfare centre. When a child is placed in the crib, a bell is rung, and the mother can leave anonymously before a carer comes to take the child. After a waiting period ranging from two to eight weeks, depending on the jurisdiction, the child is then placed for adoption.

Such boxes have spread dramatically across Europe, and can now be found in Austria, Belgium,[6] the Czech Republic, Denmark, Germany, Hungary, Italy, Latvia, Lithuania, Poland, Portugal, Russia, Slovakia and Switzerland.[7] The

---

[1]   Provided for in Article 341 Civil Code.

[2]   In Austria, the practice is somewhat different however, as will be discussed below.

[3]   Article 250 of the Civil Code does not make it mandatory for parents to recognise an illegitimate child, and if they choose not to do so, they will not be named on the birth certificate. If the child searches for information on his or her parents at a later date, this will not be disclosed if the parent wished for anonymity.

[4]   Section 67 Act No 20/1966 Sb on Care for Populace Health (as amended by Act No 422/2004).

[5]   K. BROWNE, S. CHOU, and K. WHITFIELD, *Child Abandonment and its Prevention in Europe* (2012), p. 21, available at http://resourcecentre.savethechildren.se/content/library/documents/child-abandonment-and-its-prevention-europe (last accessed 07.02.2013).

[6]   It should be noted that although the baby-box is legal in Belgium, abandoning a baby in it is illegal.

[7]   K. BROWNE, S. CHOU, and K. WHITFIELD, *supra* n. 5, p. 4. There is also an initiative to set up a baby-box in the Netherlands: RADIO NETHERLANDS WORLDWIDE, *Controversial Plan to Help Dutch Foundlings* (2011), available at www.rnw.nl/english/video/controversial-plan-help-dutch-foundlings (last accessed 22.10.2012). In many cases, the state itself has not set up the baby-boxes, and may in fact be officially opposed to them (for example in Belgium, Austria and the Czech Republic). However, where they have been established by non-governmental

number of boxes in each country varies: while only one box exists in Belgium, 45 can be found in Poland, 47 in the Czech Republic, and around 80 in Germany.[8]

While statistics are not available for all these countries, in 2009/2010 13 infants were left in Lithuania, 11 in the Czech Republic, seven in Slovakia, and six in both Austria and Latvia. In Hungary, 40 children were placed in incubators from 2000 to 2010,[9] and in Poland, 31 infants were placed from 2006 to 2010.[10] The largest numbers of children are placed in Germany, however, where 500 children were left in baby-boxes between 2000 and 2011.[11] These numbers are minimal in comparison to anonymous births in France, however, with approximately 600 women per year requesting anonymity under this legislation.[12]

2. DEFINING THE RIGHTS OF THE CHILD

The institution of 'baby-boxes' is popular among citizens – a Swiss poll in 2011 found that 87 per cent of participants thought baby-boxes were 'very useful or useful', and more than a quarter thought that every hospital should have one.[13] However, anonymous relinquishment and anonymous birth remain contentious issues from a child's rights perspective.

---

organisations, states are often reluctant to intervene, perhaps for political reasons as they fear the consequences if they shut down these facilities, and a child is found abandoned elsewhere. This was particularly obvious in Austria's discussions with the Committee on the Rights of the Child in September 2012. However, whether the state has provided the service itself, or simply allowed the establishment of baby-boxes by other entities within its jurisdiction, it is effectively sanctioning a mechanism under which children cannot know and be cared for by their own parents.

8   K. BROWNE, S. CHOU, and K. WHITFIELD, *supra* n. 5, p. 20.

9   Hungarian Department of Child and Youth Protection (2010), as quoted by K. BROWNE, S. CHOU, and K. WHITFIELD, *supra* n. 5.

10   K. BROWNE, S. CHOU, and K. WHITFIELD, *supra* n. 5, p. 9. Since there are 45 incubators placed in this country, this means that almost one third of them have not been used during this time.

11   Ibid. p. 20.

12   *Odièvre v France* [2003] ECHR 86 [36]. A similar situation exists in Austria, where in 2010 six newborns were placed in baby flaps, but 40 children were born anonymously (National Coalition for the Implementation of the UN Convention on the Rights of the Child: Austria, *Supplementary Report on the 3rd and 4th Report of Federal Republic of Austria to the United Nations, Pursuant to Article 44, Paragraph 1B of the UN Convention on the Rights of the Child* (2012), available at www.crin.org/docs/Austria_NCICRCA_CRC,OPAC,OPSC%20Report.pdf (last accessed 07.10.2012).

13   R. RAMESH, Spread of 'baby boxes' in Europe alarms United Nations (10 June 2012, *The Guardian*), available at www.guardian.co.uk/world/2012/jun/10/unitednations-europe-news (last accessed 22.09.2012). Further, the Committee on the Rights of the Child's recommendations to the Czech Republic in regard to baby-boxes created a furore of media attention and criticism, which spread over state borders to neighbouring Slovakia and Hungary, and drew recriminations from Members of the European Parliament.

First, they are in violation of Article 7 of the UN Convention on the Rights of the Child, which reads:

> 'The child shall be registered immediately after birth and shall have the right from birth to a name, the right to acquire a nationality and, as far as possible, the right to know and be cared for by his or her parents.'

Under this article, the right to 'know and be cared for' by parents is arguably joint and severable, with the right to 'know' being seen as the basis for a claim of a child to access to information on his or her origins.[14] However, the drafting is somewhat ambiguous. The term 'parent' is not defined in the Convention, and thus there has been some contention as to whether this article refers to the right of a child to know his or her *biological* parents, or his or her *legal* (e.g. adoptive) parents. In this respect, the United Kingdom lodged a declaration when ratifying the Convention, stating that: 'The United Kingdom interprets the references in the Convention to "parents" to mean only those persons who, as a matter of national law, are treated as parents'.[15]

It has also been argued that the use of the qualifying phrase 'as far as possible' indicates that children were not intended to have unimpeded access to information on their origins. The US delegation, whose wording was adopted in the final article, argued that particularly in the case of adopted children, it was not always possible or desirable for a child to know such information.[16] However, Geraldine Van Beuren rightly argues that this phrase should be read as relating to the practicality of providing the information, not the legality.[17] As will be seen below, information is not always available concerning the child's origins, which makes realisation of the right under Article 7 sometimes impossible in practice.

Perhaps as a result of this uncertainty, several states have felt the need to lodge reservations in relation to Article 7, to the effect that a failure to provide adopted children with information does not violate the Convention. For example, Poland states that:

> 'With respect to article 7 of the Convention, the Republic of Poland stipulates that the right of an adopted child to know its natural parents shall be subject to the limitations

---

[14] The English courts, for example, have made clear that this encompasses two separate rights: one to know, and the other to be cared for by, one's parents (see *Re H (Paternity: Blood Test)* [1996] 2 FLR 65).

[15] While the Committee on the Rights of the Child has indicated, albeit indirectly, that biological as well as legal parents are included under this article, and have used it as a basis for recommending that states ensure that a child can have access to information on his or her birth parents (see, for example, *Concluding Observations: France* (30 June 2004) CRC/C/15/Add.240, [23]), states have been slow to accept that this is an obligation under Article 7 as is discussed below.

[16] G. Van Beuren, Children's Access to Adoption Records: State Discretion or an Enforceable International Right? (1995) 58(1) *Modern Law Review*, pp. 37, 48.

[17] Ibid.

imposed by binding legal arrangements that enable adoptive parents to maintain the confidentiality of the child's origin.'

The Czech Republic also placed such a reservation, providing that 'the non-communication of a natural parent's name or natural parents' names to the child is not in contradiction with this provision'.

However, despite these reservations and areas of contention, the Committee on the Rights of the Child has made clear that denying the child access to information on his or her biological origins is in violation of Article 7, and that the state has a responsibility under the UNCRC to gather and conserve information concerning a child's identity.[18] As such, the Committee has taken a strong stance against the use of baby-boxes. In its Concluding Observations on the Czech Republic in 2011, the Committee strongly urged the government to end the programme as soon as possible, and instead address the root causes of child abandonment, including providing family planning, adequate counselling, social support and the prevention of risk pregnancies.[19] The Committee had previously expressed concern over the existence of such programmes in Slovakia and Austria.[20]

Anonymous birth has also been criticised, with the Committee telling France that it 'remains concerned that … the right to conceal the identity of the mother if she so wishes is not in conformity with the provisions of the Convention',[21] and recommending that it 'take all appropriate measures to fully enforce the child's right to know his or her biological parents and siblings, as enshrined in article 7 of the Convention and in the light of the principles of non-discrimination (art. 2) and the best interests of the child (art. 3).'[22] Similarly, in relation to Luxembourg, the Committee urged the state to take all necessary measures to eliminate anonymous birth and ensure that information on a child's parents is registered and kept on file to allow the child to know his or her origins at an appropriate time.[23]

---

18 United Nations Committee on the Rights of the Child, *Concluding Observations: Belgium* (18 June 2010) CRC/C/BEL/CO/3–4, [52].

19 United Nations Committee on the Rights of the Child, *Concluding Observations: Czech Republic* (4 August 2011) CRC/C/CZE/CO/3–4, [50].

20 United Nations Committee on the Rights of the Child, *Concluding Observations: Slovakia* (10 July 2007) CRC/C/SVK/CO/2, [41]; *Concluding Observations: Austria* (31 March 2005) CRC/C/15/Add.251, [29].

21 United Nations Committee on the Rights of the Child, *Concluding Observations: France* (30 June 2004) CRC/C/15/Add.240, [23].

22 United Nations Committee on the Rights of the Child, *Concluding Observations: France* (11 June 2009) CRC/C/FRA/CO/4, [44].

23 United Nations Committee on the Rights of the Child, *Concluding Observations: Luxembourg* (31 March 2005) CRC/C/15/Add.250, [28]–[29]. However, Luxembourg has submitted a reservation in relation to article 7 of the Convention, stating that it believes that this 'presents no obstacle to the legal process in respect of anonymous births, which is deemed to be in the interest of the child, as provided under article 3 of the Convention.'

In addition to these problems identified by the Committee, anonymous birth and relinquishment allow the mother to unilaterally decide the extent to which a child's rights can be exercised. This applies not only in relation to information on origins, but also concerning the right of the child to stay with his or her family where possible. It gives no opportunity to the authorities to determine whether there is a chance for the child to stay with the family if adequate assistance and support were provided, as is required by Article 19 of the UNCRC, and further prevents any investigation of the ability of members of the wider birth family to provide kinship care. More importantly, however, it deprives the child and his or her father from establishing any relationship, denying the father the chance to care for the child if he so wishes.

An example of this can be seen in France, the father of a child born under anonymous birth is denied any right to establish a relationship with his child. Even if he is aware of the child's birth, he cannot legally recognise him or her, and cannot establish paternity. This was seen in *Association Enfance et Familles v F et A*,[24] where the father legally recognised the child prior to birth. The mother told him that the child was stillborn, but eventually confessed that the child had been born anonymously. The father sought to establish paternity and custody of the child, but in the meantime, an adoption order had been made. The Court of Appeal held that the father's recognition of the child was not valid, since it related to a child who was legally deemed not to have been born to the mother.[25] As such, the mother has the opportunity to unilaterally prevent the father from establishing paternity or caring for the child, and deny the child the right to know and be cared for by his or her father.

While the French courts have accepted this situation, the Spanish Supreme Court was not similarly permissive. When declaring anonymous birth unconstitutional, the Court also noted the incongruity of the fact that while paternity can be coercively imposed on the father, the mother is free to decide whether to continue the pregnancy, or completely cut any ties with the child, and has a clear path to avoid any obligations.[26]

The right of the mother to unilaterally decide whether a child is placed for adoption, and to control the relationship between him or her and the father, has been argued to be part of the reproductive autonomy of mothers. Lori Chambers in particular has suggested that an unfettered right to release a newborn child for adoption is an essential component of a mother's autonomy and dignity, which should be exercised exclusively. She argues that if obliged to notify the father and allow him a chance to care for the child, the mother might instead

---

[24]   Court of Appeal of Riom, 16 December 1997 (1998) JCP II 10147.
[25]   The mother is deemed under French law never to have given birth, so the father could not claim paternity of her child.
[26]   Recurso de Casacion num. 2854/1994, Sentencia del TS de 21 septiembre 1999.

choose abortion.[27] Relinquishment, in her view, should be seen as an act of caring for the child, not as an act of abandonment,[28] and thus the mother should be permitted to decide how and where the child gets placed, and whether the father is involved.

The right of a child to be cared for by his or her parents is not predicated on the sex of that parent, and there is no reason why the mother should be permitted to choose the involvement of the father in the child's life, even if she has been the one who has given birth. If the mother fears that the father would harm the child, this could be dealt with by the child welfare and criminal justice systems; in all other cases, it should not be for the mother to decide the extent to which the child's right to know and be cared for by his or her parents should be exercised.

Further, in relation to a woman's reproductive autonomy, where abortion is *not* permitted, or only permitted under very limited circumstances,[29] it has been argued that anonymous birth and baby-boxes are mechanisms that can allow a woman to take back control of her body, in line with her individual rights.[30] The problem with this argument is that while abortion allows a woman the right to control her own body, once the child is born, it is not a question of the mother's reproductive rights but of her right to refuse motherhood, and to escape defined societal roles and the moral and legal obligations imposed on parents. However, these latter rights are not predicated on anonymity, but can be achieved simply through placing the child for adoption in a conventional manner.

3. COMPLIMENTARY OR CONTRADICTORY? THE BALANCING OF MATERNAL AND CHILD RIGHTS

The most comprehensive judicial discussion of anonymous relinquishment in Europe was the controversial case of *Odièvre v France*[31] before the European Court of Human Rights. In this case, the Court found that anonymous birth as traditionally practiced in France, allowing the mother to refuse to allow the

---

[27] L. CHAMBERS, Newborn Adoption: Birth Mothers, Genetic Fathers, and Reproductive Autonomy (2010) 26 *Canadian Journal of Family Law*, pp. 339, 343–5.

[28] In this respect, see the English case of *Watson v Nikolaisen* [1955] 2 QB 286, in which the High Court held that where a mother had given a child to an adoptive family she had not abandoned the child, as she had made provision for its care by placing her with people who desired to adopt her and in whom she had confidence.

[29] See, for example, Andorra, Cyprus, Ireland, Malta, Monaco, Poland.

[30] N. LEFAUCHEUR, The French 'Tradition' of Anonymous Birth: The Lines of Argument (2004) 18 *International Journal of Law, Policy and the Family*, pp. 319, 331.

[31] *Odièvre v France* [2003] ECHR 86.

child access to any identifying information, was not in violation of the European Convention on Human Rights. Interestingly, it came to this decision without referring to the child's rights under the UNCRC at any stage. This case has far-reaching implications not just for anonymous birth and relinquishment, but for the wider question of a child's access to origins in general in Europe.

The application was brought by a French woman, born in 1965, whose mother had requested that her birth be kept secret. She was thus placed for adoption anonymously. In 1990, the applicant was able to obtain non-identifying information about her natural family, but her applications for further identifying information about her parents and natural siblings were refused. She made an application to the ECtHR, complaining that her inability to obtain this information prevented her from finding out her personal history, in violation of Article 8 of the Convention.

In presenting her case, the applicant argued that mothers who asked for their identity to be kept secret did so through lack of autonomy related to social and economic issues. She contended that anonymous birth thus constituted an act of violence that was easily avoidable, and that concerns for the mother could be addressed by providing her with the necessary assistance and support, rather than promising anonymity.[32]

This argument is supported by research by Bilson and Markova, who found that in the majority of cases, women openly abandoning their babies did not want to relinquish the child, but felt that they could not care for him or her.[33] It also appears to be reinforced by the submissions of the French Government itself in *Odièvre*, which stated that there were three main categories of women who chose to give birth anonymously:

(1) young women who were not yet independent;
(2) young women still living with their parents in Muslim families originating from North African or sub-Saharan African societies in which pregnancy outside marriage was a great dishonour; and
(3) isolated women with financial difficulties (the youngest, many of whom were under 25, were single mothers; many of the older women were over 35 and for the most part separated or divorced or had been abandoned, some being victims of domestic violence, with several children to look after).[34]

Regarding the circumstances that led the women to seek the confidentiality of anonymous birth, the Government suggested that 'the stated reasons sometimes concealed more serious problems, such as rape or incest, which were not always

---

32   Ibid.
33   A. BILSON and G. MARKOVA, But You Should See Their Families: Preventing Child Abandonment and Promoting Social Inclusion in Countries in Transition (2007) 12(3) *Social Work & Social Sciences Review*, p. 29.
34   *Odièvre v France* [2003] ECHR 86 [36].

revealed by those concerned.'[35] The Government argued that protecting these women justified the practice of anonymous birth, allowing them to give birth in a controlled and safe environment, while preventing abortion or child abandonment. This was accepted by the majority of the Court, with Judge Greve in his concurring opinion arguing that at the prenatal stage, the rights and interests of the mother and child converge: in these circumstances, he held that it is in the best interests of the child to be born in a safe environment, without putting either the child's or the mother's life in jeopardy, no matter what the future consequences.

Such considerations were also characterised as a balance between the competing rights of the child himself or herself, with Judge Greve arguing that '[t]he primary interest of the child is to be born and born under circumstances where its health is not unnecessarily put at risk by birth in circumstances in which its mother tries to secure secrecy even when that means that she will be deprived of professional assistance when in labour.'[36]

These arguments do little to address the true issues at stake, which are the underlying social, economic and cultural circumstances that lead women to feel that they have no other option but to take such a step. It should not be a dichotomy between the child's safety and knowing his or her identity, but instead states should institute measures to ensure that mothers are not put in the position to have to make this choice.

The principal argument in favour of baby-boxes relies on the same justifications; that is, the right of the child to life. Those in favour argue that if baby-boxes did not exist, children would be killed by mothers unable to cope or be abandoned in unsafe places.[37] However, there is no indication that either anonymous birth or baby-boxes have had any effect on the number of abortions or children illegally abandoned or killed. Danner et al found that despite the provision of anonymous birth and baby-boxes in Austria, there are still cases of abandonment and infanticide, and suggest that the women who relinquish their children anonymously are not in fact those who are in crisis, or would otherwise kill their babies.[38] Similarly, a German study found that the number of infants abandoned illegally has not dropped since baby-boxes were introduced.[39]

---

[35]   Ibid.

[36]   *Odièvre v France* [2003] ECHR 86.

[37]   Director of the NGO 'Our Children Foundation' as quoted by R. TAIT, Baby boxes in Czech Republic: 'the first thing should be the child's right to life' (10 June 2012, *The Guardian*) available at www.guardian.co.uk/world/2012/jun/10/czech-republic-baby-box (last accessed 15.10.2012); Representative of Hamburg's SterniPark e.V., as quoted by K. MOORE, Europe: Controversial 'Baby Box' Lets Mothers Abandon Infants Safely (4 June 2005, Radio Free Europe Radio Liberty) available at www.rferl.org/content/article/1059124.html (last accessed 22.09.2012).

[38]   C. DANNER et al, Anonymous Birth and Neonaticide in Tyrol (2005) 209(5) *Z Geburtshilfe Neonatol*, p. 192.

[39]   DEUTSCHER ETHIKRAT, *Anonymous Relinquishment of Infants* (2009), p. 25. A study by Terre des Hommes in Germany found that from 1999 to 2009, over 30 infants were found abandoned in places other than baby-boxes each year (with the exception of 2005, where 29 infants were

Furthermore, in the Czech Republic, children can be placed in a baby-box up to one year of age.[40] In such cases, there appears little reason to allow a child to be placed in this manner, rather than through social services. It is no longer an issue of 'women in specific situations who unfortunately keep their pregnancy a secret and fear to approach official institutions' – as put by Members of the European Parliament[41] – but a kind of officially sanctioned alternative to traditional adoption.[42] This was confirmed by the auditor of the Foundation for Abandoned Children (Statim) in the Czech Republic, who said that the boxes were needed to solve the problem of abandoned children, as 'it quickens the adoption process, which is very slow in our country.'[43]

The use of baby-boxes for such a purpose, effectively bypassing alternative care procedures, is in clear violation of the UNCRC. The child has a right not to be placed in alternative care without an investigation into whether he or she could stay with his or her family, either with the parents themselves, or with the wider family in another form of kinship care. There is an obligation on states to undertake a fully informed determination of a child's specific situation prior to undertaking measures that would deprive him or her of these rights, a determination which anonymous relinquishment diverts and effectively prevents.

In particular, a fast track into adoption also raises serious ethical considerations where children are subsequently placed for intercountry adoption. If there has been no attempt to address the issues behind the relinquishment, including the provision of adequate support and assistance, it raises the possibility that impoverished and vulnerable families are giving up their children because they cannot cope, to be taken in by wealthy foreign families. Such a transfer of children from poor to rich should be considered very carefully.

It may also be that anonymous relinquishment actually creates a new market for legal abandonment, rather than solving problems for mothers who are actually in distress. In particular, the availability of this simple procedure, without any associated checks or assistance, may cause pressure to be placed on mothers to abandon their child, similar to the pressure that may be placed on mothers to have abortions. Although for obvious reasons little is known about the demographic of persons placing children in baby-boxes, the University of

found abandoned) (TERRE DES HOMMES, *Hilfe für Kinder in Not* (2012) available at www.tdh.de/was-wir-tun/themen-a-z/babyklappe-und-anonyme-geburt/statistik.html (last accessed 15.06.2012).

[40] K. BROWNE, S. CHOU, and K. WHITFIELD, *supra* n. 5, p. 18.
[41] Z. ROITHOVA, Letter to Professor Yanghee Lee, Chairwoman, *Committee on the Rights of the Child* (14 July 2011) available at www.eppgroup.eu/press/pdoc11/110714letter-to-un-chairwoman.pdf (last accessed 30 September 2012).
[42] This was also noted in the report by DEUTSCHER ETHIKRAT, *supra* n. 39, p. 31.
[43] R. TAIT, *supra* n. 37.

Nottingham's report on child abandonment cites anecdotal evidence provided by porters from one hospital in Hungary, in which 15 out of the 16 children placed in incubators in that hospital were placed by men, not women.[44] Similarly, reports are now emerging about abuse of the system of anonymous birth in Spain throughout the regime of Franco, when mothers were told that their children had died, only to find later that the child had been registered as an anonymous birth and subsequently adopted.[45] In these circumstances, such mechanisms may well be failing the mother, as well as the child.

In this area, anonymous birth has considerable advantages over baby-boxes, as it allows women to go anonymously to hospital and receive adequate medical care, rather than giving birth in unsafe conditions, trying to continue to conceal the pregnancy. As Maria Herczog, a member of the UN Committee on the Rights of the Child, argues, the baby-box programme 'sends out the mistaken message to pregnant women in crisis that they are right to continue with hiding their pregnancies, giving birth under uncontrolled circumstances, and then abandoning their babies anonymously, losing the possibility to connect with them again.'[46]

Anonymous birth also provides the possibility that counselling can be given to the mother, thus ensuring that her decision is not made under pressure from others, and that it is adequately informed. Research from Germany suggest that between 50 and 75 per cent of women who sought anonymity on birth changed their minds once counselling was provided,[47] further supporting the argument that anonymous birth and relinquishment stem from a failure of the state to address social, cultural and economic issues. As Simon Wright, head of Child Survival at Save the Children, stated: '[b]aby boxes are a short-cut response to a much bigger problem, and do not deal with any of the underlying reasons why babies are abandoned. Instead of setting them up, governments should concentrate on giving women choice and control over having children ... In the long run, they are not good for mothers or children.'[48]

In the case of anonymous birth, the mother can also be encouraged to leave some details for her child, so that the child has some future opportunity of gaining at least limited information about his or her parent(s). Even if this practice is still not in conformity with the UNCRC, it is better than the child

---

[44]   K. Browne, S. Chou, and K. Whitfield, *supra* n. 5, p. 29.

[45]   K. Adler, Spain's stolen babies and the families who lived a lie (15 November 2012, *BBC News*), available at www.bbc.co.uk/news/magazine-15335899 (last accessed 15.11.2012).

[46]   A. Szoboszlay, 'Baby boxes' polarise Hungary (11 June 2012, *The Guardian*) available at www.guardian.co.uk/world/2012/jun/11/baby-boxes-polarise-hungary (last accessed 19.08.2012).

[47]   Deutscher Ethikrat, *supra* n. 39, p. 28.

[48]   E. Fernandes, Abandoned... in a postbox for babies: The shocking rise of newborns being left in 'adoption hatches' by mothers unable to cope (7 July 2012, *Daily Mail*) available at www.dailymail.co.uk/femail/article-2170150/Babywiege-Newborns-abandoned-baby-boxes-German-hospital.html (last accessed 22.09.2012).

receiving no information at all. This was acknowledged by the Committee on the Rights of the Child in its 2012 Concluding Observations on Austria, when it urged the government

> 'to undertake all measures necessary to end the practice of anonymous abandonment and expeditiously strengthen and promote alternatives such as the possibility of anonymous births at hospitals as a measure of last resort to avoid abandonment and or death of the child, and to keep a confidential record of the parents to which the child could access at a later stage, taking into account the duty to fully comply with all provisions of the Convention.'[49]

This recommendation rests on the unique nature of Austrian anonymous birth, where the mother does not have to leave her name with the hospital, but must leave identifying information with the child welfare authorities for the child to access when he or she reaches 14 years of age. A similar law has recently been introduced in Germany, allowing women to give a false name to give birth in hospital and for the birth certificate, but requiring that their correct personal data be sealed and stored in a central agency for access by the child once he or she turns 16.[50]

These solutions provide a more nuanced approach to the balancing of rights in this area, allowing qualified privacy for the mother, while ensuring the child can have access to information at a later date. It is by no means satisfactory that women continue to feel the need to hide their pregnancy and motherhood, and it would be optimal if anonymous birth of any kind was not required; however, until these issues can be addressed at a deeper social, cultural and economic level, it is necessary to provide a mechanism to ensure that the rights of both women and the children they bear are protected.

Although the rights of the child are in some respect postponed in such an arrangement, this is an acceptable compromise. Unlike anonymous birth as it is traditionally practiced, with the power of veto placed in the hands of the mother, or the use of baby-boxes, the Austrian and German approaches protect the rights of both parties, giving neither paramountcy.

4. CONCLUSION

The prevalence of anonymous relinquishment and traditional anonymous birth in Europe, and the rate at which these practices are spreading, is particularly worrying from the perspective of the rights of the child.

---

[49] UNITED NATIONS COMMITTEE ON THE RIGHTS OF THE CHILD, *Concluding Observations: Austria* (5 October 2012) CRC/C/AUT/CO/3–4, [30].

[50] Gesetz zum Ausbau der Hilfen für Schwangere und zur Regelung der vertraulichen Geburt (SchwHiAusbauG) v. 28.08.2013, BGBl. I S. 3458.

As has been shown throughout the chapter, these practices violate the right of the child to be cared for by his or her parents where possible, by preventing the provision of adequate support to be given to parents and services to ensure that there is every available chance that the family can stay together. Further, they prevent a thorough examination of the other alternative care options before adoption, potentially rushing children into adoption unnecessarily.

Most importantly, however, traditional anonymous birth and 'baby-boxes' represent a failure of the positive obligation on the state to collect information on the child's origins, which effectively curtails any future search into his or her identity, in clear violation of the rights of the child under international law.

As such, there is a need to reassess the way in which society deals with the issue of child abandonment, placing a greater emphasis on the rights of the child, and achieving a real balance between these and the rights of the mother. Germany and Austria have taken the lead; it is time for other states to follow.

CROSS-BORDER SURROGACY: TIME FOR A CONVENTION?

Martin ENGEL

Contents

As the law of parentage is striving to meet the challenges of new reproductive technologies, dealing with cross-border surrogacies emerges as one of the most pressing topics in international family law. The current legal situation as regards surrogacy is quite diverse – throughout the world but also within Europe. Legal diversity has recently made a lot of people engage in so-called 'procreative tourism': coming from a country with a rather strict approach, they commission women in one of the more liberal countries to bear a child for them, and once the baby is born, they try to take it to their home country, thereby obviating the surrogacy ban that prevents them from entrusting a surrogate mother at home. European courts struggle with a coherent approach on how to treat those citizens who have gone abroad to have a baby. Meanwhile, legal research and the Hague Conference on Private International Law are thinking about a convention in order to ease the cross-border recognition of surrogacy.

1. INTRODUCTION

With the growing technical possibilities of assisted reproduction, the once monolithic idea of parenthood falls to pieces. Motherhood in particular splits up into genetic, gestational, and social motherhood – three roles that, once bound together, can now be taken over by two or even three different women. An increasingly popular and socially somewhat accepted model involving multiple mothers for one child is surrogacy: a surrogate mother commits herself to carry an embryo for another woman who for reasons of reluctance, age or medical conditions cannot or does not want to do so.[1] Usually,[2] one of the intended parents gives his sperm for the fertilisation of an egg that may stem either from the surrogate mother herself (traditional surrogacy) or from the intended mother or an egg donor (gestational surrogacy).

While surrogacy has been technically feasible for decades, it has only recently become a thriving business and thereby a notable case driver for European courts. Between 2006 and 2010, figures have increased nearly tenfold,[3] meanwhile amounting to some small four-digit number of surrogacy cases involving intended parents from European countries every year.[4] Most surrogacies take place in India, Ukraine, California, and Central America. The direct costs of a surrogacy range between about US \$15,000 and US \$100,000, depending on the price level of the respective country.[5] In India alone, the volume of business amounted to roughly €50 million in 2012.[6] New markets like Thailand are emerging and promising better service at low cost.[7]

---

[1] Whereas public opinion is split as to whether surrogacy should be supported, intended parents and their children hardly face discrimination or any other lack of acceptance; see JADVA et al., 27 *Hum. Reprod.*, pp. 3008 et seq. (2012), and in particular for Germany KATZORKE/KOLODZIEJ, in: KETTNER (ed.), *Biomedizin und Menschenwürde*, pp. 103, 119 et seq. (2004).

[2] As only in rare cases are both intended parents lacking in fertility, it is only once in a blue moon that the sperm comes from a donor.

[3] TRIMMINGS/BEAUMONT, in: TRIMMINGS/BEAUMONT (eds.), *International Surrogacy Arrangements*, pp. 483 et seq. (2013), summing up the four institutions participating in their study.

[4] There is no comprehensive survey on the number of surrogacies commissioned by European couples. However, an extrapolation of existing subsets such as the 150–200 surrogacies put out by French couples alone (PERREAU-SAUSSINE/SAUVAGE, in: TRIMMINGS/BEAUMONT (eds.), fn. 3, p. 119) or the up to 1,000 babies purportedly commissioned by Britons (see http://bit.ly/MK1Ayn [last accessed 18.01.2014]) leads to the mentioned estimation.

[5] To cite but a few: SVITNEV, 20 *Reprod. Biom. Onl.*, pp. 892, 894 (2010), for Russia; HELMS, 66 *StAZ*, pp. 114, 118 et seq. (2013) with further references.

[6] This figure results from an estimate of a low four-digit number of children born through surrogacy and a medium five-digit amount of US dollars paid per case. The Confederation of Indian Industry is frequently cited with a study according to which the predicted revenues for 2012 amounted to \$2.3 billion; see e.g., http://bit.ly/GDK80p (last accessed 18.01.2014). Those figures, relate to the whole medical tourism industry; see MOHAPATRA, 21 *Annals Health L.*, p. 191 (2012). The figure of \$450 million mentioned by MOHAPATRA, though, is not correct either, as it also relates to the whole reproductive segment of the Indian tourism market; see SMERDON, 39 *Cumb. L. Rev.*, pp. 15, 24 (2008).

[7] See e.g. the comprehensive range of surrogacy packages, available at www.newlifethailand.net/Financial (last accessed 18.01.2014). An overview of the market mechanisms in place is

Whereas the industry works quite smoothly on the national level, problems arise with respect to cross-border business. There is considerable legal diversity as to medically-assisted reproduction all over the world, leading to difficulties for courts which have to decide on the recognition of foreign official certificates and judicial decisions. Surrogacy is sometimes seen as a legitimate way to overcome infertility and to realise the desire for a child in mixed as well as in same-sex relationships.[8] At the same time, opponents of surrogacy point out the degradation of children to a merchant good and the exploitation of women in need.[9] Legal diversity leads to legal uncertainty, which in turn is mirrored by intended families experiencing a stage of factual precariousness as private international law lacks a coherent approach on the applicable law and the recognition of awards.

This paper does not comprehensively enlarge upon the legal situation in various different jurisdictions as was thoroughly done by an international research team constituted at the University of Aberdeen.[10] Instead, it attempts to give an overview of the main frictions due to legal diversity in the realm of international surrogacy laws (section 2). The article then traces the problems that European courts currently face as to the recognition of foreign decisions on the question of parenthood (section 3). Subsequently, it deals with the consequences which the missing recognition of (intended) parenthood bears for a young family with a child born by a surrogate mother (section 4). The paper eventually aims at sketching out a meaningful approach on how the law might handle surrogacy cases involving children born abroad without disadvantaging the child (section 5). The final section concludes (section 6).

2. LEGAL DIVERSITY IN INTERNATIONAL SURROGACY LAW

Surrogacy laws are everything but internationally coherent: regulations range from a total ban to liberal approaches, whereas some countries do not rule on

---

provided by BLYTH/FARRAND, 91 *Crit. Soc. Policy*, pp. 91, 99 et seq. (2005). The language of children as 'products' or 'market commodities' is analysed by FREEMAN, 4 *Int. J. Children's R.*, pp. 295 et seq. (1996). A critical example of commodification language is provided by HATZIS, in: BOELE-WOELKI (ed.), *Perspectives for the Unification and Harmonisation of Family Law in Europe*, pp. 412, 423, 429 (2003) who compares surrogate mothers with an oven, calls their economic deprivation marginal, and argues that, as surrogacy yields children, its legalisation is imperatively demanded by children's rights.

8   To cite but a few KINDREGAN, 21 *J. Am. Acad. Matrim. L.*, pp. 43 et seq. (2008); BEN-ASHER, 30 *Cardozo L. Rev.*, pp. 1885 et seq. (2009), convincingly criticising the 'cure paradigm', at the same time losing sight of human rights.

9   ATWELL, 20 *Colum. Hum. R. L. Rev.*, pp. 1 et seq. (1988). According to a longitudinal study carried out by JADVA et al., 18 *Hum. Reprod.*, pp. 2196, 2200 et seq. (2003), 12 per cent of the participating surrogate mothers were under psychological or medical treatment due to mental health problems; see also TSCHUDIN/GRIESINGER, 10 *Gyn. Endokrin.*, pp. 135, 137 (2012).

10   See TRIMMINGS/BEAUMONT (eds.), fn. 3, giving a most extensive overview of the legal situation in 25 major jurisdictions; BRUNET et al., *A Comparative Study on the Regime of Surrogacy in EU Member States* (2013).

surrogacy at all. At the same time, there is a lot of movement in the field: some of the rigid regulators currently consider allowing surrogacy at least in certain specific cases in order to cope with the factual problems of legal arbitrage, while some of the liberal countries try to ban foreigners from the market in order to prevent a systematic violation of women's rights. This leads to intended parents travelling to the most favourable jurisdiction but still facing severe problems when returning home.

2.1. CURRENT LEGISLATION ON SURROGACY

There are a couple of countries with genuinely surrogacy-friendly laws attracting the majority of worldwide surrogacy to their territories. Amongst them are the US state of California, India and Ukraine. Here, surrogacy is deliberately tolerated by the legislator which has enhanced those countries' reputation as reliable locations for the surrogacy business. Argentina is about to pass a bill which allows for gestational surrogacy even if it has to be preceded by a court judgment, but it must not be remunerated. Several European countries like Greece and the United Kingdom have also liberalised their family laws but have so far not acquired notable mandates from the international side.[11] The Netherlands has not banned surrogacy but has forbidden agencies arranging surrogacies as well as public offers by or searches for surrogate mothers.[12]

In many, if not most other European countries, surrogacy is forbidden by law.[13] A typical example of tight regulation is Germany. The German legislator attempts to avoid split motherhood, to protect the social relationship between the gestational mother and the baby, and to prevent the exploitation of poor women.[14] According to §1(1) of the German Embryo Protection Act (ESchG) and §§13c, 14b of the German Adoption Agency Act (AdVermiG), someone who assists in effecting a surrogacy or who arranges surrogacies is liable to prosecution. Any private agreement to enter into surrogacy is deemed immoral and thus void.[15] A payment claim stemming from such a contract cannot be

---

[11] Both jurisdictions demand that intended parents have at least a temporary inland domicile, which apparently discourages prospective parents; see section 54(4)(b) of the British Human Fertilisation and Embryology Act 2008 and Article 8 of the Greek Law No. 3089/2002.

[12] See CURRY-SUMNER/VONK, in: TRIMMINGS/BEAUMONT (eds.), fn. 3, pp. 273 et seq.

[13] Even in the few more liberal European countries, surrogacy agreements are not enforceable and the surrogate is initially regarded as the legal mother of the child; see TODOROVA, fn. 13, p. 19.

[14] See Bundestag paper 11/8057, pp. 12 et seq. and Bundestag paper 13/4899, p. 82; SEIDL, 8 *FPR*, pp. 402 et seq. (2002).

[15] Higher Regional Court (OLG) of Hamm, decision dated 2 December 1985, file no. 11 W 18/85; District Court (LG) of Freiburg, decision dated 25 March 1987, file no. 8 O 556/86; SACK/ FISCHINGER, in: STAUDINGER, *Bürgerliches Gesetzbuch* §138, para. 614 (2011); critical COESTER-WALTJEN, 35 *NJW*, pp. 2528, 2531 et seq. (1982).

enforced by means of public authorities. Other European countries like France and Spain have enacted similar restrictions, but with different administrative and criminal sanctions.[16] This indeed effectively averts surrogacies on their territories as it does in most if not all countries with rigid regulation.[17]

2.2. PROCREATIONAL LEGAL ARBITRAGE

The fact that surrogacy to a large extent emerges as a cross-border phenomenon is partly due to intended parents trying to exploit price differences. However, so-called 'procreative tourism'[18] is also a result of maximum legal diversity in the international realm. The legislative power of restrictive countries factually ends at their borders: so far, there is a considerable number of their citizens whom they could not effectively prevent from obtaining a baby abroad.[19]

The phenomenon of legal arbitrage is well known from other fields of law where it works perfectly well because the rather restrictive countries rarely attempt to rule on activities outside their borders.[20] This is, however, different in the ethically coined realm of family law. Here, the jurisdictions with strict approaches regarding surrogacy do not want their citizens to evade their rules.[21] And their law eventually catches the refugees as soon as they return to its reach, i.e. as soon as the intended parents bring the newborn baby home. The result is a clash between two quite different systems of family law, which materialises in the home country authorities not recognising the legal effects surrounding surrogacy in general and parenthood in particular which the intended parents were aiming at.

If the child was born in a *ius soli* country like the United States, the child will be easily issued with a passport and will often be able to follow the intended

---

16   For Spain, see Article 10 of the Spanish Assisted Reproductive Technology Act (Ley 14/2006, de 26 de mayo, sobre técnicas de reproducción humana asistida), see OREJUDO PRIETO DE LOS MOZOS, in: TRIMMINGS/BEAUMONT (eds.), fn. 3, pp. 347 et seq. For France, see Article 16-7 of the French Civil Code (Code civil) and Article 227-12 of the French Criminal Code (Code pénale), see also PERREAU-SAUSSINE/SAUVAGE, in: TRIMMINGS/BEAUMONT (eds.), fn. 3, pp. 119, 120 et seq.

17   Similar legislation has been enacted in Denmark, Norway, Austria, Sweden, and Switzerland.

18   BLYTH/FARRAND, 91 *Crit. Soc. Policy*, pp. 91, 92 (2005).

19   In theory, they might consider punishing intended parents for obtaining the baby abroad; however, so far this has not seemed to be feasible for those legislators who have thought about it; an example is France where a commission proposed in 2008 that children born to a non-authorised surrogate should pay for their parents' mistake, see MIRKOVIC, *Dalloz*, pp. 1944 et seq. (2008).

20   See e.g. EIDENMÜLLER/ENGERT/HORNUF, 10 *EBOR*, p. 1 (2009) in the field of international corporate law. There is no reasonable difference between 'legal arbitrage' and 'regulatory arbitrage'.

21   According to RAUSCHER, in STAUDINGER, *Bürgerliches Gesetzbuch* §1591, para. 14, family law is the only means which the legislator can use to prevent reproductive tourism. Meanwhile, PENNINGS, 19 *Hum. Reprod.*, pp. 2689 et seq. (2004) sees reproductive tourism as a 'safety valve that reduces moral conflict' – apparently according to the principle 'out of sight, out of mind'.

---

parents to their home country. In this case, problems do not arise before the new family could settle at home. If, however, child nationality depends on parentage, this means that the intended parents need their own jurisdiction to acknowledge their parenthood right from the beginning because without at least one of them being recognised as a legal parent, the child will not be issued with a passport from the local embassy at his place of birth.[22] To establish legal parentage here is anything but quick and easy: in the vast majority of jurisdictions, motherhood is initially attached to the woman who carried the child.[23] Furthermore, many surrogate mothers are married, which makes the laws of most countries[24] presume her husband to be the father. This impedes the child in getting the same passport as his intended parents who thus have to challenge the parenthood of the surrogate or her husband. Motherhood is contestable almost nowhere;[25] and while fatherhood is contestable almost everywhere, this takes a significant amount of time – time that intended parents are not willing to spend in a foreign country. They will thus apply for a passport on the uncertain ground of general legal principles like Article 8 ECHR or try to be immediately entered on the birth certificate – which, in turn, is not recognised by many European authorities and courts for reasons of public policy.[26]

The question thus arises as to whether intended parenthood should be internationally recognised so that the babies do not end up 'stateless and parentless'.[27] This issue is not only of momentary importance: it will remain urgent even if some European countries permit certain forms of surrogacy in the near future, because as long as there is any legal diversity in the field, legal arbitrage and therefore the problem of recognition will remain.

2.3. CURRENT DEVELOPMENTS

Taking into account the described legal and factual difficulties with cross-border surrogacies, legislators all over the world have lately noticed a need for the modernisation of their surrogacy laws. Anyway, only a few countries have already

---

[22] See §4 section 1 of the German Citizenship Act (Staatsangehörigkeitsgesetz, StAG).
[23] e.g. §1591 of the German Civil Code (Bürgerliches Gesetzbuch, BGB). See, with special regard to the French exception, SCHWENZER, in SCHWENZER (ed.), *Tensions Between Legal, Biological, and Social Conceptions of Parentage*, pp. 3 et seq. (2007).
[24] e.g. §1592 No. 1 of the German Civil Code (BGB).
[25] One example of legislation that opens motherhood to being declared void is Greece; see Article 1464 of the Greek Civil Code.
[26] See e.g. Superior Court of Justice (KG) of Berlin, decision dated 1 August 2013, file no. 1 W 413/12; an appeal is currently pending at the German Federal Court of Justice (BGH), file no. XII ZB 463/13; Spanish Directorate General of the Civil Registry and the Notary (Dirección General de los Registros y del Notariado, DGRN), decision dated 18 February 2009, file no. 2575/2008.
[27] This was the wording in the Royal High Court of Justice, decision dated 9 December 2008, file no. 2008 EWHC 3030, 'X&Y (Foreign Surrogacy)'.

reworked their laws since the turn of the millennium.[28] Interestingly, there is a drive towards a modest but conditioned liberalisation of the surrogacy market.

On the one hand, the factual availability of surrogacy options abroad makes people in restrictive countries think about cautiously liberalising their own legislation as they see that they cannot completely prevent their citizens from travelling for a baby. It might be regarded as advantageous to have surrogacy under tight control instead of being at the mercy of a foreign legislator setting loose conditions and a lower level of protection for surrogate mothers.[29] Of course, it is questionable whether a cautious liberalisation would really bring an end to procreative tourism as those intended parents who do not meet the requirements of their own country's legislation will travel anyway.

On the other hand, the heavy tourism especially to poorer countries like India allows their governments to think about protecting their female citizens from exploitation by people from wealthy nations. It is an open secret that it is first and foremost well-off people from industrialised countries who can afford to commission a surrogate and that it is frequently[30] indigent women from third world countries who – often under substantial pressure – 'opt' for surrogacy in order to improve the living conditions for themselves, their husbands, and their children.[31] A recent proposal for legislation by the Indian Union Health Ministry would – if implemented – ban foreigners from surrogacy in India.[32] Critics and pressure groups have promptly issued a warning that this might diminish the surrogacy business by 90 per cent and cause significant economic damage to a whole commercial sector.[33]

---

[28]   In Europe, these are for example Greece (2002), the United Kingdom (2002 and 2008), and Russia (2011). Currently, new legislation is under consideration in Belgium, the Czech Republic, France, Germany, and the Ukraine; however, immediate action is not expected.

[29]   This might be the rationale of the current Argentinian plans to cautiously liberalise surrogacy laws; a similar approach is taken by a German research group on a new Reproductive Medicine Act, see GASSNER et al., *Fortpflanzungsmedizingesetz, Augsburg-Münchner-Entwurf* (2013).

[30]   There is disagreement amongst legal scholars as to the extent to which surrogate mothers voluntarily and without any pressure agree to carry a baby for the intended parents. TEMAN, 67 *Social Sci. Med.*, p. 1104 (2007) indeed has a point that the exploitation of women in conjunction with surrogacy might be widely overestimated. However, her estimation of more than 99 per cent of surrogates voluntarily relinquishing the child seems highly unlikely as the studies she is referring to solely concern surrogacies carried out in the United States and the United Kingdom. For example, BLYTH, 12 *J. Reprod. Infant Psychol.*, pp. 189, 196 (1994) observes that 'the experience of being a surrogate mother is neither problem-free nor necessarily as horrendous as reported by some surrogate mothers'; in the study by BASLINGTON, 7 *J. Health Psychol.*, pp. 57, 64 et seq. (2002), three out of 14 surrogates said that leaving the baby was the worst part of their experience; however, there was a general notion that unhappy feelings soon disappeared.

[31]   RADIN, 100 *Harv. L. Rev.*, pp. 1849, 1930 (1987). Admittedly, there are a few counterexamples, especially with surrogates from richer countries such as the US; see PRETORIUS, *Surrogate Motherhood*, p. 18 (1994).

[32]   Draft Assisted Reproductive Technology (Regulation) Bill.

[33]   See for example http://read.bi/19PRXHQ (last accessed 18.01.2014) and http://ti.me/VY75g9 (last accessed 18.01.2014).

3. TRENDS IN RECENT EUROPEAN CASE LAW

Against this background of lacking, incoherent and changing regulation, European courts struggle to deal with the growing number of cases in which surrogacies have already taken place and the intended parents are fighting for the legal recognition of their parenthood.

Legal problems occasionally occur with respect to cases where child immigration and thus the recognition of parenthood is complicated by a missing genetic linkage of the child to either of the parents. However, the vast majority of cases tried in European courts concern situations in which the child is consanguineous with the intended father, but the intended parents are not willing to go through the time-consuming process of paternity acknowledgment and/or adoption before taking the baby home. These cases either relate to denied passport applications at embassies located in *ius sanguinis* countries ('child abroad') or to the rejected establishment of parenthood in the parents' home country ('child at home'). Examining overall patterns from cases recently dealt with by European courts, it is important to differentiate those two types of cases as the respective judicial decisions appear to be remarkably different in nature.

3.1. CHILD ABROAD

Many restrictive jurisdictions attempt to disincentivise surrogacies abroad by refusing to issue a passport for the newborn child, thus preventing the child from entering its territory. The reasoning behind this policy is not meant to disadvantage the child – however, it factually complicates the process of the child's immigration to the intended parents' home country. Hence, the authorities in those countries and their embassies abroad perceive this legal situation as being highly unsatisfactory because they are advised to prevent similar cases in the future by denying the child and – indirectly – the intended parents the right to enter the country in cases where prevention has already failed.

Within the last couple of years the numbers of cases contesting dismissive decisions from embassies and similar authorities has been steadily low, but however remarkable. In 2008, the English case *X & Y (Foreign Surrogacy)* caused a public stir as two children born in Ukraine had to bring suit in order to be allowed to enter the United Kingdom.[34] In *Jan Balaz v Union of India* (2009), the

---

[34] Royal High Court of Justice, decision dated December 9, 2008, file no. 2008 EWHC 3030, 'X&Y (Foreign Surrogacy)'; a similar problem emerged in the Administrative Court (VG) of Berlin, decision dated 5 September 2012, file no. VG 23 L 283.12; however, after careful consideration, the said problem turns out to be a question of conflict of laws; with regard to the VG Berlin case, this problem is meanwhile solved by the new Art. 123 of the Ukrainian Family Code.

intended parents did not succeed as the High Court of Gujarat decided that twins born through surrogacy were Indian citizens and did not assume German nationality from the intended parents.[35]

Strictly rights-based decisions, however, do not eventually prevent the intended parents from taking the baby home. Courts and other state authorities try to acknowledge the confused situation even if they are afraid to set precedents. In an attempt to cope with the deadlock, they often slur over the legal question of child nationality and sooner or later allow for child immigration. Their reasoning shows that they shrink back from perpetuating the current situation, instead they stress the exceptionality of their decision. The intended parents' passport application is often not legally successful as the child is not issued with a passport from their home country. But courts and authorities have regularly permitted them to take the baby home 'outside the rules',[36] issued a one-time travel permit,[37] or settled the dispute without any judicial decision at all.[38] Sometimes, the children born through surrogacy have had to stay in their birth countries for about a year, but there is no known case in which a child would have eventually had to stay and was never allowed to follow the intended parents to their country.[39]

3.2. CHILD AT HOME

The factual situation is somewhat different in cases where the child has already moved to the place where the intended parents live. Court decisions in these cases are no longer under the immediate pressure of the intended family living under unfamiliar circumstances. Such cases occur where the baby was born in a *ius soli* country like the United States and could easily enter the parents' European home country or where the intended parents succeeded in carrying the baby home after somehow evading the embassy or border controls. In these cases, the child is living with her intended parents according to plan, but their parenthood lacks legal recognition. Here, one does not observe patterns of non-bureaucratic decisions; instead, courts are rather relentless and tend to show

---

[35]   High Court of Gujarat, decision dated 17 November 2009, file no. LPA 2151/2009.
[36]   Royal High Court of Justice, decision dated 9 December 2008, file no. 2008 EWHC 3030, 'X&Y (Foreign Surrogacy)'.
[37]   Council of State (Conseil d'Etat), decision dated 4 May 2011, file no. 348778.
[38]   The exception proves the rule: There have been cases with strict legal decisions, such as the Administrative Court (VG) of Berlin, decision dated 26 November 2009, file no. 11 L 396.09; here, the husband of the surrogate mother had to challenge his fatherhood; then the intended father could acknowledge his fatherhood so that the child could infer his nationality on himself and thus get a passport.
[39]   In a couple of cases, intended parents and children had to stay longer than a year abroad, but could even then eventually return home. The most famous example here is the case of Baby Manji (Supreme Court of India, decision dated 29 September 2008, file no. 2008 INSC 1656).

rigour by sticking to their restrictive surrogacy laws, denying motherhood for the intended mother and referring the intended father to a formal acknowledgement of paternity. On several occasions, intended parents have unavailingly attempted to achieve recognition of a foreign birth certificate that identified them as the legal parents. Courts refer the intended parents to an acknowledgement of paternity and the adoption procedure explicitly disregarding the birth certificate for reasons of law or public policy.[40] At the same time, it should be noted that a few decisions point in a different direction, recognising foreign decisions on the parenthood of the genetic father even under the public policy restriction.[41]

It can thus be concluded that, when the best interests of the child are at stake because the newborn child has become stuck in a foreign country, courts temper justice with mercy. However, once the child is safe, the domestic laws are widely enforced;[42] exceptions prove the rule.

4. CONSEQUENCES OF LEGAL DIVERSITY IN THE RECOGNITION OF PARENTHOOD

Even though the courts obviously do their best to cushion the negative effects of international surrogacy cases on the children involved, critics argue that the problems with which young families are confronted are still considerable and have to be dealt with by an international approach.[43]

The first disadvantage children face after being born to a surrogate mother is often an extension of their stay in an underdeveloped country that the intended parents are not living in. For example, a French couple might have to stay a couple of months or even a year with the newborn child in India until the husband of the surrogate has contested his fatherhood, the intended father has acknowledged paternity, and the French embassy has eventually issued a French passport for the child. Sure enough, some local authorities issue birth certificates identifying the intended parents as the only parents of the child (even if this is against the local law), which in turn increases the chances to veil the surrogacy and to obtain a passport for the child at the foreign embassy. Anyway, this is not a solution that satisfies a lawyer. At least, many surrogacies take place in

---

[40] See e.g. Spanish Directorate General of the Civil Registry and the Notary (Dirección General de los Registros y del Notariado, DGRN), decision dated 18 February 2009, file no. 2575/2008; Administrative Court (VG) of Cologne, decision dated 20 February 2013, file no. 10 K 6710/11; Higher Regional Court (OLG) of Stuttgart, decision dated 7 February 2012, file no. 8 W 19/12; KG (Berlin), decision dated 1 August 2013, file no. 1 W 413/12.
[41] Austrian Constitutional Court (VfGH), decision dated 14 December 2011, file no. B 13/11–10.
[42] In Germany, there have even been house searches relating to investigations against people who advise on egg donation.
[43] TRIMMINGS/BEAUMONT, in: TRIMMINGS/BEAUMONT (eds.), fn. 3, pp. 439, 531 et seq.

countries which have agreed to a visa waiver programme with the intended parents' home country, enabling the intended parents to take the (legally foreign) baby home without any waiting period.

The second considerable difficulty children face arises at home out of the at least temporarily open questions of parentage: the legal uncertainty as to who is assigned legal parenthood over the child may translate into questions of custody and child maintenance. The intended parents will need the right to exercise child custody soon after the child's immigration to their home country, be it for consultations or for an application for a day nursery. Anyway, child custody largely depends on parental status. Thus, so long as paternity is not acknowledged and the intended mother has not adopted the child, most jurisdictions[44] still see the surrogate mother and her husband as the legal parents. If a personal custody decision cannot be postponed, family courts will often assign a legal guardian to make those decisions until parenthood is established.[45] The situation is further complicated where the intended parents split up before parenthood is legally arranged. If the intended parents terminate their relationship, the child will need support. The worst-case scenario here would be the intended parents denying responsibility and the child being reliant on his legal parents who live far away under possibly quite different living conditions. Some surrogacy organisations will try to avoid such a situation by asking the intended parents to reach an agreement on child support before entrusting a surrogate mother, but this is not the rule.

Anyway, there is no known case where the intended parents have denied the responsibility for child support because of a split-up before or immediately after childbirth.[46] If this happened, the child would most likely not be returned to the legal parents but – with their consent – be put up for adoption. However, in the vast majority of cases, parenthood questions will be solved before custody and maintenance problems arise – either due to a timely acknowledgement of paternity or because the registrar who is in charge of the domestic birth registration does not (want to) notice the possibility that the baby could have been carried by someone other than the intended mother.[47]

After all, it is questionable to what extent the children concerned will really sense the complications their parents face. If immigration is delayed they may suffer from being looked after by only one intended parent instead of two. If quick immigration works out but legal parentage cannot be established immediately, they will barely notice anything. Of course, if their parents separate

---

[44]   One example for a jurisdiction immediately assigning motherhood to the intended mother is the Ukraine; see Article 139 of the Ukrainian Family Code (Сімейний кодекс) and Druzenko, in: Trimmings/Beaumont (eds.), fn. 3, pp. 357, 358.

[45]   In Germany, for example, this would be done according to §1773 of the Civil Code (BGB).

[46]   Even in the case of Baby Manji, the (genetic) father tried to meet his obligations; see above fn. 39.

[47]   Of course, this is different with same-sex couples where it is obvious that both spouses cannot be the genetic parents.

before their parenthood is legally acknowledged they may incur significant disadvantages. However, such a case has not yet become public. Thus, the main factual difficulties which are the result of legal diversity are apparently caused by the intended parents. Here, it is important to remember that the rather rigid legislators have deliberately chosen to follow a restrictive approach and have hazarded the consequences on the intended parents.[48] Thus, the fact that the intended parents face severe difficulties with cross-border surrogacies does not necessarily call for criticism as they know in advance that they are following illegal plans. One can even argue that only from the struggle of those cases comes the power of prevention – and comes the invisible advantage that surrogacy mandates from citizens of countries with rather strict legislation so far remain a fringe phenomenon.

5. LEX FERENDA

The examination of the most pressing problems in recent European legislation on surrogacy shows that only in rare cases does legal uncertainty eventually materialise at the expense of the children in question. However, one might ask whether any international legal approach can still smooth out unfavourable effects for the persons involved without undermining the legitimate decisions of rigid regulators. Is there a need for an international convention on cross-border surrogacy, does parenthood have to be redefined with regard to the intention of would-be parents, or do the existing legal measures suffice for the protection of the child?

5.1. A NEW HAGUE CONVENTION

The Hague Conference on Private International Law is currently attempting to map out a convention on issues arising from international surrogacy arrangements. Building on previous work from two reports on this topic from 2011[49] and 2012[50] and drawing from a study carried out by a research team from the University of Aberdeen published in 2013,[51] the Conference has recently issued four questionnaires on the private international law issues surrounding the status of children with particular emphasis on international

---

[48]   See above fn. 21.
[49]   Hague Conference on Private International Law, *Private International Law Issues Surrounding the Status of Children, Including Issues Arising From International Surrogacy Arrangements* (2011).
[50]   Hague Conference on Private International Law, *Preliminary Report on the Issues Arising From International Surrogacy Arrangements* (2012).
[51]   TRIMMINGS/BEAUMONT (eds.), fn. 3.

surrogacy arrangements.[52] A draft convention in 2015 would be the next logical step here.[53]

The goal of such an international treaty – to protect children from the downsides of legal diversity – is honourable. However, the practical feasibility of such a convention remains questionable. An international convention brings about legal certainty, which is also brought about with the recognition of foreign decisions. As regards surrogacy, this means that the home legislations of intended parents would have to recognise certain assessments from the courts or authorities in the country where the surrogacy took place. Most likely, these assessments first and foremost concern questions of parentage as these are central to the legal problems of today. However, to ratify a new Hague Convention on international surrogacy cases would not only mean a pullback from the regulation of families living abroad, it would indeed open the floodgates to national definitions of parentage as the domestic family law could then most easily be evaded by shifting registry decisions abroad. It seems highly unlikely that the rather restrictive European jurisdictions are willing to sacrifice a fundamental principle of family law to international regulatory competition.[54]

5.2. LEEWAY FOR CROSS-BORDER RECOGNITION OF SURROGACY *DE LEGE LATA*

There are a number of renowned voices in the international realm who see sufficient leeway for a surrogacy-friendly interpretation of the prevailing European family laws. Their main reasoning can be traced back to Article 8 ECHR, which protects private and family life, and to Articles 7, 8, and 9 of the UN Convention on the Rights of the Child. The idea is that the rules on parenthood have to be reinterpreted *de lege lata* so that in surrogacy cases the intended mother is to be immediately considered to be the legal mother even though this conflicts with the letter of the law.[55] According to this approach, public policy should no longer be used to ward off the application of foreign

---

52   See www.hcch.net/index_en.php?act=text.display&tid=178 (last accessed 18.01.2014).
53   This is the reasoning by TRIMMINGS/BEAUMONT, in: TRIMMINGS/BEAUMONT (eds.), fn. 3, pp. 439, 531 et seq. (without mentioning the said time horizon).
54   BENICKE, 66 *StAZ*, pp. 101, 114 (2013); WAGNER, 65 *StAZ*, pp. 294, 299 (2012).
55   MAYER, 78 *RabelsZ*, forthcoming (2014); similarly LURGER, 33 *IPRax*, pp. 282 et seq. (2013). For a clearly more limited interpretation of Article 8 ECHR FORDER/SAARLOOS, in: ANTOKOLSKAIA (ed.), *Convergence and Divergence of Family Law in Europe*, pp. 169, 235 (2007): 'the European Court [of Human Rights], apparently, is led by principles which are determined by the Member States and not vice versa.' See also DEECH, 9 *Glob. Gov.*, pp. 425, 430 (2003): 'A right to a baby in theoretical terms would entail a duty contingent on other people to make it possible ... When procreation includes third parties beyond the confines of husband and wife, then accountability and medical ethics contribute to the decision.'

parenthood laws but be liberalised in respect of the children's rights mentioned above.[56]

However, by acknowledged legal methodology, the cited conventions can influence the interpretation of national family laws on maternity but not overrule them.[57] Furthermore, as the French Court of Cassation has put forward, Article 8 ECHR as well as Article 3 UNCRC are not violated as long as the children born through surrogacy can live with their intended parents, because here, the question of how parenthood is established turns out to be a mere technicality that the children do not effectively suffer from.[58] And even if a child has marginally suffered, the reasoning with the interests of the children might be circular: as was described above, the idea of preventive law is to discourage certain behaviour, tacitly accepting negative effects where prevention does not work. By accepting very few children to live abroad[59] for a while and to be possibly left without child support (no case is known so far!) the legislator scares many people off from international surrogacy and prevents many future children from ending up in a similar situation.[60] This calculus is reasonable not least because it is still scientifically plausible that the separation of a child from his birth mother significantly impairs his welfare.[61] Whether or not this is perceived to be a favourable legal policy is anyway not a question of legal methodology but a decision by the respective legislator.[62]

---

[56] HENRICH, in: HOFER/KLIPPEL/WALTER (eds.), *Perspektiven des Familienrechts, Festschrift für Dieter Schwab*, pp. 1141 et seq. (2005).

[57] In some countries such as in Austria, the said conventions were indeed elevated to constitutional status; however, in other legislations, the constitution overrules the convention. See CREMER, 61 *AnwBl*, pp. 159 et seq. (2011).

[58] Court of Cassation (*Cour de cassation*), First Civil Division, decisions dated 6 April 2011, file no. 09–66.486 and 10–19.053.

[59] In the view of the legislator, the child does not live 'abroad' because as long as the surrogate is his mother, her country is his country.

[60] KRAWIEC, in: BRATCHER/GOODWIN (eds.), *Baby Markets*, pp. 41 et seq. (2010), however, doubts that the preventive method works at all.

[61] The scientific picture as to whether children born through surrogacy are considerably disadvantaged is not uniform: According to GOLOMBOK, 47 *J. Child Psychol. Psych.*, pp. 213 et seq. (2006), the offspring of surrogate mothers at the age of 2 do not show abnormal socio-emotional or cognitive behaviour. However, five years later, these children have less mother-child interaction than their contemporaries, other behaviour not being noticeable; GOLOMBOK, 47 *Developm. Psychol.*, pp. 1579 et seq. (2011). The study by ROBERTSON, 13 *Ethics Collab. Reprod.*, pp. 23, 30 (1983), emphasises that it is a stress factor for children if they find out that they have been raised by someone other than their genetic parents; see also DIETRICH, *Mutterschaft für Dritte*, pp. 274 et seq. (1989); ROBINSON, 13 *Women & Pol.*, pp. 203 et seq. (1994).

[62] Many refer to the stories of Hagar, Bilhah, and Zilpah from the *Bible* (Genesis 16 and 30) to prove that surrogacy is an old phenomenon established ever since then (see e.g. HENRICH, in: HOFER/KLIPPEL/Wkalter (eds.), fn. 56, pp. 1141); however, one should not forget that even in those tales, surrogacy could only work because the surrogate was a slave; furthermore, in the case of Hagar, surrogacy led to severe problems in the interpersonal relationships.

5.3. SHIFTING THE PARENTHOOD RATIONALE FROM GENETIC LINKAGE TO INTENTION

Of course, the European legislators might want to think about a redefinition of parentage. It is a valid question to ask whether parenthood should stick to genetic linkage or be shifted or complemented by parenthood through intention.[63] The question comes up because it is only a quite recent development that motherhood can be split between the woman giving the egg and the one carrying the child. Most current European family laws irrevocably assign motherhood to the latter. The reason here is – quite surprisingly – not predominantly a closer link between the gestational mother and the child but the preventive argument mentioned above.[64] This tells us a great deal about the unsettled question of which aspect eventually matters for a modern understanding of parenthood. Is it the genetic link, the social relationship, the bare intention, or a mixture of the latter?[65]

A view on recent European jurisdiction shows that there is a growing perception that children have a right to at least know about their genetic origin.[66] The performance of such a right is somewhat hampered in the international realm as long as surrogacy-friendly states do not record data from surrogate mothers.[67] Apparently, responsibility through genetic linkage is widely perceived as disposable as long as someone else is willing to take over.[68] One might induce from this observation that parentage has to be open to contracting.[69] However, this argument turns out to be weak: as contracting on parentage is highly susceptible to child trafficking and thereby severely violating the value of human dignity from Article 1 of the Charter of Fundamental Rights of the European Union,[70] any agreement could be put on hold until some state authority has approved it. Such state approval seems necessary because human trafficking has

---

[63]   The vote for an intention-based comprehension of parentage is supported by KINDREGAN, 21 *J. Am. Acad. Matrim. Law.*, pp. 43 et seq. (2008); MORTAZAVI, 100 *Geo. L. J.*, pp. 2249, 2277 et seq. (2012); PURVIS, 24 *Yale J. L. & Feminism*, pp. 210 et seq. (2012); STORROW, 53 *Hastings L. J.*, pp. 597, 665 et seq. (2002).

[64]   See above *supra* 4.

[65]   TODOROVA, *Recognition of Parental Responsibility*, pp. 12 et seq. (2010).

[66]   See e.g. European Court of Human Rights (ECtHR), decision dated 7 July 1989, file no. 10454/83, 12 EHRR 36, *Gaskin v United Kingdom*; however, the Court did not (yet) establish a general right to know one's lineage. To deny such a right is indeed called 'expropriation of one's biography' by DAMM, 53 *JZ*, pp. 926, 932 (1998), translation by the author.

[67]   RYZNAR, 43 *J. Marshall L. Rev.*, pp. 1009, 1034 et seq. (2010). Sure enough, the same problem arises all over the world with respect to the data of sperm donors whose data are rarely stored (and made accessible) to their progeny.

[68]   In many countries, it is possible for sperm donors to remain anonymous; even where this situation changes, this is mostly due to a right of the child to know about his genetic parents and not because of an increased importance of genetics for the concept of fatherhood.

[69]   An example of legislation that is open to contracting on parentage is in Russia; see BUDZIKIEWICZ, *Contracting on Parentage*, in this book.

[70]   PAP, *Extrakorporale Befruchtung und Embryotransfer aus arztrechtlicher Sicht*, pp. 363 et seq. (1987) even goes so far as to say that human dignity does not allow intentionally splitting genetic and social motherhood; with a similar view BENDA, 38 *NJW*, pp. 1730, 1733 (1985); see

---

to be prevented, because even the intention to be parents might sometimes be (too) fungible, and because with the children, there is a voiceless third party involved which needs someone to speak up for her. To legalise surrogacy in this way might comply with children's rights as well as with the fundamental family law principles of most, if not all European countries. In fact, a legal model for such an *intentional* parenthood already coexists[71] with the parentage based on genetic linkage: it is none other than adoption.

5.4. RELYING ON ADOPTION

As etymology tells us, adoption is a model of parenthood which is not based on genetic linkage but on someone's intention.[72] Today, it functions as an emergency mechanism for cases in which the genetic parents can – for whatever reason – no longer take the responsibility to care for the child.[73] This is quite similar to what can be observed in surrogacy cases: there is some kind of a factual emergency when the intended parents try to import a baby and acquire legal parenthood even though they know they were not allowed to do so. The baby is not responsible for this awkward situation, and the law has to deal with this. Given that the intended parents deliberately chose to create the emergency, it is only just and equitable to gear the legal mechanism which deals with the situation exclusively towards the well-being of the innocent child and not towards the goals of the parents.[74] This is exactly what adoption procedures all over the world look like.[75] It is important to notice here that the best interests of the child do not necessarily argue for assigning the child to the intended parents.[76] They can indeed follow the surrogate (and possibly her husband) in

---

also STURM, in: BAUR et al. (eds.), *Festschrift für Gunther Kühne zum 70. Geburtstag*, pp. 919, 924 (2009).

[71] See the conclusion by BUDZIKIEWICZ, *Contracting on Parentage*, in this book.

[72] The Latin word *adoptare* can be translated as 'to choose'.

[73] Originally, adoption was primarily understood as a means for old-age provisions; however, this notion has considerably changed throughout the 20th century to focusing on child care.

[74] This, however, is not congruent with the intended parents' goals; see BAKER, in: TRIMMINGS/ BEAUMONT (eds.), fn. 3, pp. 411, 417: 'in the case of surrogacy a child is (pro-) created to satisfy the desire of the adult(s) for a child.'

[75] Today most legislations are slowly moving towards opening adoption even to same-sex couples and intended parents of children born through surrogacy; it is only in rare circumstances that the law bans spouses from adopting a child. Some family laws like §1741 (1) of the German Civil Code (BGB), however, grant adoptions to intended parents in surrogacy cases only if this is necessary to meet the best interests of the child; see Municipal Court (AG) of Hamm, decision dated 22 February 2011, file no. XVI 192/08; more liberally District Court (LG) of Düsseldorf, decision dated 15 March 2012, file no. 25 T 758/10; District Court (LG) of Frankfurt am Main, decision dated 3 August 2012, file no. 2–09 T 50/11; see also BOTTHOF/DIEL, 66 StAZ, pp. 211 et seq. (2013).

[76] ATWELL, 20 *Colum. Hum. R. L. Rev.*, pp. 1 et seq. (1988). With a different view, STURM, in: BAUR et al. (eds.), fn. 70, pp. 919, 931 et seq., advocating 'humanity instead of rigour'

---

their status as legal parents; however, only subject to the necessary condition that this is the best solution for the child.[77] Here, the law provides a possibility for double parenthood,[78] sure enough the sequential and not the simultaneous way.

Critics might argue that subsuming surrogacy under adoption cannot provide certainty for the intended parents that they will eventually obtain the child because – at least in theory – the child might be given to someone else. However, the question is how much certainty someone deserves who orders a child to be born as a (legal) orphan. Also, any deviation from the best interests of the child as the sole guideline for the allocation of the child result would seem iniquitous as it would mean that intended parents can take home a child whose interests would be better served by being assigned to someone else. Apart from that, it is also the rights of the surrogate which argue against 'parental certainty' for the intended parents: it is a fact that many surrogates do their job only under serious financial and social pressure and that their assurance that they are fine with relinquishing the child does not express their real feelings;[79] if this does not anyway lead to a complete prohibition of commercial surrogacy, at least it calls for the surrogate's right to eventually decide whether to keep the child only after birth. However, if the surrogate mother is granted this right, the law has to assign initial motherhood to the woman who gives birth.[80] The proponents of surrogacy thus have to decide whether they want to keep this understanding of motherhood or whether they are really willing to entitle intended parents to enforce the surrogacy agreement, if need be in the delivery room.[81]

6. CONCLUSION

Today, legal arbitrage persuades droves of Europeans to cross borders in order to have access to surrogacy services which are prohibited under their home legislation. Once the intended parents attempt to return home with the newborn

---

(translation by the author) – however, at least the cases from Third World countries also call for humanity towards women.

[77] A similar, but not identical approach is followed by LEWIS, 49 *U. Louisville L. Rev.*, pp. 371 et seq. (2011), who essentially argues that motherhood should be completely open and be assigned depending on the expected best mother-child relationship, this decision being made by a court advised by an independent board of experts.

[78] So demanded by HEIDERHOFF, 32 *IPRax*, pp. 523, 525 (2012).

[79] See above fn. 30.

[80] This also means that in surrogacy cases, there does not have to be a final parental decision at childbirth.

[81] One might argue that the legislator can circumvent this difficult decision by assigning parental rights to the intended parents but not providing enforceability to these rights, as is the case under Russian law. However, to grant someone an unenforceable right is not that different from denying it. Furthermore, to uncontestably assign motherhood to the birth mother but recognise contrary foreign court decisions means opening the maternal status and only increasing the costs of shifting maternity to the intended mother.

child, legal diversity translates into problems of legal recognition for the parental status acquired under the foreign legislation. These problems can hardly be satisfactorily solved by European courts; the judges thus tend to avoid precedents and look for informal and non-legal solutions as long as the child is still in her country of birth. The consequences of legal diversity and stagnant jurisdiction, however, turn out to be less serious than one might think: no baby born through surrogacy is known to have permanently stayed in her country of birth, and there is so far no public case in which the length of an acknowledgment of paternity or adoption procedure has made the child lose a claim for child support.

As to the *lex ferenda*, legal research does not have to decide whether to follow a restrictive or a rather open approach towards surrogacy. The range of possible legislative decisions goes from penalising the placement of a surrogacy order to the recognition of foreign decisions on parentage to entirely permitting surrogacy. Legal research should point out that, as long as there is any legal diversity and procreative tourism is not criminalised, there will definitely be legal arbitrage and the circumvention of domestic laws. For any European legislator which has decided to prohibit surrogacy, the adoption procedures are completely sufficient to meet the interests of the persons involved, placing the welfare of the child clearly above the interests of the intended parents. In order to protect weaker individuals, i.e. the children and the surrogate mothers, the focus of the discussion anyway deserves to be rather on the protection of their rights than on legalising the technically possible. And even if some European legislators should decide to liberalise their laws they cannot evade answering the fundamental question of whether they will keep their current definition of motherhood or entitle the intended parents to wrest away the newborn child from the surrogate right in the maternity room.

RE-THINKING FAMILY LAW: A NEW LEGAL PARADIGM FOR STEPFAMILIES?

Angela d'Angelo

Contents

1. INTRODUCTION

The impulse to face this issue was prompted by the consideration that the number of separations and divorces as well as the number of second marriages or cohabitations have steadily increased in most of the European countries. As a consequence, nowadays a growing number of children live within a stepfamily.[1] Nevertheless, only a few European systems have elaborated specific legal tools which are apt to regulate the complexity of the 'interconnected relationships' existing in these new family structures, while in others, like in Italy, step-parents are still considered as legal *strangers* to their stepchildren. This situation partially depends on the fact that in several EU countries family law is still based on the

---

[1] An overview of the recent demographic trends in the European Union and in Croatia, based on data provided by Eurostat, can be found in European Commission, *EU Employment and Social Situation – Quarterly Review – March 2013 – Special Supplement on Demographic Trends*, Luxembourg, Publications Office of the European Union, pp. 23–24 (2013), available at http://epp.eurostat.ec.europa.eu/portal/page/portal/product_details/publication?p_product_code=KE-BH-13-0S2 (last accessed 15.01.2014). For an interesting analysis of these trends in relation to the issues of stepfamilies see S. Navarro, Child's Life, Step-Family and Decision-Making Process, in *Beijing Law Rev.*, Vol. 4, No. 2, pp. 61–70 (2013).

traditional nuclear family's paradigm, consisting of a heterosexual couple (one mother/one father) and their own children only. But it is also the result of that recent legal trend that encourages joint parental responsibilities between both *legal* parents, regardless of their legal *status* (married or unmarried at the time of the birth, separated, divorced or no longer living together, if unmarried at the time of the birth). For instance, in Italy, as a consequence of the introduction of continued joint parental responsibilities in case of a family breakdown,[2] it becomes very difficult for the spouse of a parent to obtain a 'step-parent adoption', which up to now has been the only legal tool which enables, under certain conditions, the relationship between step-parents and their stepchildren to be legalised.[3] The above-mentioned circumstances make it clear that a comparative reflection on this matter can be useful, also from the perspective of the harmonisation of the legal solutions in the European framework.

Following this path, in this article we will summarise the main legal issues arising from stepfamilies and the related theoretical problems and then we will quickly provide a comparative overview of the legal solutions adopted at a state level in Europe. We will mainly focus on the Italian, Danish, German, Swiss, French and United Kingdom legal systems as examples of three different approaches to the controversial attribution of parental responsibilities to the step-parent. Starting from the persistent limits of the legal tools implemented in the various approaches, we argue that there is a need for a conceptual reform of family law and try to illustrate its constitutive characteristics as an entirely new paradigm, where stepfamilies are considered to be equal to a 'regular' family unit in all the phases and transitions that may occur in life. Since the term 'stepfamily' can refer to very different situations arising from second marriages or the cohabitations of divorced parents,[4] it is better to specify that, in the context of this article, a stepfamily means a family composed of a cohabiting couple of adults, whether married or not, where one or both have a pre-existing *minor*

---

[2]   Law no. 54/2006 on the separation of parents and shared custody of children, enacted on 8 February 2006 to amend, *inter alia*, Book I of the Italian Civil Code in connection with the implementation of the so-called 'principle of co-parenting'. See M. SESTA (ed.), *Codice della Famiglia*, I, Giuffrè, (II Edition), pp. 683–689 (2009); S. PATTI, L. ROSSI CARLEO (eds.), *L'affidamento condiviso*, Giuffrè (2006).

[3]   In this sense, Cass. Civ., 10 May 2011, No. 10265, *infra*, para. 3.1.

[4]   Significantly, in some languages, like in Italian common vocabulary, there is no specific term to define this new family structure. For this reason, some Italian scholars have coined new words aimed at indicating the phenomenon and, at the same time, at clarifying which situations they are focusing upon. See D. BUZZELLI, *La famiglia 'composita'. Un'indagine sistematica sulla famiglia ricomposta: i neo coniugi o conviventi, i figli nati da precedenti relazioni e i loro rapporti*, Jovene (2012); S. BELLONI, *La famiglia polinucleare. Studio comparato sui profili personali, patrimoniali e successori della famiglia fra prima e nuove unioni*, Aracne (2011); F. UCCELLA, Dalla 'famiglia pluriematica' alla 'famiglia putativa' come soggetto giuridico: prime considerazioni, in *Familia*, pp. 447–459 (2005); T. AULETTA, La famiglia rinnovata: problemi e prospettive, in *Familia*, pp. 19–51 (2005); S. MAZZONI, *Nuove costellazioni familiari. Le famiglie ricomposte*, Giuffrè (2002).

child or children who live with them and/or the other child or children of the couple themselves. The key factor here is the presence, in the new family, of *at least* one minor child who is not legally related to both the adults, because in these situations the step-parent may play the role of a 'parental figure', in addition to the biological/legal parents, without actually taking their place *in legal terms*.

My premise, in essence, is that all parental figures who actively contribute as care providers in the upbringing of minor children may have a great influence on their educational, moral and religious development, regardless of their legal *status*, and, as a consequence, it might be unreasonable not to recognise their importance from a legal perspective. Moreover, in some cases, it might contrast with the best interests of minor children that always have to be given primary consideration, especially in matters affecting their material, educational and emotional needs as well as their personal and family interests.

2. STEPFAMILY ISSUES AND RELATED THEORETICAL PROBLEMS

The existing dichotomy between the step-parents' 'social role' and their 'legal *status*' contributes in complicating the lives of these new families in different ways and may contrast with the interests of stepchildren.[5] For instance, due to the absence of formally recognised relationships between minors and their parent's partner/spouse, step-parents may encounter many obstacles in assisting stepchildren with many daily tasks, especially when they have to deal with the public authorities (e.g. schools, hospitals, etc.).

Moreover, although stepbrothers and/or stepsisters live together in the same household, they may be discriminated against by statutory provisions that recognise, for instance, some family benefits in connection with the 'parent' that they do not have in common.

Yet it is possible that contrasts occur in the decision-making process between the non-residential parent of the stepchild and the step-parent effectively involved in the child's upbringing. The matter becomes even more complex in the case of a stepfamily breakdown, when the legal irrelevance of the 'social link' between some family members makes it very difficult to protect their interests before a court.

---

[5]   See M. DIMSEY, *Multi-parent families in the 21th century*, in K. BOELE-WOELKI, T. SVERDRUP (eds.), *European Challenges in Contemporary Family Law*, Intersentia, pp. 101–111 (2008); I. SCHWENZER, Tensions between Legal, Biological and Social Conceptions of Parentage, in *Electronic Journal of Comparative Law*, Vol. 11.3 (December 2007), available at www.ejcl. org/113/article113–6.pdf (last accessed 15.01.2014).

On the contrary, it could be useful, when appropriate, to still maintain continuity and stability for the minors involved. Traditional family law considers the care, maintenance and education of minor children as exclusive prerogatives of their parents and places these obligations at the heart of the concept of parental responsibility. Nevertheless, in the reality of many stepfamilies, many tasks related to the stepchildren's daily lives and upbringing are, in fact, spontaneously carried out by an adult who is not *ipso iure* considered to be the holder of these responsibilities.

As a matter of fact, in most European jurisdictions the legal concept of parental responsibility is extended beyond its traditional limits and, in view of the best interests of the child, not only legal parents but also other persons or public bodies can be regarded as rights holders. For this reason, the Principles of European Family Law Regarding Parental Responsibilities, drafted by the Commission on European Family Law (CEFL), expressly consider their exercise by parents and by third persons.[6] According to the CEFL Principles, on the one hand both legal parents should have parental responsibilities for the child, regardless of the dissolution of their marriage/informal relationship and whenever possible they should exercise them jointly (especially with regard to important decisions);[7] on the other hand, a third person may acquire parental responsibilities in whole or in part, or may exercise some or all of them in addition to or instead of the parents. The parent's partner may take part in decisions on daily matters unless the other legal parent objects.[8] Despite the important guideline provided by the CEFL Principles, in many practical situations it is not always easy to distinguish between decisions on daily matters and important decisions concerning matters such as education or the child's residence.

Furthermore, the automatic exclusion of step-parents from the decision-making process when there are objections by the other legal parent may contrast with the interests of the stepchild. This is particularly true when the step-parent is effectively involved in the child care while the non-residential parent does not have frequent contact with the child and, consequently, it is reasonable to suppose that the step-parent should have a better understanding of the child's developmental needs. In this sense, we can argue that stepfamilies challenge contemporary family law to solve the problem of how to legally recognise the parallel (or additional) parental figures when more than two adults play a significant role in a minor child's life.

---

[6] See K. BOELE-WOELKI, F. FERRAND, C. GONZÁLEZ BEILFUSS, M. JÄNTERÄ-JAREBORG, N. LOWE, D. MARTINY, W. PINTENS (eds.), *Principles of European Family Law Regarding Parental Responsibilities*, Intersentia (2007); see also K. BOELE-WOELKI, The CEFL Principles Regarding Parental Responsibilities: Predominance of the Common Core, in K. BOELE-WOELKI, T. SVERDRUP (eds.), *supra* n. 5, pp. 63–84.

[7] CEFL Principles 3:8; 3:10–13.

[8] CEFL Principles 3:9; 3:17–18.

3. A COMPARATIVE ANALYSIS OF LEGAL SOLUTIONS IN THE EUROPEAN FRAMEWORK

On account of this, a number of European national legislators and courts have elaborated innovative legal solutions aimed at balancing the role of the biological/legal parents with the role of the step-parent who is actually involved in the child care. Even though several EU Member States have already regulated some aspects of the stepfamily's life, only a few jurisdictions have elaborated specific legal tools which are apt to legally recognise the step-parents' 'social role' as 'additional parental figures', so there are still significant differences between European legal systems in approaching this issue.[9]

Our comparative analysis identifies three different legal approaches:[10]

(1) An *'exclusionary-model approach'*: where there is no possibility to recognise the legal relevance of step-parents as 'additional parental figures'.
(2) A *'replacing-model approach'*: where formal or informal agreements between legal parents may delegate – totally or partially – some parental rights and duties to a third person. However, it should be noted that these agreements are only allowed when one parent has sole parental responsibilities.
(3) An *'inclusive-model approach'*: where a statutory provision can entrust parental responsibility to a third person (and in particular the step-parent) without depriving the legal parents of their own responsibility. Here, more than two adults may legally share parental rights, duties and responsibilities.

3.1. THE 'EXCLUSIONARY-MODEL APPROACH'

In compliance with the first approach only parents can hold parental responsibility concerning their child/children, so there is no possibility to recognise the legal relevance of the step-parent as an additional parental figure.

Indeed, in these jurisdictions, only the legal *status* of a parent entitles an adult to enjoy all the related rights and benefits, while requiring the undertaking of all duties and responsibilities towards the child. Consequently, adoption is the

---

9   An exhaustive overview of the legal instruments adopted at the State level in Europe can be found in S. Navarro, *supra* n. 1, pp. 65–68. See also S. Belloni, *supra* n. 4, pp. 72–86, M. Bruggeman, Le statut du beau-parent par-delà les frontières, in *Droit de la famille*, 6 (2009); G. Ferrando, Famiglie ricomposte e nuovi genitori, in T. Auletta (ed.), *Bilanci e prospettive del diritto di famiglia a trent'anni dalla riforma*, Giuffrè, pp. 285–304 (2007).
10   See A. D'Angelo, La famiglia nel XXI secolo: il fenomeno delle famiglie ricomposte, in D. Amram, A. D'Angelo (eds.), *La famiglia e il diritto fra diversità nazionali ed iniziative dell'Unione Europea*, Cedam, pp. 13–47 (2011).

only way to attribute a legal 'vestige' to the new relationship between the step-parent and his/her stepchild/children.

However, according to the traditional nuclear family paradigm, by adopting the stepchild, the step-parent acquires the legal *status* of a parent but this result, in general, is associated with the consequent exclusion of one legal parent from his/her parental authority.

In some European countries, *ad hoc* rules have been enacted to facilitate the adoption of the stepchild by the new spouse, without breaking the ties between the adopted minor and the other biological parent. In this sense, we can refer to step-parent adoption as provided for by Article 44 b) of Italian Adoption Law 184/1983 (as amended in 2001).[11]

Indeed, this specific form of adoption confers the *status* of an adoptive parent upon the step-parent without breaking the ties between the adopted minor and the other biological parent (and his/her relatives), but the provision applies only to the married partner of the minor's legal parent, so it cannot be extended to non-married, 'merely' cohabiting partners.

It is interesting to note that while, by law, the other biological parent's consent is always required, in the past the courts progressively admitted the step-parent's adoption even against opposition by the other biological parent, every time such opposition was considered to be manifestly in contrast with the best interests of the child who had been well integrated into the new family.[12] But, as anticipated, after the entry into force of Law no. 54/2006 on continued joint parental responsibilities after a family breakdown, the Italian Supreme Court has recently overruled this progressive case law trend, thereby affirming that opposition by the other biological parent is preclusive, even if he or she has never actually lived with the child.[13]

3.2. THE 'REPLACING-MODEL APPROACH'

Other European countries adhere to the second approach, the 'replacing-model' one. Here, if one legal parent has sole parental authority for the child, formal or informal agreements between legal parents may delegate, totally or partially, the rights and responsibilities of parental authority to the partner of this parent and this may, in some circumstances, be recognised by the courts.

An exemplary application of this second approach can be found in Denmark, where Article 11 of the Danish Act on Parental Authority and Contact provides that the spouse of a parent who has sole parental authority can obtain parental

---

[11] A. FINOCCHIARO, M. FINOCCHIARO, *Adozione e affidamento dei minori: commento alla nuova disciplina (L. 28 marzo 2001 n. 149 e D.L. 24 aprile 2001 n. 150),* Giuffré (2001).
[12] In this sense, *ex multis,* Cass. Civ., 5 August 1996, No. 7137.
[13] Cass. Civ., 10 May 2011, No. 10265, case note by G. FERRANDO, L'adozione in casi particolari del figlio naturale del coniuge, in *Corriere Giuridico,* p. 91 (2012).

authority by means of an agreement with the other parent. The agreement will be approved if it does not contrast with the best interests of the child, but the other parent has to consent to the transfer of parental authority.[14] The same replacing mechanism can be found in Germany, where two provisions of the German Civil Code and of the Registered Partnership Act entitle the spouse or the registered partner of a parent with sole parental responsibilities to participate in decision-making on matters relating to the child's everyday life (so-called 'limited parental responsibilities').[15]

Indeed, in both examples, the attribution of parental responsibilities to the step-parent cannot interfere with the other legal parent who has already been deprived of his/her parental responsibility.

3.3. THE 'INCLUSIVE-MODEL APPROACH'

In the European context it is also possible to find clear examples of a 'more inclusive' approach, where the position of a step-parent can be lawfully recognised, without the requirement that one of the legal parents renounces his/her parental rights and duties.

According to this last approach, a statutory provision vests a third person (and in particular the step-parent) with parental responsibility, or with certain rights and duties concerning the day-to-day upbringing of the child, without depriving the legal parents of their own parental responsibility.

Thus, in these jurisdictions more than two adults legally share parental rights, duties and responsibilities, thereby generating the phenomenon of so-called 'multiple parentage'.

Examples of this approach can be found in Switzerland, France and the United Kingdom where different legal tools have been adopted in order to recognise the legal relevance of the step-parent or, more broadly, of other adults who actively contribute in the upbringing of children without being their legal parents.

In this sense, it is interesting to observe the solution provided for by Article 299 of the Swiss Civil Code, according to which, in the case of a second marriage, *'each spouse must provide the other with assistance in an appropriate manner in the exercise of parental responsibilities in relation to the other spouse's children and stand in for the other if circumstances require'.*[16]

On the basis of this duty to provide assistance in the exercise of his/her spouse's parental responsibility, the married step-parent automatically acquires

---

14   See K. BOELE-WOELKI, B. BRAAT, I. CURRY-SUMNER (eds.), *European Family Law in Action, Vol. III: Parental Responsibilities*, Intersentia, p. 391 (2005).

15   According to §1687 b para. 1 German CC and §9 Registered Partnership Act, see K. BOELE-WOELKI, B. BRAAT, I. CURRY-SUMNER (eds.), *supra* n. 14, p. 396.

16   See K. BOELE-WOELKI, B. BRAAT, I. CURRY-SUMNER (eds.), *supra* n. 14, p. 407.

the position of an 'auxiliary parental figure': he/she has a legal duty to contribute to the upbringing of the stepchild, but he/she is not authorised to act if the law requires the consent of the legal parents.

Switzerland is the only legal system where the collaboration of the step-parent in parental prerogatives is considered mandatory. Nevertheless, the 'vicarious' position assumed by the step-parent under the Swiss Civil Code avoids the problem of a necessary coordination with the position of the other legal parent, the non-residential parent.

Another interesting legal tool can be found in Article 377-1 of the French Civil Code, according to which '*if the child's educational needs require it, the family judge can provide that the father and the mother, or only one of them, share the exercise of their own parental responsibility with a third person*' (the so-called *délégation-partage de l'autorité parentale*).[17]

This institution significantly differs from the simple delegation of parental authority to a third person (the so-called *délégation-volontaire*) provided for by Article 377 of the French Civil Code, because it allows the legal parents, who remain the original holders of parental responsibility, not only to delegate to a third person (*délégataire*) the exercise of their own parental responsibility over the child, but also to share this exercise with the third *délégataire*.

Both parents have to agree to such a delegation, and they are considered, together with the *délégataire*, as acting with the consent of all the others regarding the usual acts of parental responsibility in relation to the child.

In any case, the agreement has to be approved by the Family Court, which is also appointed to help the parties to reach a settlement in the case of conflicts or difficulties arising from the shared exercise of parental responsibility. It should be noted, however, that this provision is not specifically addressed to step-parents. At the same time, the difficulties in defining the concept of 'usual acts of parental authority' have not encouraged stepfamilies to make use of this legal tool.[18]

Finally, the United Kingdom provides a clear example of a 'more inclusive' approach which is expressly addressed to step-parents. Here, a new specific provision of the Children Act allows the spouse of the child's parent to acquire parental responsibility for the child, in addition to both legal parents, through an agreement with them or by a court order.[19]

---

[17]   Art. 377-1 French CC, introduced by Law n° 2002/305 of 4 March 2002 on parental authority. See F. Boulanger, Modernisation ou utopie?: la réforme de l'autorité parentale par la loi du 4 mars 2002, in *Recueil Dalloz*, p. 1571 (2002).

[18]   V. Depadt-Sebag, La reconnaissance juridique des tiers beaux-parents: entre adoption simple et delegation-partage, in *Recueil Dalloz*, p. 2494 (2011).

[19]   Section 4A of the Children Act (1989), amended by the Adoption and Children Act (2002) and by the Civil Partnership Act (2004), according to which: 'where a child's parent who has parental responsibility for the child is married to, or is a civil partner of, a person who is not the child's parent ("the step-parent") – (a) parent or, if the other parent of the child also has parental responsibility for the child, both parents may by agreement with the step-parent provide for the

Unlike the French solution, section 4 A of the Children Act allows the step-parent to hold parental responsibility for his/her stepchild in addition to both legal parents, and not only to share the exercise of such responsibility with them. Moreover, parental responsibility can be acquired even as a result of an agreement among all the pre-existing holders, without the need for the court's approval.

Thus, all these simultaneous holders of parental responsibility have almost the same legal *status* and, as a consequence, they can equally take part in the decision-making process concerning the upbringing of the child. However, it is not clear how to solve the potential conflicts which may arise due to the greater number of adults entitled to take decisions concerning the same child.

4. A POSSIBLE DIFFERENT PERSPECTIVE

This comparative overview makes clear that despite the relevance of the *ad hoc* solutions adopted so far, the legal tools which are able to bridge the gap between current family law and the social reality of stepfamilies are still far from perfect.

It is worthwhile highlighting that almost all the solutions analysed require a marriage between the step-parent and the stepchild's legal parent. This precondition makes it impossible to satisfy the needs of the growing number of unmarried stepfamilies. At the same time, as already stressed by scholars, none of the legal tools aimed at attributing parental responsibilities to the step-parent requires a minimum period of time during which the step-parent and the stepchild live together and develop a real emotional bond.[20]

Moreover, legal tools inspired by a 'substitutive' ideology may contrast with the best interests of the stepchild, in so far as they may interrupt his/her relations with the other legal parent. On the contrary, legal tools based on a more 'inclusive' family model, by simply increasing the number of adults entitled to take part in decisions relating to the minor's life, potentially expose stepchildren to an increasing number of conflicts with serious consequences for their psychological well-being. These limits suggest an opportunity to develop a completely different approach to the problem, where emphasis is placed on the position of the minor stepchildren and their right to live with their own family.

In fact, it is universally recognised that the role of the family is that of a 'fundamental group unit of society', which for children represents 'the natural environment for growth and well-being'.[21] This is confirmed at an international

---

step-parent to have parental responsibility for the child; or (b) the court may, on the application of the step-parent, order that the step-parent shall have parental responsibility for the child.'

20   See, S. NAVARRO, *supra* n. 1, p. 67.

21   In these terms, *ex multis* the Convention on the Rights of the Child, adopted and opened for signature, ratification and accession by General Assembly Resolution 44/25 of 20 November 1989.

and national level by several examples of preferential protection being accorded to family life and children's rights as family members.[22]

Despite the lack of a common definition of a 'family' in the international and European framework, both the European Court of Human Rights (ECtHR) and the Court of Justice of the European Union (ECJ) have interpreted the concept of 'family life' in a broader perspective, by offering protection under this concept to *de facto* family relations and, in some cases, also to stepfamilies.[23] Hence, according to this line of interpretation, one can argue that a conceptual reform of family law has already started where a variety of different family structures can be included within the concept of the 'family', as commonly accepted and protected at the EU level.

In addition, the full equality of the wife and the husband in jointly determining their family life can be considered to be a common rule of EU family law. A similar rule can be applied to cohabiting partners, in so far as their relationship could be included within the concept of 'family life'.

Thus, if we consider a stepfamily as a 'regular' family unit, we have to take into account the stepchild's right to be considered a full member of the family where he/she is growing up and with whom he/she is developing significant emotional ties. At the same time, we cannot neglect the position of the step-parent in determining his/her own family life together with his/her actual partner, and the need to avoid interferences from third persons or public bodies in decisions regarding the stepfamily's reorganisation, which necessarily affect the stepchild's daily life and upbringing (e.g. the family residence or domicile, holidays abroad, etc.). Here, the position of the step-parent may conflict with the non-residential parent's right to take decisions for his/her own child, especially when the parental responsibilities are still exercised jointly by both legal parents after the dissolution of their marriage or unmarried relationship.

Building on these theoretical assumptions, the legal paradigm we propose for the stepfamily suggests that national legislators and courts should take into account new criteria in balancing the position of step-parents and the other legal parent, who may be considered, in some cases, as a 'third' party with regard to

---

[22] At the European level it is worth mentioning, on the one hand, the general principle of the protection of family life provided for by Articles 8 and 12 of the European Convention on Human Rights (ECHR) as well as by Articles 7 and 9 of the Charter of Fundamental Rights of the European Union (Nice Charter, 2000) and by Article 33 of the Nice Charter, which ensures that *'the family shall enjoy legal, economic and social protection'*; on the other hand, there is recognition of the rights of children as family members, provided for by Article 24 of the Nice Charter, as well as by Article 3 of the Convention on the Rights of the Child.

[23] In the ECJ case law, two leading cases have to be stressed: *Baumbast and R. v Secretary of State* (C-413/99, ECR I-7091) and *Carpenter v Secretary of State* (C-60/00, ECR I-6279). Concerning the ECtHR case law, we can refer to the judgment of the 27 October 1984 in the case of *Kroon and others v The Netherlands* (App. No. 18535/91). Regarding the difficult common definition of a 'family' in the EU context, see F.D. BUSNELLI, M.C. VITUCCI, Frantumi europei di famiglia, in *Riv. Dir. Civ.*, 4, p. 767 (2013).

the new family unit where his/her minor child or children actually live. Indeed, in our opinion, the potential conflicts arising from these situations cannot be solved either by the *ex ante* distinction between daily and important decisions or through the preventive attribution of the decision-making power concerning specific matters to the step-parent.

On the contrary, it may be reasonable to 'limit' the legal powers of the other parent, who lives apart from the stepfamily, whenever they may be in conflict with the personal and family interests of the child. To put it differently, a possible solution could be not to extend the step-parent's parental responsibility, but to set limits on the exercise of parental responsibility by the non-residential parent, according to the circumstances of the case.

Such limits should obviously be related to the best interests of the stepchild since the attribution of parental responsibility is aimed at promoting and safeguarding his/her welfare.[24]

The validity of this thesis could be proven in the field of decisions concerning a change to the stepfamily's residence: the national courts could scrutinise and decide upon an objection by the non-residential parent to the relocation of his/her minor child by taking into account the stepchild's interest in moving together with the new family within which he/she is well integrated. Moreover, it could be considered legally possible to limit the parent's rights to oppose the step-parent's participation in the decision-making process when the courts find that the stepchild's best interests requires this, and the non-residential parent's opposition amounts to an abusive interference in the stepfamily's life.

5.   CONCLUSIONS

In light of the above considerations, we can underline some final remarks.

In our opinion, the proposed legal paradigm for stepfamilies, based on a new concept of stepchildren's family life, could offer important guidelines for the legal recognition of these new family structures.

First of all, it suggests that the opportunity to assure the legal recognition of the step-parent's 'social role' depends on the possibility to consider him or her as a member of the stepchild's own family. The main consequence of the aforementioned statement should be a reaffirmation of the stepchild's right to be heard and to express his or her opinion and wishes concerning his or her family life.[25] Of course, we are aware that this new paradigm requires some important changes in the current family law culture.

---

24   CEFL Principles 3:1, 3:3.
25   Art. 12 CRC, see L. SMITH, Recent developments in Child Law, in K. BOELE-WOELKI, T. SVERDRUP, *supra* n. 5, p. 56.

Firstly, in compliance with the mentioned progressive case law trend of both the European Court of Human Rights and the Court of Justice of the European Union, national legislators and courts need to increasingly extend the concept of 'children's family life' in order to protect the social ties between all the stepfamily's members, not only the relationship between the stepchild and the non-residential parent.

Secondly, in all disputes regarding the stepchild's daily life and upbringing, the national courts should elaborate upon an 'abusive' exercise of parental responsibilities by the non-residential parent, in order to balance his or her position and the step-parent's position in the decisions which eventually affect the stepfamily's organisation.

Finally, national legislators and public authorities should encourage alternative dispute resolution mechanisms such as family mediation in all disputes regarding the upbringing of stepchildren, in order to promote friendly settlements among all the adults effectively involved in child care. Moreover, since these mechanisms contribute to developing a collaborative climate among the adults concerned, they are considered suitable for the direct participation of stepchildren in all or part of such informal procedures.

As we have said, there are still significant differences between European jurisdictions in approaching these issues, but we are strongly persuaded that every effort aimed at promoting the best interests of children involved in these situations will contribute to the further harmonisation of family law in Europe.

PART FOUR
INTERNATIONAL FAMILY
RELATIONSHIPS

THE PROPOSAL FOR A REGULATION ON MATRIMONIAL PROPERTY

A Critique of the Proposed Rule on the Immutability of the Applicable Law

Andrea BONOMI

Contents

1. INTRODUCTION

The 2011 Proposal for a Regulation on jurisdiction, applicable law and the recognition and enforcement of decisions in matters of matrimonial property regimes (hereinafter, 'the Proposal') is designed to fill in a very serious gap in the process of the European unification of private international law rules in the field of family law.

The main aspects of the Proposal have already been analysed in detail by several distinguished scholars.[1] Subject to some qualifications and possible

---

[1]   See in particular: KATHARINA BOELE-WOELKI, Property Relations of International Couples in Europe: The Interaction between Unifying and Harmonizing Instruments, in: *Festschrift für Bernd von Hoffmann*, Bielefeld 2011, pp. 63–72; MARKUS BUSCHBAUM/ULRICH SIMON, Les propositions de la Commission européenne relatives à l'harmonisation des règles de conflit

improvements, most of the solutions envisaged are very reasonable and deserve clear and unqualified support. This is true with respect to all the main areas covered by the proposed instrument, i.e. jurisdiction, applicable law, and the recognition and enforcement of decisions and authentic instruments.

In particular, the choice of submitting, to the jurisdiction of the courts of one single country, questions of the dissolution of matrimonial property regimes and the connected issues of succession and divorce (Articles 3 and 4 of the Proposal) is very sensible. With respect to the determination of the applicable law, the adoption of a unitary system (Article 15) and the broad admission of party autonomy (Articles 16 and 18 of the Proposal) are also entirely satisfactory.

However, in our view, the weakness of the proposed system lies in the choice of an immutable connecting factor for the determination of the law which is applicable to the matrimonial property regime. In this contribution we focus on the shortcomings of this solution and on the possible alternatives.

2. THE IMMUTABILITY SYSTEM FROM A COMPARATIVE LAW PERSPECTIVE

Pursuant to Article 17(1)(a) of the Proposal, the applicable law is – in the absence of a choice of law by the spouses – 'the law of the State of the spouses' first common habitual residence after the marriage'.

The reference to the *first* common habitual residence implies that a change of the common habitual residence of the spouses during the marriage does not entail any change of the law governing the matrimonial property. A *'conflit mobile'* is excluded through a crystallisation of the applicable law, as determined immediately after the marriage.[2]

---

de lois sur les biens patrimoniaux des couples mariés et des partenaires enregistrés, *Rev. crit. DIP* 2011, pp. 801–816; BEATRIZ CAMPUZANO DÍAZ, The Coordination of the EU Regulations on Divorce and Legal Separation with the Proposal on Matrimonial Property Regimes, *YPIL* 2011, pp. 233–253; NINA DETHLOFF, Güterrecht in Europa – Perspektiven für eine Angleichung auf kollisions- und materiellrechtlicher Ebene, in: *Festschrift für Bernd von Hoffmann*, Bielefeld 2011, pp. 73–88; DIETER MARTINY, Die Kommissionsvorschläge für das internationale Ehegüterrecht sowie für das internationale Güterrecht eingetragener Partnerschaften, *IPRax* 2011, pp. 437–458; MARIEL REVILLARD, L'harmonisation du droit international privé de la famille dans la pratique notariale, in: *Mélanges en l'honneur d'Hélène Gaudemet-Tallon*, Paris 2008, p. 789; ILARIA VIARENGO, The EU Proposal on Matrimonial Property Regimes – Some General Remarks, *YPIL* 2011, pp. 199–215.

2   Under the proposed text, it is not clear whether the rule of Article 17(1)(a) only applies when the spouses have a common habitual residence immediately after the marriage, or also when they establish it later on: on this point, see DIETER MARTINY (fn. 1), p. 450. Moreover, it is unclear whether this rule necessarily implies – as its wording seems to suggest – a 'common' habitual residence, or also comes into play when the spouses – without living together – have their habitual residence in the same State. In any case, these points should be clarified in the final text of the Regulation.

The spouses can only derogate from this immutability system by means of an intentional choice of the law which is applicable to their regime during the course of their marriage. As stated in Article 18 of the Proposal, 'the spouses may, at any time, make their matrimonial property regime subject to a law other than the one hitherto applicable'. In principle, the effects of this voluntary change of the applicable law are limited to the future (*ex nunc*), but the spouses can provide that this choice of law has retrospective effect (Article 18, second and third sentence).

From a comparative law perspective,[3] the immutability of the law which is applicable to the matrimonial property regime has been adopted in several national choice-of-law systems, for example in German law.[4] However, other countries have opted for an 'automatic' mutability of the applicable law. This means that a change in the factual elements, which are used as connecting factors (in particular a change of the common domicile, of the common habitual residence, or of the common nationality of the spouses), may involve – even in the absence of a party's choice – an *ipso iure* change of the applicable law. In turn, this change of the applicable law brings about a (more or less dramatic) change of the spouses' matrimonial property regime.

In a mutability system, a change to the applicable law can occur immediately after a variation of the connecting factor (e.g. at the time of the change of the spouses' common habitual residence), or it can be made subject to other conditions (such as the concurrence of the common habitual residence and the common nationality, or the passing of a certain period of time). Under Article 7 of the 1978 Hague Convention on the Law Applicable to Matrimonial Property Regimes,[5] for instance, a change of the spouses' common habitual residence results in a modification of the applicable law when the spouses move to the country of their common nationality, or when they become nationals of that State, or, failing that, when the spouses have lived in the country of their new habitual residence for a period of not less than ten years.

Another important difference among the mutability systems relates to the effect of the change in the applicable law. In some systems, the mutability only affects the assets which the spouses, or one of them, acquire(s) after the change of the applicable law. This non-retrospective (*ex nunc*) change of the applicable law results in the subsequent applicability of two (or possibly more) laws (and matrimonial property regimes) during the marriage. This is the case under the 1978 Hague Convention; pursuant to Article 8(1) of that Convention, a change of

---

3   For a comparative overview of the choice-of-law rules which are applicable to matrimonial property, see ANDREA BONOMI, Les régimes matrimoniaux en droit international privé comparé, in: Andrea Bonomi/Marco Steiner, *Les régimes matrimoniaux en droit comparé et en droit international privé*, Genève 2006, pp. 59–75.
4   Article 15(1) EGBGB. A similar rule is applicable in Austria, Greece, Portugal and Spain.
5   Convention of 14 March 1978 on the Law Applicable to Matrimonial Property Regimes. The Convention is only in force in France, Luxembourg and the Netherlands.

the applicable law under Article 7 'shall have effect only for the future, and property belonging to the spouses before the change is not subject to the new applicable law'. By contrast, in some national systems, the new applicable law retroacts to the moment of the celebration of the marriage with the consequence that it becomes applicable even to property belonging to the spouses, or to one of them, prior to the change.[6]

3. THE DRAWBACKS OF THE IMMUTABILITY SYSTEM

A comparison between the different systems briefly described above demonstrates that all these systems present advantages and drawbacks, so that it would be naïve to believe that an absolutely perfect rule can be proposed. Nevertheless, we consider that in the specific framework of the creation of uniform European conflict-of-law rules for matrimonial property, the immutability rule, proposed by the Commission, is the less convincing solution.

Its more evident drawbacks are that it frequently results in a lack of proximity between the spouses and the designated law, and in the necessity for the court or other authorities to apply a foreign law. It also results in a lack of coordination with the rules governing other closely connected issues.

3.1. LACK OF PROXIMITY

The lack of proximity results from the fact that, in the case of a change of the common habitual residence by the spouses, the immutability rule normally leads to the application of the law of a country where the spouses no longer reside at the relevant time.

This is well illustrated by two cases recently decided by the French *Cour de cassation*.[7] In both cases the spouses had resided, for several years, in France. Nonetheless, their matrimonial property was still subject to the rules of the country where they had lived during the first years of their marriage.[8]

---

[6]   This is the case under Article 55(1) of the Swiss Private International Law Act. A similar rule is applicable in Italy, although Italian private international law does not clearly specify this: see Tito Ballarino, *Diritto internazionale privato*, Padua 1999, p. 428.

[7]   *Cour de cassation*, 29.02.2012 and 12.04.2012, *Rev. crit. DIP* 2012, p. 864, with comments by Caroline Kleiner. The commentator also refers to a similar, unreported case (*Cour de cassation*, 26.10.2011) in which the application of the law of the first common habitual residence (Algerian law) led to very harsh results for one of the spouses.

[8]   In the first case, the Turkish spouses had married in Turkey in 1984, but moved to France one year after the marriage. In the second case, the French spouses had married in New York in 1999, then returned to France also one year after their marriage.

In such situations, the immutability rule leads to a result which is not fully consistent with the choice of the common habitual residence as the main connecting factor. The application of the law of the spouses' common habitual residence makes sense because this is the place where the spouses have established the 'centre of their life', in particular the centre of their common life. However, if we do not apply the law of their current common habitual residence, but rather the one of their first common habitual residence after the marriage, we end up with the law of a country where the spouses no longer have the centre of their life. This approach is not entirely compatible with the rationale underpinning the connecting factor of the common habitual residence.[9] For this reason we consider that the immutability rule fits better within a system where matrimonial property is subject to the law of the common nationality of the spouses (as in the present German system), but is less in line with a system based – at least in principle – on the spouses' common habitual residence.

The immutability rule is also not fully in harmony with the last connecting criterion of the 'cascade' system provided for in Article 17(1)(c) of the proposed regulation. Failing a (first) common habitual residence and a common nationality of the spouses, the applicable law will be that of the State with which the spouses 'jointly have the closest links, taking into account all the circumstances, in particular the place where the marriage was celebrated'. The rationale of this rule – as that of the connecting factor based on the common habitual residence – is clearly the search for proximity between the spouses and the applicable law. By virtue of this rule, such circumstances like the place of the celebration of the marriage or the place of the habitual residence of each spouse can be taken into account – although only on a subsidiary basis – for the purpose of determining the law which is applicable to the matrimonial property regime. By contrast, since Article 17(1)(c) only comes into play when the spouses never had a common habitual residence, a very significant contact such as the present or last common habitual residence of the spouses is never relevant for that purpose.[10] In our opinion, this is not fully consistent with the idea of proximity, which clearly underlies Article 17(1).

3.2. APPLICATION OF FOREIGN LAW

Whenever a couple have changed their common habitual residence during the marriage, the connecting factor of Article 17(1)(a) leads to the application of the law of the country of their first common habitual residence. In such

---

9   For similar reasoning, see Bernard Audit/Louis D'Avout, *Droit international privé*, 7th ed., Paris 2013, p. 866 ('Si c'est le centre d'intérêt des époux qui importe, le réalisme suggère de tirer les conséquences d'un déplacement définitif de cet élément en cours du mariage').

10   Obviously, unless it coincides with the first common habitual residence.

circumstances, however, based on the Proposal itself and on the other existing European regulations, jurisdiction normally lies with the courts of the Member State of the present or last habitual residence of the spouses, and not with the court of the State of their first habitual residence. In all of these cases, the court seized will have to apply a foreign law.

This is so in the event of the death of one of the spouses. Under Article 4 of the Succession Regulation, the courts of the *last* habitual residence of the deceased have jurisdiction to rule on the succession. By virtue of Article 3 of the Proposal, the courts seized of an application concerning the succession will also have jurisdiction to rule on matters relating to the matrimonial property regime in connection with that application. However, the law applicable to these matters will be that of the spouses' first common habitual residence, i.e. a foreign law.

There are, of course, some special and subsidiary rules under the Succession Regulation, which can lead to attributing jurisdiction to the courts of the State of the nationality of the deceased (Articles 5 to 9), or to the courts of the place where the inheritance property is located (Article 10), or to some other courts having sufficient contacts (Article 11), but none of these rules will necessarily point to the courts of the State of the first common habitual residence of the spouses.

The same difficulty arises in divorce and separation cases. Certainly, under Articles 3 to 5 of the Brussels II *bis* Regulation, jurisdiction can be based on alternative grounds subject to the choice of the claimant. However, none of these criteria point to the State of the *first* habitual residence of the spouses although they can, under particular circumstances, lead to jurisdiction being allocated to the courts of that State (this is the case, for instance, when, after the marriage has broken down, one of the spouses has moved back to the country of the spouses' first common habitual residence). Moreover, in the absence of an agreement between the spouses, the court seized for divorce or separation purposes under Brussels II *bis* will not necessarily have jurisdiction to rule on matters of matrimonial property.[11] In such a case, jurisdiction will normally lie – under Article 5(1)(a) and (b) of the Proposal – with the courts of the spouses' common habitual residence at the time of the proceedings or, failing that, with the courts of their last common habitual residence. Once again, if the spouses have changed their residence during the marriage, the court seized will have to apply foreign law.

Some may argue that the applicability of foreign law is a normal occurrence in international situations. However, nobody will deny that the ascertainment and the application of foreign law is one of the most difficult tasks that a court

---

[11] Under Article 4 of the Proposal '[t]he courts of a Member State called upon to rule on an application for divorce, judicial separation or annulment under Regulation (EC) No. 2201/2003, shall also have jurisdiction... to rule on matters of the matrimonial property regime arising in connection with the application', but only 'where the spouses so agree'. Failing such an agreement, 'jurisdiction is governed by Articles 5 *et seq.*'

can face. The area of matrimonial property is not an exception in this regard. We are all aware of the difficulties raised by the application of the domestic rules on matrimonial property regimes, which are very often based on very technical and complex criteria such as the distinction between personal and marital property, or those concerning the evaluation of the assets. The application of the homologous notions of a foreign law can turn into a judicial nightmare.

If the courts of certain Member States are sufficiently well equipped for this task, others are manifestly unprepared and try to avoid the application of foreign law by all possible means. Of course, the European Union and the Hague Conference are presently looking into this issue in order to develop some efficient mechanism of co-operation, but it seems unlikely that miracle solutions can be elaborated in the short term.[12]

One should also consider that, in a system based on the universal (*erga omnes*) application of the choice-of-law rules (see Article 21 of the Proposal), the law of the first common habitual residence can be that of a non-Member State. The access to this law and its application is often more difficult than the access to and the application of a Member State's law. Moreover, the level of protection granted by this law to the financially weaker spouse is often lower than that provided for by the law of the Member State of the forum.[13]

When a problem can hardly be solved, it is prudent to try to prevent it from occurring too frequently. This is the approach adopted in the Succession Regulation, where the rules on jurisdiction and applicable law have been drafted for the purpose of reducing the instances where foreign law might be applied. According to recital 27 '[t]he rules of this Regulation are devised so as to ensure that the authority dealing with the succession will, in most situations, be applying its own law.' Of course, even in the system of that regulation, this objective is not always met since other considerations have sometimes prevailed over the policy of favouring the *lex fori*. Nevertheless, the Succession Regulation clearly goes in the right direction.

The same concern about promoting the application of *forum* law also inspired the 2007 Hague Protocol, which has been incorporated into the Maintenance Regulation. The reinforced role of the *lex fori*, which is promoted for claims made by certain 'privileged' classes of creditors to the rank of a principal criterion (Article 4(3)), is one of the main innovations of that instrument, as compared to the 1973 Hague Convention.[14]

---

12 See the interesting suggestion by SHAHEEZA LALANI, A Proposed Model to Facilitate Access to Foreign Law, *YPIL* 2011, pp. 299–313.

13 See, for example, the French decision referred to (in fn. 7) by CAROLINE KLEINER (*Cour de cassation*, 26.10.2011), in which the separation of property regime provided for by Algerian law was considered applicable to a French couple who – after two years of marriage in Algeria – had returned to France in 1962 and lived there since then.

14 See our Explanatory Report, Nos. 20 and 64 to 67.

By contrast, for the important area of matrimonial property, and for the quite common situation of a change of the common habitual residence, Article 17(1)(a) of the Proposal almost systematically leads to the application of foreign law. This is unfortunate and should be corrected.

3.3. APPLICATION OF DIFFERENT LAWS TO CONNECTED ISSUES

Questions relating to the property of the spouses arise in quite different situations, very often in parallel with issues pertaining to a different, but related area of the law, such as divorce, maintenance, succession, contracts, real property, and bankruptcy. In international situations, it is of course highly desirable that all of these different issues are subject to a single law.

Unfortunately, the immutability principle leads, in the case of a change of residence by the spouses, to the submission of the matrimonial property to the law of the *first* common habitual residence of the spouses. This law frequently differs from the law which is applicable to other connected issues under the existing European regulations or national choice-of-law rules.

Thus, when matrimonial property questions arise after the death of one of the spouses, the law applicable to such issues will generally be distinct from that governing the succession of the deceased, i.e., in the absence of a choice, the law of his/her *last* habitual residence (Article 21(1) of the Succession Regulation).[15]

In the case of divorce or separation, the law applicable to the division of the matrimonial property will frequently be different from the law which, in the absence of the spouses' choice, is applicable to divorce and separation under the Rome III Regulation, i.e. the law of the common habitual residence of the spouses at the time the court is seized or the law of their last common habitual residence (Article 8 Rome III Regulation).[16] A similar discrepancy will also result with respect to the law applicable to maintenance – which is normally, under the 2007 Hague Protocol, the law of the State of the *current* habitual residence of the creditor (Article 3) or the law of the State to which the spouses

---

[15] On the lack of coordination between the two instruments, see ANDREA BONOMI, The Interaction among the Future EU Instruments on Matrimonial Property, Registered Partnerships and Successions, *YPIL* 2011, pp. 217–231.

[16] Under Article 8(b) of the Rome III Regulation, the law of the State where the spouses were last habitually resident is applicable to divorce or legal separation 'provided that the period of residence did not end more than 1 year before the court was seized, in so far as one of the spouses still resides in that State at the time the court is seized.' Failing these conditions, the applicable law is that of the State of the common nationality or, failing that, the law of the forum. In any case, not one of these criteria points to the law of the State of the spouses' first common habitual residence.

are more closely connected, in particular that of their *last* common habitual residence (Article 5).[17]

These kinds of difficulties can also arise when questions related to the matrimonial property arise during the marriage on the occasion of a sale or another transaction concerning the assets of one of the spouses, in particular when the assets are situated in the country of the habitual residence of the spouses at the time of the transaction – as is frequently the case. The law of the country where the property is located (*lex rei sitae*) will normally govern – under national choice-of-law rules – the transfer of title over the property and, when required, the registration of the transaction. This same law will also govern, in the great majority of cases, the sales or the other underlying contract; under the Rome I Regulation the contract of sale is normally governed, for immovable property, by the *lex rei sitae* (Article 4(1)(c)), or otherwise by the law of the habitual residence of the seller (Article 4(1)(a)). By contrast, the law of the first common habitual residence of the spouses will be applicable to the issue of matrimonial property under Article 17(1)(a) of the Proposal, and the same law will also govern the effects of the matrimonial property regime on the legal relationship between the spouse(s) and a third party (Article 35(1) of the Proposal), i.e. the purchaser of the property or another third party contractor.

To protect the *bona fide* third party, however, the drafters of the Proposal were obliged to provide for a derogation from the general rule. Thus, Article 35(2) and (3) of the Proposal allow the State of the current habitual residence of the spouses (or of one of them) and the State of the location of the immovable property to provide that a spouse may not rely on the law applicable to the matrimonial property regime in dealings with a third party if the conditions of disclosure or registration set up by the law of that State are not satisfied, unless the third party was aware (or ought to have been aware) of the law applicable to the matrimonial property regime. This special and complex rule would in most cases have been superfluous if the matrimonial property regime were made subject to the law of the State of the current habitual residence of the spouses.

Finally, if one of the spouses is subjected to bankruptcy proceedings, the applicable law is normally the law of the State where the proceedings are instigated (Article 4 of the Insolvency Regulation). This is the State where the centre of the debtor's main interests is situated (Article 1 of the Insolvency Regulation), and coincides, in the case of a physical person, with the debtor's habitual residence at the time of commencing the proceedings. If the spouses are not separated, this leads to the application of the law of the country where they have their habitual residence at the time of the proceedings. Once again, the matrimonial property issues that can be of great importance during the proceedings will be governed, under Article 17(1)(a) of the Proposal, by a different law – that of the first habitual residence of the spouses.

---

17   See BEATRIZ CAMPUZANO DÍAZ (fn. 1), pp. 245 *et seq.*

In all of these cases, the immutability rule leads to the concurrent application of two or more different laws to questions which arise within the framework of the same transaction or the same proceedings, and which are closely connected to each other.

This circumstance may create serious problems of characterisation and adaptation. Thus, the submission of the matrimonial property regime and the succession of one of the spouses to two different laws raises difficult questions concerning the classification of certain national law rules or institutions, which are on the borderline between these two areas of the law.[18] The same is also true with respect to divorce and its financial consequences. For instance, the distinction between the division of matrimonial property regimes and the maintenance obligations between spouses can be very difficult if the law applicable to one of these issues is that of a common law country where the law does not clearly distinguish between these two legal categories and gives the competent court wide discretion to rule on all financial consequences of divorce or legal separation.

4.   THE POSSIBLE ALTERNATIVES

The criticism of the immutability rule can only be conclusive if one can show that another, more convincing, solution is available. Among the possible alternatives mentioned above, only a rule based on the retrospective (*ex tunc*) mutability of the applicable law really provides, in our view, more satisfactory results.

Such a rule should be based on the application of the law of the country of the habitual residence of the spouses at the time when the question of the matrimonial property regime arises (the 'relevant moment'). The relevant moment is, depending on the circumstances, that of death, legal separation or divorce, or that of a transaction relating to one of the spouses' assets or the opening of bankruptcy proceedings. If the spouses do not have their habitual residence in the same country at the relevant moment (e.g. in the case of previous separation or death), the applicable law should be that of the State in which they had their last common habitual residence.

Such a rule avoids most of the drawbacks we have previously emphasised. In particular:

–   The law of the present or last common habitual residence of the spouses normally satisfies the goal of proximity, on which the choice-of-law rules in this area should be based. As a matter of fact, the spouses can in no instance

---

[18]   For some examples, see ANDREA BONOMI, The Interaction among the Future EU Instruments on Matrimonial Property, Registered Partnerships and Successions, *YPIL* 2011, pp. 219–221.

be regarded as having weak contacts with the country where they have fixed the centre of their life, i.e. of their common personal and patrimonial interests. Contrary to the criteria of the spouses' first common habitual residence, that of their current or last common habitual residence never leads to the application of the law of a country that is now too remote to the spouses, or insignificant with respect to their present interests. Thus, this solution is entirely consistent both with the choice of the habitual residence as the main connecting factor, and with the search for the closest link as the last subsidiary rule in the 'cascade' system of Article 17 of the Proposal.

– Since judicial jurisdiction is frequently based, in this area of the law, on the current or last habitual residence of the spouses or of one of them, the application of the law of that same country will significantly reduce the instances in which a foreign law is applicable to the merits. The frequent application of the *lex fori* is regarded as one of the most important advantages of the retrospective mutability rule in the countries that have adopted that rule.

– The law of the current or last common habitual residence of the spouses will frequently coincide with the law applicable to other connected issues, such as divorce or legal separation and their financial consequences, the succession of one of the spouses, the transactions and the real rights relating to assets belonging to the spouses, and the insolvency proceedings opened in relation to the assets of one of the spouses.

In theory, another possible alternative to the immutability rule is a system based on the non-retrospective mutability of the law applicable to the matrimonial property regime. Such a solution would also satisfy the quest for proximity, and probably to an even higher degree than the retrospective mutability rule we propose. As a matter of fact, a rule of *ex nunc* mutability generally leads to the submission of each individual item of the spouses' property to the law of their habitual residence at the time of the acquisition of such property.

However, such a system would not entirely avoid the other drawbacks of immutability, i.e. the need to apply a foreign law to at least part of the assets, and the concurrent application of different laws to intertwined questions. Moreover, the *ex nunc* mutability rule would add a further element of complexity by imposing the successive application of two (or several!) different laws to the property acquired by the spouses at different moments of their married life. By doing so, such a rule would contradict one of the fundamental policies on which the Proposal rests, i.e. the principle of the unity of the applicable law (Article 15 of the Proposal).

For of all of these reasons, a rule based on retrospective mutability is, in our view, preferable.

5. THE ALLEGED FLAWS OF A RETROSPECTIVE MUTABILITY RULE

As mentioned above, all conceivable solutions to the questions raised by a change of the spouses' habitual residence have their advantages and disadvantages. The retrospective mutability rule, which we propose as the most appropriate solution for the purpose of unifying the choice-of-law rules on the matrimonial property regime in Europe, has also been the object, in the past, of very strong criticism. In the opinion of its detractors, this approach contains at least two main flaws. On the one hand, it leads to an automatic change of the applicable law and of the matrimonial property regime, which can be very surprising for the spouses concerned. On the other hand, such an automatic change of the matrimonial property regime can result in the loss of rights or expectations protected by the rules that were applicable prior to the change.

5.1. THE SURPRISE EFFECT

The first criticism is, in our opinion, not entirely convincing. It should be noted that, under the system of 'pure' mutability, which we propose, the change of the applicable law arises directly from the change of the common habitual residence of the spouses and not simply as a result of the passage of time, as is sometimes the case under the 1978 Hague Convention.[19] It is true that if the applicable law (and the property regime) changes with the passage of time, such a modification can be totally unperceived by the spouses and very surprising to them. The criticism addressed to this rule of the Hague Convention is therefore justified.[20]

However, it is submitted that the 'surprise effect' is much less evident when the change is an immediate consequence of the change of habitual residence. When the spouses move the 'centre of their life' to a different country, will a change of the rules applicable to their matrimonial property be so surprising to them?

Consider that when a person moves his or her habitual residence to a different country, most of the rules that constitute his or her legal 'environment' change. This is true with respect to personal and family life since the law of the new habitual residence will generally become applicable – either under existing European regulations or under national choice-of-law rules – to several aspects, such as the personal relationships between the spouses, their reciprocal financial

---

[19] See *supra*, section 2.
[20] See RICHARD CRÔNE, Le changement automatic de loi applicable au regime matrimonial: une bombe à retardement, Défrénois 2001, No. 37396; ERIC FONGARO, Le changement de regime matrimonial en droit international privé – Entre present et avenir, *Droit & Patrimoine* 2012, pp. 87–91, at p. 90.

rights and obligations, the personal and financial relationships with their children, the conditions and main effects of legal separation and divorce, and their rights in a future succession. More generally, the law of the new habitual residence becomes applicable to a very significant part of the professional and patrimonial interests of the persons concerned: it will govern many of the contractual relationships which they enter into, among other things, for housing and employment; it will also govern their social security rights and tax obligations. The law of the country to which the person has moved will also dictate the rules governing the person's general behaviour and determine the civil and penal consequences of his or her acts.

If, in such an overall changing context, the law of the new habitual residence becomes applicable to the property consequences of the marriage, where is the surprise? On the contrary, it could even be argued that the continuous application of the law of the first common habitual residence is surprising to the spouses, in particular when the change of residence occurred shortly after the marriage.[21]

One should also consider that spouses are generally unaware of the specificities of the matrimonial property regime governing their marriage. They often only become interested in and aware of the applicable rules when they have to sell some property (in particular immovable property), or when the matrimonial property is to be divided as a consequence of the death of one spouse or divorce. At the relevant moment, the spouses will normally seek legal advice, which will be easier to obtain in the country where they live, and will be based on local law rather than on the foreign law of their first common habitual residence.

Of course, in some cases spouses are very well informed about the rules which are applicable to the matrimonial property. This is more frequently the case for persons with significant wealth, or a higher level of education. However, a couple in this situation will normally gather information about the consequences of an intended change of their habitual residence, in particular for tax reasons, so that the risk of an unexpected change is reduced. In such instances, spouses frequently enter into a marriage contract regulating their property relations: if that is the case, an exception to the mutability rule should be provided so that the validity of the contract is not affected by the change in habitual residence.[22]

Finally, positive measures could be envisaged to further reduce the danger of a surprise effect. The European Union could easily require its Member States to set up an information mechanism for persons benefiting from freedom of movement. Normally, persons admitted for residence in a Member State must comply with some administrative requirements, and in particular ask for a

---

[21]   See the French cases referred to *supra*, fn. 6.
[22]   See *infra*, section 5.2.

residence permit. It would be very helpful if, in the course of such administrative procedures, applicants were provided with some basic information on the possible legal consequences of a change in habitual residence not only with respect to their matrimonial property, but also with respect to all other changes of the applicable law rules mentioned. Not to mention that in a constantly growing area of European private international law, parties are permitted to choose the law which is applicable to their private relationships (and thus to avoid an undesired change of the governing rules). The suggested information system would also have the function of instructing the persons concerned about such choices, thus reducing the gap between informed and uninformed migrants.

5.2. THE LOSS OF RIGHTS AND EXPECTATIONS

The second criticism aimed at the retrospective mutability approach is that this system, by leading to an *ex tunc* change of the rules applicable to the matrimonial property regime, entails, in certain situations, a loss of rights and expectations, which had accrued to the spouses, or to one of them, by virtue of the previously applicable law.

This objection is more serious than the previous one, and it specifically targets the retrospective application of the new law, which is ironically one of the most appealing features of the proposed mutability rule. To address this concern, it is important to first define and restrain the instances of the retrospective application of the law of the new common habitual residence of the spouses.

It seems obvious, on the one hand, that the suggested *ex tunc* application of the law of the new habitual residence should not affect the validity of previous transactions entered into under the law of a former habitual residence. If the spouses, or one of them, have validly alienated, or otherwise disposed of, specific assets in compliance with the requirements set up by the law of their common habitual residence at the time of the transaction, the validity and the effects of such a transaction should not be raised again as a consequence of the change of the habitual residence. By the same token, the right vested in third parties as an effect of such transactions should also be respected. These safeguards are normally provided for in all cases of the retrospective application of new rules of law. The Proposal itself includes an express provision to that effect in the last sentence of Article 18 with the aim of limiting the retrospective effect that spouses may decide to confer to the choice of law they are allowed to make at any time during the marriage.

Moreover, it is submitted that the proposed mutability rule should not apply when the spouses have entered into a marriage contract under the law of their previous habitual residence. In such a case, the change of the common habitual residence should not retrospectively disturb the validity of the property arrangements made by the spouses under the then applicable law. This solution is expressly provided for under Article 7(2) of the 1978 Hague Convention and under Article 55(2) of the Swiss Private International Law Act (PILA). To a certain extent, the same philosophy (*favor validitatis*) has also inspired the provisions of the Succession Regulation concerning the admissibility and the substantive validity of dispositions upon death (Articles 24 and 25).

A third qualification of the retrospective mutability rule should result from the rather broad admission of the spouses' choice of the applicable law under the Proposal. Since under Article 18 of the Proposal the spouses 'may, at any time during their marriage, make their matrimonial property regime subject to a law other than the one hitherto applicable', they should *a fortiori* be permitted – within the framework of a system providing for the retrospective mutability of the applicable law – to decide that the law of their previous habitual residence continues to be applicable notwithstanding a change of residence. Such a choice would amount to an agreed exclusion of the mutability of the applicable law. This is also permitted under Article 7(2) of the 1978 Hague Convention and under Article 55(2) of the Swiss PILA.

Notwithstanding the qualifications suggested above, the danger of a loss of rights or expectations still exists, to a certain extent, in the instances where the spouses have neither entered into a marriage contract, nor excluded the retrospective mutability. In our view, however, such a risk should not be overestimated.

First, one should consider that the fundamental purpose of matrimonial property regimes consists of granting, to the spouses, specific rights at the time of the dissolution of the regime. As such, it is not disturbing if the applicable law, and thus the applicable regime, are determined at the moment of dissolution, provided that the validity and effects of previous contracts and transactions are not affected.[23]

This is obviously the case when the property regime is based on the allocation to each of the spouses of a claim of participation in the acquisitions of the other spouse during the marriage (e.g. the German regime of the *Zugewinnausgleich*), or on the 'deferred' constitution of community property rights (e.g. the Danish and Swedish community property regimes).[24] In such systems, the value of the

---

[23]   It is true that under many matrimonial property regimes the spouses are already granted some specific rights *during the marriage*. In particular, the consent of both spouses is often required for the validity of acts of disposition concerning certain assets, and sometimes even for the administration thereof. Under a mutability system these rights will not be disregarded, but will instead be determined by the law which is applicable at the time of each act of disposition or administration of the assets concerned, i.e. by the law of the spouses' habitual residence at the relevant time. Therefore, it cannot be said that such rights are lost in the case of a retrospective change of the applicable law: they are just substituted by the equivalent rights granted by the new applicable law.

[24]   In Denmark, this regime is called '*formuefællesskab*', in Sweden '*giftorättssystem*'. See the study 'Les conséquences patrimoniales du divorce', by the French Senate, available at www.senat.fr/lc/lc72/lc72.pdf (last accessed 20.11.2013).

marital property is shared equally between the spouses upon the dissolution of the matrimonial property regime, but until that time, each of the spouses continues to own and control his or her property as if it were separate property. Since under such a regime no actual right in the other spouse's assets vests during the marriage, a retrospective change of the applicable law does not destroy any existing or protected legal position.

This is *a fortiori* the case when the law of the previous habitual residence is based on the discretionary power of the courts to divide the spouses' property in the case of divorce, legal separation, or succession, as is often the case in common law systems.

At first sight, this might seem different when the property regime provided by the law of the first common habitual residence is that of community property[25] since the effect of such a regime is to immediately confer, on each of the spouses, property rights in a share of the common assets. One has to consider, however, that even in such systems the main effects of the community property only become apparent at the time of the dissolution of the regime, when each of the spouses can claim the sharing of the common property. Until that moment, the spouses do not have any property rights on *specific* assets. Therefore, even in these situations, it cannot be said that a retrospective change of the applicable law destroys property rights in specific assets.

Of course, even if existing rights in specific assets are not affected by an automatic change of the applicable law (and of the matrimonial property regime), such a change can very seriously impact the spouses' expectations. This is for instance the case when a community property or participation regime is replaced by a separation of property regime, or vice versa.

This might seem harsh. One should consider, however, that this results from the fact that, under a mutability system, the migrant spouses will be submitted to the law of the country where they have chosen to establish their common habitual residence, and will therefore be treated in exactly the same way as all other spouses living in that country. This does not seem to be particularly shocking.

Moreover, the risk of a blatant lack of protection for the financially 'weaker' spouse is *de facto* very limited. One should consider that the proposed retrospective mutability rule would be applicable in the Member States of the European Union and that – for the reasons that we have already illustrated – it would most frequently lead to the application of the law of the forum State. Most European Union Member States provide in their internal law for quite a high level of protection for the 'weak' spouse, even if the chosen technical modalities may differ from one country to another (community property, deferred community property, participation in acquisitions, the power of the court to

---

25   This is the case in the law of several Member States, such as Belgium, Bulgaria, France, Italy, Portugal, Spain, etc.

equitably distribute the assets after divorce or legal separation, etc.). The change from one of these systems to another does not generally entail a serious impairment for the financially weaker spouse.[26]

The risk of a lack of protection can only become concrete in the few countries where the legal property regime is the separation of property (for instance in Catalonia). In this situation, however, compensation mechanisms are normally provided.[27] If not, the rules on maintenance obligations after divorce can also be used to prevent results that are too harsh.

6. CONCLUSION

To sum up, we consider that the reference to the spouses' first common habitual residence in Article 17 of the Proposal should be replaced by a reference to their current habitual residence or, failing that, to their last common habitual residence. The subsidiary connecting factors based on the common nationality or on the closest links should be applicable only when the spouses do not have and never have had a common habitual residence. The reference to the 'common' habitual residence should be intended as referring to the simultaneous habitual residence of the spouses in the same country.

Under this system, a change of the common habitual residence would lead to a retroactive change of the law governing the matrimonial property regime, without affecting the validity of previous transactions entered into under the law of a former habitual residence. Moreover, when the spouses have entered into a marriage contract under the law of their previous habitual residence, a change of the common habitual residence should not retrospectively disturb the validity of such a contract. In any case, the spouses should be permitted to exclude the mutability by deciding that the law of their previous habitual residence continues to be applicable notwithstanding a change of residence.

Finally, the Member States should be required to set up a mechanism providing immigrants with information on the legal consequences of a change in habitual residence and, where applicable, on the possibility to avoid some of these consequences by a choice of law.

---

[26] As mentioned above, the application of the law of the first common habitual residence often leads to harsher results, in particular when it is the law of a non-Member State (see *supra*, fn. 12).

[27] For instance, Article 41 of the Catalan Family Code, pursuant to which 'the spouse who has worked for the household or for the other spouse without payment in exchange, or with insufficient payment, is entitled to obtain economic compensation from the other spouse, in the event that this fact has produced a situation of inequality between the patrimonies of both spouses which implies an unjust enrichment of one spouse.'

'HABITUAL RESIDENCE' IN EUROPEAN FAMILY LAW

The Diversity, Coherence and Transparency of a Challenging Notion

Katharina Hilbig-Lugani

Contents

1. INTRODUCTION

Habitual residence has long been a well-established criterion in private international and international procedural law. But recently, its use in legislative acts in the field of European family law has strongly multiplied and diversified, thus creating new challenges when applying the concept of habitual residence. The following observations provide a little guidance in handling the habitual residence concept in its new leading role.

1.1. UBIQUITY OF THE HABITUAL RESIDENCE CONCEPT IN MODERN EUROPEAN FAMILY LAW ACTS

Habitual residence is the predominant or at least a very important criterion in a large number of European family law acts – the Brussels II *bis* Regulation,[1] the Rome III Regulation,[2] the Maintenance Regulation,[3] the Hague Protocol on Maintenance 2007[4] and the Draft Marital Property Regulations.[5] It is thus the guiding principle both in jurisdiction and in applicable law in divorce, maintenance and (will probably in the future be in) matrimonial property: for jurisdiction in divorce matters see Art. 3 para. 1(a) nos. 1–6 Brussels II *bis* Reg., for the applicable law in divorce matters see Art. 5 para. 1(a) and (b) as well as Art. 8(a) and (b) Rome III Reg. For jurisdiction in maintenance matters see

---

[1] Council Regulation (EC) No. 2201/2003 of 27 November 2003 concerning jurisdiction and the recognition and enforcement of judgments in matrimonial matters and matters of parental responsibility, repealing Regulation (EC) No. 1347/2000, OJ L 338, 23 December 2003, pp. 1–29.

[2] Council Regulation (EU) No. 1259/2010 of 20 December 2010 implementing enhanced cooperation in the area of the law applicable to divorce and legal separation, OJ L 343, 29 December 2010, pp. 10–16.

[3] Council Regulation (EC) No. 4/2009 of 18 December 2008 on jurisdiction, applicable law, recognition and enforcement of decisions and cooperation in matters relating to maintenance obligations, OJ L 7, 10 January 2009, pp. 1–79.

[4] Protocol of 23 November 2007 on the Law Applicable to Maintenance Obligations.

[5] Proposal for a Council Regulation on jurisdiction, applicable law and the recognition and enforcement of decisions in matters of matrimonial property regimes, COM (2011) 0126 final. The corresponding Proposal for registered partnerships is not governed by the residence principle and will not be regarded further in the present text.

Art. 3(a) and (b) as well as Art. 4 para. 1(a) and (c) no. ii Maintenance Reg., for the applicable law see Arts. 3, 4 para. 3, Arts. 5 and 8(b) Hague Protocol 2007. For jurisdiction in matrimonial property see Art. 3 Draft Marital Property Reg. in conjunction with Art. 4 Succession Reg., Art. 4 Draft Marital Property Reg. in conjunction with Art. 3(a) Brussels II *bis* Reg., Art. 5 para. 1(a) to (c) Draft Property Reg. and for the applicable law Art. 16(a) and (b), Art. 17 para. 1(a) as well as Art. 18(a) Draft Property Reg.

This tendency is very strong in, but is not restricted to, family law. The situation is similar in the Succession Regulation[6] – see especially Art. 4, Art. 13 for jurisdiction and Art. 21 para. 1, Art. 24 para. 1, Art. 25 paras. 1 and 2, Art. 27(d), Art. 28(b) Succession Reg. for the applicable law – in Rome I Regulation[7] – see Art. 4 para. 1(a), (b), (d), (e), (f), para. 2, Art. 5 para. 1, para. 2 subpara. 1, subpara. 2(a) and (b), Art. 6 para. 1 and many more as well as Art. 19 Rome I Reg. – in Rome II Regulation[8] – see Art. 4 para. 2, Art. 5 para. 1 subpara. 1(a), subpara. 2, Art. 10 para. 2, Art. 11 para. 2, Art. 12 para. 2(b), Art. 23 Rome II Reg. – and even the Insolvency Regulation.[9] The 'centre of main interest' which governs jurisdiction and applicable law (Arts. 3 and 4 para. 1 Insolvency Reg.) for physical persons is interpreted by the ECJ to generally refer to the habitual residence.[10] A central exception is the old[11] and new[12] Brussels I Regulation which primarily focuses on domicile instead of on habitual residence.

---

[6] Regulation (EU) No. 650/2012 of the European Parliament and of the Council of 4 July 2012 on jurisdiction, applicable law, recognition and enforcement of decisions and acceptance and enforcement of authentic instruments in matters of succession and on the creation of a European Certificate of Succession, OJ L 201, 27 July 2012, pp. 107–134.

[7] Regulation (EC) No. 593/2008 of the European Parliament and of the Council of 17 June 2008 on the law applicable to contractual obligations (Rome I), OJ L 177, 4 July 2008, pp. 6–16.

[8] Regulation (EC) No. 864/2007 of the European Parliament and of the Council of 11 July 2007 on the law applicable to non-contractual obligations (Rome II), OJ L 199, 31 July 2007, pp. 40–49.

[9] Council Regulation (EC) No. 1346/2000 of 29 May 2000 on insolvency proceedings, OJ L 160, 30 June 2000, pp. 1–18.

[10] ECJ, 25 October 2011, C-509/09 and C-161/10 – *eDate Advertising GmbH/ X and Martinez/ MGN Limited*, no. 49.

[11] Council Regulation (EC) No. 44/2001 of 22 December 2000 on jurisdiction and the recognition and enforcement of judgments in civil and commercial matters, OJ L 12, 16 January 2000, pp. 1–23.

[12] Regulation (EU) No. 1215/2012 of the European Parliament and of the Council of 12 December 2012 on jurisdiction and the recognition and enforcement of judgments in civil and commercial matters, OJ L 351, 20 December 2012, pp. 1–32.

1.2. COMMON CORE OF THE HABITUAL RESIDENCE NOTION

Positive secondary European Union law contains no definition of the habitual residence of a physical person acting for private purposes.[13] There is a common core of the habitual residence notion on which most authors in European jurisdictions would agree. It can be summarised as follows: (1) Habitual residence can be described as the actual centre of one's living. (2) A certain initial minimum physical presence is necessary to establish habitual residence but not under all circumstances to maintain it. Physical presence of a certain duration is a first important factor when ascertaining habitual residence. (3) Integration into the social environment is the second important factor. (4) The third one is the intention to reside.[14] (5) The duration of the presence, the social integration and the intention to reside are communicating factors among which the surplus of one can to a certain extent compensate for the lack of another.

1.3. CURRENT STANDARDS FOR INTERPRETATION

What can one say about the interpretation standards applied today for the habitual residence notion? The notion is subject to an autonomous interpretation, independent from national concepts. Whether habitual residence can be taken as given has to be established on a case by case basis. It is debated whether and to what extent the habitual residence notion can or should be subject to a uniform interpretation. Is it the same in all acts? Can it be the same in autonomous provisions, in international conventions and in European regulations? Within the European regulations is it the same in all jurisdictional provisions, on the one hand, and in all applicable law provisions, on the other? Or is it the same in certain substantive areas such as family law, the law of succession, the law of contracts, or smaller within family law in the fields of divorce, maintenance, property, care?

In examining the actual approach currently applied by doctrine and the courts we find that they deal with the notion in a very pragmatic, interactive, not

---

[13] For professional physical persons and juridical persons see Art. 19 Rome I Reg. and Art. 23 Rome II Reg. An attempt by the European Parliament to include a basic definition and guidelines for interpretation in Rome III (see EP, 19 September 2008, A6–0361–2008, pp. 7 et seq.) remained unsuccessful.

[14] This criterion is highly disputed. The majority in German doctrine are in favour of the relevance of a (manifested) *animus manendi*. See K. THORN, in: T. Rauscher, *EuZPR/EuIPR*, 2011, Art. 19 Rom I-VO no. 15; K. THORN, in: PALANDT, *BGB*, 72nd ed. 2013, Art. 19 Rom I-VO no. 6. In depth M.-P. WELLER, "Der 'gewöhnliche Aufenthalt' – Plädoyer für einen willenszentrierten Aufenthaltsbegriff", in: S. LEIBLE/H. UNBERATH (eds.), *Brauchen wir eine Rom 0-Verordnung?*, 2013, pp. 293 et seq.

to say creative manner. Often the authorities referred to stem from autonomous, international and European sources from all ages and substance matters. Often the commentators refer to the comments on other, presumably more central provisions and advocate the application of the principles developed for those other provisions, thereby often generating chain references and sometimes even circular references. So there is a great deal of interaction between the different branches – which is a good thing. But it is not always completely transparent how the actual pragmatic approach goes together with the theoretical approach on uniform interpretation. Often we find a certain tendency to divide the habitual residence concept into two large blocks – one interpretation for family and succession law (Brussels II *bis* Reg., Rome III Reg., Maintenance Reg., Hague Protocol, Succession Reg.) and one for (purely) economic issues (Rome I Reg., Rome II Reg., Insolvency Reg.).[15]

2. DIVERGENCE FACTORS

The central part of this contribution consists of identifying factors which create divergences in interpretation.

2.1. DIFFERENT LEGAL CONSEQUENCES IN JURISDICTIONAL AND APPLICABLE LAW PROVISIONS AS WELL AS IN OBJECTIVE CONNECTING FACTORS AND IN CHOICE OF LAW PROVISIONS

The first factor is the difference in the results of assuming or denying habitual residence.

2.1.1. Broadening the Options

Jurisdiction provisions typically establish concurring jurisdiction, thus assuming that habitual residence opens a broader range of competent courts to the applicant, typically favourable to the interests of the parties involved (see, for example, Art. 3 para. 1(a) Brussels II *bis* Reg., Art. 3(a) and (b) Maintenance Reg., Art. 5 Draft Marital Property Reg. and the former Art. 5 no. 2 Brussels I Reg.).

---

[15] In this sense J. KROPHOLLER/J. VON HEIN, *Europäisches Zivilprozessrecht*, 9th ed. 2011, Art. 3 EuMVVO, no. 3. Those two blocks blend into each other in Art. 5 no. 2 (old) Brussels I Reg., the (former) international jurisdiction provision for maintenance claims (see U.P. GRUBER, in: T. RAUSCHER (ed.), *EuZPR/EuIPR*, 2010, Art. 3 EG-MahnVO, no. 12).

Also in the choice of applicable law provisions, thus assuming that habitual residence typically leads to a broader range of laws from which the parties can choose (see, for example, Art. 5 para. 2 subpara. 2(a) and (b) as well as Art. 7 para. 3 subpara. 2(b) Rome I Reg., Art. 5 para. 1(a) and (b) Rome III Reg., Art. 8(b) Hague Protocol 2007 and Art. 16(a) and (b) Draft Marital Property Reg.).

Similarly, in provisions allowing for choice of court agreements, thus assuming that habitual residence typically broadens the scope of eligible jurisdictions (see, for example, Art. 15 no. 3 and Art. 19 no. 3 Brussels II *bis* Reg. as well as Art. 4 para. 1(a) and (c) no. ii Maintenance Reg.).

2.1.2. *Blocking Subsidiary Options*

In contrast, when habitual residence forms one of the objective connecting factors for the applicable law, assuming that habitual residence typically bars access to the next step on the ladder of objective connections and denying habitual residence allows access to the next step (see, for example, Art. 4 paras. 1, 2, 4 Rome I Reg., Art. 4 paras. 2, 3 and Art. 12 para. 2(c) Rome II Reg., Art. 8(a) and (b) Rome III Reg. and Art. 17 para. 1(a) Draft Marital Property Reg.).

Thus to the extent that approving the existence of a habitual residence is in the interests of both parties[16] the notion can be dealt with more generously than where habitual residence is employed to establish the applicable law in the absence of a choice of law clause. Furthermore, in both types of provisions, the question of multiple habitual residences may be answered differently, as well as the question of an alternating habitual residence.

2.2. DIVERGING (GROUPS OF) PERSONS CONCERNED

The second factor concerns the differences arising from the different persons addressed. The habitual residence may be that of a person independently of his or her position in a family relationship network (Rome I Reg., Rome II Reg., Insolvency Reg.) or that of children (see e.g. Art. 4 para. 1(c) Hague Protocol 2007, Arts. 8 and 10 Brussels II *bis* Reg.), spouses (see e.g. Art. 3 Brussels II *bis* Reg., Arts. 5, 8 Rome III Reg., Art. 4 para. 1(c) Maintenance Reg., Art. 5 Hague Protocol 2007, Arts. 5, 16, 17, 18 Draft Marital Property Reg.) or of other family members or family members in general (Arts. 3, 4 Maintenance Reg., Arts. 3, 4 para. 1(a) and (b), para. 3 Hague Protocol 2007).

---

[16]   e.g. when it broadens the scope of laws which are capable of being chosen in a fair and reasonable choice of law agreement or when it leads to an additional competent forum which does not result in any inconvenience for the defendant.

Although neither children nor spouses can be considered dependent, the habitual residence of children follows different rules than the habitual residence of adults.[17] The younger they are, the more their habitual residence is closely connected to that of the parent(s) in whose care they are. The younger they are, the faster they will be able to establish a new habitual residence. The plans of a working adult for his or her life in the years to come carry more weight than a young child's ideas about the future. when appreciating the common habitual residence of spouses, the plans of the partner and the family plans will carry more weight than when appreciating the habitual residence of a person independent from his family context. More generally: when confronted with a person addressed by the lawmaker by his or her position in the family relationship network, the focus of the relevant questions and test will be different from those applicable when confronted with a person addressed by the lawmaker merely by his professional quality as a seller, consumer or debtor.

2.3. METHODOLOGICAL DIFFERENCES IN APPLYING THE HAGUE PROTOCOL 2007 AND EU REGULATIONS

Divergences are thirdly raised by the fact that interpretation standards for the Hague Protocol 2007 diverge from interpretation standards for acts of the European Union. The Hague Protocol 2007 remains an international convention and does not have the character of European Union law. The specific set of interpretation rules developed for secondary European Union law will thus not apply to it. The Maintenance Regulation, pursuant to its consideration no. 8, has to be interpreted in the light of the Hague Protocol. So we are confronted with three different sets of interpretation rules: for the Hague Protocol purely international convention methods, for the Maintenance Regulation a mix of international convention and European Union methods and for all others purely European Union methods.

2.4. DIFFERENT COURT STRUCTURES FOR THE INTERPRETATION OF THE HAGUE PROTOCOL 2007 AND EU REGULATIONS

Similarly and fourthly, the interpretation of EU regulations including the Maintenance Regulation takes place in the hierarchical court structure superseded by the ECJ while the interpretation of the Hague Protocol is not controlled by one supreme instance.

---

17   For recent case law see ECJ, 2 April 2009, C-523/07 – A, FamRZ 2009, p. 843 and ECJ, 22 December 2010, C-497/10 PPU – Mercredi/Chaffe, FamRZ 2011, p. 617.

2.5. DRAFTING DIFFERENCES

When it comes to the structure of the habitual residence provision itself, the relevant rules represent large-scale drafting differences.

2.5.1. Establishing Habitual Residence Today or at a Point in Time in the Past

The task may be about establishing habitual residence in the present or many years ago. As examples of the first type see Art. 6 para. 2 and Art. 8(a) and (b) Rome III Reg., Art. 4 para. 1 subpara. 2 Maintenance Reg. (application to the court), Art. 15 para. 3(a) Brussels II *bis* Reg. (a point in time after an application to the court), Art. 4 and Art. 21 para. 1 Succession Reg. (the death of the deceased), and Art. 3 Draft Marital Property Reg. in conjunction with Art. 4 Succession Reg. (the death of the spouse). As examples for the second type see Art. 8 para. 1(b) Hague Protocol 2007, Art. 5 para. 1(a) Rome III Reg., Art. 4 para. 1(a), (c) no. 2 Maintenance Reg., Art. 16(b) and 18(a) Draft Marital Property Reg. (the time of the choice of law or choice of court agreement) and Art. 17 para. 1(a) Draft Marital Property Reg. (the time of the celebration of the marriage). Where habitual residence has to be established for a point in time in the far past, two modifications might occur. First, the density and precision of the facts and the conviction required to establish habitual residence might be lower. Second, objective aspects might reasonably take the lead over subjective aspects (the intention to reside), because the subjective aspects might become typically impossible to establish for events in the far past.

2.5.2. Establishing Habitual Residence for a Certain Point in Time or for a Certain Duration

Numerous provisions require habitual residence at only one moment in time while some ask whether habitual residence exists or has ceased to exist for a certain duration of time. As examples of the second type see Art. 4 para. 1(c) no. 2 Maintenance Reg., Art. 8(b) Rome III Reg., Art. 3 para. 1(a) no. 5 Brussels II *bis* Reg. (one year) and Art. 3 para. 1(a) no. 6 Brussels II *bis* Reg. (six months). Depending on whether a point in time or a longer duration is concerned, the set of facts which we have to take into account will vary and given the flexibility of the entire appreciation, it is very well possible that for one specific moment our decision on whether or not a habitual residence existed might have a different outcome based on the two different sets of facts.

2.5.3. Affirming or Dismissing the Existence of a Habitual Residence

Sometimes it is asked whether a habitual residence exists, sometimes whether it has been terminated; e.g. in the provisions requiring the last common habitual residence of the spouses given that one spouse still maintains this habitual residence – Art. 5 para. 1(b) Draft Marital Property Reg., Art. 3 para. 1(a) no. 2 Brussels II *bis* Reg. and Art. 5 para. 1(b) Rome III Reg. Of course, the thresholds for establishing (and terminating) habitual residence A and (establishing and) terminating habitual residence B are identical, but focusing in an isolated manner on establishing or terminating the habitual residence shifts the balance of appreciation so that the same facts might acquire a different relevance in one scenario or the other.

2.5.4. Exceptional Character

Whether or not the rule containing the habitual residence criterion contains an exception or not will influence whether we interpret the habitual residence criterion in a restrictive or an extensive manner. Examples of exceptions can be found in Art. 15 para. 3(a), (b), (d) Brussels II *bis* Reg. as well as in Art. 6(a) Succession Reg.

2.6. DIFFERENCES IN LEGITIMACY/ACCEPTANCE

An important source of divergence lies in the different levels of legitimacy and/ or acceptance of the rules concerned.

For example, many people criticise Art. 5 para. 1(b) Rome III Reg. which provides that the spouses can choose as the law applicable to their divorce the law of their last common habitual residence if one spouse still maintains this habitual residence. Authors rightly criticise that this does not represent a law with which both spouses are really closely connected.[18] They might thus tend to lean towards a restrictive interpretation of the last common habitual residence and/or of the maintained habitual residence. Another example is jurisdiction nos. 5 and 6 in Art. 3(a) Brussels II *bis* Reg., which were not as universally agreed upon as jurisdiction nos. 1–4.[19] Furthermore, Art. 5(d) Rome III Reg. is surprising because it requires not necessarily more than a unilateral link between one spouse and the law chosen (e.g. if the *lex fori* based on the opponent's habitual residence is chosen).[20] Moreover, the close connection between the spouses and the law chosen in Art. 5 Rome III Reg. only needs to

---

[18] D. COESTER-WALTJEN/M. COESTER, "Rechtswahlmöglichkeiten im Europäischen Kollisionsrecht", in: R. MICHAELS/D. SOLOMON (eds.), *Liber Amicorum Klaus Schurig*, 2012, pp. 33 et seq., 38.

[19] For more details, see A. BORRÁS, in: U. MAGNUS/P. MANKOWSKI (eds.), *European Commentaries on Private International Law: Brussels IIbis Regulation*, 2012, Art. 3 nos. 10 et seq.

[20] The necessity of a close link between the spouses and the law chosen is underlined in consideration nos. 14 and 16.

exist at the moment when the choice of law is made without there being room for an adaptation to changed circumstances, even though the connection might have been dissolved some 20, 30 or 40 years ago.[21]

2.7. INFLUENCE OF GENERAL LEGISLATIVE GUIDELINES

As a seventh point we must take into account general legislative guidelines underlying the provision containing the habitual residence criterion.

2.7.1. Protection of the Weaker Party

The rule's goal to protect the weaker party might influence our understanding of habitual residence in the form requirements for the choice of divorce law (Art. 7 paras. 2 and 4 Rome III Reg.), in the limit on maintenance proceedings (Art. 8 para. 1 Maintenance Reg.) or in the choice of law limits with regard to a renunciation of the right to maintenance (Art. 8 para. 4 Hague Protocol 2007).

2.7.2. Strengthening Party Autonomy

The commitment to allow for more party autonomy is celebrated as one of the main innovations of the Hague Protocol.[22] We might thus tend to lean towards an extensive interpretation of the habitual residence notion in Art. 8 para. 1(b) Hague Protocol 2007 on the eligible jurisdictions.

2.7.3. Others

Other legislative aims influencing our interpretation might for example be the tendency to make divorce easy to obtain (*favor divortii*, see Rome III Reg.),[23] the

---

21   See K. BOELE-WOELKI, "For better or for worse: the Europeanization of International divorce law", *YbPIL* 12 (2010), 1, 16 and P. FRANZINA, "The law applicable to divorce and legal separation under Regulation (EU) no. 1259/2010 of 20 December 2010", *Cuadernos de Derecho Transnacional (CDT)* 3 (2011), pp. 85 et seq., 110, 111, no. 47.

22   A. BONOMI, *Rapport Explicatif*, 2009, no. 109; A. BONOMI, "The Hague Protocol of 23 November 2007 on the Law Applicable to Maintenance Obligations", *YbPIL* 10 (2008), 333, 351; A. BOICHÉ, "Propos introductif: entrée en vigueur du règlement CE n° 4/2009 sur les obligations alimentaires", *AJ Famille* 2011, 236; J. HIRSCH, "Das neue Haager Unterhaltsübereinkommen und das Haager Protokoll über das auf Unterhaltspflichten anzuwendende Recht", in: D. COESTER-WALTJEN/V. LIPP/E. SCHUMANN/B. VEIT (eds.), *Europäisches Unterhaltsrecht: Die Bedeutung der Haager Übereinkommen und der UnterhaltsVO für das englische und deutsche Recht. 8. Göttinger Workshop zum Familienrecht*, 2010, pp. 17 et seq., 34.

23   See C. KOHLER, "Einheitliche Kollisionsnormen für Ehesachen in der Europäischen Union: Vorschläge und Vorbehalte", *FamRZ* 2008, pp. 1673 et seq., 1680 with further references; P. FRANZINA, "The law applicable to divorce and legal separation under Regulation (EU) No. 1259/2010 of 20 December 2010", *Cuadernos de Derecho Transnacional (CDT)* 3 (2011), pp. 85 et

intention to minimise the relevance of nationality in favour of habitual residence (e.g. Arts. 5 and 8 Rome III Reg.),[24] the interest in the continuity of the applicable law to enable a planned and orderly family life over decades,[25] the aim to have a coincidence of *ius* and *forum* (very visible in the interaction between the Brussels II *bis* Reg. and the Rome III Reg.)[26] and the tendency to enable valid dispositions of property upon death (*favor testamenti*, Art. 27 Succession Reg.).

2.8. INFLUENCE OF SURROUNDING PROVISIONS

Furthermore, we cannot appreciate the habitual residence notion in an isolated manner as we have to take the system of surrounding provisions into account. When appreciating the habitual residence criterion in a provision on choice of law, we might be influenced by whether or not the act in question provides sufficient safeguards for the weaker party in the choice of law agreement. For example, such a safeguard mechanism is contained in Art. 8 para. 5 Hague Protocol 2007 while it is lacking – according to the dominant opinion[27] – in the Rome III Regulation. When finding a habitual residence proves to be difficult, the result of our search might be influenced by whether or not the act in question contains a viable default rule, such as is the case in Art. 13 para. 1 Brussels II *bis* Reg.

2.9. DIFFERENT HABITUAL RESIDENCES FOR DIFFERENT ASPECTS OF LIFE?

A very tricky question is whether one might even consider whether a person can have differing habitual residences for different aspects of life. In the same way as

---

seq., 98 et seq., nos. 21 et seq. Similarly the former German Minister of Justice S. LEUTHEUSSER-SCHNARRENBERGER in a Press Release of 3 December 2010 (available at www.bmj.bund.de), and D. LOOSCHELDERS, "Scheidungsfreiheit und Schutz des Antragsgegners im internationalen Privat- und Prozessrecht", in: D. BAETGE/J. VON HEIN/M. VON HINDEN (eds.), *Die richtige Ordnung: Festschrift für Jan Kropholler zum 70. Geburtstag*, 2008, pp. 329 et seq., 350.

24   See P. HAMMJE, "Le nouveau règlement (UE) n° 1259/2010 du Conseil du 20 décembre 2010 mettant en oeuvre une coopération renforcée dans le domaine de la loi applicable au divorce et à la séparation de corps", *Revue critique de droit international privé (RCDIP)* 2011, pp. 291 et seq., no. 35 and EPEC, *Study to inform a subsequent Impact Assessment on the Commission proposal on jurisdiction and applicable law in divorce matters*, Draft final report, April 2006, Table 6.7., p. 54.

25   See D. COESTER-WALTJEN/M. COESTER, "Rechtswahlmöglichkeiten im Europäischen Kollisionsrecht", in: R. MICHAELS/D. SOLOMON (eds.), *Liber Amicorum Klaus Schurig*, 2012, pp. 33 et seq., 42.

26   See COM (2006) 399 final, p. 11; COM (2010) 105 final, p. 8.

27   Disagreeing and advocating content control on the European level is C. KOHLER, "Le choix de la loi applicable au divorce – Interrogations sur le règlement 'Rome III' de l'Union européenne", in: H. KRONKE/K. THORN (eds.), *Grenzen überwinden – Prinzipien bewahren. Festschrift für Bernd von Hoffmann zum 70. Geburtstag*, 2011, pp. 208 et seq., 217.

one might establish a habitual residence more easily for the sale of a car than for the purposes of succession after death, one might establish habitual residence more easily for the purpose of a maintenance claim than for the purpose of the spouses' property.

Take the following example: a 35-year-old German national born and raised in Bonn moved to Marseille, France, two years ago to work as a car dealer. He then dies in a car accident. One aspect of the case is whether one of the last cars he sold was defective and which law is applicable to the sales contract – what is the seller's habitual residence for the purpose of Art. 4 para. 1(a) Rome I Reg.? Another aspect of the case is which law governs the succession after his death – what is the habitual residence of the deceased for the purposes of Art. 21 para. 1 Succession Reg.? If one asks those two questions in two different oral examinations, I assume that the students will have no problem in assuming habitual residence for the purpose of Rome I Regulation – two years of living and working in a new environment will surely be regarded as sufficient. I suppose that they will be much more hesitant when it comes to the succession questions. The students will, if possible, ask further questions: What were the young man's plans for the future – did he envisage returning home to Bonn? What was his family situation, did he have a wife or partner and/or children in Bonn or Marseille? What other links did he maintain with Bonn – maybe he maintained close ties with his old friends, casual business transactions, frequent visits to his parents? Where did he have most of his assets, especially immovables – in Germany or in France? Did he contemplate his death in any way? Depending on the answers to these questions, in one and the same case we might assume and deny a habitual residence depending on which aspect of life is concerned. The students' tendency to treat the two cases differently is supported by considerations 23 et seq. of the Succession Reg. which outline a very proper and restrictive understanding of habitual residence for the purposes of the Succession Regulation.

This effect will not only appear in succession and contract cases or the like, but also in pure family law cases: there will be much more hesitation to assume a habitual residence for establishing the law applicable to matrimonial property than for the purposes of jurisdiction in a maintenance proceeding.

The next question is whether this approach – probably not always entirely conscious – to differentiate between areas of life should be admitted or whether it would be better to stick to the notion that one person has the same habitual residence no matter whether we look at his contractual liability, his marriage or his death. To the extent that different understandings are not dictated by EU law,[28] I would advocate a uniform approach for all areas of life. The reason for this is simple: given all the divergence factors discussed above, the numerous

---

[28] The exact impact of considerations 23 et seq. Succession Reg. is not yet fully clear.

divergence factors multiplied by the numerous different areas of life,[29] accompanied by different doctrine and case law for all those areas of life, will most probably result in an atomised notion of habitual residence which will completely lack any common strains.

3. CONCLUSIONS: TRANSPARENT STANDARDS FOR INTERPRETATION

The above observations result, as a first conclusion, in the call for a commitment to more transparency, to a more transparent handling of principles relied upon and a more transparent handling of the divergence criteria. The differences in and the difficulties of habitual residence provisions should be clearly displayed and labelled in that way instead of being hidden beneath the seemingly attractive idea of uniformity in interpretation.

The above observations have demonstrated that there can be no large general areas of uniform interpretation of 'habitual residence' in EU family law acts (and beyond). Interpretation may be surprisingly uniform between two very distant provisions and it might be very distinct for two neighbouring provisions. Even if we decide to decline the legitimacy of certain divergence factors – saying, for example, that no difference should be made between different areas of life or pursuant to the systematic surroundings of the provision – we will most probably not be entirely successful. This is due to the fact that the lawyer applying a certain provision typically lacks the synoptic view which revealed the divergence criteria to us. When his or her interpretation is influenced by one of those 'inadmissible' divergence criteria, he or she might not even necessarily be aware of it.

What is suggested here is not to give new content to the habitual residence concept. It is rather about employing a more open and more detailed method when testing the existence of a habitual residence. This will raise consciousness among lawyers of the different facets of habitual residence and help to improve the predictability and comparability of the results.

On the level of fact gathering we should standardise the facts taken into account in order to either – whatever we finally opt for – eliminate or at least to control the influence of the subject matter/area of life concerned, so that we are aware that we are gathering facts which are very specific to successions or marriage or contract. On the level of appreciation we should first determine the time scale of the appreciation, which varies according to whether a certain point in time or a time span is relevant. We should secondly give consideration to

---

29   There is no real consensus on what one area of life is – whether it is the "family" or whether the field family has to be subdivided into marriage, marital property, divorce, maintenance, care etc.

potential specific interdependences with other persons (e.g. children, spouses). Thirdly, we should be clear about the applicable factors dictating a wide or narrow interpretation (such as the level of acceptance, the general legislative guidelines, the systematic surroundings, the exceptional characteristics, etc.). Finally, we should determine what relevance should be attributed to subjective factors and this relevance should diminish with the distance between the relevant point in time and today.

NEW APPROACHES TO SAME-SEX MARRIAGE

The End of Nationality as a Connecting Factor?

Stuart DAVIS

Contents

The use of nationality and domicile as a connecting factor for private international law questions over same-sex relationships has already been abandoned in Belgium and the Netherlands, whenever such use would deny giving effect to a same-sex marriage. Recent French developments mark a further remarkable shift away from its use as a means to determine personal law. Finally, England may find itself forced to reconsider its approach to the use of domicile as a connecting factor, once the implications of its new law on same-sex marriage are properly understood.

1. INTRODUCTION

In the United States, the approach taken by the courts in determining the validity of a marriage from another state is generally to presume validity if the necessary conditions, both as to form and capacity, are fulfilled under the law of the state where the marriage was celebrated, the *lex loci celebrationis*.[1] Rebutting this presumption depends on a properly formulated application of the public policy exception.[2] This causes tensions where an increasing number of US jurisdictions now permit same-sex marriages, whilst others remain vehemently opposed.[3] Section 2 of the Defense of Marriage Act 1996[4] confuses matters as it purports to enshrine a right not to recognise an out-of-state same-sex marriage,[5] but this does not override the basic principle that the refusal needs to be based on a legitimate use of the public policy exception. The debate on the scope and nature of this exception, and the limits which may be imposed on its use by US constitutional protections, has been continuing for many years.[6]

European jurisdictions, on the other hand, need not always invoke a public policy exception to refuse recognition to an otherwise valid foreign same-sex marriage. Frequently, their private international law rules provide an additional peg on which to hang a refusal. The formal validity of a marriage still depends on adherence to requirements in the place of celebration, but questions as to the capacity of the parties to marry are governed by each individual's 'personal law', usually the law of his or her nationality or domicile.

The Netherlands and, later, Belgium each had to find a solution to this dilemma of personal incapacity based on nationality when they introduced same-sex marriage, discussed in section 2 below. More recently France, known for her adherence to a strict approach towards capacity based on national personal law, has also expanded the institution of marriage to include same-sex couples.[7] In doing so, her existing rules on capacity have been recognised as no

[1] *Restatement (Second) of Conflict of Laws* (1971), §283, discussed by BARBARA COX, 'Same-Sex Marriage and Choice-of-Law: If we marry in Hawaii, are we still married when we return home?' (1994) *Wis L Rev*, p. 1033, at p. 1063.
[2] JOANNA GROSSMAN, 'Resurrecting Comity: Revisiting the Problem of Non-Uniform Marriage Laws' (2005) 84 *Oregon LR*, p. 101.
[3] CNN, 'Same Sex Marriage Fast Facts', available at http://edition.cnn.com/2013/05/28/us/same-sex-marriage-fast-facts/index.html (last accessed 14.09.2013).
[4] 10 Stat. 2419.
[5] The US Supreme Court judgment of 26 June 2013 in *US v Windsor* struck down Section 3 (but not Section 2) of the Defense of Marriage Act as a breach of the Equal Protection provisions of the US constitution: hence the ban on recognition of same-sex marriages at the federal level was found unconstitutional but the express choice for individual US states to deny recognition to another state's same-sex marriages remains unaffected, at least for now.
[6] LARRY KRAMER, 'Same-Sex Marriage, Conflict of Laws, and the Unconstitutional Public Policy Exception' (1996–97) 106 *Yale LJ*, p. 1965.
[7] Loi no. 2013–404 du 17 mai 2013 ouvrant le mariage aux couples de personnes de même sexe.

longer suitable, leading to a further move away from nationality as a connecting factor, discussed in section 3. England and Wales, which also now allow same-sex marriage,[8] use a similarly strict approach, basing capacity under personal law on 'domicile', a concept closely related to nationality in that it is inherited at birth, does not vary according to habitual residence, and can be difficult to change. England has yet to recognise the problems which remain unsolved in its new legislation, but I argue the new law will need to bring with it a significant change in the use of domicile as a connecting factor, discussed in section 4.

2. REMOVING THE YOKE OF CITIZENSHIP: BELGIUM AND ELSEWHERE

The use of personal law to determine capacity for marriage means those affected find it difficult to circumvent any prohibitions or incapacities imposed on them by their 'home' state, even if they exercise their free movement rights to move elsewhere within the EU. On a strict application of the principle it means that Italian nationals, for example, lacking capacity to enter into a same-sex marriage under Italian law, are not only unable to conclude a same-sex marriage in Italy, but also find themselves unable to form a same-sex marriage in any other country, even one which permits same-sex marriage for its own nationals (or which allows marriages for nationals of such other countries which also permit same-sex marriage). This also affects the ability of already-married same-sex couples to enjoy other EU treaty freedoms, such as where they own property in a Member State and want to assert their married status there for tax, succession or other reasons.

2.1. DISREGARD OF INCAPACITY UNDER FOREIGN PERSONAL LAW

To avoid this scenario, European jurisdictions which have introduced same-sex marriage have also normally introduced provisions to ensure that marriages celebrated on their own territory are not rendered void by virtue of the nationality of one or other of the couple. Usually these provisions ensure the validity of marriages where at least one of the couple is a resident or national of the country in question. They also enable the country performing the marriage to avoid imposing a discriminatory ban on its own citizens to the effect that they can only marry certain foreigners and not others. The Netherlands, the first country to introduce same-sex marriage, was already able to rely on provisions

---

8   Marriage (Same Sex Couples) Act 2013, effective since 29 March 2014.

which refer questions of essential validity to Dutch law where one of the future spouses is Dutch or habitually resident in the Netherlands.[9] These mirror Article 3(1) of the 1978 Hague Convention on the Celebration and Recognition of the Validity of Marriages,[10] although only the Netherlands, Australia and Luxembourg have ratified the Convention.[11] Dutch law also mirrors the Convention in how it recognises a foreign same-sex marriage, namely that its validity depends on the law of the place of celebration.[12] This means, importantly, that the capacity of the parties to enter into the marriage will also be determined by the *lex loci celebrationis* which may or may not refer to the nationality of the parties.

Belgium, by comparison, did not originally modify its private international law rules when it introduced same-sex marriage in 2003, but in 2004 introduced a specific exception in Article 46(2) Belgian Code of Private International Law.[13] Since then, whilst capacity to marry is still primarily governed by personal law, any incapacity to enter into a same-sex marriage will be disregarded if one of the couple has the nationality of a jurisdiction permitting same-sex marriage, or has his habitual residence in such a jurisdiction.

This effectively meant that French citizens living in Belgium could enter into a same-sex marriage there when this was still prohibited in France. It also meant a French citizen could, in Belgium, marry a Belgian of the same sex even if both were living in France, and even that a French citizen still living in France could marry someone of any nationality as long as the latter was habitually resident in Belgium.

Understandably, both the Dutch and Belgian solutions triggered a negative reaction in France from those who saw these private international rules as unnecessarily 'flexible'.[14] It might have been seen as an unwarranted extension of sovereignty – why should Belgian law purport to determine the capacity of a

---

[9] Article 2(a) Wet Conflictenrecht Huwelikj 7 September 1989, Stb. 1989, 392, now replaced in the same form by Article 10:28 Dutch Civil Code.

[10] Available at www.hcch.net/index_en.php?act=conventions.text&cid=88 (last accessed 14.09.2013).

[11] There is some debate as to whether the Convention was intended to apply to same sex marriages: IAN CURRY-SUMNER, 'Private International Law Aspects of Homosexual Couples: The Netherlands Report' (May 2007) Vol. 11.1 *Electronic Journal of Comparative Law*, available at www.ejcl.org/111/art111-8.pdf (last accessed 04.09.2013), but there is nothing in the wording of the Convention itself to suggest otherwise.

[12] Article 10:31 Dutch Civil Code.

[13] Loi 16 juillet 2004 portant le Code de droit international privé, Moniteur Belge 27.07.2004. See AUDE FIORINI, 'The codification of private international law: the Belgian experience' (2005) 54 *ICLQ*, p. 499.

[14] For example HUGUES FULCHIRON, 'Mariage et Partenariats Homosexuels en Droit International Privé Français' (2006) *RIDC*, p. 409, at p. 425.

French citizen to marry, particularly one still living in France rather than in Belgium?[15]

2.2. CAPACITY ISSUES IN RECOGNISING FOREIGN SAME-SEX MARRIAGES

One further consequence of the Belgian reforms is that they apply not only to marriages conducted in Belgium, but also affect the way Belgian law regards marriages conducted elsewhere. Article 46(2) does not say simply that any incapacity to enter a same-sex marriage is disregarded if one of the couple is a Belgian national or habitually resident in Belgium. If it had, the effect would be limited to confirming that a Belgian resident or national is not restricted as to the nationality or residence of the same-sex partner he or she wants to marry in Belgium.[16] Instead, the provisions refer, in the abstract, to residence in 'a state' which permits same-sex marriage.[17] The formalities for a Belgian marriage require this condition to be satisfied in any event, in that at least one of the couple must be a resident or a national of just such a country (namely, Belgium) in order to marry there, so the wording must be intended to have a wider application: incapacity under personal law is to be disregarded if one of the couple is habitually resident in, or a national of, *any* country which permits same sex marriage. The rule thus also implicitly applies to marriages conducted outside Belgium. In other words, Belgian law goes further than simply applying the *lex loci celebrationis* to determine capacity, and disregards incapacities to marry a same-sex partner irrespective of whether the marriage takes place in Belgium, or the place of habitual residence of one or both of the couple, or anywhere else where same-sex marriage is permitted. As discussed in section 4 below, this has interesting consequences for same-sex marriages which might now be conducted in England between non-domiciliaries, as these could end up being valid in Belgium but void in England.

---

[15] Although it did not mean, of course, that the Belgian marriage in question would necessarily be recognised or given any effect in France, so to this extent French sovereignty is unaffected.

[16] This is effectively the situation under the equivalent Dutch provisions and Article 3(1) of the Hague Convention, which apply only where one of the couple is a national or resident of the country in which the marriage is celebrated.

[17] Article 46(2) reads, in the original, 'L'application d'une disposition du droit désigné en vertu de l'alinéa 1er est écartée si cette disposition prohibe le mariage de personnes de même sexe, lorsque l'une d'elles a la nationalité d'un Etat ou a sa résidence habituelle sur le territoire d'un Etat dont le droit permet un tel mariage.' Translation: 'The application of a provision of law deemed applicable by virtue of subsection (1) is set aside where this provision prohibits the marriage of persons of the same sex and where one of them is a citizen of, or has his or her habitual residence in, a State whose law permits such a marriage.'

2.3. DISREGARD OF INCAPACITY BY FOREIGN JURISDICTIONS RESPECTED BY FORUM STATE

Whilst Belgium appears to impose its own notions of capacity even to foreign marriages, other countries adopt a different solution. To recap, the problem relates not to marriages performed on home territory involving foreign citizens who might otherwise lack capacity, but instead concerns the effect of marriages performed in another jurisdiction involving nationals who lack capacity under their personal law. Take, for example, Yves, a French citizen living in France, whose Italian boyfriend Luca lives in Brussels. The couple get married in Belgium. As discussed above, whilst this marriage would not until recently have been recognised in France, it remains a valid marriage in Belgium by virtue of the 2004 provisions, which now look to the law of Luca's *habitual residence* to accord capacity to marry. But other countries now have a choice – do they, as did France, treat the marriage as void because neither party had capacity to marry under their personal law based on nationality or prior domicile, or do they, like Belgium, treat it as valid by looking at something other than nationality as the relevant connecting factor?

The 1978 Hague Convention, and, in ratification thereof, the Netherlands,[18] use the *lex loci celebrationis*. The marriage will be recognised as valid under Dutch law because the conditions of essential validity are satisfied under Belgian law, the law of the place of celebration. This is the case even though the conditions of essential validity are not satisfied under Dutch law (as neither party is Dutch or resident in the Netherlands) and the same marriage could not (even now) be validly concluded in the Netherlands. Switzerland also looks to the law of the place of celebration, even though it will then 'convert' the marriage into a registered partnership.[19] The same solution was used in the UK, although, as discussed in section 4, this changed recently with interesting consequences. Prior to the change, although English law normally referred questions of capacity to the law of the place of domicile of the spouses at the time of the marriage, it replaced this for same-sex marriages (converted into registered partnerships) with a test based on capacity under the law of the place of celebration. In short, England looked to Belgian law to determine the validity of Yves' and Luca's marriage.

Whilst not the topic of this paper, it is worth pausing to consider whether residence would in any event be a better connecting factor than the domicile or nationality of one or other spouse, or even the place of celebration. In Yves and Luca's case, does Belgian law really have the better claim to influence the validity under English or Swiss law of a marriage between two people resident in France,

---

[18]   Article 5(1) Wet Conflictenrecht Huwelijk, now Article 10:31 Dutch Civil Code.
[19]   Article 45(3) Loi fédérale de droit international privé, 18 decembre 1987 as amended, available at www.admin.ch/ch/f/rs/2/291.fr.pdf (last acessed 28.03.2013).

only one of whom is Belgian? French law might well appear the more logical choice and the law with the better claim to decide to the matter.[20]

3. FRENCH DEVELOPMENTS

3.1. THE TRADITIONAL APPROACH: NATIONALITY ABOVE ALL

Until the recent reforms, the French approach towards recognition of same-sex marriages concluded in other countries reflected a 'classic' approach to private international law. Only formal validity was governed by the law of the place of celebration, whilst essential validity (capacity) continued to be governed by the law of the nationality of the parties. It followed that any same-sex marriage involving a French citizen would not be valid under French law, even one which had been lawfully celebrated elsewhere.[21] Conversely, a foreign marriage would be valid under French law and be allowed to produce such effects in France as were not contrary to French public policy (such as the filing of joint tax returns to take advantage of shared allowances for married couples),[22] as long as both parties had capacity to marry under their personal law.

This approach, whilst conceptually coherent, would have resulted in some surprising results had it been allowed to reach its logical conclusions. For example, marriages involving American nationals, whose domicile does not restrict their ability to marry elsewhere if another state allows it, could have expected a variety of treatments as French law struggled to identify the state, as opposed to federal, 'nationality' of the citizen in question. A marriage celebrated in Massachusetts between a Dutch woman and her New York partner might well have been recognised in France, as would a marriage between a Dutchman and a Portuguese man performed in New York, but a New York marriage between a Dutchman and his Texan partner might have been void in France for lack of capacity of the Texan.[23]

---

20 See also RUTH LAMONT 'Habitual Residence and Brussels II bis: Developing Concepts for European Private International Family Law' (2007) 3 *Journal of Private International Law*, p. 261; PAUL LAGARDE, 'Développements futurs du droit international privé dans une Europe en voie d'unification: quelques conjectures' (2004) 68 *RabelsZ*, p. 225; MYRIAM HUNTER-HENIN, 'Droit des personnes et droits de l'homme: Combinaison ou confrontation?' (2006) *Rev. Crit DIP*, p. 743.

21 Réponse ministérielle, n° 886; J.O. Sénat, Q 24 janvier 2008, p. 161; note E. FONGARO, (2008) n° 6 chron. n° 16, *Dr. Famille*, p. 14 et seq.

22 JEAN-PIERRE STROOBANTS, 'La France reconnaît le mariage d'un couple d'hommes néerlandais' *Le Monde* 5 September 2008, available at www.lemonde.fr/europe/article/2008/09/05/la-france-reconnait-le-mariage-d-un-couple-d-hommes-neerlandais_1091846_3214.html (last accessed 06.10.2013).

23 The treatment of marriages abroad not involving French citizens might have given rise to an opportunity to make use of the French doctrine of attenuated effects even if one of the couple

---

A strict application of the rule denying effect to marriages involving French citizens, wherever celebrated, would have caused even greater concern. A Frenchman married to a Spaniard in Spain would still logically have been regarded as single under French law, even perhaps to the extent of then being at liberty to marry a woman in France, resulting (bigamy aside) in him being married to one person under Spanish law, and a different person under French law. The same Spanish man would have had far fewer problems under French law had he instead married a Belgian, as in that case many incidents of his marriage would have been recognised. For the Frenchman, a denial of his married status might be regarded as justifiable on the basis that he had attempted a fraud on French law in seeking deliberately to evade a prohibition under his personal law. For the Spaniard, however, the fact that French law recognises his marriage to a Belgian but not to a Frenchman is the point where conflicts rules show their unacceptable basis of discrimination on grounds of nationality. In my opinion this is the case even if at first sight marriage remains a matter left to the Member States and harmonisation of substantive family law is outside the scope of the Treaties.[24] In *Johannes* the Court of Justice found that using nationality as a connecting factor was not in itself unjustifiable discrimination on grounds of nationality in breach of the Treaties.[25] However, the facts of *Johannes* are quite specific, concerning an attempt by a retired, divorced German EU official to avoid a newly-introduced rule of German law concerning the apportionment of pension rights with his former wife, something he claimed would not have applied had he not been German. The alleged different treatment in question was therefore permitted '*discrimination à rebours*', i.e. treating one's own nationals less favourably than others, and the justification for the different treatment was based in any event on a desire to protect the wife's interest. These specific factors call into question the usual authority given to the judgement[26] as a blanket justification for the use of nationality as a connecting factor.

---

lacked capacity under his own personal law, but public policy might well still have prevented recognition if the couple in question were living in France. See further HUGUES FULCHIRON, 'Le Droit Français et les mariages homosexuels étrangers' (2006) *RIDC*, p. 1253.

24 MASHA ANTOKOLSKAIA, 'Harmonisation of substantive family law in Europe: myths and reality' (2010) 22 *CFLQ*, p. 398.
25 C-430/97 *Johannes v Johannes* [1999] ECJ I-3475.
26 For example MICHAEL BOGDAN, 'The EC Treaty and the Use of Nationality and Habitual Residence as Connecting Factors in International Family Law', Chapter 9 in Johan Meeusen, Marta Pertegás, Gert Streatmans and Frederik Swennen (eds), *International Family Law for the European Union* (2007, Intersentia), p. 307. See also the discussion by TITO BALLARINO and BENEDETTA UBERTAZZI, 'On Avello and Other Judgments: A New Point of Departure in the Conflict of Laws' in Petar Sarcevik et al (eds), *Yearbook of Private International Law*, Vol. 6 (2004), (2005, Sellier), p. 85.

3.2. THE NEW FRENCH APPROACH: TEMPORARY RESIDENCE SUFFICES

The new French law opening marriage to same-sex couples adopts the same solution as used in Belgium:

> 'Art. 202-1 – Les qualités et conditions requises pour pouvoir contracter mariage sont régies, pour chacun des époux, par sa loi personnelle.
> Toutefois, deux personnes de même sexe peuvent contracter mariage lorsque pour l'une d'entre elles soit sa loi personnelle, soit la loi de l'Etat sur le territoire duquel elle a son domicile ou sa résidence, le permet.'[27]

This was the wording originally used in an 'avant-projet' – an early draft of the proposed legislation[28] – as well as the wording finally adopted. However, it was not the text originally presented for consideration to the French legislature in November 2012,[29] which envisaged a different wording, namely:

> 'La loi personnelle d'un époux est écartée, sous réserve des engagements internationaux de la France, en tant qu'elle fait obstacle au mariage de deux personnes de même sexe, lorsque la loi de l'Etat sur le territoire duquel est célébré le mariage le permet.'[30]

Had this version been adopted instead, it would have constituted a definitive move away from nationality or even residence as a connecting factor in favour of the *lex loci celebrationis*. For example, a same-sex marriage celebrated in New York between an Italian and a Greek national, both living in Italy, would then have been treated as valid in France, notwithstanding that neither of the couple has capacity under personal law, and, moreover, despite the fact that New York requires neither of the couple to be domiciled or resident there in order to conclude a same-sex marriage.[31]

---

27   Fn. 8 above. Translation: 'The attributes and conditions required for entering into a marriage are governed for each of the spouses by his or her personal law. However, two persons of the same sex may enter into marriage when one of them is permitted to do so, either by his or her personal law or by the law of the State on whose territory he or she is domiciled or resident.'

28   HUGUES FULCHIRON, 'Le "mariage pour tous" en droit international privé: le législateur français a la peine...' (January 2013) no 1 *Droit de la Famille*, p. 31.

29   Projet de loi ouvrant le mariage aux couples de personnes de même sexe, JUSC1236338L, 7 November 2012, available at www.legifrance.gouv.fr (last accessed 03.02.2013).

30   Translation: 'A spouse's personal law will be set aside, subject [only] to France's international engagements, insofar as it prevents the marriage of two persons of the same sex, where the law of the State on whose territory the marriage is celebrated permits the marriage in question.'

31   See www.cityclerk.nyc.gov/html/marriage/same_sex_couples_faq.shtml (last accessed 20.09.2013). Strictly speaking, whether that marriage is subsequently treated as valid in New York will still depend on the parties having capacity to enter into the marriage under the laws of their domicile, hence a marriage between an Italian and a Greek both continuing to be

Unsurprisingly, this was a step too far. Instead France's adoption of the 'Belgian' solution ostensibly retains a link to nationality as the main connecting factor but adds, by exception to the nationality principle, a reference to the residence of one of the partners if this is needed to render the marriage valid. In reality, with most jurisdictions still denying same-sex marriage to their own nationals, the 'residence exception' will become the main connecting factor for a large number of international same-sex couples wanting to marry and live in France.

For marriages which take place in France it will of course be a matter of French law whether one of a couple, otherwise lacking capacity under personal law, has become resident in France. In principle a marriage can take place in France after a continuous presence of only one month,[32] and even this can be subject to a flexible interpretation.[33] But, just as with the Belgian provisions, the wording of Article 202-1 suggests that, in order to be meaningful, it applies equally to marriages conducted outside France. For these foreign marriages the question of residence in a particular jurisdiction will need to be determined by the law of that jurisdiction rather than reverting to French law. For example, the Belgian concept of 'habitual residence', needed to marry in Belgium, presupposes a three-month stay. An Italian could marry a Greek in Belgium and then be recognised as married in France, but only if one of them had been resident in Belgium at the time of marriage, and that question will need to be determined under Belgian rules (three months' presence) rather than French ones (one month's presence). The situation is more complex for marriages celebrated in common law jurisdictions which do not usually impose minimum residency requirements as part of the formalities of marriage. For example, our Italian-Greek same-sex couple could marry in New York. New York itself will not care how long the couple have been there in order to perform the ceremony, but in order to be treated as married under French law one of them will need to show that they had become 'domiciled or resident' in New York (or another jurisdiction permitting same-sex marriage) prior to the marriage. Logically, a period of less than one month would not be sufficient to confer residence by French standards, but New York does not use notions of 'residence' in marriage law, and it may be possible for a person to be 'resident' in New York after only a few hours. The references to *son domicile ou sa résidence* in Article 202-1 might of course not be alternatives but instead require the application of the prevailing connecting factor in use in the place of celebration, or perhaps in the jurisdiction in which domicile or residence is claimed. If so, one of the couple may need to show not residence, but domicile, in a jurisdiction allowing same-sex marriage.

---

domiciled in Italy may later be at risk of challenge. However, personal capacity will not be tested or need to be proven at the time of the marriage.

32   Code Civil (France), Article 74.
33   HUGUES FULCHIRON (fn. 28), para. 9.

3.3. RESIDUAL PROBLEMS LINKED TO NATIONALITY

Despite confusions which can arise over domicile or residence, nationality at least will no longer be a barrier to the recognition of same-sex marriages in France, whether the marriages were concluded by French nationals or foreigners living in France, or foreigners living abroad. However, there is one exception to this – the problem of 'international engagements' mentioned in the proposed draft has not gone away. Although not now expressly set out in the law, the French government still takes the view that it cannot override incapacities imposed by a personal law deemed applicable by virtue of conventions concluded with other counties.[34] This concerns nationals of eleven jurisdictions, mostly former French colonies and the former Yugoslavian republics. The status of these conventions following the introduction of the new law has already been called into question.[35]

In addition to the question of compatibility with French public policy, of particular interest here is that it purports to apply to nationals of two other EU Member States, Poland and Slovenia, who will continue to be denied the ability to marry in France and whose same-sex marriages conducted elsewhere will also be denied recognition under French law. A clearer case of discrimination on grounds of nationality is difficult to envisage. Under the former French rules there was already a largely incomprehensible and unjust incongruity in that a French court could tell a Spanish man his marriage to a Frenchman (or a German, or a Texan) was non-existent, whilst it would have upheld a marriage as giving rise to legally enforceable obligations had the same man married a Belgian (or a New Yorker, or a Swede). Now, under the new rules, we could find a French court telling a Spanish woman that her marriage to a Polish woman, celebrated in the Netherlands whilst both were resident there, is not recognisable in France. If so, given the effect this would have on the couple's real ability to enjoy their EU free movement rights, it might well lead the Court of Justice, given the opportunity, to reconsider the *Johannes* reasoning. An indication of such a potential change of approach, where using nationality to determine personal law

---

34 'Circulaire du 20 mai 2013 de présentation de la loi ouvrant le mariage aux couples de personnes de même sexe (dispositions du Code civil)' Bulletin Officiel du Ministère de la Justice du 31 mai 2013, JUSC1312445C, available at www.textes.justice.gouv.fr/art_pix/JUSC1312445C.pdf (last accessed 27 September 2013).

35 In September 2013 a public prosecutor prevented a same-sex marriage between a Moroccan and a Frenchman on the basis that it contravened the Franco-Marrocan convention. The TGI Chambery lifted the restriction in a judgment on 11 October 2013, stating that the new law had implicitly modified French international public policy ('*ordre public international français*'). See SHAHZAD ABDUL, 'Un tribunal autorise le mariage gay d'un Marocain et d'un Français', *Le Monde* 12 October 2013. Further appeals to higher courts against this or other similar decisions are likely to take place which may clarify whether here, as is the case with *talaq* divorces and adoption cases involving Muslims, '*ordre public*' takes precedence over international conventions.

leads to a restriction on free movement rights and other treaty freedoms, can already be seen in recent cases such as *Garcia Avello*[36] and *Grunkin-Paul*.[37]

4. ENGLISH DEVELOPMENTS

Like France, England (although, for now, not yet Scotland) has now amended its laws to extend marriage to same-sex couples. With the coming into force of the Marriage (Same Sex Couples) Act 2013 England will also need to change the way it deals with conflicts and capacity problems, but the way it will do so is still unclear. The background to this is the former UK method of recognising foreign same-sex marriages as civil partnerships. As already mentioned, overseas same-sex marriages were recognised, but converted to a civil partnership, if the marriage was valid by the laws of the place of celebration.[38] The reference to the foreign law applies not only to the formal validity of the marriage, but also to the capacity of the parties to marry.[39] As a clear application of the *lex loci celebrationis,* this meant, for example, that the New York marriage referred to earlier between a Greek and an Italian same-sex couple would be treated as valid (although converted to a civil partnership) even though neither party was resident or had spent any time at all living in New York.

However, the new Act does not answer the question whether the rules applicable to the recognition of overseas marriages as partnerships will now be extended to the recognition of those marriages *as marriages*, or whether the 'old' rules for the recognition of overseas marriages will now apply. Given the move towards *lex loci celebrationis* for registered partnerships, it might have been thought that the same rule will continue to apply for assessing the validity of overseas marriages. If so, then a French same-sex marriage between, for example, Stavros, a Greek man living in Cyprus and Gianni, an Italian who has been living in the Netherlands, would be valid simply on the basis that French law treats Gianni's residence in the Netherlands as sufficient to confer capacity to marry. That would be the solution under the old law, albeit the relationship would be renamed a civil partnership. However, it would wrong to assume that the new law will simply treat the couple as married rather than partnered. Whilst the Act *repeals* the provision which converts overseas marriages into registered partnerships, it also, perhaps inadvertently, also removes the provision which made the law of the place of celebration govern questions of capacity.[40]

---

36   C-148/02 *Carlos Garcia Avello v Belgium* [2003] ECR I-11613.
37   C-353/06 *Grunkin v Grunkin-Paul* [2008] ECR I-7639.
38   Civil Partnership Act 2005 s215(1)(a).
39   Capacity is determined according to the 'relevant law', defined as 'the law of the country or territory where the relationship is registered (including its rules of private international law)', Civil Partnership Act 2005, s212(2).
40   Schedule 2, s5(2) Marriage (Same Sex Couples) Act 2013.

Thus, whilst a foreign same-sex *civil union* will continue to be treated as a valid civil partnership, section 10(1)(b) of the new law now provides, somewhat obliquely, simply that *a marriage* under the law of any country outside the UK 'is not prevented from being recognised' under English law only because it is the marriage of a same-sex couple.

This is very unsatisfactory. The usual rules on capacity for determining the validity of a marriage under English law are similar to the classic French rules, in that they are based on the law applicable under the domicile of *each* of the parties at the time of the marriage.[41] If these rules are applied, it will mean that Gianni's marriage to Stavros referred to above will not be valid under English law, *either* as a civil partnership *or* as a marriage, due to the incapacity of at least one (in fact both) of the couple under the laws of their antenuptial domicile.

The application of those rules would also mean a same-sex marriage previously validly conducted in Belgium between a Belgian national and an Italian domiciled in Italy will now *not* be recognised in England as a valid marriage, due to the incapacity of the Italian under English conflicts law, and this will now be the case despite the marriage being valid in Belgium under Article 46(2) Belgian Code of Private International Law. Again, even though that same marriage would until now have been recognised as a civil partnership, the disapplication of the Civil Partnership Act to overseas marriages means that the Belgian marriage is now at risk of not being recognised *either* as a marriage *or* as a registered partnership. The provision in the Marriage (Same Sex Couples) Act that the marriage 'is not prevented from being recognised' does not mandate recognition, and existing English conflicts rules call into doubt its ongoing validity.

For marriages which take place in England the position is not much better, although one helpful rule of English law disregards any incapacity of one of the parties if one of the couple at least is domiciled in England and Wales at the time of the marriage. The case of *Sottomayer v De Barros (No 2)*[42] established that 'the validity of a marriage celebrated in England between persons of whom the one has an English, and the other a foreign, domicile is not affected by an incapacity which, though existing under the law of such foreign domicile, does not exist under the law of England'.[43] Foreigners seeking to marry a British same-sex partner in London may take comfort from this 1879 rule, but should take heed (and legal advice) if the partner might be domiciled in Scotland or Northern Ireland rather than England or Wales. However, if neither partner is domiciled in England the situation is less satisfactory. Like New York, England

---

41   Rule 74 in Collins and others (eds), *Dicey, Morris and Collins on the Conflict of Laws* (15th edition, 2012, Sweet & Maxwell), p. 939.

42   (1879) 5 PD 94.

43   Peter Machin North and James Fawcett, *Cheshire and North's Private International Law* (13th edition, 1999, Butterworths), p. 731, fn. 18, quoting Collins and others (eds), *Dicey and Morris on the Conflict of Laws* (12th edition, 1993, Sweet & Maxwell), p. 679.

does not insist on either party being resident or a national in order to marry in England, meaning many international couples can be expected to marry in London where neither of the couple is domiciled there. In such cases, if *one* of the couple is domiciled in a country which does not permit same-sex marriage, the application of normal English conflict rules could again lead to a finding that the marriage is void, even if the *other* partner was domiciled in a country which does now permit same-sex marriage, such as France.

Ironically, for such English marriages, the wording of both the French and Belgian laws could have the consequence of making them valid in France or Belgium even if they might be void under English law, the *lex loci celebrationis*. Take, for example, a marriage which takes place in London between a Spanish woman previously resident in Paris and a Polish woman who is resident, but not domiciled, in London. No formalities as to capacity will prevent the marriage taking place, but if the couple later split up one of them could successfully argue that the marriage was void under English law for lack of capacity of the Polish woman under the law of her domicile. If successful, this would prevent an English court being able to grant a divorce or make financial judgments concerning the couple. However, French and Belgian law would continue to regard them as married, given that at least one of them (and possibly both) had capacity under the laws of their residence, and a Spanish court could reasonably be expected to take the same position.

Thus, whilst there is some scope to suppose at least that *lex loci celebrationis* will apply to capacity to form foreign (same-sex) marriages just as it does currently for registered partnerships, the status under English law of English marriages between non-domiciliaries remains most uncertain. It would be optimistic to conclude that the normal rules on capacity based on domicile are no longer expected to apply. If so, the possibility of these marriages being found void under English law whilst remaining valid under foreign laws should be seen as a potential embarrassment to the English legislature, but these arguments met with no reaction when submitted to the legislative committee debating the new Act.[44] It may well be the case that the judiciary, through case law, will need to continue to re-address these problems unless the English Parliament confronts the issues head on.

---

[44] STUART DAVIS, '*Memorandum to the Public Scrutiny Committee debating the Marriage (Same Sex Couples) Bill*' (February 2013), available at www.publications.parliament.uk/pa/cm201213/cmpublic/marriage/memo/m11.htm (last accessed 20.09.2013).

PROTECTION ORDERS ACROSS EUROPE

First Remarks on Regulation No. 606/2013

Eva DE GÖTZEN

Contents

The present essay will deal with EU Regulation No. 606/2013 on mutual recognition of protection measures in civil matters, which has been recently adopted on the basis of Article 81 TFEU in order to ensure the free circulation of such measures throughout the EU.[1] To that end, firstly certain key issues which have arisen so far in the context of cross-border *ex parte* measures will be tackled as well as their enforcement abroad. Subsequently, a short overview of the new Regulation and of its main features will be presented. Finally, a few considerations focusing on the interrelationship between the EU uniform rules and the Italian legal system shall be addressed.

---

[1] Regulation (EU) No. 606/2013 of the European Parliament and of the Council of 12 June 2013 on mutual recognition of protection measures in civil matters, OJ L 181, 29.06.2013, p. 4. It shall apply from 11 January 2015. The UK and Ireland have decided to take part in this instrument. Denmark is not bound by it or subject to its application.

1. CONTEXT OF THE EU LEGISLATIVE PROPOSAL

According to certain surveys, around one European woman in five has suffered from violence, such as physical assault or psychological harm, at least once during her adult life. In the majority of cases, such violence has been domestic violence. However, this kind of violence is not limited to (ex-)spouses and relatives. In fact, it also includes victims who are stalked by acquaintances, by strangers, or sometimes even by ex-partners with whom they were not married or did not enter into a registered partnership. Moreover, the victims may be indirect, such as family members, especially children, who also suffer from the consequences of violence committed by and among their parents.[2] Therefore, in order to satisfy the need for protection shown by these victims, from the 1970s onward several Member States started to enact *ad hoc* legislation. Such legislation provides for the possibility to adopt temporary and preventative remedies – generally aimed at removing the offender of domestic violence from the protected party's home and/or workplace for a limited period of time – regardless of whether or not the violent conduct amounts to the commission of a crime and independent from divorce proceedings.[3]

Until now, by their very nature, the effects of such legal remedies have been confined within the territory of the issuing Member State. As such, when a protected person exercised his/her right to free movement, the protection gained through a national order was irremediably lost unless an additional order was issued in the Member State of destination. However, the most compelling need of a victim of violence fearing (often imminent) additional assaults is to obtain immediate protection even in a cross-border situation, without going through expensive and time-consuming procedures.

Against this background, in the context of a legislative package which aims at strengthening the rights of victims in the EU, including a directive on minimum standards on the rights, support and protection of victims of crime[4] and another legal instrument on the mutual recognition of protection measures taken in criminal matters,[5] the EU legislator has finally adopted a simple and effective EU instrument based on the mutual recognition and adaptation of

---

[2]   S. VAN DER AA, Protection Orders in the European Member States: Where Do We Stand and Where Do We Go from Here?, in *European Journal on Criminal Policy and Research*, 2012, pp. 183–204.

[3]   Such protection orders are provisional as they are granted for a specific period of time during which their effects reach as far as the effects of the main proceedings.

[4]   Directive 2012/29/EU of the European Parliament and of the Council of 25 October 2012 establishing minimum standards on the rights, support and protection of victims of crime, and replacing Council Framework Decision 2001/220/JHA, OJ L 315, 14.11.2012, pp. 57–73.

[5]   Directive 2011/99/EU of the European Parliament and of the Council of 13 December 2011 on the European protection order (the so-called EPO Directive), OJ L 338, 21.12.2011, pp. 2–18.

precautionary measures in civil matters,[6] Regulation No. 606/2013, which is expected to overcome the practical hurdles which victims of violence have faced in a cross-border setting.

2. *EX PARTE* PROTECTION ORDERS AND THE FORMER EU PRIVATE INTERNATIONAL LAW UNIFORM INSTRUMENTS

On the one hand, domestic violence, stalking and violence against (or in front of) children are considered to be tortious conducts between private persons. Moreover, court orders aimed at stopping and preventing unlawful behaviour between private parties should be qualified as *'civil matters'* pursuant to Article 1(1) Regulation No. 44/2001 ('Brussels I').[7] Therefore, the free circulation throughout the EU of temporary remedies affecting the behaviour of a known aggressor should be, supposedly, ensured under the Brussels I Regulation.[8] Needless to say, remedies against (domestic) violence relate in the slightest degree to the scope of this Regulation, which mainly deals with economic redress. As a consequence, the mechanism used in such an instrument, even though it deals with mutual recognition in civil matters as well, may not be the suitable solution in order to meet the needs arising from the specific situation of a person at risk.

On the other hand, not only are many protection orders taken in civil matters in a Member State provisional but they are also ordered upon the request of the

---

[6] The new Regulation deals only with protection measures taken in civil matters. Otherwise, injunctions taken out in criminal matters are covered by Directive 2011/99/EU (Article 1/ Recital 9), see fn. 5.

[7] Council Regulation (EC) No. 44/2001 of 22 December 2000 on jurisdiction and the recognition and enforcement of judgments in civil and commercial matters, OJ L 12, 16.01.2001, p. 1 ss. See the opinion of Advocate General Mengozzi delivered on 5 April 2011, case C-406/09, *Realchemie Nederland BV v Bayer CropScience AG*, ECR 2011 p. I-09773, no. 62–67. According to AG Mengozzi, court orders aimed at preventing unlawful behaviour are civil matters, while orders intended to sanction unlawful behaviour are criminal matters. From this perspective, protection orders must be qualified as civil matters as they shall halt and prevent assaults between private parties.

[8] The inclusion of interim measures within the scope of the Brussels I Regulation is determined not by their own nature but by the nature of the rights that they serve to protect (ECJ, judgment of 27 March 1979, case 143/78, *de Cavel*, ECR 1979, p. 1055, no. 8; judgment 26 March 1992, case C-261/90, *Reichert and Kockler v Dresdner Bank AG*, ECR 1992, p. I-2149, no. 32; and judgment 17 November 1998, case C-391/95, *Van Uden Maritime BV v Firma Deco-Line*, ECR 1998, p. I-7091, no. 33); see M. PERTEGÁS, Article 31, in U. MAGNUS, P. MANKOWSKY, *Brussels I Regulation*, Munich, 2012, 2nd ed., pp. 609–620. More generally, if there is a dispute between two private persons and the action is intended to protect private rights, such a legal relationship between the parties must be classified as *'a private law relationship'*, thus falling within the scope of the Brussels I Regulation (CJ, 18 October 2011, case C-406/09, *Realchemie Nederland BV v Bayer CropScience AG*, ECR 2011, p. I-09773, no. 41).

person at risk without the addressee being heard at first instance, particularly in case of urgency (*ex parte* procedures). According to the well-known ECJ judgment in *Denilauler,*[9] the concept of a (recognisable) judgment in the sense of Article 32 Brussels I Regulation includes only provisional and protective measures given after hearing the debtor.[10] As a consequence, measures granted subsequent to unilateral proceedings and not subsequently confirmed in the light of the respondent's explanations are not 'judgments' within the meaning of Article 32 Brussels I Regulation.[11] Therefore, *ex parte* remedies against domestic violence, as one-sided orders, should be excluded from the regime of the Brussels I Regulation.

Notwithstanding this, given the solution outlined by the ECJ in later cases,[12] *ex parte* measures are now clearly covered by the concept of provisional measures within the understanding of the new Article 2(a) Regulation No. 1215/2012 ('Brussels I recast').[13] Accordingly, a decision granting any *ex parte* measure is to be recognised and enforced abroad like any other decision. However, the mutual recognition of such measures is now subject to some further restrictive

---

[9]   See ECJ, judgment of 21 May 1980, case 125/79, *Denilauler v Couchet Frères*, ECR 1980, p. 1553, no. 18: 'Judicial decisions authorizing provisional or protective measures, which are delivered without the party against which they are directed having been summoned to appear and which are intended to be enforced without prior service do not come within the system of recognition and enforcement provided for by the Judgment Convention'.

[10] B. Hess, T. Pfeiffer, P. Schlosser, *The Heidelberg Report on the Application of Regulation Brussels I in 25 Member States (Study JLS/C4/2005/03)*, Munich, 2008, para. 527; P. Wautelet, Article 32, in U. Magnus, P. Mankowsky, *Brussels I Regulation, supra* fn. 8, para. 22: the liberality of the regime set up under the Brussels I Regulation was only possible because of the protection afforded to the defendant in the original proceedings. It is essential that before the judgment is delivered, an *inter partes* procedure takes place – or could have taken place if the defendant had chosen to appear.

[11] B. Hess, T. Pfeiffer, P. Schlosser, *The Heidelberg Report, supra* fn. 10, para. 744 according to which, as the case law of national courts demonstrates, the cross-border enforcement of provisional measures becomes possible subsequent to its confirmation after the respondent has submitted his comments.

[12] ECJ, judgment of 13 July 1995, case C-474/93, *Hengst Import BV and Anna Maria Campese*, ECR 1995, p. I-02113, nos 14 and 19: it has been held that an order issued following summary proceedings brought *ex parte* is entitled to benefit from the smooth mechanism of the Brussels I Regulation if the defendant has the possibility to challenge the order before it becomes enforceable. See ECJ, judgment of 14 October 2004, case C-39/02, *Mærsk Olie & Gas A/S v Firma M. de Haan en W. de Boer*, ECR 2004, p. I-09657, no. 50.

[13] Regulation (EU) No. 1215/2012 of the European Parliament and of the Council of 12 December 2012 on jurisdiction and the recognition and enforcement of judgments in civil and commercial matters, OJ L 351, 20.12.2012, p. 1 ss. See C. Honorati, Provisional Measures and the Recast of Brussels I Regulation: A Missed Opportunity for a Better Ruling, in *Rivista di diritto internazionale privato e processuale*, 2012, p. 525–544; M. Bogdan, The Proposed Recast of Rules on Provisional Measures under the Brussels I Regulation, in E. Lein (ed.), *The Brussels I Review Proposal Uncovered*, London, 2012, p. 133; P. Kiesselbach, The Brussels I Review Proposal – An Overview, in E. Lein (ed.), *The Brussels I Review Proposal Uncovered*, pp. 7, 15, 28; A. Kramer, Abolition of exequatur under the Brussels I Regulation: effecting and protecting rights in the European judicial area, in *Nederlands Internationaal Privaatrecht*, 2011, p. 638.

preconditions set up by the EU legislator being met. Therefore, not even the solution provided for by the Brussels I recast Regulation would be suitable for the specific provisional measures addressed herein.[14]

Finally, Regulation No. 2201/2003 ('Brussels II *bis*')[15] only refers to divorce proceedings, legal separation and the annulment of marriages (Article 1(1)(a)). As such, it does not deal with remedies which would permit the protection of the victimised spouse in the period prior to the process of separation or divorce.[16]

Therefore, the EU legislator was pressed to adopt a specific instrument devoted to the peculiarity of the measures at hand also for the purpose of filling in the current gaps in the EU civil law procedures.

3. MAIN FEATURES OF REGULATION NO. 606/2013

The new Regulation provides for some autonomous definitions so as to outline its specific scope of application. 'Protection measures' are defined in Article 3(1) as preventive and temporary measures imposing rules of conduct on a person causing danger, such as obligations or prohibitions, comprehensively forbidding the addressee from having any contact with the victim. The second definition is the notion of 'issuing authority'. It is now taken for granted that the nature of the authority ordering a protection measure is not determinative for the purposes of assessing the civil character of a protection measure (Recital 10).[17] Hence, unlike other areas of judicial cooperation, the new Regulation should apply to decisions rendered not only by courts or tribunals but also by administrative authorities and other issuing authorities designated by a Member State as having competence in matters falling within the scope of the Regulation at hand.[18] As far as the definition of 'cross-border situation' is concerned, the new Regulation deals only with the recognition of a protection measure sought in a Member State other than the Member State of origin (Article 2(2)). From a private international law point of view, this is the only cross-border perspective dealt with by the new Regulation since acts of domestic violence are generally not

---

[14] See below at §5.

[15] Council Regulation (EC) No. 2201/2003 of 27 November 2003 concerning jurisdiction and the recognition and enforcement of judgments in matrimonial matters and the matters of parental responsibility, repealing Regulation (EC) No. 1347/2000, OJ L 338, 23.12.2003, p. 1 ss.

[16] Moreover, according to the ECJ case law (judgment of 15 July 2010, case C-256/09, *Bianca Purrucker v Guillermo Vallés Pérez*, ECR 2010, p. I-07353, nos 83 and 87), provisional measures granted under Article 20, Brussels II *bis* Regulation cannot be recognised under Articles 21 and 23 of such Regulation. Only legal redress aimed at protecting children from domestic violence, since this issue is strictly connected with parental responsibility matters under Article 1(1)(b), can be enforced under the Brussels II *bis* Regulation.

[17] The national legal traditions in the area of protection measures are highly diverse. In some national laws protection measures are regulated by civil law, in others by criminal law and some regulate them under administrative law.

[18] Only measures issued by police authorities are expressly excluded, see Article 3(4); Recital 13.

committed in cross-border settings. Therefore, since most of the cases under consideration herein are purely only of a domestic nature, the new Regulation does not provide for either heads of jurisdiction or conflicts of law rules.

Nevertheless, in exceptional cases the parties may be domiciled in different EU Member States. For instance, following the end of a personal relationship, a person may be victimised in a Member State other than the Member State of origin. In this context, issues of jurisdiction may arise. Since the current general rules concerning heads of jurisdiction in civil matters are left untouched, jurisdiction shall be based on the criteria provided for by the Brussels I Regulation, and in the future by the Brussels I recast Regulation.[19] Moreover, in order to determine the law applicable to cross-border relationships, domestic violence, stalking and violence against children can be qualified as tortious conducts. Therefore, despite the fact that the Rome II Regulation does not include family relationships within its scope (Article 1(2)(a)), violence within families, in so far as it amounts to tortious conduct, is nevertheless covered by the scope of the Rome II Regulation which thus prevails over the conflicts of law rules of the Member States.[20]

4. RECOGNITION AND ENFORCEMENT UNDER REGULATION NO. 606/2013

The new Regulation provides for a speedy and efficient mechanism to ensure that the Member State to which the person at risk moves will swiftly recognise the protection measure issued by the Member State of origin without any intermediate formalities and any declaration of enforceability (the so-called *exequatur*).

Following the rationale of existing EU instruments on judicial cooperation in civil and commercial matters, namely the Brussels I recast Regulation and the Brussels II *bis* Regulation,[21] Regulation No. 606/2013 has introduced a standardised EU-wide certificate (Article 5). This certificate includes all information relevant for the recognition and, where applicable, enforcement of the protection measure (Article 7(f)). It is issued by the competent authority of the issuing Member State at the request of the protected person and the same

---

[19] As far as protection orders are related to parental authority and the right of access, the heads of jurisdiction are provided for by the Brussels II *bis* Regulation, namely Articles 8, 9 and 13. Additional grounds are provided by Article 20, although these provisional measures are excluded from the recognition system under the Brussels II *bis* Regulation. See fn. 15.

[20] Regulation (EC) No. 864/2007 of the European Parliament and of the Council of 11 July 2007 on the law applicable to non-contractual obligations (Rome II), OJ L 199, 31.07.2007, p. 40 ss. See A. DICKINSON, *The Rome II Regulation*, Oxford, 2008, para. 3.153.

[21] The rationale of Articles 41 and 42 of the Brussels II *bis* Regulation, dealing with decisions on the right of access or the return of the child, has been followed.

authority will then serve the measure on the person causing the risk, informing him or her about the geographical extension of the foreign protection measure and any sanctions which will be applicable in case of its violation (Article 8). By presenting the certificate, the victim will immediately obtain the relevant protection of the Member State of enforcement by the competent authority (Article 4). Therefore, the certificate acts as a kind of 'passport' for quick and easy recognition of the protection measure when the protected person moves or travels to another Member State.

The procedure for enforcement is then governed by the law of the Member State addressed (Article 4(5)). According to a fundamental principle of mutual recognition in civil matters, even if the foreign protection measure is unknown under the national law of the Member State addressed, this State must have recourse to the relevant provisions of its national law in order to ensure compliance with the foreign coercive measure (Article 11).[22]

Moreover, in view of removing obstacles to the free movement of protection measures, not only does the new Regulation provide for the abolition of intermediate procedures, but also the grounds for non-recognition that can be invoked in the Member State where enforcement is sought are kept to a minimum (Article 13). The first one coincides with the grounds for refusal pertaining to the irreconcilability of the judgment. It is noteworthy that this ground is more liberal than other EU uniform instruments where the *exequatur* has been abolished since these instruments specifically require that only an earlier judgment is concerned.[23] The second one is the general public policy exception which may justify, in exceptional circumstances, the courts of the Member State addressed being allowed to refuse the recognition or enforcement of a protection measure.

Finally, the recognition of the protection measure may not be refused on the ground that the law of the Member State addressed does not allow for such a measure based on the same facts and mutual trust shall in no case result in a review either of the substance of the decision to be recognised and enforced or of the competence of the court of the State of origin.[24]

---

[22] According to the case law of the ECJ, a Member State must recognise coercive measures by the courts of other Member State even if its national law does not provide for a similar measure. See judgment of 4 February 1988, case 145/86, *Hoffman v Krieg*, ECR 1988, p. 645.

[23] See Regulation No. 805/2004 creating a European Enforcement Order for uncontested claims (OJ L 143, 30.04.2004, p. 15), Article 21; Regulation No. 1896/2006 creating a European order for payment procedure (OJ L 399, 30.12.2006, p. 1), Article 22; Regulation No. 861/2007 establishing a European Small Claims Procedure (OJ L 199, 31.07.2007, p. 1), Article 22. A Proposal for a new EU Regulation amending Regulation No. 861/2007 and Regulation No. 1896/2006 has been presented on 19 November 2013 (COM(2013)794 final).

[24] See Articles 12 and 13(3).

5. THE BRUSSELS I RECAST SYSTEM AND PROTECTION ORDERS ISSUED *EX PARTE*: IRRECONCILABILITY

As was pointed out before, preventive remedies may be taken either in proceedings on notice to both parties or in *ex parte* proceedings where, generally, the person causing the risk was not served with the document instituting the proceedings or an equivalent document and remedies are generally issued following summary proceedings.

As already highlighted, these legal remedies may now be equally enforced under the Brussels I recast Regulation in all Member States without the need for any *exequatur* proceedings but complying with the following requirements:

(1) the judgment containing the measure must be issued by a court having jurisdiction as to the substance of the matter (Recital 33, Article 2);[25]

(2) such a judgment must be enforceable in the Member State of origin before the issuing of the certificate provided for by Article 53 (Article 42(2)(b)(ii));

(3) such a judgment must be served by the interested party upon the defendant prior to enforcement (Recital 33, Article 42(2)(c)). Therefore, it is now expressly provided that a foreign interim measure, granted in unilateral proceedings without the defendant being heard, can be subject to mutual recognition throughout the EU provided that the defendant has been served with a copy of the order.[26] However, it may be doubtful whether the enforcement of a served *ex parte* measure must also comply with the additional requirement that such a measure was later confirmed at the end of the *inter partes* (main) proceedings or, at least, after the period for challenging the *ex parte* order has expired. Apparently, the most deplorable shortcoming of the Brussels I recast Regulation is the lack of any special provision vesting the court of the Member State of enforcement with the power to suspend the effects of the enforcement in case the *ex parte* measure is challenged in the Member State of origin.[27] As a matter of fact, the court of the Member State addressed is in any case vested with the power to suspend

---

[25]   Where provisional, including protective, measures are ordered by a court of a Member State not having jurisdiction to determine the substance of the claim, the effect of such measures should be confined, under the Brussels I recast Regulation, to the territory of that Member State (Recital 33).

[26]   In such a case the surprise effect may be attenuated since automatic enforcement may imply that both parties have been heard in the Member State of origin.

[27]   See Article 44(3), *Proposal for a Regulation of the European Parliament and of the Council on jurisdiction and the recognition and enforcement of judgments in civil and commercial matters (Recast)*, COM(2010)748 final of 14 December 2010, now abolished. See L. SANDRINI, *Tutela cautelare in funzione di giudizi esteri*, Padova, 2012, p. 442, fn. 103.

the effects of the enforcement of any judgment if this judgment is subject to a challenge in the Member State of origin or when the time for such an appeal has not yet expired (Recital 31, Article 51). Therefore, even *ex parte* orders which are still challengeable become entitled to automatic recognition under the Brussels I recast Regulation.

Being suitable as a starting point, various arguments have led to the conclusion that this mechanism would not have been the best solution for *ex parte* measures issued against domestic violence.

Firstly, protection orders against domestic violence may be legal remedies which are different and autonomous from the ones afforded by and through proceedings on the substance of the matter (divorce and similar matters/ criminal offences). Therefore, by allowing for their free circulation only when they were granted by the court having jurisdiction on the merits could lead to a substantial denial of justice for the victim of violence.

In the second place, it should be noted that instituting additional formal proceedings before the issuing of the EU-wide certificate, such as the notification of the restrainee by the victim of violence, could considerably delay the protection afforded to the latter. Victims may shy away from serving the *ex parte* order as they fear the reaction of the person responsible for the risk.

Finally, the specific object of the type of measures at hand is expected to produce a surprise effect intended to safeguard the victim. Stipulating that the automatic recognition of *ex parte* measures must be subject to their prior service on the other party would lead to the further, unintended, result of depriving the applicant of any surprise effect, thus rendering these remedies totally meaningless.

So, in the light of the above, the very core solutions of the new Regulation seem to be as follows.

Firstly, it is not required that the issuing authority has jurisdiction to hear the substance of the case.

Secondly, due to the specific need of the victim of violence to obtain immediate protection, the service required under the Brussels I recast Regulation does not apply to *ex parte* protection measures against (domestic) violence falling within the scope of the new Regulation. However, it is worth adding that the abolition of *exequatur* is intended to apply to such measures complying with the different additional requirement that the defendant has the right to comment on the application to grant the provisional or protective order under the national law of the Member State of origin even at a later stage of the proceedings (Article 6(3)).

Thirdly, the new Regulation makes it clear that the EU-wide certificate may be issued as soon as the protection measure is enforceable in the Member State of origin, regardless of whether the period for challenging such a measure has expired (Recital 25). In other words, due to the typical urgency of the cases in question, this certificate may be issued regardless of whether or not the restrainee has actually submitted his defence and, what is more, regardless of whether such a measure, following the resolution of the main (*inter partes*) proceedings, would subsequently not be confirmed in the light of the restrainee's explanation in the Member State of origin.[28]

Finally, it is noteworthy that in order to strike a balance between the victim's protection and the right of free circulation of the restrainee, the effects of recognition under the new Regulation are, by way of an exception, limited to a period of 12 months from the issuing of the EU-wide certificate, irrespective of whether the protection measure itself has a longer duration (Article 4(4)).

6. THE NEW REGULATION AND THE FORMER EU PRIVATE INTERNATIONAL LAW UNIFORM INSTRUMENTS

The new Regulation establishes special rules in relation to the recognition of protection measures issued in civil matters. Therefore, by following a general principle of law, it shall supersede the general rules set out by the Brussels I and Brussels I recast Regulations.

The situation is different as regards the Brussels II *bis* Regulation. This Regulation aims at centralising all proceedings relating to a given divorce or legal separation, while the new Regulation deals with interim measures issued irrespective of divorce or legal separation proceedings. Therefore, given the partially different and broader scope of such Regulations, all protection measures taken in the context of ongoing proceedings relating to a divorce or legal separation and, for that reason, falling within the scope of the Brussels II *bis* Regulation shall continue to be governed by this instrument. Otherwise, protection measures which do not fall under the application of the Brussels II *bis* Regulation, among which protection measures concerning a non-married couple, same-sex partners or neighbours are included, will be covered by the new Regulation (Article 2(3)).

---

[28] It cannot be overlooked that when a protection measure is suspended or withdrawn in the Member State of origin, the competent authority of the Member State of recognition suspends or withdraws the effects of recognition and, where applicable, the enforcement of the protection measure (Article 14).

7. THE ITALIAN PROTECTION ORDER AGAINST DOMESTIC VIOLENCE

In 2001 the Italian legislator introduced a protection order against domestic violence and this is contained in Article 342 *bis-ter* of the Italian Civil Code. The Italian protection order is issued when domestic violence is concerned or when stalking takes place in the context of cohabiting partners, irrespective of a matrimonial relationship. Therefore, such an order grants protection even among *more uxorio* relationships. As a matter of fact, in the present state of affairs it is debated whether cohabitation is required in order for the protection measure to be granted under Article 342 *bis* of the Italian Civil Code.[29]

Moreover, Article 342 *ter* provides for a protective measure in civil matters, aiming at enforcing a separation from a violent partner, including obligations or prohibitions imposed on the person causing the risk. The duration of such a measure cannot exceed one year, although it may be extended upon the request of a party but only if there are serious reasons for doing so and only until this is strictly necessary. For these reasons, the Italian protection order shall fall within the scope of Regulation No. 606/2013.

According to the Italian Civil Procedural Code (Article 736 *bis*), the application is filed with the court of the place where the applicant is a resident or is domiciled. The judge, upon hearing the parties, may issue an order which is immediately enforceable. Otherwise, in urgent cases the court may issue an *ex parte* protection measure, without the defendant being summoned to appear. In the absence of any legislative guidance, due to the need to provide immediate protection to the victim of violence, Italian legal doctrine deems that even such an *ex parte* measure is immediately enforceable.[30] The judge then schedules a hearing which both the parties should attend within a period no later than eight days from the service of the application and the order on the defendant. At this hearing the judge is entitled to uphold, amend or discharge the protection order. Although the final decision may be challenged, it does not prevent the protection order from being temporarily enforceable. Due to the appropriate safeguards aimed at securing the fundamental rights of the offender, an Italian protection measure ordered *ex parte* meets the requirements for mutual recognition set forth by Regulation No. 606/2013.

Lastly, it is worth addressing the relationships between the Italian protection order and the process of separation or divorce under Italian procedural law. If during the process of separation or divorce, the spouses have already attended a

---

29   A. SCALERA, Gli ordini di protezione contro gli abusi familiari, in *Giurisprudenza Merito*, 2013, pp. 231 et seq., §4; V. ZIANTONA, Note sugli ordini di protezione contro gli abusi familiari, in *Teoria e storia del dritto privato*, 2011, §2.

30   F. GIANFILIPPI, Sugli ordini di protezione contro la violenza nelle relazioni familiari, in *Giurisprudenza Merito*, 2004, p. 465.

hearing in which the judge has ordered measures whose contents were akin to protection orders, then orders under Article 342 *bis* of the Italian Civil Code cannot be adopted. Accordingly, the protection orders under Article 342 *bis* of the Italian Civil Code may be requested only during the time between the filing of the divorce or separation application and the court hearing of the spouses, but they automatically lose their effectiveness once similar measures in matrimonial matters are adopted.[31]

Therefore, if the protection measures are issued under Article 342 *bis* of the Italian Civil Code before the first hearing regarding the conjugal relationship, they freely circulate within the EU under Regulation No. 606/2013. Otherwise, if the protection order is issued in the context of the first hearing regarding the conjugal relationship it then deals with matrimonial matters and, as such, shall circulate under the Brussels II *bis* Regulation.

In the light of the above it seems fair to conclude that the Italian protection order appears to be a valid example in understanding the choices made by the EU legislator in the field of temporary measures against domestic violence.

8. CONCLUSION

We should now turn to investigate whether the solutions proposed by Regulation No. 606/2013 meet the needs outlined at the beginning.

- The new Regulation simplifies the formalities for recognition and establishes quick enforcement procedures for all protection measures taken in civil matters in a Member State, even for *ex parte* orders not yet served on the addressee.
- All measures available from any and all national courts having jurisdiction under their own laws to order protection measures against domestic violence may now take effect in all Member States. Thus access to justice for victims of violence will be improved.
- Moreover, the new Regulation enables victims to move freely and safely within the EU, allowing them to take advantage of domestic provisions anywhere in the EU.

---

[31] See Tribunale of Bari, 3 March 2009, in *Giurisprudenza Italiana*, 2010, p. 654 et seq. and T.C. COMBERIATI, Spunti in tema di ordine di protezione contro gli abusi familiari emesso nel corso di una separazione, in *Rivista Trimestrale di Diritto e Procedura Civile*, 2012, pp. 257–277; E. D'ALESSANDRO, Gli ordini civili di protezione contro gli abusi familiari: profili processuali, in *Rivista Trimestrale di Diritto e Procedura Civile*, 2007, p. 225, §4.

- Furthermore, by sweeping away non-essential formal requirements for the purpose of enforcement abroad the new Regulation respects the fundamental rights of victims of violence such as the right to life and to gender equality.[32]
- Of course, the focus seems to be primarily on the interests of the victim of the domestic violence. However, it must not be forgotten that an *ex parte* measure may interfere with the perpetrator's life and privacy without the latter being able to put his side of the argument and the interim enforcement can be very dangerous for the restrainee, preventing him from freely moving across the EU. Actually, the simple availability of an effective remedy against the *ex parte* order even at a later stage of the proceedings seemed to be an appropriate safeguard for ensuring the restrainee's fundamental procedural rights.[33]

After a first evaluation, I have come to the conclusion that the new Regulation is expected to provide greater protection for potential victims of violence when they move abroad, making the administrative procedure more straightforward for them in compliance with the fundamental rights of the individual. However, the main problem still remains, in my opinion, at a national level, where it often occurs that victims of violence refrain from seeking legal intervention, even from reporting the violence, due to the fact that they fear the reaction of the person causing the risk. Without any national order against domestic violence to be enforced abroad, no protection can be granted across the EU.

---

[32]   See, for instance, the case *Opuz v. Turkey* (Application no. 33401/02) in which the ECtHR ruled that the failure of the State to provide adequate protection to women against domestic violence constitutes a violation of the right to life (Article 2 ECHR) and a violation of gender equality (Article 14 ECHR).

[33]   See Articles 47–48 of EU Charter of Fundamental Rights and Article 6 ECHR.

PART FIVE

TRANSNATIONAL FAMILIES:
ACROSS NATIONS AND CULTURES

FAMILY LIFE AND EU CITIZENSHIP

The Discovery of the Substance of the EU Citizen's Rights and its Genuine Enjoyment

Katharina KAESLING

Contents

First and foremost, families in the European Union have to look to the national bodies of law regulating their legal relationships. On the EU level, the conflicts of laws as well as jurisdiction and the recognition and enforcement of judgments in family matters have been dealt with, but there is virtually no EU substantive family law. The same is true for the regulation of immigration. Article 79 TFEU allows for limited legislative action in accordance with the underlying principles of subsidiarity and proportionality in the areas of law enumerated in Article 79(2) TFEU. In spite of that commitment, the development of a common EU immigration policy is still a dream for the future. Family reunification policy has not been agreed upon within the European Union. However, on the basis of

European Union citizenship, a remarkable body of case law regarding the family life of EU citizens with third country nationals has emerged. Hence, EU law increasingly influences family life in the European Union.

1. EU CITIZENSHIP AS A TRIGGER FOR FUNDAMENTAL EVOLUTIONS

EU citizenship is intrinsically related to the EU's integration process and has brought about significant evolutions.

1.1. MOVING BEYOND THE MARKET RATIONALE

Moving beyond the market rationale, EU citizenship was introduced by the Treaty of Maastricht,[1] thus at a time when the European Economic Community transformed into the European Union. The original Treaty of Rome presupposed not only Member State nationality, but also economic activity in order to enjoy the fundamental freedoms.[2] However, these economically active 'market citizens'[3] only represent a portion of EU citizens.

EU citizenship shows that the European Union's aspirations go beyond the traditional economic rationale. Free movement is no longer for economically active persons only.[4] Instead, EU citizenship is designed to be the fundamental status of the nationals of all Member States, as the Court of Justice of the European Union (CJEU) has repeatedly held[5] and as EU legislative acts

---

[1]   Cf. The Maastricht Treaty, Provisions amending the treaty establishing the European Economic Community with a view to establishing the European Community, Maastricht, signed on 7 February 1992, Title II, Part C; Treaty of Amsterdam amending the Treaty of the European Union, the Treaties establishing the European Communities and certain related acts, signed on 2 October 1997; it has also been put forward that the Treaty of Maastricht only codifies pre-existing assumptions, cf. D. KOCHENOV and R. PLENDER, EU Citizenship: From an Incipient Form to an Incipient Substance? The Discovery of the Treaty Text, (2012) 37 EL.Rev., p. 369, pp. 372.

[2]   Cf. for economic activity as a decisive factor for the free movement of persons Case C-281/06, Jundt v. Finanzamt Offenburg [2007] ECR I-12231, para. 33; C. BARNARD, The Substantive Law of the EU: The Four Freedoms, 3rd edition, Oxford University Press, 2010, p. 223.

[3]   See M. EVERSON, The legacy of the market citizen, in J. SHAW and G. MORE (eds), New Legal Dynamics of the European Union, Oxford, Clarendon Press, 1995.

[4]   For further analysis see F. WOLLENSCHLÄGER, A New Fundamental Freedom beyond Market Integration, (2011) 17 ELJ, pp. 1; D. KOSTAKOPOULOU, Ideas, Norms and European Citizenship: Explaining Institutional Change, (2005) 68 Modern L.Rev., p. 233.

[5]   Case C-184/99 Grzelczyk [2001] ECR I -6193, para. 31, mirroring AG La Pergola's opinion in Case C-85/96 Martinez Sala [1998] ECR I – 2691, para. 20, 'a new individual legal standing'; Case C-413/99 Baumbast and R. [2002] ECR I-7091, para. 82.

confirm.[6] All EU citizens have a right to move and reside freely within the Union and corresponding rights are granted to their family members, irrespective of their nationality, but under certain conditions.[7] These conditions are in particular laid out in the Citizens' Rights Directive.[8] EU citizens shall not be discouraged from exercising their rights to free movement, as the CJEU has emphasised.[9] In this respect, migration of EU citizens and their family members across borders within the European Union is certainly regulated by EU law. But what about EU citizens who choose to refrain from exercising their rights to free movement and their family life with third country nationals? Does EU citizenship also induce a move beyond cross-border logic?

1.2. MOVING BEYOND CROSS-BORDER LOGIC?

Traditionally, the application of EU law requires the establishment of a link to EU law via the exercise of one of the fundamental freedoms. Articles 45, 49 and 56 TFEU do not only presuppose an economic activity, but also involve a cross-border element. Likewise, the directive on the right of citizens of the Union and their family members to move and reside freely within the territory of the Member States[10] is not applicable to situations that lack a traditional cross-border element. But the CJEU has also dealt with family reunification involving EU citizens on the basis of the citizenship provisions in primary law.

According to Article 20 TFEU, EU citizenship follows Member State nationality.[11] However, EU citizenship has also proven to entail limitations for the Member States when exercising their powers[12] and thus to affect the

---

6 See Citizens' Rights Directive, Recital 3; for the European Commission's take also see EU citizenship report 2010 – Dismantling the obstacles to EU citizens' rights, Brussels, 27.10.2010, COM (2010) 603 final.
7 Member States may refuse entry and residence rights upon a case-by-case examination on grounds of public policy, security or public health; the directive also allows for the refusal, termination and withdrawal of rights in the case of an abuse of rights or fraud, like marriages of conveniences.
8 Directive 2004/38 of the European Parliament and of the Council of 29 April 2004 on the right of citizens of the Union and their family members to move and reside freely within the territory of the Member States amending Regulation (EEC) No. 1612/68 and repealing Directives 64/221/EEC, 68/360/EEC, 72/194/EEC, 73/148/EEC, 75/34/EEC, 75/35/EEC, 90/364/EEC, 90/365/EEC and 93/96/EEC, *Official Journal of the European Union*, 30.04.2004, L 158/77.
9 Cf. Case C-127/08 Metock et al. [2008] ECR I-6241, para. 59 and 82; Case C-109/01 Akrich [2003] ECR I-9607, para. 53 and 54; Case C-434/09 McCarthy [2011] ECR I-3375, para. 28.
10 Cf. note 8.
11 Expressly asserted by the Treaty of Amsterdam amending the Treaty on the European Union, the Treaties establishing the European Communities and certain related acts, Amsterdam, signed on 2 October 1997, Article 2 (9).
12 Case C-369/90 Micheletti [1992] ECR I-04239, para. 10, in the context of the Member States' competence to determine the conditions for the acquisition and loss of nationality.

delimitation of EU and national competences. In *Rottmann*,[13] a citizen risked losing his Member State nationality and thus also his status as an EU citizen. The CJEU held that this situation fell within the material scope of EU law by reason of the nature of EU citizenship. Consequently, the Member State measure interfering with the citizenship status had to be proportionate.[14] Relying on that reasoning in *Rottmann*, the CJEU held in the context of family reunification in *Ruiz Zambrano* that 'Art. 20 TFEU precludes national measures which have the effect of depriving citizens of the Union of the genuine enjoyment of the substance of the rights conferred by virtue of their status as citizens of the Union'.[15] The CJEU hereby introduced the 'genuine enjoyment formula', based upon the substance of citizenship rights, which remains to be discovered.

Initially, the CJEU stressed that EU citizenship 'is not intended to extend the scope ratione materiae of the Treaty also to internal situations'.[16] Yet, in both *Rottmann* and *Ruiz Zambrano*, the Grand Chamber justified its jurisdiction on the ground of the severity of the Member State's interference with citizenship rights.[17] Subsequently, the CJEU applied the genuine enjoyment formula in other cases concerning the rights of third country nationals to reside with their static EU citizen family members in their home state.

2. THE RIGHTS OF THIRD COUNTRY NATIONALS TO RESIDE WITH THEIR STATIC EU CITIZEN FAMILY MEMBERS

EU citizens' rights to live with their family members who are nationals of non-Member States have been dealt with by the CJEU in three cases. Following the fundamental Grand Chamber decision in *Ruiz Zambrano* in 2011, the CJEU was presented with situations regarding the refusal to allow third country nationals to reside with their EU family members in *McCarthy*[18] and *Dereci et al.*[19]

---

[13] Case C-135/08 Rottmann [2010] ECR I-1449.
[14] Cf. Rottmann, para. 42 and para. 55.
[15] Case C-34/09 Gerardo Ruiz Zambrano v. Office national de l'emploi [2011] ECR I-01177, para. 42.
[16] Joint cases C-64/96 and C-65/96 Uecker and Jacquet [1997] ECR I-3171, para. 23; Case C-148/02 Garcia Avello [2003] ECR I-11613, para. 26.
[17] Cf. M. HAILBRONNER and S. SÁNCHEZ, The European Court of Justice and Citizenship of the European Union: New Developments Towards a Truly Fundamental Status (2011) *ICL Journal*, pp. 498, 500.
[18] Case C-434/09 McCarthy [2011] ECR I-3375.
[19] Case C-256/11 Dereci et al. [2011] ECR I-11315.

2.1. FROM *RUIZ ZAMBRANO* TO *DERECI*

Having recalled the facts of the cases *Ruiz Zambrano*, *McCarthy* and *Dereci et al.* (section 2.1.1), the CJEU's decisions shall be exposed (section 2.1.2) in order to analyse the application of the genuine enjoyment formula in this jurisprudence (section 2.2).

2.1.1. Recalling the Facts

In *Ruiz Zambrano*, the Colombian national Mr Ruiz Zambrano had applied for work and residence permits in Belgium, where he lived with his Colombian wife, one Columbian child and two minor Belgian children. The Belgian children had been born in Belgium and had never left their home state.

The Jamaican national Mr *McCarthy* requested leave to remain with his wife Mrs McCarthy, an Irish and UK citizen, in the UK. Notwithstanding her dual nationality, Mrs McCarthy was born in the UK and had always lived there. She was in receipt of state benefits and therefore did not qualify as a worker or a self-employed or self-sufficient person.

In *Dereci et al.*, the Court was presented with five sets of facts involving EU citizens who had never exercised their rights to free movement. The third-country nationals Mr Maduike and Mr Dereci wanted to live with their static Austrian spouses in Austria. Not unlike the situation in *Ruiz Zambrano*, Mr Dereci had three minor Austrian children. Finally, Mr Kokollari and Mrs Stevic sought reunification with an Austrian parent who they claimed was maintaining them. The EU citizens concerned were not dependent on their third country national family members.[20]

In all three cases, the court applied the genuine enjoyment formula.

2.1.2. Decisions

In *Ruiz Zambrano*, the Grand Chamber of the Court introduced the genuine enjoyment formula according to which national measures are precluded if they deprive EU citizens of the genuine enjoyment of the substance of their citizens' rights. The CJEU derived a right to reside and work directly from Article 20 TFEU. Three months later in *McCarthy*, this formula was applied by the CJEU's Third Chamber side by side with the traditional cross-border test. The Chamber appears to have focused on Mrs McCarthy's dual nationality, which alone was not considered sufficient to establish a cross-border element. She was considered to be a static EU citizen.[21] The Court did not find any indication of a deprivation of the genuine enjoyment of Mrs McCarthy's rights. The decision in *McCarthy*

---

20 Dereci et al., para. 32.
21 See McCarthy, para. 41.

does not appear to be easily reconcilable with the Court's assessment in *Ruiz Zambrano*. It is true that the Supreme Court of the United Kingdom referred two questions regarding the applicability of the Citizens' Rights Directive to the CJEU for a preliminary ruling in *McCarthy*. But the CJEU was quick to note that it remains free to provide 'the national court with all the elements of interpretation of European Union law which may be of assistance in adjudicating on the case before it'[22] and it 'reformulated'[23] the Supreme Court's question regarding Art. 16 of the Citizens' Rights Directive into the question of 'whether Art. 21 TFEU is applicable' to a static Union citizen.[24] When assessing the applicability of Art. 21 TFEU, the Court firstly determined that Mrs McCarthy's right to move and reside freely was not affected.[25] It then went on to say that in the case of a static citizen, like it had already found Mrs McCarthy to be, Article 21 TFEU could still be applicable in the case of a deprivation of the genuine enjoyment of the substance of the rights conferred by virtue of her status as a citizen of the Union.[26] Curiously, and in spite of what the CJEU had previously underlined as to its assistance to the national court by providing it with all the useful elements, it did not then further elaborate upon the issue of applicability due to a deprivation of genuine enjoyment – even though the facts bear more than a little resemblance to the situation in *Ruiz Zambrano*.

In *Dereci et al.*, the CJEU slightly modified the terminology of the genuine enjoyment formula, as it stipulated that the Member State measure must not lead to a *denial* of the genuine enjoyment of the substance of citizens' rights. The Court then left it to the national courts to apply the genuine enjoyment test to the five situations at hand on the basis of the 'provisions on citizenship of the Union'.

The decisions in *McCarthy* and *Dereci* show that there are limits to the rights conferred by virtue of the status of EU citizenship, but they do not call the essence of the *Ruiz Zambrano* formula into question. The genuine enjoyment formula is repeated and employed in all cases. Even when the court stresses the applicability of EU law to transborder situations, it confirms the relevance of the intensity of the Member State's interference with citizenship rights.[27] The Court's Third Chamber did not abandon the Grand Chamber's logic of *Ruiz Zambrano* in *McCarthy*. The Grand Chamber's wording in *Dereci et al.*, demanding a denial of the genuine enjoyment of the substance of the rights conferred by virtue of the European Union citizen status, insinuates that the Member State measure must have a substantial impact for the genuine enjoyment formula to come into play. However, the validity of the genuine enjoyment

---

[22] McCarthy, para. 24.
[23] McCarthy, para. 44.
[24] McCarthy, para. 44.
[25] McCarthy, para. 49.
[26] See McCarthy, para. 56.
[27] See only McCarthy, para. 56.

formula was confirmed in both *McCarthy* and *Dereci et al.* It has become a second jurisdiction test. Member State measures touching upon the substance of citizens' rights have to be compatible with EU law. It is thus essential to determine the scope of this substance and when its genuine enjoyment is called into question.

2.2. APPLICATION OF THE GENUINE ENJOYMENT FORMULA IN THE CJEU'S JURISPRUDENCE: IN NEED OF GUIDELINES

Specifically in *Dereci*, the CJEU underlined the importance of the national courts' assessment.[28] The genuine enjoyment formula evidently requires a thorough evaluation of the specific circumstances of the individual case. National courts are best situated to assess whether the Member State measure amounts to a denial of the genuine enjoyment of the substance of citizens' rights. Yet the CJEU has to enable them to make this assessment by providing clear guidelines at the EU level.

So far, the paramount criterion seems to be whether the Union citizen has to, in fact, leave EU territory. This criterion was referred to in all three cases. In *Ruiz Zambrano*, it appears to be decisive that the children would have to follow their parent if the latter was expelled.[29] However, the Court did not see why Mrs McCarthy should not remain in the UK without her husband. In *Dereci et al.*, the CJEU maintained that it is not sufficient that it might appear desirable to live together in the citizen's home state for economic reasons or in order to keep the family together.[30] At the same time, the Court stressed that it wants to adopt a functional approach, focussing on the effectiveness of Union citizenship enjoyed by EU citizens.[31] Legally, no citizen of a Member State can be forced to leave that very Member State as the prohibition on the expulsion of the State's own nationals is a principle of public international law,[32] which the CJEU reaffirmed both previously[33] and specifically in *McCarthy*.[34] In fact, not only children, but also spouses like Mrs McCarthy might feel compelled to leave in order to maintain their matrimonial community. Does the Court differentiate between categories of familial relationships? Are spousal relations not sufficient, while parental relations are? Or is the genuine enjoyment formula specifically designed

---

28   Dereci et al., paras 72 and 74.
29   Ruiz Zambrano, para. 44.
30   Dereci et al., para. 68.
31   Dereci et al., para. 67.
32   Cf. Art. 3 of Protocol No. 4 to the ECHR.
33   C-370/90 Singh [1992] ECR I-4265, para. 22; C-291/05 Eind [2007] ECR I-10719, para. 31; for the right to enter the territory and remain there for any reason see Case 41/74 van Duyn [1974] ECR 1337, para. 22 and Case C-257/99 Barkoci and Malik [2001] ECR I-6557, para. 81.
34   Para. 29.

to protect minors rather than adults? In *McCarthy*, self-sufficiency appears to be a relevant factor,[35] and with that, even the reintroduction of the condition of an economic activity seems to be possible. So a number of criteria (might) have played a role in the CJEU's decision-making, but other than the citizen's right not to be forced to leave the territory of the Union none of them gained consistent substantiation in the CJEU's jurisprudence.[36] The preliminary ruling in *Ruiz Zambrano* was characterised by its brevity and laconicism, reminiscent of the Court's style in early fundamental cases.[37] In spite of the Advocate General's hint in *Dereci*,[38] the Court did not make use of the opportunities to further clarify its argumentation. This body of case law thus gives rise to considerable legal uncertainty as to the interpretation and application of the genuine enjoyment formula.

Curiously, the right to respect for family life has so far not been accorded particular importance in the context of family reunification. In fact, the Court dismissed its relevance in both *Ruiz Zambrano* and *McCarthy* with no further ado. In *Dereci et al.*, the Court finally seemed to deal with the right to respect for family life.[39] Sadly, the Court then settled for a mere reiteration of the general principles of the protection of fundamental rights at the EU level by stating that the right to respect for private and family life is only relevant to situations covered by EU law. It did not elaborate upon its value for the interpretation and application of the genuine enjoyment formula.

3. FOR AN INTERPRETATION IN THE LIGHT OF THE RIGHT TO RESPECT FOR PRIVATE AND FAMILY LIFE

Notwithstanding the limitation of the impact of fundamental rights to matters within the ambit of EU law, the substance of the rights flowing from the EU citizen status has to be defined in consideration of the right to respect for private and family life as set out in Article 7 of the Charter of Fundamental Rights of the European Union (Charter) and Article 8 ECHR. Article 52(2) of

---

[35] See to that effect D. KOCHENOV, The Right to Have What Rights? EU Citizenship in Need of Justification, 19 *ELJ* 2013/ SSRN, p. 10.

[36] See D. KOCHENOV, The Right to Have What Rights? EU Citizenship in Need of Justification, 19 *ELJ* 2013/ SSRN, p. 17.

[37] M. HAILBRONNER, M. and S. IGLESIAS SANCHEZ, The European Court of Justice and Citizenship of the European Union: New Developments towards a Truly Fundamental Status, (2011) *ICL Journal* Vol. 5(4), pp. 498, 500.

[38] AG MENGOZZI specifically reminded the court in its Opinion in Dereci et al. that the state of jurisprudence was not 'very satisfactory from the point of view of legal certainty', Opinion AG Mengozzi, para. 49; also see D. KOCHENOV, The Right to Have What Rights? EU Citizenship in Need of Justification, 19 *ELJ* 2013/ SSRN, p. 14.

[39] Cf. para. 70.

the Charter states that the interpretation of EU law shall be carried out in the light of the Charter and the rights enshrined therein. When the CJEU is interpreting the TFEU's citizenship provisions, it is clearly interpreting EU law in the sense of Article 52(2) of the Charter. It is thus bound to consider the right to family life.

As we have seen, the severity of the Member State's interference with citizenship rights has been held decisive by the CJEU. Alas, relying on intensity as the focal factor risks creating blurred demarcation lines. So far, there is considerable legal uncertainty as to the relevant criteria for interpreting and applying the genuine enjoyment formula. This is all the more deplorable as it goes to the core of the protection of family life with third-country nationals in the EU. In order to avoid a defragmentation of the rights derived from EU citizenship, guidelines at the EU level are needed.

The contours of the right to respect for private and family life, on the other hand, have already been developed, especially by the ECHR.[40] Also under the ECHR, the right to respect for private and family life is not absolute, but is subject to a number of limitations.[41] These outlines should be put to use in the context of family reunification on the basis of EU citizenship as a minimum standard. The CJEU's evaluation of a Member State measure's proportionality is a threefold test. The CJEU assesses, firstly, its necessity, secondly its suitability, and thirdly it considers the excessive effects for the persons concerned.[42] When the ECHR evaluates whether a Contracting State's interference with the right to respect for private and family life can be justified on grounds of the particular gravity of the circumstances, it also carries out a proportionality analysis.[43] In its jurisprudence, a list of rather specific criteria for this assessment can be

---

[40]   As to the notion of 'family life' see Marckx v. Belgium, judgment of 27 April 1979, Series A No. 31, para. 31; K. and T. v. Finland, judgment of 12 July 2001, Application No. 25702/94, para. 150; the notion of private life is broader, but certainly includes the right to establish and develop relationships with other human beings, see only Niemitz v. Germany, judgment of 16 December 1992, Application No. 13710/88.

[41]   According to Art. 8(2) ECHR, an interference with the right to respect for private and family life is justified if the Contracting State's measure is based on and adopted in accordance with the law, a legitimate aim is pursued and the measure is necessary, meaning that it is specifically proportionate to the legitimate aim pursued. Families may be expected to relocate, see only ECtHR, Gul v. Switzerland, judgment of 19 February 1996, Application No. 23218/94, and it has been established that the birth of a child as such does not give rise to an entitlement to stay under the ECHR, see ECtHR Darren Omoregie and Others v. Norway, judgment of 1 July 2008, Application No. 265/07, para. 66.

[42]   The test whether the measure has an excessive effect can also be seen as one of the limbs of the necessity test, see T. TRIDIMAS, Proportionality in Community Law: Searching for the appropriate standard of scrutiny, in: E. ELLIS (ed.), The Principle of Proportionality in the Laws of Europe, Hart Publishing, 1999, p. 68. The CJEU uses differing formulas, see Case C-368/95 Familiapress [1997] ECR I-3689; Case C-265/06 Commission v. Portugal [2008] ECR I-2245; Case C-244/06 Dynamic Medien Vertriebs GmbH [2008] ECR I-505, para. 44.

[43]   See only ECtHR, Rodriguez da Silva v. Netherlands, judgment of 31 January 2006, Application No. 50435/99.

found, among them the length of the third country national's stay in the host country, the nationalities of the various persons concerned, the length of the marriage and the factors shaping the effectiveness of the family life as well as the concerned children's age,[44] the social, cultural and linguistic ties to the host and home country[45] and specifically the best interests of children.[46] These criteria should be reflected in the application of the genuine enjoyment formula.

While this approach acknowledges the Member State's legitimate interest in controlling immigration, it also sets limits as the gravity of the particular circumstances is susceptible to outweigh the Member State's interest. Member State measures that eliminate all prospects of private and family life for their national should be qualified as a denial of the genuine enjoyment of the substance of EU citizens' rights, as they effectively render the right to respect for private and family life an empty shell.

The EU Charter of Fundamental Rights draws on the ECHR.[47] Following the EU's accession to the ECHR as envisioned by Article 6(2) TEU, the rapport between the role of fundamental rights within European Union law and within the system of the Council of Europe will be further strengthened and the protection of fundamental rights will be reinforced.[48]

National courts determine whether EU law is applicable by applying both the traditional cross-border test and the genuine enjoyment formula.[49] The cases brought before the CJEU cast doubt on the sufficiency of the Member States' obligation to respect Article 8(1) ECHR under public international law.[50] The right to respect for private and family life have to be considered as a matter of EU law within the parameters of its scope of application – especially with regard to the development of EU citizenship and the continuing integration process. The European Union has a vested interest in considering the fundamental right of respect for private and family life in the context of family reunification insofar as it has a bearing on EU citizenship and its *effet utile*.

---

[44] See for a list of criteria for the assessment of the necessity and proportionality of an expulsion ECtHR, Amrohalli v. Denmark, judgment of 11 July 2002, Application No. 56811/00, para. 35.

[45] See ECtHR, Omjudi v. The United Kingdom, judgment of 24 November 2009, Application No. 1820/08; ECtHR, Omoregie et al. v. Norway, judgment of 31 July 2008, Application No. 265/07.

[46] Cf. ECtHR, Nunez v. Norway, judgment of 28 June 2009, Application No. 55597/09; ECtHR, Maslov v. Austria, judgment of 22 March 2007, Application No. 1638/03.

[47] See C. BARNARD, *The Substantive Law of the EU: The Four Freedoms*, 3rd edition, Oxford University Press, 2010, p. 421.

[48] See Draft accession agreement of the European Union to the European Convention on Human rights, finalised 5 April 2013; Cf. C. BARNARD, *The Substantive Law of the EU: The Four Freedoms*, 3rd edition, Oxford University Press, 2010, p. 421f.

[49] Cf. in that respect Dereci, para. 74: 'the denial of the genuine enjoyment of the substance of the rights conferred by virtue of [one's] status as a citizen of the Union ... is a matter for the referring court to verify'.

[50] Hinted at by the Court in Dereci, para. 72.

4. A SENSIBLE DELIMITATION OF EU AND NATIONAL SPHERES: A NEW DEFINITION OF THE CATEGORY OF PURELY INTERNAL SITUATIONS

It has been argued that the doctrine of purely internal situations should be brought to an end rather than setting up a rather complicated jurisdiction test like the genuine enjoyment formula.[51] However, leaving the category of purely internal situations intact is preferable to an abolition of reverse discrimination. Rather than granting EU family reunification rights to all static and migrant EU citizens, a sensible demarcation line should be drawn using the genuine enjoyment formula.

As one of the fundamental doctrines of EU law, the purely internal situation doctrine has been developed by jurisprudence since the 1970s.[52] According to that doctrine, situations that are wholly internal to one Member State do not fall within the scope of EU law.[53] Traditionally, those were situations where no adequate link to the exercise of fundamental freedoms within the EU could be shown.[54] In more recent cases, the CJEU has also accepted more tenuous links,[55] but the category of purely internal situations has not been abandoned. In *Ruiz Zambrano*, the Court resisted the temptation[56] to abolish this doctrine. Yet the introduction of the genuine enjoyment formula results in an adjustment of the definition of purely internal situations. In addition to the traditional cross-border situations, situations involving Member State measures that encroach on the substance of citizens' rights are no longer considered to be purely internal situations. Within that sphere, reverse discrimination to the detriment of the nationals of the acting Member State is prohibited and fundamental rights are to

---

[51] See the Opinion of Advocate General SHARPSTON in Ruiz Zambrano, paras 86 and 144, proposing to rely on Art. 18 TFEU to prohibit reverse discrimination.

[52] See Case 175/78 Saunders [1979] ECR 1129, para. 11, which the Court later repeated in the context of all fundamental freedoms.

[53] See D. HANF, "Reverse Discrimination" in: EU Law: Constitutional Aberration, Constitutional Necessity, or Judicial Choice, *Maastricht Journal of European and Comparative Law* 2 (2011), p. 29; for a critical analysis of the purely internal situation rule, see A. TRIFONYDOU, 'Purely Internal Situations and Reverse Discrimination in a Citizen's Europe: Time to "reverse" reverse discrimination?', in: P.G. XUEREB (ed.), *Issues in Social Policy: A New Agenda*, Progress Press, 2009, pp. 11 – 29.

[54] See e.g. Case 292/86 Gullung [1988] ECR 111, para. 12; Case C-415/93 Bosman [1995], ECR 1995 I-04921, para. 13.

[55] See Case C-60/00, Carpenter [2002] ECR I-06279, para. 39, regarding Art. 56 TFEU. The CJEU found it sufficient that Mr Carpenter would be impeded in providing services in other Member States if his wife was not allowed to live with him in his home state. Moreover, the CJEU has not declined jurisdiction in cases where EU law was not applicable as such, but gained relevance due to a non-discrimination clause in national constitutions, see Joined Cases C-515, 519–524 and 526–540/99 Reisch et al. [2002], ECR I-2157, para. 25–27; Case C-448/98 Guimont [2000] ECR I-10663, para. 2024.

[56] In the form of AG SHARPSTON's invitation, see the Opinion of Advocate General Sharpston in Ruiz Zambrano, para. 84.

be applied as a matter of EU law.[57] At least for now,[58] the CJEU has upheld this underlying distinction between EU and national legal spheres.

Neither has the category of purely internal situations been given up, nor should it be relinquished in the near future. While the equal treatment of all EU citizens might be desirable in principle, this approach neglects the fact that the EU only has certain, specific objectives that cannot serve as a basis for policy choices in the area of family reunification – which would then have to be made by the Court. At this point in the integration process, the Member States' national lawmakers are called upon to lay down immigration policies, while EU law sets standards flowing from a functional reading of the free movement and citizenship provisions. In that way, the EU's influence is limited to cross-border situations and severe interferences with the EU citizen status and the substance of EU citizens' rights as determined in accordance with the genuine enjoyment formula. Instead of abandoning purely internal situations, the CJEU has opted for an extension of the type of situations covered by EU law as a consequence of the recognition of the EU citizenship status and corresponding rights. Key to a workable solution is the definition of the rights conferred upon all EU citizens by virtue of their status according to EU guidelines, in consideration of their right to respect for family and private life as laid out above.

5. CONCLUSIONS

The status of EU citizens involves consequences for the immigration of third country nationals and their family life with EU citizens. By consistently employing the genuine enjoyment formula in the light of the right to respect for private and family life, the effects of reverse discrimination to the detriment of static EU citizens are significantly mitigated. Making use of the criteria developed in the jurisprudence on the right to respect for private and family life is susceptible to reducing legal uncertainty as to the interpretation of the genuine enjoyment formula and thus to the limits of the Member States' latitude. A sufficient margin of discretion is left to the Member States, while EU citizenship prohibits Member States from undermining the right to respect for private and family life with third country nationals and thereby calls the genuine enjoyment of the substance of the citizenship rights into question.

---

[57] See for the requirements of EU law concerning the effective protection of the fundamental rights conferred on EU citizens also Joined Cases C-372/09 and C-373/09, Josep Penarroja Fa. [2011] ECR I-01785; as O'Leary remarked almost a decade ago, in general one of the main objectives of establishing the status of citizenship is the protection of (fundamental) rights against abridgement by the state, see S. O'LEARY, The Relation between Community Citizenship and the Protection of Fundamental Rights in Community Law, CMLR 2 (1995), pp. 519, 520.

[58] In Joined Cases C-372/09 and C-373/09 Josep Penarroja Fa. [2011] ECR I-01785, the CJEU hints at future developments as to the relevance of fundamental rights in EU law.

PRIVATE AND FAMILY LIFE *VERSUS* MORALS AND TRADITION IN THE CASE LAW OF THE ECtHR

Geoffrey WILLEMS

Contents

1. INTRODUCTION

For approximately thirty years now, the European Court has constantly been reshaping the relations between individuals, the family and the State.

On the one hand, the autonomous concepts of private life and family life have been given a totally unexpected width. On the other hand, the obligations imposed on States in this ever-enlarging field have also become heavier. Article 8 requires States not only to abstain from undue interferences, but also to protect individuals from each other and to adopt positive measures designed to ensure the effectiveness of rights.

However, the rights guaranteed by the Convention may suffer restrictions on different grounds. The second paragraph of Article 8 of the Convention foresees that States may limit individual rights in order to pursue different legitimate aims such as the security or the economic well-being of the country, the protection of the rights and freedoms of others or the protection of morals. The pattern of justifications imposed on States regarding actions and abstentions in the ambit of personal and family life is evolving: at first sight, one could think that morals and traditions are much less efficient today than they used to be in the early case law of the Court. If this would be consistent with the contemporary favour for 'liberal pluralism',[1] recent decisions suggest that the Court is still ready to uphold national solutions inspired by 'legal moralism'.[2]

This contribution studies, firstly, how moral and traditional views seemed to have been progressively delegitimised as justifications for restrictions to personal autonomy and equality between people and family forms (section 2) and, secondly, how, for a couple of years, majoritarian conceptions of morality appear reinvested with considerable weight while traditional views on family relations are treated in a schizophrenic way by the European judges (section 3).

2. FROM A DELEGITIMISATION OF MORALS AND TRADITION AS JUSTIFICATIONS FOR RESTRICTIONS ON RIGHTS

The protection of morals has often been invoked by States trying to justify restrictions on individual freedom in sexuality-related matters (section 2.1). The protection of the traditional family has rather been advanced as an argument

---

[1]   For some authors, morals and traditions should be suppressed from the legitimate aims list. States' justifications should be, in other words, 'value-free'. An author claims that the reference to the protection of morals is 'at best repetitive' of the protection of the rights of others (C. NOWLIN, "The Protection of Morals Under the European Convention of Human Rights and Fundamental Freedoms", *Human Rights Quarterly*, 2002, p. 285). As regards traditions, we can rely on the objective affirmed by another author to 'delegitimize tradition as a legitimate aim' (A. TIMMER, "Delegitimizing tradition as a "legitimate aim": inspiration for Strasbourg from California", *Strasbourg observers*, 11 August 2010). See also: C. WARNOCK, "Sex Work in New Zealand: The Re-Importation of Moral Majoritarianism in Regulating a Decriminalized Industry", *Canadian Journal of Women and the Law*, 2012, pp. 414–438.

[2]   According to T.S. Petersen, a professor at Roskilde University, 'legal moralism can be defined as follows: the immorality of an act of type A is a sufficient reason for the criminalization of A, even if A does not cause someone to be harmed'. Herbert Hart would have been the first to use the term (T.S. PETERSEN, "What is Legal Moralism", *SATS Northern European Journal of Philosophy*, 2011, vol. 12, pp. 80–81). See also: H.L.A. HART, "Positivism and the Separation of Law and Morals", *Harvard Law Review*, 1958, vol. 71 pp. 593–629.

justifying the differentiated treatment of unconventional families and inequalities between men and women (section 2.2).

2.1. SEXUAL MORALITY AND AUTONOMY

The approach of sexual morality by the ECHR was developed in the case law relating to Article 10 and was then applied in homosexuality and sadomasochism cases.

2.1.1. Freedom of Expression

The 1976 *Handyside v United Kingdom*[3] case is undoubtedly the foundational leading case in the ECHR morals case law. The editor Richard Handyside had published a controversial book entitled *The Little Red Schoolbook*. The book was conceived for children and contained advice regarding drugs and sexuality. There were complaints and the Public Prosecutor initiated criminal proceedings. The books were seized and destroyed and the editor was fined. He complained before the ECHR that his right to freedom of expression had been violated. The European judges held that 'it [was] not possible to find in the domestic law of the various Contracting States a uniform European conception of morals' as 'the view taken by their respective laws of the requirements of morals varies from time to time and from place to place' and that 'by reason of their direct and continuous contact with the vital forces of their countries, State authorities [were] in principle in a better position than the international judge to give an opinion on the exact content of these requirements as well as on the "necessity" of a "restriction" or "penalty" intended to meet them' (§48). Having examined the content of the litigious book – including advice concerning pot smoking and the use of pornography[4] – and stressed that it was aimed at children and adolescents, the Court considered, by thirteen votes to one, that the UK court's judgment pursued the legitimate aim of protecting the morals of the youth (§52) and that the interferences complained of were proportionate to this aim (§59), even if the

---

3   ECtHR, *Handyside v UK*, 7 December 1976.
4   See §32. For instance: 'Maybe you smoke pot or go to bed with your boyfriend or girlfriend – and don't tell your parents or teachers, either because you don't dare to or just because you want to keep it secret. Don't feel ashamed or guilty about doing things you really want to do and think are right just because your parents or teachers might disapprove. A lot of these things will be more important to you later in life than the things that are "approved of"' and 'Porn is a harmless pleasure if it isn't taken seriously and believed to be real life. Anybody who mistakes it for reality will be greatly disappointed. But it's quite possible that you may get some good ideas from it and you may find something which looks interesting and that you haven't tried before'.

same book had appeared and been circulating in the majority of the member States (§57).

About ten years after this, in the fairly similar *Müller v Switzerland*[5] case, the Court held that 'there is a natural link between protection of morals and protection of the rights of others' (§30)[6] and that it was still not possible to find 'a uniform European conception of morals' (§36) so that the Swiss court could reasonably decide to confiscate obscene paintings and fine the organisers of their exhibition, even if 'conceptions of sexual morality [had] changed in recent years' (§§36 and 43).[7] In the much more recent judgment in *Akdas v Turkey* dated 16 February 2010, concerning the Turkish edition of Guillaume Apollinaire's pornographic novel *Les Onze Mille Verges*, the Court maintained that, having regard to the relative character of moral conceptions in Europe, a certain margin of appreciation must be allocated to the States, but it considered that 'the recognition of cultural, historical and religious singularities of the member States did not go as far as to forbid the access to a work of art which is a part of the European literary heritage' (§§29–30).[8]

So morals were and still are a potential justification for restrictions on the freedom of expression. The principles exposed in *Handyside* still constitute the conceptual framework for the adjudication of moral cases today. However, unlike books or exhibitions, private sexuality does not affect the public at large.

2.1.2. Homosexuality and Sadomasochism

Five years after *Handyside*, the Court was asked to assess the acceptability of the Northern Irish laws repressing consenting sexual intercourse between men.

In the 1981 *Dudgeon v United Kingdom* case, the Strasbourg judges reaffirmed that the requirements of morals are intrinsically relative – in time and space – and that domestic authorities are better placed than an international court to

---

[5] ECtHR, *Müller v Switzerland*, 24 May 1988.

[6] See also: ECtHR, *Otto-Preminger-Institut v Austria*, 20 September 1994, sp. §§46–57; ECtHR, *Wingrove v United Kingdom*, 25 November 1996, sp. §§45–64; ECtHR, *Vereinigung Bildender Künstler v Austria*, 25 January 2007, sp. §§29–39.

[7] According to the Sarine District Criminal Court: 'In the instant case, although Mr. Müller's three works are not sexually arousing to a person of ordinary sensitivity, they are undoubtedly repugnant at the very least. The overall impression is of persons giving free rein to licentiousness and even perversion. The subjects – sodomy, fellatio, bestiality, the erect penis – are obviously morally offensive to the vast majority of the population. Although allowance has to be made for changes in the moral climate, even for the worse, what we have here would revolutionize it. Comment on the confiscated works is superfluous; their vulgarity is plain to see and needs no elaborating upon. ... Nor can a person of ordinary sensitivity be expected to go behind what is actually depicted and make a second assessment of the picture independently of what he can actually see. To do that he would have to be accompanied to exhibitions by a procession of sexologists, psychologists, art theorists or ethnologists in order to have explained to him that what he saw was in reality what he wrongly thought he saw' (§14).

[8] Author's own translation.

define their content and to evaluate the necessity of an interference intended to meet them (§52). According to the Court, the general prohibition on male homosexual conduct constituted an interference in the applicant's right to private life (§41) and this interference was aimed at the protection of morals and at the protection of the rights of others, the distinction between those two aims being, in this context, 'somewhat artificial' (§§45–47).[9] It was beyond doubt, for the Court, that 'some degree of regulation of male homosexual conduct, as indeed of other forms of sexual conduct, by means of the criminal law can be justified' (§49). In this context, 'the moral climate in Northern Ireland in sexual matters' could legitimately be taken into account and the fact that 'similar measures [were] not considered necessary in other parts of the United Kingdom or in other member States' did not mean that they were not necessary in Northern Irish society (§§56–57). However, the Court finally decided that, in a context of better understanding and growing acceptance of homosexuality – even in Northern Ireland – and since sexuality was 'an essentially private manifestation of human personality', there was 'no sufficient justification provided by the risk of harm to vulnerable sections of society or by the effects on the public' (§60) to admit the general criminalisation of private homosexual relations between consenting adult males (§61).[10]

---

[9]   See §47: 'It is somewhat artificial in this context to draw a rigid distinction between "protection of the rights and freedoms of others" and "protection of morals". The latter may imply safeguarding the moral ethos or moral standards of a society as a whole (see para. 108 of the Commission's report), but may also, as the Government pointed out, cover protection of the moral interests and welfare of a particular section of society, for example schoolchildren (see the *Handyside* judgment of 7 December 1976, Series A no. 24, p. 25, para. 52 in fine – in relation to Article 10 para. 2 (art. 10–2) of the Convention). Thus, "protection of the rights and freedoms of others", when meaning the safeguarding of the moral interests and welfare of certain individuals or classes of individuals who are in need of special protection for reasons such as lack of maturity, mental disability or state of dependence, amounts to one aspect of "protection of morals" (see, mutatis mutandis, the *Sunday Times* judgment of 26 April 1979, Series A no. 30, p. 34, para. 56)'.

[10] See, however, the dissenting opinions of Judge Zekia, Matscher and Walsh. The latter opposed the legal philosophies of Devlin and Hart: '[Devlin] claims that the criminal law of England not only "has from the very first concerned itself with moral principles but continues to concern itself with moral principles". Among the offences which he pointed to as having been brought within the criminal law on the basis of moral principle, notwithstanding that it could be argued that they do not endanger the public, were euthanasia, the killing of another at his own request, suicide pacts, duelling, abortion, incest between brother and sister. These are acts which he viewed as ones which could be done in private and without offence to others and need not involve the corruption or exploitation of others. Yet, as he pointed out, no one has gone so far as to suggest that they should all be left outside the criminal law as matters of private morality' (§9), while '[t]he opposite view, traceable in English jurisprudence to John Stuart Mill, is that the law should not intervene in matters of private moral conduct more than necessary to preserve public order and to protect citizens against what is injurious and offensive and that there is a sphere of moral conduct which is best left to individual conscience just as if it were equitable to liberty of thought or belief' (§11). According to the judge 'sexual morality is only one part of the total area of morality and a question which cannot be avoided is whether sexual morality is "only private morality" or whether it has an inseparable social

The *Dudgeon* principles were reaffirmed in *Norris* and *Modinos*.[11] In the 1999 *Smith and Grady* and *Lustig-Prean and Beckett* cases, the Court went one step further by deciding that the 'negative attitudes' of the 'heterosexual majority' could not justify the revocation of homosexuals from the Royal Air Force or the Royal Navy.[12]

The United Kingdom was again condemned in the 2000 *A.D.T.* case where the applicant had been sentenced by the national courts because he had taken part in homosexual group sex at his home.[13] The European judges affirmed that 'at some point, sexual activities can be carried out in such a manner that State interference may be justified ... for the protection, for example, of health or morals' but, since the applicant had only engaged 'in private, in non-violent sexual activities with up to four other men', the maintenance of the legislation as well as the prosecution and conviction of the applicant were contrary to Article 8.[14] In 2003, Austria was condemned in the *L. and V.* case where the applicants had been convicted by the national courts because they had had homosexual intercourse with consenting adolescents between the ages of 14 and 18. For the European judges, 'the Criminal Code embodied a predisposed bias on the part of a heterosexual majority against a homosexual minority' and 'these negative attitudes [could not] ... amount to sufficient justification for the differential treatment any more than similar negative attitudes towards those of a different race, origin or colour' (§52).[15]

Moral views about homosexuality could thus no longer justify criminalisation or discrimination as far as consensual and non-violent sexual relationships were concerned. But what if sex is violent and/or not consensual?

---

dimension' (§15) and to him 'the law has a role in influencing moral attitudes and if the respondent Government is of the opinion that the change sought in the legislation would have a damaging effect on moral attitudes then in my view it is entitled to maintain the legislation it has' (§20).

[11] See: ECtHR, *Norris v Ireland*, 26 October 1988; ECtHR, *Modinos v Cyprus*, 22 April 1993.

[12] ECtHR, *Smith and Grady v United Kingdom*, 27 September 1999, §97; ECtHR, *Lustig-Prean and Beckett v United Kingdom*, 27 September 1999, §90.

[13] While heterosexual or lesbian group sex was not criminalised by the Sexual Offences Acts 1967 (see §§18–19).

[14] ECtHR, *A.D.T. v United Kingdom*, 31 July 2000, §37.

[15] Heterosexual or lesbian sex with consenting adolescents was not criminalised by Article 209 of the Austrian Criminal Code (see §34). See also ECtHR, *Santos Couto v Portugal*, 21 September 2010, §§37–44. On the evolution of the sexuality case law up until *A.D.T.*, see e.g.: M. GRIGOLO, "Sexualities and the E.C.H.R.: Introducing the Universal Sexual Legal Subject", *European Journal of International Law*, 2003, pp. 1024–1035.

In the 1997 *Laskey, Jaggard and Brown*[16] case concerning consensual,[17] but very violent,[18] sexual practices involving numerous men,[19] the Court held that the prosecution and conviction of the applicants was not contrary to Article 8 since they could be considered necessary and proportionate to the aim of protecting health. It was thus not necessary to determine whether the interference was also justified by reference to morals but 'this finding … [must] not be understood as calling into question the prerogative of the State on moral grounds to seek to deter acts of the kind in question' (§51).[20]

However, seven years later, the Court decided another sadomasochism case – *K.A. and A.D. v Belgium*[21] – without a single reference to morals or to any kind of other public interest. The Court considered that there had been no violation of Article 8 since the applicants had been convicted by the national judges notably because they had not stopped their assault even when the victim had withdrawn her consent by using a pre-agreed safeword.[22] Even if the judicial minimalism of the ECHR is well known, the absence of any consideration related to morals or health has sometimes been interpreted as implying that, from then onwards, the only legitimate limit that a State could place on sexual freedom was the exigency of the full and persistent consent of all people involved.[23]

---

16   ECtHR, *Laskey, Jaggard and Brown v United Kingdom*, 19 February 1997.

17   If the 'facts' part of the judgment says that 'these activities were consensual' (§8), Judge Pettiti asked in his concurring opinion if one can 'consider that adolescents taking part in sado-masochistic activities have given their free and informed consent where their elders have used various means of enticement, including financial reward'?

18   'The acts consisted in the main of maltreatment of the genitalia (with, for example, hot wax, sandpaper, fish hooks and needles) and ritualistic beatings either with the assailant's bare hands or a variety of implements, including stinging nettles, spiked belts and a cat-o'-nine tails. There were instances of branding and infliction of injuries which resulted in the flow of blood and which left scarring' (§8).

19   From their point of view, their sexual activities concerned only 'private morality' and were none of 'the State's business' (§45). According to the government, their condemnation was justified not only by the necessity to protect public health but also by broader moral considerations and by the respect that human beings owe to each other (§40).

20   For concurring Judge Pettiti the Court should have stressed that the State is entitled 'to regulate and punish practices of sexual abuse that are demeaning even if they do not involve the infliction of physical harm'.

21   ECtHR, *K.A. and A.D. v Belgium*, 17 February 2005.

22   According to the applicants, in 'a permissive, liberal and individualist society', people would no longer be shocked by sadomasochist practices even if the 'slaves' involved in the considered sexual games were paid (§50). From the point of view of the Belgian authorities, 'acts of torture couldn't be tolerated in a democratic society where respect owed to each other by human beings is an essential value' (§67).

23   As in *Laskey*, money played an obscure role in *K.A. and A.D.* since it was admitted by the applicants that their victim had sometimes been paid to act as a slave in specialised clubs (see for instance §71). The influence of money on consent in sexual matters is also illustrated by the *Tremblay v France* case where the Court emphasised that compelled prostitution was contrary to the rights and the dignity of the human being and that, for some, prostitution was never freely consented to and always at least constricted by socio-economic reasons (ECtHR, *Tremblay v France*, 11 September 2007, §§25–26).

2.2. TRADITIONAL FAMILY AND EQUALITY

As morality seemed to progressively vanish from the sexuality case law in favour of an exclusive consent criterion, the traditional conception of the family appeared less and less able to justify the different treatment of 'unconventional' families or inequalities between men and women.

2.2.1. Unmarried and Homosexual Couples

As early as 1979, the Court affirmed in the *Marckx v Belgium* case that 'support and encouragement of the traditional family was in itself legitimate or even praiseworthy'.[24]

In 1986, the Commission held – in the *Lindsay*[25] case – that even if 'in some fields, the de facto relationship of cohabitees [was] ... recognised, there still [existed] differences between married and unmarried couples, in particular, differences in legal status and legal effects'. In 2000, the Court confirmed – in *Schackell*[26] – that if 'there [was] ... an increased social acceptance of stable personal relationships outside the traditional notion of marriage ... [it remained] an institution which [was] widely accepted as conferring a particular status on those who enter it'.[27] As a consequence, unmarried and married couples could not be compared for the purposes of the non-discrimination test and differences could exist between heterosexual *de facto* cohabitees and heterosexual spouses as regards – for instance – income tax or survivors' benefits. However, in *Marckx*[28] and in *Johnston*[29] the Court made it clear that this could not justify disadvantages for children born outside of marriage. In the former, the European judges condemned the 'law whereby the establishment of ... maternity [was] conditional on voluntary recognition or a court declaration' for illegitimate children (§39) while, in the latter, they decided that a child born out of an adulterous relationship 'should be placed, legally and socially, in a position akin to that of a legitimate child' (§74).

In the 2003 *Karner v Austria*[30] case, the Court considered that the aim of protecting the traditional family was 'a weighty and legitimate' aim, but emphasised that that aim was 'rather abstract' and could thus be achieved by 'a broad variety of concrete measures'. In this context, the Court found that it had not been demonstrated that depriving homosexuals of the right to succeed to their partner's tenancy, whereas heterosexual cohabitees were entitled to that

---

[24] ECtHR, *Marckx v Belgium*, 13 June 1979, §40.
[25] ECmHR, *Lindsay v United Kingdom*, 1 November 1986.
[26] ECtHR, *Schackell v United Kingdom*, 27 April 2000.
[27] See also: ECtHR, *Johnston and others v Ireland*, 18 December 1986, §§68 and 75; ECtHR, *Muñoz Dias v Spain*, 8 December 2009; ECtHR, *Serife Yigit v Turkey*, 2 November 2010.
[28] ECtHR, *Marckx v Belgium*, 13 June 1979.
[29] ECtHR, *Johnston v Ireland*, 18 December 1986.
[30] ECtHR, *Karner v Austria*, 24 July 2003, §§40–41.

benefit, was necessary in order to protect the traditional family.[31] This standard determined by *Karner* has been described as very high since 'granting ... rights and benefits to another group does not result in the groups who already had those rights and benefits losing them' and 'nor do such rights and benefits necessarily become "diluted" or less valuable simply because someone else receives them'.[32] In the 1999 *Salgueiro*[33] case, the Court had condemned Portugal since the domestic court had awarded parental responsibility to a mother on the basis of the father's homosexuality relying on the affirmation that 'the child should live in ... a traditional Portuguese family' (§34). In the 2008 *E.B.*[34] case, it condemned France since the French authorities had refused authorisation to adopt as a single person to a woman on the sole ground of her homosexuality invoking notably 'the lack of a paternal referent' and 'the lifestyle' of the applicant (§§87, 88 and 94).[35]

On the one hand, marriage is a particular status that creates heavy duties between spouses and it is then understandable – says *Lindsay* or *Schackell* – that this institution also implies some benefits for those who enter into it. However, children should not be penalised by their parents' conjugal situation: illegitimate and adulterous children have to be placed at least in a substantial position akin to that of a legitimate child. On the other hand, homosexual non-married couples must be treated in the same way as heterosexual non-married couples as regards substantial 'rights and benefits' related to conjugality such as tenancy transfers or insurance cover extensions, says *Karner*. Homosexual persons also have the right – according to *Salgueiro* and *E.B.* – to be treated equally as a separated parent or as a candidate for adoption as a sole person.

What about the differences between non-married homosexuals and married heterosexuals? Are they legitimate differences based on conjugal status or illegitimate differences based on sexual orientation? In the 2008 *Courten v United Kingdom* case, the Court decided that such a difference could be acceptable because of the special status of marriage *even if* homosexuals could not make the choice to marry.[36] In a context characterised by the equalisation of

---

31   See also: ECtHR, *Kozak v Poland*, 2 March 2010, sp. §§98 and 99; ECtHR, *P.B. and J.S. v Austria*, 22 July 2010.

32   J. SCHERPE, "The Legal Recognition of Same-Sex Couples in Europe and the Role of the European Court of Human Rights", *The Equal Rights Review*, 2013, p. 92.

33   ECtHR, *Salgueiro da Silva Mouta v Portugal*, 21 December 1999.

34   ECtHR, *E.B. v France*, 22 January 2008.

35   The Court decided in *Burden v United Kingdom* that a non-conjugal relationship was different by 'nature' or by 'essence' from the relationship between married couples or homosexual civil partners. As a consequence, the applicants, two sisters who had lived together for their whole life, could not be compared to couples for the purposes of inheritance taxation, ECtHR (Gr. Ch.), *Burden v United Kingdom*, 29 April 2008, §62. See also: ECtHR, *Korelc v Slovenia*, 12 May 2009, §92.

36   ECtHR, *Courten v United Kingdom*, 4 November 2008.

family types, this circular reasoning[37] is unsatisfactory. The argument according to which marriage confers specific rights and duties on those who enter into it cannot be opposed to people who are unable to marry.[38]

2.2.2. Inequalities between Men and Women

The invocation of the traditional family does not appear able to justify differences between men and women.

In the 2004 *Ünal Tekeli v Turkey*[39] case, the applicant – a Turkish female lawyer – challenged the impossibility for her to continue to bear only her maiden name after her marriage. As she argued that this constituted discrimination on the ground of sex, the government explained that the litigious rule reflected 'a traditional arrangement whereby family unity was reflected in a joint name' (§§43–46).

Having reaffirmed that 'the advancement of the equality of the sexes is today a major goal in the member States' (§59), the European judges considered that the main question was 'whether the tradition of reflecting family unity through the husband's name could be regarded as a decisive factor' and their answer was that 'this tradition derived from the man's primordial role and the woman's secondary role in the family' and that 'nowadays the advancement of the equality of the sexes in the member states of the Council of Europe prevented States from imposing [it] on married women' (§63).

3. TOWARDS A RELEGITIMISATION OF MORALS AND TRADITION AS JUSTIFICATIONS FOR RESTRICTIONS ON RIGHTS?

Around 2010, the Court was suddenly invited to decide different hard cases in personal and family law including sexual relationships between siblings, abortion, assisted procreation, same-sex marriage and same-sex adoption. If it is beyond doubt that morals are back in the case law relating to sexuality and the beginning of life (section 3.1), the legitimacy of the invocation of traditional views when the cardinal institutions of family law (i.e. marriage and filiation) are at stake is unclear (section 3.2).

---

[37] See: P. JOHNSON, "Adoption, Homosexuality and the European Convention on Human Rights: Gas and Dubois v France", *Modern Law Review*, 2012, p. 1147.

[38] See also: ECtHR, *Mata Estevez v Spain*, 10 May 2001; ECtHR, *M.W. v United Kingdom*, 23 June 2009; ECtHR, *Manenc v France*, 21 September 2010.

[39] ECtHR, *Ünal Tekeli v Turkey*, 16 November 2004.

3.1. MORALS ARE BACK

3.1.1. Incest

In the 2012 *Stübing v Germany*[40] case, the applicant had been convicted by a criminal court because he had had consensual incestuous sexual relations with his sister.[41] The Court considered that the litigious conviction was aimed at the protection of morals and of the rights of others and reaffirmed – referring to *Handyside*[42] – that national authorities were better placed to give an opinion on the content and requirements of morals (§60). Then, in an European context where incestuous relations between siblings were 'neither accepted by the legal order nor by society as a whole' (§61), the Strasbourg judges chose – without any reference to *Dudgeon, Norris, Modinos, Laskey* or *K.A. and A.D.* – to uphold the national court's decision considering that the imposition of criminal liability was justified by a combination of objectives, including the protection of the family, self-determination and public health (§63).

While it is surely important to note the formal comeback of morals in the sexuality case law, its substantial significance in *Stübing* should not be overestimated. It must effectively be stressed that, in this case, the applicant's sister suffered from personality disorders and that this specific point carried a great deal of weight in the Court's reasoning (see §64). The ruling could thus be interpreted in the sense that the most legitimate aim pursued by the German jurisdiction was the protection of the sexual determination of the applicant's younger sister whose genuine consent was doubtful in the light of her established psychological weakness.

Two Grand Chamber cases seem to be much more significant in revealing the renewed efficiency of morals as a justification for restrictions on rights guaranteed by Article 8.

---

[40] ECtHR, *Stübing v Germany*, 12 April 2012. About this case: K. DYER, "The need to re-evaluate incest in the age of assisted reproductive techniques: Stübing v. Germany", *Family Law*, 2012, p. 1144; D. SOKOL, "What's so wrong with incest? The case of Stübing v Germany", available at http://ukhumanrightsblog.com/2012/04/15/whats-so-wrong-with-incest-the-case-of-stubing-v-germany/(last accessed 07.11.2013).

[41] See §7: 'In 1984, the applicant's biological sister, S. K., was born. The applicant was unaware of his sister's existence until he re-established contact with his family of origin in 2000. Following their mother's death in December 2000, the relationship between the siblings intensified. As from January 2001, the applicant and his sister had consensual sexual intercourse. They lived together for several years'.

[42] The Court also referred to *A., B. and C. v Ireland*. See *infra*.

3.1.2. Abortion and Procreation

In *A., B. and C. v Ireland*,[43] the Court was for the very first time invited to evaluate the acceptability of the prohibition of abortion for reasons of health or well-being.[44] Once more relying on the *Handyside* judgment, it considered that the impugned restrictions were based on 'profound moral values' shared by the Irish people (§226). Having said so, it neutralised the European consensus about abortion for reasons of health or well-being by affirming that 'even if it [appeared] … that most Contracting Parties [permitted] a greater legal access to abortion, this consensus [could not] be a decisive factor in the Court's examination' (§237)[45] and held that a large margin of appreciation had to be recognised to States because of 'the acute sensitivity of the moral and ethical issues raised' (§233). In this context, the Court did not 'consider that the prohibition of abortion for health and well-being reasons, based on the profound moral views of the Irish people as to the nature of life and as to the consequent protection to be accorded to the right to life of the unborn' exceeded the margin of appreciation of Ireland (§241).

One year later, in *S.H. and others v Austria*,[46] the Court had to take a position on the Austrian prohibition of heterologous *in vitro* fertilisation.[47] The Strasbourg judges held that this restriction pursued the legitimate aims of protecting 'health or morals' as well as 'the rights and freedoms of others' (§90). As in *A., B. and C.*, they decided that, even if 'there was a clear trend in the legislation of the Contracting States towards allowing gamete donation for the purpose of in vitro fertilization, which reflected an emerging European consensus', this consensus 'did not decisively narrow the margin of appreciation

---

[43]   ECtHR (Gr. Ch.), *A., B. and C. v Ireland*, 16 December 2010.
[44]   It was not, however, the first time that the Court had had to deal with abortion. In the 1992 *Open Door and Dublin Well Woman v Ireland* case, which concerned the interdiction to inform Irish women about the possibilities of abortion outside Ireland, the Court decided that the wide discretion recognised to the State in the ambit of morals was even wider 'on matters of belief concerning the nature of human life' (ECtHR, *Open Door and Dublin Well Woman v United Kingdom*, 29 October 1992, §68). See also, on the matter of effective access to abortion where it is legally permitted: ECtHR (Gr. Ch), *Tysiac v Poland*, 20 March 2007; ECtHR, *R.R. v Poland*, 26 May 2011.
[45]   The Court referred to the *Vo v France* case concerning an involuntary abortion where it had decided that 'the question of when the right to life begins came within the States' margin of appreciation because there was no European consensus on the scientific and legal definition of the beginning of life, so that it was impossible to answer the question whether the unborn was a person to be protected for the purposes of Article 2. Since the rights claimed on behalf of the foetus and those of the mother are inextricably interconnected …, the margin of appreciation accorded to a State's protection of the unborn necessarily translates into a margin of appreciation for that State as to how it balances the conflicting rights of the mother (§237)'.
[46]   ECtHR (Gr. Ch.), *S.H. and others v Austria*, 3 November 2011.
[47]   i.e. *in vitro* fertilisation with sperm or ova from a donor (see §14).

of the State' (§§96–97).[48] Having conferred such a wide margin of appreciation on the respondent State, the Court ruled that 'the prohibition of the donation of gametes' did not exceed the power of appreciation of the national legislature since it 'was a controversial issue in Austrian society, raising complex questions of a social and ethical nature on which there was not yet a consensus in the society and which had to take into account human dignity, the well-being of children thus conceived and the prevention of negative repercussions or potential misuse' (§113).[49]

In those two Grand Chamber cases, the moral conceptions prevailing in the Member State were thus considered to carry sufficient weight to override the emerging European consensus. Both decisions have given rise to strong dissent between the European judges. In *A., B. and C.*, six dissenting judges considered that the prohibition of abortion violated article 8 of the Convention. According to them, 'it was the first time that the Court had disregarded the existence of a European consensus on the basis of "profound moral views" and it was a real and dangerous new departure in the Court's case-law'.[50] In *S.H. and others*, four judges disagreed with the majority and were convinced that the prohibition of heterologous *in vitro* fertilisation was contrary to the Convention. From their point of view, the reasoning of their colleagues implied that 'States' positions of principle must now take precedence over the European consensus, which [was] a dangerous departure from the Court's case-law considering that one of the Court's tasks is precisely to contribute to harmonising across Europe the rights guaranteed by the Convention'.[51]

---

48 According to the Court, 'there is now a clear trend in the legislation of the Contracting States towards allowing gamete donation for the purpose of in vitro fertilisation, which reflects an emerging European consensus. That emerging consensus is not, however, based on settled and long-standing principles established in the law of the member States but rather reflects a stage of development within a particularly dynamic field of law and does not decisively narrow the margin of appreciation of the State' (§96). So, '[s]ince the use of IVF treatment gave rise then and continues to give rise today to sensitive moral and ethical issues against a background of fast-moving medical and scientific developments, and since the questions raised by the case touch on areas where there is not yet clear common ground amongst the member States, the Court considers that the margin of appreciation to be afforded to the respondent State must be a wide one' (§97).

49 See also: ECtHR, *Costa and Pavan v Italy*, 28 August 2012, sp. §§59 and 68.

50 Joint partly dissenting opinion of Judges Rozakis, Tulkens, Fura, Hirvelä, Malinverni and Poalelungi, §9. Different authors agreed with the minority and expressly wrote that the Court here failed to follow its *Dudgeon* case law where the Irish perceptions about homosexuality were not considered sufficient to trump the development of a European consensus (F. DE LONDRAS and K. DZEHTSIAROU, "Grand Chamber of the European Court of Human Rights, *A., B. & C. v Ireland*, Decision of 17 December 2010", *International and Comparative Law Quarterly*, 2013, pp. 252–254 and B. WEINSTEIN, "Reproductive Choice in the Hands of the State: the Right to Abortion under the European Convention on Human Rights in Light of A, B & C v. Ireland", *American University International Law Review*, 2012, pp. 421–424).

51 Joint dissenting opinion of Judges Tulkens, Hirvelä, Lazarova Trajkovska and Tsotsoria, §10. See also: S. McGUINNESS, "Health, human rights and the regulation of reproductive technologies in S.H. and others v. Austria", *Medical Law Review*, 2013, pp. 157–158;

It appears that, in those two controversial cases, the majority judges themselves were at least uncomfortable and tried to rely on two additional justifications to strengthen the decision they had reached. The first argument is a procedural one: in both cases, the Court expressly insisted on the fact that the internal solution had only been adopted after an extensive national debate about abortion[52] and IVF[53] respectively, which meant that the national legislature had itself carefully realised a balance of the competing interests.[54] The second argument is spatial: in both cases, the Court considered that the fact that the applicants were allowed to cross the borders in order to benefit, in another State, from the litigious techniques – abortion or IVF – was a relevant element to assess the European acceptability of the litigious restrictions.[55]

3.2. TRADITIONS: CULTURAL CONNOTATIONS OR MERE STEREOTYPES?

In the context of the reaffirmation of morals as a legitimate aim which is able to justify restrictions on sexual and procreative autonomy, are traditional views about the family also relegitimised as a potential justification for inflections of the equality rule?

3.2.1. Same-Sex Marriage and Same-Sex Filiation

After *Marckx*, *Johnson* and *Karner*, it seemed that traditions could not justify, as such, the differentiated treatment of couples or children. At the most, marriage, as a special status implying heavy duties, could justify some extra benefits for married couples.[56]

In 2010, when the Court was asked to take a frontal position on the ground of same-sex marriage, the pertinence of traditional views about the family were firmly reaffirmed.

J. SCHERPE, "Medically assisted procreation: this margin needs to be appreciated", *Cambridge Law Journal*, 2012, pp. 276–279; G. WILLEMS, "Cour de Strasbourg et procréation médicalement assistée avec tiers donneur: des choix interprétatifs empreints de *judicial self-restraint*", *Revue trimestrielle de droit familial*, 2012, pp. 509–532.

52 ECtHR (Gr. Ch.), *A., B. and C. v Ireland*, 16 December 2010, §239 (on 'the lengthy, complex and sensitive debate in Ireland').

53 ECtHR (Gr. Ch.), *S.H. and others v Austria*, 3 November 2011, §114 (on 'the careful and cautious approach adopted by the Austrian legislature in seeking to reconcile social realities with its approach of principle in this field').

54 This is an illustration of the growing tendency of the Court to insist on the procedural dimension of human rights when confronted with very sensitive and highly political matters.

55 ECtHR (Gr. Ch.), *A., B. and C. v Ireland*, 16 December 2010, §241; ECtHR (Gr. Ch.), *S.H. and others v Austria*, 3 November 2011, §114.

56 See also: ECtHR (Gr. Ch.), *Van der Heijden v the Netherlands*, 3 April 2012, §69.

In this *Schalk and Kopf v Austria*[57] case, where two men claimed the right to marry, the Court held that 'a cohabiting same-sex couple living in a stable *de facto* partnership, [fell] within the notion of "family life", just as the relationship of a different-sex couple' (§94) and that 'the right to marry enshrined in Article 12 must [not] in all circumstances be limited to marriage between two persons of the opposite sex' (§61). However, it considered that marriage '[had] deep-rooted social and cultural connotations which may differ largely from one society to another' and that 'the Court must not rush to substitute its own judgment in place of that of the national authorities' (§62). For some authors, relying on the 1987 *F. v Switzerland*[58] case, this reference to 'cultural connotations' could mean that the Court is inclined – just as in *A., B. and C.* and *S.H. and others* – to neutralise the European consensus mechanism on the question of gay marriage.[59]

But three years later, when the Court was confronted with the sensitive question of same-sex adoption, it took a radically different position about traditional views concerning filiation.

In the 2013 *X. and others v Austria* case,[60] the applicants were two women living together in a stable relationship and who challenged the prohibition of the adoption of one partner's child by the other partner in the case of same-sex couples as such an adoption was permitted for unmarried heterosexual couples.[61] The Strasbourg judges repeated that the protection of traditional family and the protection of the interests of the child were legitimate aims (§138) and considered that the responding government had to establish that 'protection of the family in the traditional sense and, more specifically, the protection of the child's interests, require the exclusion of same-sex couples' (§141).[62] The Grand Chamber considered in this regard that Austrian law was lacking coherence since 'the legislature … accepted that a child may grow up in a family based on a same-sex couple [but] insisted that a child should not have two mothers or two

---

57   ECtHR, *Schalk and Kopf v Austria*, 24 June 2010.

58   The European judges had affirmed that marriage was 'closely bound up with the cultural and historical traditions of each society and its deep-rooted ideas about the family unit' and that as a consequence 'the fact that, at the end of a gradual evolution, a country finds itself in an isolated position as regards one aspect of its legislation does not necessarily imply that that aspect offends the Convention' (ECtHR, *F. v Switzerland*, 18 December 1987, §33).

59   F. Hamilton, "Why the Margin of Appreciation is Not the Answer to the Gay marriage Debate", *European Human Rights Law Review*, 2013, pp. 47–55; J.-P. Marguénaud, "Enterrement du mariage homosexuel et naissance de la vie familiale homosexuelle", *Revue trimestrielle de droit civil*, 2010, p. 739.

60   ECtHR (Gr. Ch.), *X. and others v Austria*, 19 February 2013. See also: ECtHR, *Gas and Dubois v France*, 15 March 2012 (where the Court transposed the circular argument of *Courten, M.W. and Manenc* [*supra*] to the question of same-sex second-parent adoption).

61   See §10: One of the women had a son born from an anterior heterosexual relationship. His father had recognised him but the mother had sole custody. The two applicants and the children had been living together since the second applicant's son was five years old.

62   Available space here precludes an investigation of this connection between the protection of the traditional family and the protection of the interests of the child.

fathers' (§144) and that the 'repeated requests' to prohibit second-parent adoption in same-sex couples made during the elaboration of the 2010 Registered Partnership Act[63] 'merely reflected the position of those sectors of society which are opposed to the idea of opening up second-parent adoption to same-sex couples' (§143).[64]

Marriage and filiation are thus not dealt with in the same way by the European Court: while traditional views about marriage ('deep-rooted social and cultural connotations') are considered very weighty and justify the exclusion of homosexuals from this institution,[65] traditional conceptions about filiation ('the position of [some] sectors of society') are considered mere stereotypes and cannot justify the legislature's wish to avoid a situation in which a child has two mothers or two fathers.[66] Such an asymmetry is difficult to understand since there is a strong connection in family law between marriage and filiation.[67] Above all, it seems difficult to perceive what exactly distinguishes the venerable deep-rooted social and cultural connotations related to marriage in *Schalk and Kopf* and the inacceptable stereotypes associated with filiation in *X. and others*.[68]

---

[63] The exclusion of second-parent adoption for gay couples had only been expressly introduced in Austrian law by the Registered Partnership Act in 2010 (§142).

[64] See also: ECtHR, *Fretté v France*, 26 February 2002, sp. §41 and ECtHR, *E.B. v France*, 22 January 2008. Those two cases concerned adoption by a single homosexual. In *Fretté*, the Court decided that it was 'quite natural that the national authorities, whose duty it [was] in a democratic society also to consider, within the limits of their jurisdiction, the interests of society as a whole, should enjoy a wide margin of appreciation when they [were] asked to make rulings on such matters. By reason of their direct and continuous contact with the vital forces of their countries, the national authorities [were] in principle better placed than an international court to evaluate local needs and conditions' (§41) (there is an interesting joint partly dissenting opinion of Judges Sir Nicolas Bratza, Fuhrmann and Tulkens). The *E.B.* judgment overruled *Fretté* and the Court held that 'if the reasons advanced for such a difference in treatment were based solely on considerations regarding the applicant's sexual orientation this would amount to discrimination under the Convention' and that 'French law allows single persons to adopt a child … thereby opening up the possibility of adoption by a single homosexual, which is not disputed' and 'the reasons put forward by the Government cannot be regarded as particularly convincing and weighty such as to justify refusing to grant the applicant authorization' (§§93–94).

[65] ECtHR, *Schalk and Kopf v Austria*, 24 June 2010.

[66] ECtHR (Gr. Ch.), *X. and others v Austria*, 19 February 2013.

[67] Even the French Judge Jean-Paul Costa emphasised this connection in his concurring opinion in the *Gas and Dubois* judgment (ECtHR, *Gas and Dubois v France*, 15 March 2012, concurring opinion of Judge Costa joined by Judge Spielmann). See also, for example, on the so-called "marriage-and-kinship-based model": B.C. HAFEN, Individualism and Autonomy in Family Law: the Waning of Belonging, *Brigham Young University Law Review*, 1991, p. 5.

[68] See, for a deeper analysis: G. WILLEMS, "Orientation sexuelle et adoption: l'Autriche condamnée par la Cour européenne des droits de l'homme", *Revue trimestrielle de droit familial*, 2013, pp. 1024–1042.

3.2.2. Men and Women

While the conflict between traditional conceptions of marriage or filiation and the growing exigency of equality between couples is characterised by this strange asymmetry, traditional gender roles today seem to be totally insufficient to justify any differentiated treatment of men and women.

In the 2012 *Konstantin Markin v Russia*[69] case, the applicant – a Russian male military radio operator – challenged the impossibility for him to benefit from parental leave. He maintained that this constituted discrimination on the ground of sex. The government argued – just as the Russian Constitutional Court (§34) – that the regulation of parental leave was grounded on 'the special social role of women associated with motherhood' (§139).

Nevertheless, according to the Strasbourg Court, 'contemporary European societies [had] moved towards a more equal sharing between men and women of responsibility for the upbringing of their children' (§140). So, 'the difference in treatment [could not] be justified by reference to traditions prevailing in a certain country' since 'States may not impose traditional gender roles and gender stereotypes' (§142). As a consequence, 'the reference to the traditional distribution of gender roles in society [could not] justify the exclusion of men, including servicemen, from the entitlement to parental leave' (§143).[70]

4. CONCLUSION

As an international human rights court, the ECtHR has to regulate the intervention of the State in personal and family matters. This task implies deciding on whether majoritarian views are pertinent and sufficient motives for restrictions on individual autonomy or differences between family types or whether moral conceptions and traditional perceptions prevailing in a national society should be suppressed from the legitimate aims list in the name of liberal pluralism.[71]

---

69   ECtHR (Gr. Ch.), *Konstantin Markin v Russia*, 22 March 2012.

70   See also: ECtHR, *Petrovic v Austria*, 27 March 1998; ECtHR, *Weller v Hungary*, 31 March 2009; ECtHR, *Andrle v the Czech Republic*, 17 February 2011. In the latter, the Court decided to admit a difference between men and women for the calculation of pensions since 'the original aim of the differentiated pensionable ages based on the number of children women raised was to compensate for the factual inequality between men and women' and 'in the light of the specific circumstances of the case, this approach continues to be reasonably and objectively justified on this ground until social and economic changes remove the need for special treatment for women' (§60).

71   Basically, the question is whether 'the State should play a major role in reinforcing the type of sexual mores that have historically defined marriage as the only appropriate form of sexual expression' or whether 'the decision to marry or not marry, to engage or not engage in sexual relationships, to bear children within a relationship with a parental partner, without a partner, or not at all, [are] matters of private choice in which the state should not intrude'

The European judges certainly appear reluctant to allow restrictions on sexual autonomy on the sole ground of morals. Even in *Stübing*, the fundamental limit to sexual freedom seems rather to be the genuine consent of the people involved. However, when assisted procreation and abortion are at stake, as in *A., B. and C.* and *S.H. and others*, moral views prevailing in society become really weighty and are even able to dismiss an emerging or even consolidated European consensus.

This approach, vehemently contested by dissenting judges in those two cases, may effectively appear problematic: when there is a well-settled European consensus, the Court could or should take the responsibility to crystallise this common conception into substantial requirements instead of simply relying on the quality of the domestic debate and/or the possibility for the applicant to cross borders.

The Strasbourg Court considers that the protection of the traditional family is a legitimate but abstract purpose which implies a heavy evidentiary burden on the State. Nevertheless, traditional marriage and its socio-cultural connotations occupy a totally specific situation in the law of the European Convention and it seems – to some commentators on *Schalk and Kopf* – that national perceptions about this institution could even overrule a hypothetical future European consensus about gay marriage. Surprisingly, the European judges did not recognise that such weight should be given to filiation and the majority's conceptions about this other structural pillar of family law were depicted – in *X. and others* – as mere stereotypes.

In our opinion, this differentiated treatment of marriage and filiation is inconsistent. As was advised by Judge Costa, those two institutions should be dealt with in the same way: if the recognition and protection of same-sex conjugal relationships do not necessarily imply the opening of same-sex marriage then the recognition and protection of same-sex parental relationships do not necessarily imply the opening of same-sex coparental adoption. Instead of choosing such a coherent perspective, the Court has adopted a rather schizophrenic approach to those two institutions. In a context characterised by the absence of any European consensus, maybe the European Court should focus, at least temporarily, on the full realisation of substantial equality. Institutional identity – i.e. marriage and filiation – is not the only way for the law to recognise and protect homosexual families and one important step could be to ensure the allocation of the same pragmatic prerogatives to all families.

(J. CARBONE, "Morality, Public Policy and the Family: The Role of Marriage and the Public-Private Divide", *Santa Clara Law Review*, 1996, pp. 267–286).

REAL-LIFE INTERNATIONAL FAMILY LAW

Belgian Empirical Research on Cross-Border Family Law

Jinske Verhellen

Contents

1. INTRODUCTION

In 2004 Belgium codified its private international law. This Code of Private International Law (PIL Code) encompasses the three pillars of private international law: (1) rules on international jurisdiction, (2) rules on the applicable law, and (3) rules on the recognition and enforcement in Belgium of foreign judgments and authentic acts.[1]

With support from the Flanders Research Foundation (FWO-Vlaanderen), I conducted research into the concrete application of the PIL Code in the field of family law.[2] I examined whether or not the objectives set out by the Belgian

---

[1] For an English translation of the Belgian PIL Code (Law of 16 July 2004), see *Yearbook of Private International Law*, 2004, Vol. 4, pp. 319–375.

[2] J. Verhellen, *Het Belgisch Wetboek IPR in familiezaken. Wetgevende doelstellingen getoetst aan de praktijk*, Brugge, 2012, p. 513 (free translation: *The Belgian Code of Private*

legislator have been achieved in practice and whether or not the Belgian PIL Code is a sufficiently adequate instrument to deal with 'real-life' international family law matters. For this study I had access to a vast amount of empirical sources which offered a clear picture of how courts and (local) authorities apply the PIL rules.

My field-test research revealed several discrepancies between the legislative ambitions and the practice of the courts and administrations, some of which can be attributed to the context within which private international law functions. At the national level, for instance, migration policy exerts considerable pressure on international family law. The research demonstrates a true instrumentalisation of private international law by migration (law) policies, leading, amongst other things, to all kinds of limping family law relationships (limping names, limping fatherhoods, limping marriages and divorces, etc.).

This contribution first outlines the empirical research method (section 2) and briefly illustrates the added value of empirical research in legal studies (section 3). It then reflects a few of the research findings: the nexus between private international law and migration law and their different normative approaches to identical family situations (section 4.1) and the issue of party autonomy which is not used though possible in certain fields of family law and not possible though useful in other areas of family law (section 4.2).

2. EMPIRICAL RESEARCH IN THE FIELD OF PRIVATE INTERNATIONAL LAW

The research was divided into two consecutive phases. Firstly, I focused on the objectives and choices of the Belgian legislator in drafting the PIL Code provisions in the field of family law. In a second phase these legislative objectives were compared to the actual practice of judicial and administrative authorities.

For the field-test of the legislative intentions I relied on three empirical sources: court decisions (section 2.1), in-depth interviews with judges (section 2.2) and a database of queries for advice submitted to one of the Belgian Centres for Private International Law (section 2.3). These empirical data allowed for a thorough *bottom-up* evaluation of the Belgian PIL Code.

2.1. COURT DECISIONS DATABASE

This database was set up for the purposes of the research and contains 656 court decisions. It includes both published and unpublished judgments, Belgian and

---

International Law in family matters. Field-test research of legislative intentions and the actual practice of courts and administrations).

foreign decisions and decisions of the European Court of Human Rights and the European Court of Justice.

2.2. IN-DEPTH INTERVIEWS

In 2010, 16 Belgian judges specialising in cross-border family law were interviewed. The selection of these interviewees was based on two main considerations: (1) the 'verifiable' PIL expertise (based on the decisions of the judge in question), and (2) the 'expected' expertise (taking into consideration the multicultural/international character of the place in which the judge has jurisdiction).

The interviews with the judges have been a valuable addition to the available court decisions. For example, it was not an obvious choice to undertake a study of party autonomy in Belgian divorce proceedings given that hardly any case law concerning this party autonomy is available. In 2004 the Belgian legislator took a very innovative approach by introducing a provision for the parties involved in a divorce case to choose the applicable law.[3] The lack of applications by the courts suggested that this new element in the PIL Code was/is never used in practice. In order to support this conclusion, I discussed the possibility for the parties to choose the applicable law in divorce cases with several judges. The results of this part of the research are interesting; also in the light of the Rome III Regulation.[4]

2.3. PIL CENTRE DATABASE

At the end of 2005, the Belgian government established two Centres for Private International Law, one Dutch-speaking[5] and the other French-speaking.[6] These legal clinics became a point of contact for both individuals and professionals with PIL questions regarding family law matters. The queries for

---

3   Article 55, §2 PIL Code: 'The spouses may however choose the law, which will apply to the divorce or the legal separation. They can only designate one of the following laws: 1) the law of the State of both spouses' nationality when the action is introduced; 2) Belgian law. The choice has to be expressed at the time of the first appearance in court.'

4   Council Regulation No. 1259/2010 of 20 December 2010 implementing enhanced cooperation in the area of the law applicable to divorce and legal separation, *OJ* L 343 of 29 December 2010. Belgium is one of the EU Member States taking part in the enhanced cooperation in the area of the law applicable to divorce and legal separation.

5   Embedded in the non-profit organisation 'Kruispunt Migratie en Integratie' (www. kruispuntmi.be).

6   Embedded in the non-profit organisation 'Association pour le droit des étrangers' (www. adde.be).

advice range from very simple questions posed to the helpdesk to more elaborate and difficult ones.

The database of the Dutch-speaking PIL Centre proved to be a unique source of information – not least because of its size. During the period chosen for the research (January 2006 to December 2010), this PIL Centre dealt with 3,369 queries for advice.[7]

3. ADDED VALUE OF EMPIRICAL RESEARCH

The empirical sources allowed for a combination of qualitative and quantitative analysis. The research first and foremost reflects a qualitative analysis of the empirical data, but it did not avoid a quantitative approach. Without being completely bound up in numbers, I provided numbers so as to give an insight into the extent of certain problems. The numbers indicate the type of problems judges and administrations are struggling with; they also indicate which issues are recurring. I will give one illustration: the analysed data showed that courts and administrations very often take into account the *fraude à la loi* when reviewing foreign marriage acts.[8] The evasion of the law was mentioned in 77 of the 111 analysed court decisions, i.e. in 70% of the cases. I was able to analyse the use of *fraude à la loi* qualitatively (when and on what grounds do Belgian judges conclude that parties are evading the law?), but the numbers as such were relevant too. They confirmed an 'impression' that existed among legal scholars for a longer period of time.

The empirical data also allowed me to stay close to the actual applications in practice. This was a considered choice. After all, private international law does not take care of abstract problems, but of the problems of people and their families.

Analysing the queries for advice received by the PIL Centre revealed many difficulties and developments that are not immediately apparent in the decisions of the courts. For instance, Belgium has no (reported) jurisprudence on the consequence of marriage on the subsequent name of the couple in question, and more specifically on the possibility the PIL Code offers in

---

7   So as to ensure that privacy was protected, the research was based only on the database of the Dutch-speaking PIL Centre. The national Commission for the Protection of Privacy authorised this PIL Centre to make the relevant data available for the purpose of scientific research; however, this was restricted to certain data. With the enquiries handled by the Dutch-speaking PIL Centre being entered systematically into an electronic database, it was 'technically' possible to omit a number of fields containing specific information (e.g. the personal details of whoever was making the enquiry or giving advice). As a result I had a database at my disposal that was sufficiently anonymous so as not to breach any right to privacy. The fact that the queries handled by the French-speaking Centre are only available on paper made the same kind of privacy protection impossible.

8   Articles 18 and 27 PIL Code.

choosing a surname following a marriage.[9] The absence of court decisions could give the impression that there are no problems concerning this matter. The PIL Centre database clearly contradicts this and made a profound study of several recurring issues possible, such as the problems of Turkish women who are registered under different surnames in different Belgian registration systems.

Furthermore, the PIL Centre database opened up certain administrative practices, not to be evaluated otherwise. I will give one illustration. Certain authorities refuse to recognise Pakistani marriage certificates with a specific clause – I refer to the clause that denies the wife the right to a divorce.

Question (person concerned, April 2009):
'In June 2008 the [Antwerp] city administration would not recognize my marriage due to the clause that the husband refuses his wife the right to a divorce. The administration has since asked the public prosecutor for advice. ... I've been waiting for almost a year now for the municipality's answer.'

According to Pakistani law the man can delegate his repudiation right to his wife. This is an option for the man. This delegation right can be seen in the Pakistani marriage contract (clause no. 18 – 'Has the husband given the right of divorce to his wife, if so on what conditions?'). When the specific clause in the marriage contract mentions that the wife does not have the right to divorce, this indicates that the husband has not delegated his right of repudiation to his wife. However, this does not mean that the wife cannot end the marriage in any other way. After all, the law of Pakistan recognises different forms of divorce that are also accessible to the wife.[10] The Belgian Immigration Office considers such a clause to be contrary to the principle of equality between women and men. As a result the marriage certificate cannot be recognised, as it is considered to be contrary to public policy. Consequently the people involved cannot receive a visa or a residence permit based on this foreign marriage. The PIL Centre database reveals even more. The Belgian Immigration Office advises those involved to apply for a correction of the marriage certificate through the courts in Pakistan. This administrative practice of the

---

9   Article 38, para. 2 PIL Code: 'When the law of the State of the nationality of one of the spouses permits him to choose a name on the occasion of the marriage, the civil servant registers this name on the marriage certificate.'

10   See among others C. APERS, "L'acte de mariage pakistanais comportant une clause relative au divorce et sa reconnaissance en Belgique", *Revue du droit des étrangers*, 2009, No. 151, pp. 633–644; M. MUNIR, "Stipulations in a Muslim Marriage Contract with Special Reference to *Talaq Al-Tafwid* Provisions in Pakistan", *YIMEL*, 2005–06, Vol. 12, p. 248; L. CARROLL, "Talaq-i-Tafwid and Stipulations in a Muslim Marriage Contract: Important Means of Protecting the Position of the South Asian Muslim Wife", *Modern Asian Studies*, 1982, Vol. 16, No. 2, pp. 277–309.

Immigration Office is clear in the PIL Centre database but (for now) is not visible in court decisions.

Question (person concerned, November 2008):
'Our marriage certificate from Pakistan was not recognized after the [Belgian] consulate made a remark about a divorce clause. We now have a certificate from the Pakistani judge that the marriage can be annulled. Now the consulate has no further remarks.'

Question (type of enquirer unknown, December 2009):
'The Belgian Immigration Office refuses a visa because of the clause in the Pakistani marriage certificate that denies the wife the right to a divorce. The Belgian Immigration Office asks for new documents to reopen the case. The new document they request is a modified marriage certificate. What is that?'

Question (registrar of births, marriages and deaths, March 2010):
'Last year we registered a marriage certificate of a Belgian woman, married in Pakistan, into our Civil Register. This certificate mentioned that the wife had no right to divorce. The person involved is now presenting us with an amended judgment that does give her this right. Can you tell us how we should proceed?'

4. SELECTION OF RESEARCH FINDINGS

4.1. CROSS-BORDER OPENNESS OF PRIVATE INTERNATIONAL LAW *VERSUS* BORDER-CHECK CLOSE UP OF MIGRATION LAW

Private international law should first and foremost be the branch of law which can respond to migration and its influence on the family lives of people. However, private international law – as a bridge builder between different legal systems – does not stand on its own. It is also being drawn into the global migration issue. Certain migration procedures in Belgium often lead to far-reaching regulations of family relations because a specific migration policy is being pursued rather than cross-border harmony – which is characteristic of private international law. Granting the foreign wife of a Belgian husband a family reunification visa requires a stance on the marriage that this couple concluded abroad, the foreign marriage act being the ground for the visa application. When a decision on that foreign marriage not only requires a PIL investigation but also a fraud investigation in the largest sense of the term (into documents, sham marriages and even criminal networks of human trafficking), private international law unintentionally and unwittingly ends up in the broader – politically and socially very sensitive – migration debate. And in this debate private international law and migration law take a different, even an opposite normative stance which I would describe as the 'cross-border openness' of private international law versus the 'border-check close up' of migration law.

The data analysed reveal numerous contradictions between the approach of identical family situations either from a private international law perspective or from a migration policy perspective. This article is necessarily limited to two examples that illustrate this field of tension between private international law and migration law: the recognition of foreign acts and the use of double standards depending on the nature of the foreign act and the approach of polygamy annex repudiation cases.

The tension between the different normative stances of private international law and migration law is clear from the way judges and (local) authorities give a different meaning to the evasion of the law (*fraude à la loi*) and the public policy exception depending on whether they are dealing with foreign marriage acts or with foreign birth certificates in cases of surrogacy abroad. The comparative analysis of the court decisions on the recognition of foreign acts – foreign marriage acts, on the one hand, and foreign birth certificates after surrogacy, on the other – revealed the application of double standards. Belgian couples who turn to a surrogate mother abroad can count on more understanding and legal creativity/flexibility than couples who marry abroad and seek to obtain a residence permit in Belgium. I compiled this under the title 'Fighting fraud versus tailor-made family planning'.

A second illustration deals with the complicated immigration (policy) constructions of the Belgian Immigration Office: through the non-recognition of foreign marriage dissolutions the person(s) involved are considered to be bigamous and the family reunification visa is subsequently denied. I described this as 'polygamy annex repudiation' cases.

Article 57 PIL Code provides in a specific recognition rule for foreign marriage dissolutions based on the will of the husband. The basic principle of Article 57 is the non-recognition of the repudiation. Two elements are defining in this: the unilateral character of the marriage dissolution and the fact that the repudiation is the husband's prerogative. When these two elements are present, recognition is not possible, unless a number of restrictive conditions are cumulatively met: (1) the deed has been approved and sanctioned by a judge in the State of origin; (2) at the time of the court approval neither of the spouses had the nationality of a State whose law does not know this form of marriage dissolution; (3) at the time of the court approval neither of the spouses had their habitual residence in a State whose law does not know this form of dissolution; (4) the wife has accepted the dissolution in an unambiguous manner and without coercion; and (5) none of the grounds of refusal provided for in Article 25 (= general recognition rules) prohibits the recognition (general public policy clause, rights of defence, etc.). These cumulative requirements should allow judges and administrations to evaluate the repudiation on a case-by-case basis in the light of the relevant circumstances. The circumstances are evaluated rather than the repudiation institution itself. With this functional approach to foreign repudiations the Belgian legislator expressed its respect for the foreign legal order.[11]

Article 57 was the object of long debates in Parliament, primarily of a political nature. There were two leading principles when drafting this provision: equality and reasonableness. Repudiations are contrary to the principle of equality between women and men, but an absolute refusal to grant recognition could lead to unjust results for the women involved.

In practice this provision which aims at protecting the equal rights of women and men is in danger of being used by a restrictive migration policy at the expense of the fundamental right to family life.[12] When Belgian embassies and consulates for instance legalise foreign divorce documents they tend to qualify marriage dissolution documents from Islamic countries rather pro forma as repudiations, even documents from countries where repudiations do not exist, e.g. Tunisia. This qualification results in the application of Article 57 and the use of the 'Article 57 sticker' in the framework of legalisation. This sticker has a huge impact. The 'Article 57 sticker' or the stance of the Ministry of Foreign Affairs under which the embassies and consulates fall, takes the form of a binding opinion which other administrations, such as the immigration office and local authorities in Belgium, then simply take over. Civil servants rarely question the embassies' and consulates' judgment, as they are considered to be in the best position to assess these matters locally. Based on this qualification the recognition of a divorce/repudiation of a Moroccan man, for instance, is easily refused. When this man marries again with another Moroccan woman and this woman requests a family reunification visa, this visa will be easily denied for reasons of polygamy (the man still being considered to be married to this first wife when he remarried in Morocco). The resulting question is then whether it is still really about the incompatibility of polygamy with public policy, or whether it has become about finding ways to control the flow of immigrants from certain countries (Morocco, Tunisia or Pakistan).

4.2. PARTY AUTONOMY: NOT USED THOUGH POSSIBLE, NOT POSSIBLE THOUGH USEFUL

As mentioned above, party autonomy for divorce was an important innovation in Belgian PIL. Article 55, §2 of the PIL Code allows the spouses to choose

---

[11] Explanatory Memorandum, Parliamentary Records of the Belgian Senate, Session Extraordinaire 2003, No. 3-27/1, p. 90.
[12] See also C. HENRICOT, "L'application du Code marocain de la famille, à la croisée des jurisprudences belge et marocaine en matière de dissolution du mariage", *Journal des Tribunaux*, 2011, pp. 648–650.

between the law of the State of both spouses' nationality and Belgian law. With this choice of law, the legislator wanted both to improve international harmony and to show respect for people's cultural ties. After all, this possibility to choose the applicable law allows spouses to prefer the law of their country of origin. Not only does this allow them to confirm their connection with the culture of their country of origin, it also ensures the spouses that the Belgian decision will have effect abroad each time the foreign law subjects the recognition of a judgment to a control of the applicable law.[13]

The research reveals that this major innovation is barely seen in practice: people are not or are only scarcely making use of the possibility to choose the applicable law. And if by way of exception they do, they make a very pragmatic choice for Belgian law. People mainly want a quick divorce and for that Belgian law offers them all the possibilities. And even when people are concerned with their Belgian divorce being recognised in their country of origin, this concern has (so far) not resulted in a choice for the application of the foreign law.

> *Interview (judge of Court of First Instance):*
> 'I have never seen that. Well, the application of Belgian law is usually almost always possible based on one of the other provisions of Article 55... I have never seen it myself because Article 55 is so broad I can almost always go with Belgian law.'

> *Interview (judge of Court of First Instance):*
> 'Ah non, moi je n'ai jamais eu ce cas-là. C'est même le contraire. Quand ils sont ici, ils vivent ici, ils ne comprennent même pas qu'on leur parle de leur droit national.'

> *Interview (judge of Court of First Instance):*
> 'Lawyers will always choose Belgian law because they are all so busy. And when they choose to use Belgian law, it saves them from having to look up the foreign law. Would that not be it?'

> *Interview (judge of Court of First Instance):*
> 'Je n'ai jamais eu de demande de choix pour une autre loi que la loi belge, peut-être parce que la loi belge est devenue d'une facilité déconcertante. ... J'ai déjà appliqué le droit étranger, mais pas sur base du choix. Quand il y a un choix, ça a toujours été la loi belge qui a été choisie.'

> *Interview (judge of Court of First Instance):*
> 'Quand un Marocain veut qu'on applique sa loi, bien souvent, il va divorcer au Maroc. Bien souvent il s'est marié au Maroc et il va divorcer au Maroc. ... C'est très théorique... [L]es divorces, je pense que les gens sont pragmatiques... Donc s'ils veulent divorcer vite, ils ne vont pas souligner le fait qu'ils sont marocains.'

---

13   Explanatory Memorandum, Parliamentary Records of the Belgian Senate, Session Extraordinaire 2003, No. 3–27/1, p. 86.

Moreover, the PIL database shows that people are often preoccupied with matters other than the choice of the applicable law. They are regularly faced with difficult problems regarding the documents they have to present (for instance, the presentation of a 'legalised' marriage certificate) or they worry about the impact the divorce will have on their residence status. *Hic et nunc* the formal-administrative aspect and the aspect of the right of residence prevail over the family law aspect of their migration story.

These are without doubt interesting findings in the light of the Rome III Regulation that uses party autonomy as a starting point. These findings also make us think about party autonomy in other areas of family law. It may not seem a priority in divorce matters, but in issues surrounding the family name, for instance, it appears that there should be more attention to the choice of the persons concerned.

Regarding the matter of the name, the Belgian legislator very clearly chose the law of the State of which the person has its nationality.[14] The reference to the national law was not questioned at all. This choice of the Belgian legislator was based on the substantive law principle of the stability of the name and the fear for the loss of legal certainty, which immediately shows how interwoven private international law and the Belgian substantive name law are. For Belgium the continuity and stability of the name are essential. Consequently more freedom of choice is inconceivable, both in substantive law and private international law.[15] My empirical data revealed, however, that courts often take people's wishes and expectations into consideration, especially in the field of names.

The analysis of the collected data also confirmed that the nationality criterion, combined with an unconditional preference for the Belgian nationality in cases of dual nationality,[16] inevitably leads to many limping names (children having a national passport under one name, another passport under a different name). As a Belgian PIL scholar I am very uncomfortable with the fact that the Belgian legislator has still not taken any steps to remedy the situation of limping names for which it was condemned by the European Court of Justice in the *Garcia Avello* case.[17] The PIL Centre database shows that there are still many

---

[14] Arts. 37–38 PIL Code.

[15] Yet it is about time the Belgian legislator stops separating both branches of the law. For it has to be said, this distinction seems to be merely a theoretical one. After all, in essence it is simply about the choice of a name. See e.g. the discussion between Monéger and Gaudemet-Tallon on more freedom of choice. Does it have to be about the choice of the applicable law or a choice for the name? Monéger rightly asks herself *'Ne choisit-on pas une loi en fonction d'un nom?'*, F. MONÉGER, "Actualité du nom de famille en droit international privé", *Droit International Privé. Travaux du comité français de droit international privé. Années 2004–2006*, Paris, 2008, p. 21.

[16] Art. 3, §2, 1° PIL Code: 'The references in the present statute to the nationality of a natural person, who possesses two or more nationalities, refer to: the Belgian nationality, if it is one of the nationalities'.

[17] ECJ 2 October 2003, case C-148/02.

Garcia Avello scenarios in Belgium and that this matter is not restricted to compound Spanish and Portuguese names. For instance, when a Belgian/Dutch child is born in Belgium and the parents subsequently request a name change in the Netherlands, the Belgian authorities apparently cannot enter the Dutch name change directly into the Belgian registers. Parents are referred to the Federal Ministry of Justice to obtain a name change for their child. Being able to obtain a name change through an administrative procedure should – according to the Belgian administration – suffice to comply with the requirements of EU law. After all, the Federal Ministry of Justice changes names without many problems or costs. However, the obligation to systematically follow and pay for an administrative procedure might very well be considered a restriction of the free movement of people. Especially since there is now a less time-consuming and cost-free alternative available, i.e. allowing the persons involved to choose the applicable law. But it is too soon to tell. First, let us await whether the infringement procedure which was recently initiated by the European Commission will lead to a new case against Belgium before the European Court of Justice.[18]

5.   CONCLUSION

Although my research focused on Belgian private international law and its daily practice, the empirical research method can be inspiring for further research elsewhere. I am convinced that it should be more common practice in legal research to use – apart from the classic text analysis of the regulations and the study of the jurisprudence – other sources as well. In studying the PIL Centre database I ventured onto paths unfamiliar to a legal scholar. This database gave me an insight not just into the legal *decisions* but also into the real-life legal *questions* of the persons and families involved. In the end this is where law starts.

---

[18]   See press release of 27 September 2012, IP/12/1021: 'The European Commission decided today to refer Belgium to the Court of Justice of the European Union for hindering the right to free movement of children born in Belgium who have one Belgian parent and one parent of another EU Member State nationality. For the moment, Belgian municipalities refuse to register these children under a surname other than their father's name – even if the child has already been registered under a double name in the consulate of another EU Member State.'

TRANSNATIONAL FAMILY RELATIONS INVOLVING MOROCCAN NATIONALS LIVING ABROAD: AN ANALYSIS OF THE IMPLEMENTATION OF THE MOROCCAN FAMILY CODE

Brief report on research in progress*

Marie-Claire FOBLETS

Conents

*   At the conference on *Family Law and Culture in Europe: Developments, Challenges and Opportunities* held in Bonn from 29 to 31 August 2013 at the initiative of the Commission on European Family Law I presented a research project on a subject that is closely related to the topic of the conference, but which is still in progress. It would therefore be premature to draw conclusions before publishing the results. For the purposes of this volume I present in broad outline the subject and aims of the research project discussed as well as a brief overview of the methodology adopted by the partners involved in the research. The principal investigator of this research project is the author of this brief report. She is since 2012 the director of the Department of Law and Anthropology at the Max Planck Institute for Social Anthropology (Halle, Germany) and provides the scientific coordination of the project presented here. Thanks are due to Dr Monica Sandor for her invaluable help in the preparation of the English version of this contribution. The publication of the volume in which the research results will be presented and amply commented is planned for autumn 2014. For information on the next stages of the research project and the conference being planned, please contact foblets@eth. mpg.de.

1. PROJECT DESCRIPTION

By voting for Law no. 70.03 in 2004, the Moroccan Chamber of Representatives and the Chamber of Councillors adopted a new Family Code (MFC).[1] The MFC was the subject of much commentary at the time, which helped familiarise people, especially abroad, with this new legislative instrument and especially the many changes it brought to the regulation of family relationships in Moroccan domestic law.[2] Some have considered that the Moroccan legislators had revolutionised family law, while others described the exercise as minimalist.

The research project[3] presented briefly here does not seek to take a position within this debate, which in the end is essentially a debate on the evolution of Moroccan domestic law, but to study certain very specific effects of this legislative process which is nothing short of remarkable. The aim of the project is to produce, on the occasion of the tenth anniversary of the entry into force of the new Moroccan Family Code (2004–2014), a collective publication that addresses various questions around the *concrete application*, in Morocco and in several European countries, of provisions that have a particular impact on the family situation of Moroccan nationals living abroad (MNAs).

---

[1]   Dahir no. 1.04.22 of 12 *hija* 1424 (3 February 2004) promulgating Law no. 70.03 enacting the Family Code, *Bulletin officiel* no. 5358 of 6 October 2005, 667ff.

[2]   See i.a.: A.E. Young, *Irreconcilable differences?: Shari'ah; human rights and family code reform in contemporary Morocco*, in: K.M. Clarke, M. Goodale (eds), *Mirrors of Justice: Land and Power in the Post-Cold War Era*, Cambridge U.P., 2010, 191–207; J.G. Luengos, *La reforma de la Mudawana en Marrueos: debate e implicaciones en torno a la identidad Marroqui*, in: C. de Cueto, A. Sid Ahmed (eds), *Droits humains et diversité ethnoculturelle dans l'espace méditerranéen: réalités et perspectives*, Paris, Publisud, 2007, 47–56; J. Pruzan-Joergensen, *Liberalization and Autocracy in Morocco: the puzzle of the Moudawana reform*, Saarbrücken, LAP Lambert Academic Publishing, 2012; F. Talhaoui, *La nouvelle loi marocain sur la famille: des chaînes à plus d'égalité entre hommes et femmes dans le ménage?*, in: B. Khader, e.a. (eds), *Penser l'immigration et l'intégration autrement*, Brussels, Bruylant, 2006, 337–347; M.-C. Foblets, J.-Y. Carlier, *Le Code marocain de la famille: incidences au regard du droit international privé en Europe*, Brussels, Bruylant, 2005; L. Buskens, *La droit de la famille au Maroc*, in: N. Bernard-Maugiron, B. Dupret (eds), *Ordre public et droit musulman de la famille en Europe et en Afrique du Nord*, Brussels, Bruylant, 2012, 97–126; M. Loukili, *L'ordre public en droit international privé marocain de la famille*, in: *ibid.*, 127–160; L. Jordens-Cotran, *Muslims in the Dutch legal order: subjects to local civil laws and to muslim family law*, in: S. Haas (ed), *Family, Law and Religion: debates in the Muslim world and Europe and their implications for co-operation and dialogue*, Vienna, ÖOG, Austrian Development Co-operation, 2009, 55–84.

[3]   Title in French: '*Le Code de la famille marocain – une analyse de l'application des dispositions du Code portant en particulier sur les situations familiales transnationales et/ou impliquant des ressortissants marocains résidant à l'étranger*'.

2.   A RESEARCH PROGRAMME WITH FIVE COMPONENTS

The research project consists of five components. The *first* involves performing an analysis, as detailed as possible, of the case law available since 2004 for the five European countries with the largest population of Moroccan residents: France, Italy, the Netherlands, Spain and Belgium. The aim is to undertake an in-depth analysis of the case law that can help provide a more concrete idea of the problems raised by the application of the MFC since 2004 and especially of the legal problems affecting the family lives of MNAs. The study devotes special attention to the way in which in practice the provisions of the MFC relating to marriage, divorce and filiation are applied – or rejected. In the event that they are rejected, the analysis focuses on the reasons adduced for the rejection.[4]

The analysis of the case law of the European countries selected has been entrusted to national experts in the area: for France, the work is being carried out by Professors Françoise Monéger and Hugues Fulchiron; for the Netherlands by Dr Leila Jordens-Cotran; for Belgium by Dr Jinske Verhellen and Ms Hélène Englert; for Italy by Professor Roberta Aluffi; and for Spain by Professor Anna Quiñones.

The *second* component, which is indispensable for this research, is a study of the Moroccan case law concerning MNAs. Thanks to the contribution of Professor Mohamed Loukili (Rabat-Agdal) of the Faculty of Law of the Mohammed V University in Rabat (Agdal), where he has been teaching private international law for many years, we have been able to examine more than 100 unpublished court decisions. He has also taken it upon himself to inventory the published case law. He has provided not only a summary of each decision but also translated these into French. The translation of the decisions was co-supervised by Professor emeritus Michèle Zirari, who for many years held the chair in criminal law at the same law faculty in Rabat (Agdal). Professor Loukili also agreed to carry out a detailed analysis of all the Moroccan decisions inventoried – both published and unpublished, since 2005.

The *third* component of the research is slightly different in nature: in this case we have also undertaken a modest field study at three Moroccan consulates located in medium-sized cities in three different countries in the centre of Europe (Rotterdam, Lille and Antwerp). The field study focused on the regularisation practices for marriage certificates and registrations of marriages entered into by MNAs. The field study was carried out by Dr Aboulkasem Ziani[5] and was made possible by the kind cooperation of the consular officials in the aforementioned cities.

---

4   For illustrations of this rejection, see also: N. Bernard-Maugiron, B. Dupret (eds), *supra* n. 2.

5   Dr Aboulkasem Ziani teaches sociology at the University of Marrakech.

A particularly important component of the research project is the *fourth* aspect, which has to do with the daily experience of judges in *Morocco* of applying the Code to situations involving MNAs and with the way in which those judges seek solutions to the specific cases that come before them. Professor Mohamed Loukili and Dr Ziani undertook to interview a number of these judges. A detailed questionnaire was drawn up for this purpose focusing on the thorny questions that emerged from the case law. The idea behind the initiative of interviewing Moroccan judges was to shed light on the concrete application of the Code by the Moroccan judges who have been asked to rule on family disputes among MNAs. Provided judges were open to the initiative and willing to share their experience, it was felt that surveying them could contribute to greater awareness on the part of legal practitioners in Europe – judges, administrations, lawyers, etc. – of the difficulties faced by the judicial and administrative authorities in Morocco when called upon to apply the MFC and in particular the new provisions that entered into force in 2004. For a sound understanding of the family law situation of MNAs, both from the perspective of their situation in Europe and under Moroccan law, the position taken by Moroccan judges responsible on a day-to-day basis for interpreting the Code seems absolutely essential. The aim of these interviews was to give a group of Moroccan judges the opportunity to clarify their position, by responding to a number of preselected questions.

A meeting with Moroccan judges and officials is also planned, to be held probably in Rabat in autumn 2014. This will constitute the *fifth* component of the research project. The aim of the meeting is to gather responses from the Moroccan judges and officials to the results of the research carried out in the five European countries mentioned above, in order to be able to take their reactions into consideration before proceeding to the final stage of the project, namely, the publication of a collective volume. The event will take the form of a working meeting.

The ensuing volume will, in turn, be presented at a public conference to be held either in 2014 (tenth anniversary of the new Moroccan Family Code) or, if that should not prove practicable, in early 2015. The date remains to be determined.

The five components of the research are complementary. The aim is to understand the family situation of MNAs and thereby to contribute, in the short term, to enhancing international harmonisation in their regard. Today, some ten years after the new MFC came into force, the judiciary in Europe still does not have the information necessary to guarantee transparency regarding the effective application of the provisions of the Code relating to Moroccan nationals living within its borders. But the same is true for the exportability of European (national) courts to Morocco: several arguments can be advanced in favour of greater visibility and more widespread information about the practices in this area, in order to provide practitioners of family law in Europe with clear and reliable insight into the way in which judicial decisions and documents issued by the competent civil and family law authorities in the MNAs' countries of residence are received within Moroccan internal law.

The motivation of the university partners to this project is ambitious yet simple: that greater familiarity with the provisions of the MFC as they relate to MNAs, including the way in which these have been received in Morocco since 2005, and with foreign judgments and administrative family documents which directly or indirectly concern MNAs, will contribute to a more professional and correct approach to the provisions in question on the part of those who are called upon to apply these on a day-to-day basis.

3. PRINCIPAL THEMES STUDIED

Taking legal practice as its starting point, the project identifies several specific judicial problems regularly encountered by MNAs in organising their family life. In order to gain a more concrete idea of the types of questions being addressed by the research, a few of the principal themes discussed in depth with the Moroccan judges and emerging from the analyses of the case law for each of the five European countries – relating to marriage and its effects, divorce and filiation – are set out in what follows. Each of the themes will be analysed in greater detail in the published volume, which will include a comparison of the findings for the different countries. The aim is, among others, to highlight the solutions that make it possible to achieve a viable and sustainable balance between the demands and conditions imposed by the various domestic legal systems (in both family law and private international law) involved and the particular situations of the MNA families concerned.

- The reports drawn up by several of the researchers mention the difficulty encountered by couples married civilly in Europe to have the effects of their marriage recognised in Morocco upon production of the (civil) marriage certificate from the wedding celebrated according to the law of their habitual residence. In some cases the particular difficulty is to produce acceptable proof of the marriage.
- A new provision of the 2004 Code was that found in Article 49. This provision allows spouses to indicate in their marriage contract how they wish to divide up any property acquired during the marriage. There is to date little information about the concrete application of this provision. The analysis conducted in the course of this project, in particular of Moroccan case law in the first ten years of the Code, should make it possible to fill this gap. The specific situation of MNAs is at times so complex from a legal point of view that it is to be expected that couples who marry either in Europe or in

Morocco would be better protected if they availed themselves of the opportunity offered in Moroccan law to insert in their contract clauses that take account of their personal situation. In practice, however, this possibility is rarely used. The comparative study of this project explores the reasons for the lack of interest in this option: is it due to a lack of understanding or a misunderstanding on the part of the spouses as to the (wide) margin of negotiation between them offered by Moroccan law in order to set the terms of their marriage as best suits them, or is it a matter of custom (one simply does not negotiate one's marriage)? The observations to this effect by Dr Ziani in the various consulates suggest it is mainly the latter reason. Nevertheless, the present situation means that a unique possibility which Moroccan law offers to spouses, namely to organise their marriage on an egalitarian basis and one suited to their individual situation, remains underutilised.

- As regards the dissolution of marriage, the study concentrates on the most frequent forms of divorce. In 2004 it was generally agreed that divorce based on 'irreconcilable differences' between the spouses (*chiqaq*; Article 94 of the MFC) constituted one of the major elements of the reform. The study of Moroccan case law shows, however, that the courts remain cautious, fearing appeals deemed excessive. The study reveals how, in practice, the rights of the wife and children are determined in the event of dissolution of marriage on grounds of *chiqaq*; it also examines the somewhat sensitive question of how compensation for the damage suffered by the wronged spouse, where relevant, is calculated.

- Two other, very frequent forms of marriage dissolution are divorce by mutual consent (Article 114 MFC) and divorce by *khôl* (Article 115 MFC). The introduction of divorce by mutual consent (Article 114) was received in 2004 as another considerable step forward, as it allows the spouses to agree to terminate their conjugal union *without conditions*. In Europe, the courts still frequently confuse *khôl* divorce and divorce by mutual consent, a confusion that results from the formulation of Article 115 of the Code, which provides that '[t]he spouses may agree on divorce in exchange for compensation [*khôl*] according to the provisions of Article 114 above'. Our study shows that a not insignificant consequence of this confusion is that it is not unusual for European courts to treat divorce by mutual consent as equivalent to *khôl* divorce and therefore to refuse to recognise its effects, on grounds that respect for the principle of equality between the sexes is not guaranteed.

- The study also shows how, exactly, the provision of Article 128 on the enforcement of decrees of divorce issued by European judges is applied. This provision could justifiably be considered innovative when adopted in 2004. In accordance with Article 128 of the Code, '[d]ecisions rendered by foreign courts concerning repudiation, divorce, divorce in exchange for compensation or annulment shall be admissible when they are issued by a court with jurisdiction over the matter and are based on grounds for terminating the marriage relationship that do not contradict those contained in this Code'. In other words, the Moroccan courts have to find a parallel between the ground for the dissolution of the marriage decreed abroad and a ground recognised in Moroccan law. Little was known hitherto about the way in which Moroccan judges in practice go about finding such a parallel: do any forms of divorce recognised in European family codes pose particular difficulty? A question in which this research project has taken particular interest is whether irretrievable breakdown of the marriage, which is an increasingly frequent ground invoked for divorce in Europe today, constitutes a reason that Moroccan courts consider compatible with domestic Moroccan law. The answers to this question range widely.

- A very sensitive question but one that is addressed via the various analyses of case law in the six countries (including Morocco) examined in this study is that of the best interests of the child. How are the interests of the child taken into account in the course of marriage dissolution proceedings, whether by means of a *chiqaq*, *khôl* or divorce by mutual consent? The interviews with Moroccan judges provide very valuable information on this question; to cover the subject adequately, one would have had to interview European judges on this issue as well. Doing so was beyond the bounds of this research project, however, and will have to be the task of a future project.

- Finally, probably the most contested form (in Europe) of the dissolution of marriage is that provided for in Article 78 of the Code, which states that divorce 'under judicial supervision' is intended for 'the dissolution of the bonds of matrimony exercised by the husband and wife, each according to his or her respective condition, under judicial supervision and according to the provisions of this Code'. In the French translation of the Code, the term '*répudiation*' (*talaq*) was replaced throughout by the term '*divorce*', thereby creating difficulties in understanding on the part of European courts and administrations dealing with requests for recognition of divorces decreed in Morocco on the basis of Article 78. These difficulties in understanding are to some extent fed by the new role granted to the Moroccan judge upon dissolution of a marriage under Article 78: the role of Moroccan judges seems quite limited, since it does not provide either for opposing the dissolution of marriage or for verifying the motives for the dissolution, nor does it involve enquiring as to the wishes of the wife.

4. ROLE OF CONSULAR OFFICIALS

As stated above, the study has also examined the role of the consular officials in applying the MFC to families including MNAs. The consular officials play a particular role in accompanying the family lives of MNAs. Every morning dozens of MNAs, if not hundreds, appear at the consulates in many European cities in order to seek regularisation of marriage documents, to register children born abroad or to gain recognition of civil marriages contracted before the authorities of the country of habitual residence; in some cases they simply wish to obtain information about their legal situation and about the conflict of law rules that apply to them (the application of Moroccan law or of the country of habitual residence; the competent courts, etc.). The services provided by the consulates thus play an absolutely essential role for MNAs, even if not all of them by any means make use of them.

Since so little is known about the reality on the ground, the types of services provided by the Moroccan consular officials in Europe and in particular since the entry into force of the new MFC, our study also comprises field study carried out in three consulates, as indicated above: in Lille, Rotterdam and Antwerp. The resulting observations are most interesting: they show the role of consulates, in particular as regards the application of Article 14 of the MFC, namely, the registration of civil marriages contracted before the authorities of the country of habitual residence, and how the consular officials handle the recognition of the validity of these civil marriages between MNAs if the marriages were not celebrated in the presence of two Muslim witnesses, as required by the MFC.[6]

Where a civilly married couple wishes at the same time to have the children (already) born of their union registered (that is, born since the civil marriage), it usually happens that the consulates claim not to be competent and tell the parties to seek regularisation of their family situation from the Moroccan judicial authorities. This procedure appears to be in accordance with what the MFC requires, but it does not facilitate things for the couples concerned.[7]

---

[6]   In practice, the *adouls* draw up a supplementary adular act known as ICHHAD, which mentions marriage contracted according to the law of the country of residence and that involves the presence of two Muslim witnesses, the mention of the *sadaq*, where applicable, and possibly the presence of the *wali* or any other clause in accord with the MFC. This supplementary document, once entered in the appropriate register, is attached to the civil marriage certificate and the two documents are sent to the Moroccan civil registrar for registration.

[7]   The provision of Article 14 is thus without effect on the filiation of the children. To register children as the legitimate offspring of the couple, the latter must submit a copy of the said certificate within three months to the civil registrar at the Moroccan consulate competent for the district where the certificate had been drawn up, as well as to the division of the family court of the place of birth of both of the spouses.

5. WHY FOCUS ON THE LEGAL ASPECTS OF THE FAMILY LIVES OF MNAS?

The research project is of course not yet finished. But we can already venture an answer to the question: why focus on the family lives of Moroccan nationals living abroad?

One quite innovative aspect of the 2004 MFC is that it takes into account the situation of transnational families. The past thirty or so years have seen an increasing number of Moroccan nationals affected by the internationalisation of family life: whether this involves family situations created in Morocco but lived out abroad and therefore falling under the jurisdiction of a foreign State, or situations that arise outside of Morocco involving Moroccan nationals who live abroad but wish to have the effects of their family situation recognised in Moroccan domestic law.

By showing an openness – in principle – to recognising the new reality experienced these days by thousands of Moroccan families around the world, and in particular in Europe, Morocco adopted, in 2004, the internationalist ideal held by many practitioners of family law today, who argue for greater openness by national legislators to the reality of cross-border family life.

By recognising, in particular, the possibility for MNAs to contract marriage according to the administrative procedures of the country of residence (Article 14), and by allowing for the recognition – albeit provided certain conditions are met – of judicial decrees of divorce handed down abroad that terminate a marriage involving MNAs (Article 128), the Moroccan legislators have shown trust in the administrative and judicial authorities of other countries, agreeing to recognise certain effects of their decisions within the Moroccan domestic legal order.

This study seeks to verify the extent to which this internationalist position found in the Moroccan Family Code is reflected in the facts on the ground, after ten years of application of the new MFC.

The internationalist option clearly cannot be unilateral. Its success depends on the reception of the MFC abroad as well. Our study has therefore also examined the attitude taken by the judicial and administrative authorities in Europe since 2004 when called upon to interpret the court decisions and administrative actions of Moroccan authorities involving MNAs.

On the one hand, the judicial and administrative authorities in Europe are required, when applying foreign law (in this case that of Morocco) to apply it 'in accordance with the interpretation given to it in the foreign country'.[8] This makes the application of foreign law very difficult: how is one to know precisely what this interpretation may be? On the other hand, given that Moroccan case

---

[8] See especially Article 15, 1, para. 2 of the Belgian Code of Private International Law.

law in family matters is generally very poorly understood by experts and practitioners abroad, some prejudices continue to exist. The resulting recourse to the public policy exception is frequent if not the rule. Finally, there is the question of the treatment of family law institutions unknown in European family law, such as the *sadaq* (a form of dower), and in some cases the resulting maintenance payable during the period of continence (*idda*), the consolation gift (*mut'a*) or the right of the woman to remain in the conjugal home during the period of continence, to give but a few examples.

These various factors arising from unfamiliarity with Moroccan law in turn serve to maintain a gap between the different judicial systems, in spite of the desire for openness on the part of legislators in adopting the 2004 Code; this frequently turns against the Moroccan families concerned, who thus find themselves in limping situations, i.e., their family situation does not, in legal terms, enjoy the same recognition in the different countries with which they retain very close ties. As a result, the above-mentioned openness on the part of the Moroccan legislators as expressed in the 2004 Code does not always produce the desired effect.

This study brings together a number of unpublished testimonies by practitioners in the field, including magistrates, regarding these questions of interpretation. In general, it can be said that the case law of both European and Moroccan courts relating to questions of the family lives of MNAs is inadequately known on the opposite sides of the Mediterranean. Certain prejudices continue on both parts, leading to erroneous interpretations of the provisions of the 2004 MFC.

By way of conclusion, we see two principal reasons for continuing to focus on the legal aspects of the family lives of MNAs.

The *first* argument has to do with the trust on the part of European judicial and administrative authorities in the way their decisions are treated within the Moroccan internal legal order. Given that Moroccan case law in family matters is very poorly known by experts and practitioners abroad, certain prejudices continue to exist. Consequently, recourse to the public policy exception is frequent if not the rule. This suspicion on the part of the European authorities in turn serves to maintain the gap between the different legal systems, in spite of the entry into force of the new Code in 2004.

The *second* argument is related to the first: greater familiarity with Moroccan case law would enable European practitioners – be they judges, lawyers or civil servants responsible for civil matters – to take it systematically into account. This would help prevent the multiplication of limping situations, by informing the parties involved (often spouses or partners) *in advance* that the situation they envisage entering into in Europe will necessarily meet with a refusal of recognition in Moroccan internal law. Conversely, the courts in Europe could in this way refer in their judgments on the dissolution of marriage to grounds that would help facilitate the recognition of the decision in Moroccan domestic law, without necessarily being incompatible with the laws that a European judge is required to enforce.

In sum, greater visibility of Moroccan case law in family matters involving MNAs would have the highly desirable consequence of greater professional familiarity with that case law abroad, and in particular with the way in which the foreign court decisions and administrative documents affecting the family lives of MNAs have been received in Morocco since 2005. Properly documented knowledge of Moroccan case law depends, in the first instance (1) on that case law being made available and, subsequently, (2) if possible, by means of a thorough and reliable analysis thereof for the purposes of the practice of Moroccan family law abroad. It is this twofold process that this research project seeks to undertake. The ultimate goal is to contribute to ensuring greater international harmony, in the medium term, in family situations involving MNAs. But this is probably asking too much from a modest academic project such as this one.

FAMILY LAW AS CULTURE

Werner GEPHART

Contents

1. INTRODUCTION AND OVERVIEW: WHY FAMILY LAW SHOULD BE LINKED TO THE CULTURAL BASICS OF SOCIETY

The aim of my article is to apply the 'law as culture perspective' of the Käte Hamburger Center for Advanced Study in the Humanities named 'Law as Culture' to questions of family law. I will start with the fundamental question of why culture should matter at all in family law affairs. I shall do this even though the burden of proof seems like it ought to be the other way around, that is one should have to explain why in matters so deeply related to tradition, religion and the nation as family structures and their regulations, culture should not matter at all (section 2). This is indeed not a completely innocent kind of inquiry because there is or has been at least an important debate about the 'cultural restraints argument'. To answer this question is of crucial importance for the basic orientation of our centre.

All this presupposes that we are talking about the same subject, that is to say that we are treating family – not its normative regulation but the conception of what 'family' means – as identical across different times and different civilisations. A look at family semantics in the world could reveal a wide range of differences.

Next I want to remind you of the importance family law had for the founding fathers, sons, nephews and grandchildren of the discipline I try to stand for: sociology. Especially in Durkheim's writings, the analysis of family law is a privileged methodological tool to grasp by way of the law the structures of family life (section 3).

I then have to mention the difference of law in the books and the living law approach in order to foresee what contemporary debates in European family law may mean for this fundamental distinction. We cannot avoid taking a look at the concept of law used in this context. The more we project culture into the concept of law, by way of including symbolic and ritual elements of the force of law, the easier it becomes to retrace the cultural traits of family law as well, without necessarily calling it a constraint (section 4).

This has to be tested with regard to the well known image of family law that is fraught with religious and cultural meaning (section 5).

Beyond the convergence debate of different family law cultures the encounter of models may be interesting. What does it mean when so called archaic, pre-modern family structures meet with the postmodern family, kinship ties with the weak ties of a nearly disbanded family traces (section 6)?

What we know about the world, we know by way of the media. How can family life and its legal forms impregnate our life by way of TV series, court TV shows, Hollywood A and B movies? Whether we like it or not: the representation of family worlds is part of social reality (section 7).

Finally, I would like to raise the question of what is meant by 'European' in the kind of family law that is so controversially discussed (section 8). Shall we conceive of Europe as a space where common family principles are possible? Because of the legitimising force of the experts or because of some inner communality arising from a value community?

A very last glimpse at the cultural importance (*Kulturbedeutung*) of family law analysis may be allowed in order to conclude.

2. CULTURE MATTERS: AS A CONSTRAINT OR AS A CONDITION?

The first commandment of an analysis of family law in the light of a cultural sociology of the law, as done at the Käte Hamburger Center for Advanced Study in the Humanities 'Law as Culture',[1] might be formulated as follows: You have to take 'culture' seriously!

---

[1]   For a description of the centre's program see W. GEPHART (ed.), *Rechtsanalyse als Kultur-forschung*, Frankfurt am Main 2012.

Some people might be reluctant to a perspective that gives 'culture' such a central place in the conceptualisation of a systematic access to the study of law. Why not 'civilisation'? Is the word 'culture' not contaminated politically by an attitude of superiority of those who declare themselves to be the bearer of 'culture'? And especially in a German context 'culture' has also this connotation of a horrible experience. Wolf Lepenies has told those ambivalent tales in his book *Kultur und Politik*.[2]

On the other hand, the culture-civilisation difference, so much cherished by Norbert Elias, transfers the characteristic of 'civility' to the French tradition of the court society, the centralisation of power at Versailles and the civilisation of collective feelings to the role of manners. This is an interesting perspective, but I insist however on a broad concept of culture, including the high and the lower levels in society, but primarily referring to a value connotation that brings 'culture' out of a politically and morally contaminated context.

If it is true that 'culture matters', what I will try to show in this article and which is in a certain tension to a pure and sometimes poor positivistic reading of the sphere of law, then we must take 'culture' seriously, understanding the static elements of cultural tradition as well as the dynamic forces of cultural complexity. If it would be possible also to preserve a value loaded concept of 'culture' – when Weber speaks about the 'transcendental precondition' of all *Kulturwissenschaften*, namely to take a standpoint in the world, that is *Stellungnahme*, and to give a sense to the world – *Sinnstiftung*[3] – then an interaction, a *Wechselwirkung* of 'law and culture' or 'culture and justice' may lead us back to some profound and value-laden questions of the humanities.

But is this a shared conviction among the members of the Commission on European Family Law? One could interpret the aims and intentions of that commission as incompatible with a cultural bias assumption that anthropologists and sociologists and even the European Council proclaim when stating that family law 'is very heavily influenced by the culture and tradition of national (or even religious) legal systems, which could create a number of difficulties in the context of harmonization'.[4] Masha Antokolskaia has prominently argued against the so-called 'cultural constraint argument'. It entails – as far as I see – two

---

2   W. LEPENIES, *Kultur und Politik. Deutsche Geschichten*, München/Wien 2006.

3   It is obvious that those preconditions of any kind of *Kulturwissenschaften*, *Sinnstiftung* and *Stellungnahme* intervene with the protestant's attitude towards the world. This circle has been firstly analysed, in: W. GEPHART/H. WALDENFELS (ed.), *Religion und Identität. Im Horizont des Pluralismus*, Frankfurt am Main 1999.

4   Council report on the need to approximate Member States' legislation in civil matters of 16 November 2001, 13017/01 justciv 129, p. 114, in: M. ANTOKOLSKAIA, Family Law and National Culture: Arguing against the cultural constraints argument, in: *Utrecht Law Review* 4, 2008, p. 25–34 (p. 25). See also by K. BOELE-WOELKI, Building on Convergence and Coping with Convergence in the CEFL Principles of European Family Law, in: M. ANTOKOLSKAIA (ed.), *Convergence and Divergence of Family Law in Europe*, Antwerpen/Oxford 2007, pp. 253–270 (p. 256).

elements: on the one hand an empirically meant statement that family laws are embedded in different and unique cultural contexts, composed of heritage and traditions, and on the other hand that these differences are unbridgeable, and can neither spontaneously converge nor deliberately be harmonised.

One has to go deeply into the legal culture debate in order to identify some differences between Lawrence Friedman,[5] on the one hand, and perhaps David Nelken,[6] on the other, who have done most impressive studies in the field. We do not have the time to go over this debate in fast forward. But let me remind you of some of the arguments against the thesis of unique particularism: cross-cutting affiliations simply go beyond the national borders, wherein a plurality of cultural orientations (such as the south–north dimension, for example) might prevail. Instead, progressive and conservative subcultures would have much more explanatory power, for example in the acceptance of same-sex marriage patterns and divorce rules.

Beyond those differences on the progressive–conservative scale, all-embracing European values would cut across the cultural constraint argument of unbridgeable diversity, that is a kind of European family culture centred around 'individualism and rationalism, personalism and intellectualism, rights-consciousness and dissolution of traditional authority, and respect for human rights',[7] as the aforementioned Masha Antokolskaia has formulated, in other words: patterns of modernity.

Though the cultural constraint argument is refuted, the importance of a common culture, a pan-European culture at best embedded in human rights convictions seems to be an underlying premise of the impressive work of the Commission on European Family Law. We could also interpret the findings of Marie-Claire Foblets in the sense that the cultural otherness, 'harmonised' at length within the multitude of European family legal orders, still finds an expression in the context of Islamic family law traditions.

3. FAMILY LAW AS A METHODOLOGICAL TOOL: A DURKHEIMIAN LEGACY

René König's work aside,[8] Emile Durkheim's sociology of family has received far too little attention. That said, there is a latent influence on an entire direction

---

5   Cf. L. FRIEDMAN: Legal culture and social development, in: *Law & Society Review* 4/1, 1969, pp. 29–44.

6   Cf. D. NELKEN: Using Legal Culture: Purposes and Problems, in: id. (ed.): *Using Legal Culture*, London 2012, pp. 1–51.

7   M. ANTOKOLSKAIA, Family Law and National Culture, *supra* n. 4, p. 33.

8   Reprinted in: R. KÖNIG, *Emile Durkheim zur Diskussion. Jenseits von Dogmatismus und Skepsis*, München 1978.

of sociology at the heart of which lies the sociological anthropology by Claude Lévi-Strauss.[9]

Family, marriage and kinship have taken up much space in the *Année sociologique*, and Lévi-Strauss incidentally dedicated his structural anthropology to its 'inventor'.[10] Going through the numerous reviews, a sociology of family can be reconstructed that goes beyond the fragments represented by the '*famille conjugale*'[11] and the relevant passage in *Division du travail social*.[12] The introductory lecture to the *Cours de science sociale*, which opens a lecture on the sociology of family, represents a particularly fruitful source.

Durkheim selected 'family' as a subject both thematically and didactically suited to explain what he regards as the fundamental problem in sociology, namely the change in forms of solidarity from mechanical to organic solidarity. In order to illustrate this structural change, Durkheim directs his attention to the both simplest and oldest grouping: family. As a first step, Durkheim develops a 'model' of the elements of family.

The distinction between goods and persons is fundamental. Durkheim arrives at the following conception of structure and function, in which the aspect of exchange is further systematised. He differentiates a cycle of goods from a cycle of personal relationships in which parents and children, the respective groupings of relatives as well as the state and pre-state collective general order, are distinguished.[13]

Family is portrayed as a 'system': 'The complete system of these relations that collectively constitute *family life*'.[14] The epistemological objective is the analysis of the *social life* of families, which is made up of the basic elements of property and personal relations. Having accepted this problem statement, how can the specific form of family be grasped?

From the perspective of phenomenological sociology, the task would be to trace the composition of the *lebenswelt* of families as a meaningful constitution of the 'world' and its objective, spatial, temporal and social 'structure'.[15] Durkheim also targets the family's *structure*: 'In summary, what we must seek to reconstruct is the *internal structure* of family, which alone is of scientific

---

9   C. Lévi-Strauss, *Les structure élémentaires de la parenté*, Paris 1949.
10   Cf. C. Lévi-Strauss, Ce que l'ethnologie doit à Durkheim, in: *Annales de l'Université de Paris 1*, 1960.
11   E. Durkheim, La famille conjugale, published posthumously, in: *Revue philosophique 90*, 1921, pp. 2–14 (reprinted in: Textes 3, pp. 35–49).
12   Cf. E. Durkheim, *De la division du travail social*, p. 184.
13   Cf. the chart in W. Gephart, *Gesellschaftstheorie und Recht. Das Recht im soziologischen Diskurs der Moderne*, Frankfurt 1993, p. 344. This can be verified by examining the way the relationships are arrayed, in: Introduction à la sociologie de la famille, in: *Annales de la faculté des lettres de Bordeaux 10*, 1888, pp. 257–281 (reprinted in: Textes 3, pp. 9–34, at p. 13).
14   'Le système complet de ces relations dont l'ensemble constitue *la vie de la famille se trouve*', in: Introduction à la sociologie de la famille, *supra* n. 13, p. 12, emphasis added. This and the following passages translated by the present author.
15   Cf. W. Gephart, *Gesellschaftstheorie und Recht*, Part I, Chap. 2 (pp. 55 et seq.).

interest'.[16] However, Durkheim maintains that this structure can be gleaned neither from observations of the living environment by a 'stranger', nor from authentic representations from its inhabitants. The latter are at most of literary value: 'Generally speaking, such reports and descriptions, that may certainly be of literary interest or even possess moral authority, need to be rejected as they are not sufficiently objective documents'.[17] There is but one single way to discover these structures – that from the outset are intended to be exclusively objective – and that is to grasp them personally. But where might these structures be located? The answer can be found in *Science positive de la morale en Allemagne*: 'In these manners of acting consolidated by usage that we call customs, law, morals';[18] Durkheim's reasoning once again clarifies the implicit concept of structure: 'For customs is precisely that which is shared and constant in all human conduct'.[19] In other words, *structure* refers both to concrete individuals and to a *constancy of relations* that transcends diverse time runs.[20] If this constancy can now be discerned in law and customs, it seems reasonable to draw conclusions from *law* for *structure*: 'Customs describes precisely the *structure* of the family or rather, *it represents this structure itself*'.[21]

Let us take a moment to summarise this train of thought. The object of sociological analysis is the 'life' of the family. This can only be grasped by means of objective documents that can be found in law and customs, as they represent temporally and individually persistent structures and ultimately are, in fact, identical to these structures. Narratives can be left for literati, as they do not possess the necessary objectivity.

Sociology is structural analysis, and since structures are focused in law, sociology necessarily needs to be equated to the analysis of law. In the early period of French sociology, social science was therefore *only* conceivable as legal analysis if – as Durkheim maintains – the methodological postulate of objectivity was to be respected. *Sociology is an analysis of family law!* This family law bias reaches so far as to enter Durkheim's definition of the scope of sociology, which is to cover the ontological region of the social as the realm of the *faits*

---

[16] 'En résumé ce que nous devons chercher à reconstituer c'est la *structure interne* de la famille qui seule présente un intérêt scientifique', in: Introduction à la sociologie de la famille, *supra* n. 13, p. 18, emphasis added.
[17] 'Il faut donc, en général, récuser ces récits et ces descriptions qui peuvent avoir un intérêt littéraire et même une autorité morale mais qui ne sont pas des documents suffisamment objectifs', ibid.
[18] 'Dans ces manières d'agir consolidées par l'usage qu'on appelle les coutumes, le droit, les mœurs', ibid.
[19] 'Car la coutume est justement ce qu'il y a de commun et de constant dans toutes les conduites individuelles', ibid., p. 19.
[20] For a comparative overview of structural-theoretical approaches in sociology, cf. P. M. BLAU (ed.), *Theorien sozialer Strukturen. Ansätze und Probleme*, Opladen 1978.
[21] 'Elle [la coutume] exprime donc exactement la *structure* de la famille ou plutôt *elle est cette structure elle-même*', in: Introduction à la sociologie de la famille, *supra* n. 13, p. 19, emphasis added.

sociaux. A *fait social*, so Durkheim, can be discerned wherever 'I uphold my duties as a brother, as a husband [i.e. familial duties] or as a citizen; when I observe my contractual obligations, fulfil tasks defined not by myself and my acts, but by law and morals'.[22]

This closes the loop: it is only the analysis of law that grants access to the fluid epistemological object of family life by representing a congealed form of social life that nonetheless possesses normative power. The birth of sociology from the spirit of jurisprudence – as I once termed it in my work *Gesellschaftstheorie und Recht*[23] 20 years ago by now – has *family law* as its inception point.

Family, however, can only be grasped as a locus of social life for the cultural-sociological perspective if its symbolic forms, without which social life would be unthinkable, are reinforced by the dynamic forces of social life as described in the *Formes élémentaires de la vie religieuse*.[24]

Yet from where does this normative power[25] stem? Does it come from the habits of the heart, the *'habitudes de Coeur'*, from religious traditions or from the wisdom of European experts? Before addressing this question, we direct our attention to that miserable problem of finding a concept of law that is neutral to legal cultures without forfeiting the ability to answer the question what 'family law as culture' might mean.

4.   A MULTIDIMENSIONAL CONCEPT OF LAW

As a thesis I would like to formulate as follows: 'law' is to be understood as the contrafactual symbolical generalisation of normative expectations, backed by an enforcement agency, framed by ritual procedures and embedded in a community, we call *'Rechtsgemeinschaft'*.

It is obvious that elements of Luhmann's concept of law, especially the role of normative expectations going back at least to Weber, are combined with the cultural dimension of symbols and rituals as we find them in Durkheim's *Elementary forms of social life* on the one hand and the role of the *Erzwingungsstab*, the coercive element very prominent in Weber's writings on the law, on the other.

---

22   'Quand je m'acquitte de ma tâche de frère, d'époux ou de citoyen, quand j'exécute les engagements que j'ai contractés, je remplis des devoirs qui sont définis, en dehors de moi et de mes actes, dans le droit et dans les mœurs' in: E. DURKHEIM: *Les règles de la méthode sociologique*, Paris: PuF 1993 (1895), p. 3.

23   W. GEPHART, *Gesellschaftstheorie und Recht. Das Recht im soziologischen Diskurs der Moderne*, Frankfurt am Main 1993.

24   On how to read DURKHEIM as a cultural sociologist, cf. the volume edited by J.C. ALEXANDER: *Durkheimian sociology: cultural studies*, Cambridge 1992.

25   This old fashioned type of questioning has not yet found a satisfying answer, as the conference about 'The Normative Complex. Legal cultures, validity cultures, normativities' (9–10th of April 2014) at the Center has demonstrated!

In choosing to conceive of law in this fashion, I was fully aware of the challenges this choice entails:

(1) One major problem is whether such a definition is culturally biased: in other words, whether it is able to cover the wide range of legal spheres in the global world, encompassing for example Islamic legal forms as well as those of Hindu society and the legal orders of indigenous people.
(2) A second problem would concern the applicability in the diachronic direction; the ability to grasp legal and social change.
(3) A third one seems to be the relationship to other normative orders, that is the place of law in the realm of normativity.

The aforementioned definition excludes the question of validity, both as factual one and as one that is normatively conceived. Therefore, a complementary concept of *Geltungskultur*[26] – validity culture – should be introduced as a way of justifying the normativity of norms and identifying its sources. In other words: the 'reason' of law and the 'basis' of its 'deontic power' – to use the language of Searle.

One important aspect should be maintained: by way of pursuing a pure concept of the law defined by the logic of norms and sanctions, the symbolic and the ritual dimension brings in the cultural factor without external imputation. 'Culture' is thereby built into the concept of the law. Marriage ceremonies, symbolic representation of parenthood in the mass media, the presentation of politicians in everyday life with their sexual orientations and legal interests to make their choices legally binding: all those differences may persist despite a harmonising effect at the level of norms.

The question of validity brings us back to one major field of debate at our centre, that is the close relation of law and religion.

5. SHAPES AND SHADOWS: RELIGIOUS IMAGES AND THEIR TRACES

Though the CEFL approach has been very optimistic concerning the bridgeability of cultural differences, including religiously based ones, the sociologist remains attentive to the reason of a cultural and religious foundation of family images and concepts.

---

[26] See the publication of the aforementioned conference about 'The Normative Complex' (forthcoming) and – for a first formulation: W. GEPHART/R. SAKRANI, "Recht" und "Geltungskultur". Zur Präsenz islamischen Rechts in Deutschland und Frankreich, in: W. GEPHART (ed.), *Rechtsanalyse als Kulturforschung* [Schriftenreihe des Käte Hamburger Kollegs "Recht als Kultur", ed. by W. GEPHART, Bd. 1], Frankfurt am Main 2012, p. 103–137.

The religious factor, so to speak, plays at two levels: first at that of the relationship of law to other societal spheres in general and secondly by way of an intimate relation between family structures and conceptions and the religious sphere.

(a) The *nearness or the 'elective affinity' of law and religion, its structural resemblances, in other words, is evident.* It is therefore all the more important to make analytical distinctions and empirical observations of how law and religion is interwoven.

The borders of law provide a view onto the abyss of *violence*, which – in turn – is connected with the *Sacred*, as René Girard puts it in his mimetic theory. And thus – once more – *religion* comes into play for the purpose of a humanities-based analysis of law without the necessity of criticising an innocently maintained secularisation thesis. Law is not only based on implicit religious prerequisites within the metaphorical meaning of a 'theology of the modern constitutional state'; prerequisites that are not just virulent and even inhibiting in the religious laws of Judaism, Christianity and Islam: they also pervade the legal-normative sphere of 'modern societies' as some kind of civil-religious ferments.

Within the framework of the International Centre for Advanced Studies 'Law as Culture', the complex relationship of these two basic spheres of human societies must be considered under this twofold focus of a religious-denominational relativity and orientation of legal orders and in terms of a structural affinity between law and religion, both of which appear as increasingly delivering an identity-generating potential. This issue is being addressed in many parts of the world. The reference to the Sharia after the Arab Spring is the most recent example for this identity-confirming function. Any crucial achievement in this domain requires further dynamic interaction between cultural sciences, humanities including religious studies and legal theory.

(b) What are the consequences of those general reflections for the field of family law?

The tale of family law in Europe[27] cannot be told in terms other than those of a religious history of medieval canon law including its roots in Roman law, the role of the Protestant Reformation, the Enlightenment and the exportation of the legal secular transplants promulgated by the *code civile*. In the nineteenth century, the picture becomes more complex: according to Masha Antokolskaia, the progressive–conservative divide emerged during this period and emcompasses agrarian Catholic countries as well as modernising Nordic countries with a historical protestant background. Besides human rights law that intervenes in family law traditions (Article 8 of the European Convention on Human Rights), secularisation and de-ideologisation of family law seems to

---

[27]   See M. ANTOKOLSKAIA, *Harmonisation of Family Law in Europe: A Historical Perspective. A Tale of Two Millenia*, Antwerpen/Oxford 2006.

prescribe a general trend in the evolution of European family law(s). Divorce, non-marital cohabitation and its recognition, illegitimate children, new family structures and the new property regime. The legal system has not refused to respond to changes in society. Yet the question remains whether religious affiliations in accepting non traditional forms of family life can be simply reduced to the progressive–conservative distinction or whether confessional lines demarcate differences in the openness to embrace or firmness to resist change.

According to my appraisal of the field, to the extent I am familiar with it, an inquiry about the confessional influence in family law projects remains an empirical necessity. How the churches react not only to the prevalence of civil marriage, but to forms of cohabitation, divorce and legal separation, partnership models and the revival of formalism in family law when it comes to same-sex-marriage; all this seems to be of the greatest empirical and comparative interest allowing a better insight into how the discourse about legal regulation of family life in Europe is embedded in religion.

We remain so far within the same family of family law in Europe. The family law of the 'other' is represented by Islamic law and different Muslim communities in Europe. I leave aside the problem that in Andalusia, Sicily and as some historians say even in the common law, the traces of Islamic legal traditions should be reevaluated. The whole matter is very complex, even though the 'otherness' is remarkable: polygamy, divorce proceedings, marriage of minors, dowry, parental responsibilities in the case of divorce – all these institutes are incompatible with traditional values and legal practices in Europe. The announced clash of legal cultures is however less grave than some theorists predicted. Private international law on the one hand and minority jurisprudence on the other is the normative ground where conflict resolution is settled. But this is another story and would deserve further reflections.

6. CONFLICTS OR DIALOGUES: THE ENCOUNTER OF FAMILY CONCEPTIONS AND REALITIES

If we do not take account of the facticity of the global age[28] we stick to the restrictions of methodological nationalism. The tools employed by this conference transcend such nationalism. In other words, does globalisation affect family structures? And what are the judicial necessities to deal with this change on the stage of family landscapes.

---

[28] See M. ALBROW, *The Global Age. State and Society Beyond Modernity*, Cambridge 1996; see also M. ALBROW, *Sociological Essays for the Global Age*, Frankfurt am Main 2014 [Schriftenreihe "Recht als Kultur", vol. 5, forthcoming].

Theories of migration, as one major cause of globalisation, explain the success of migrants in dependence of their ability to use family networks in the society they migrate to. One of my doctoral students was even able to identify the effect of family ties comparing legal and illegal immigrants in the city of Bonn.[29] Elisabeth Beck-Gernsheim made a strong argument that perhaps the so-called premodern family structures with broad affiliations may be much better suited to respond to challenges of globalisation in order to produce solidarity, as Parsons might have said. This represents an alternative narrative to that of the nuclear family, so cherished in a former phase of debates on family due to their supposed adaptation to the conditions of 'modernity'.[30] If family communities live at distant places without losing the chance to communicate through the internet (e.g. via Skype), those so-called archaic kinship networks may become a new model of family ties. This would be an example of how globality reaches out to the proper space of family structures and reverses traditional images of family by way of re-traditionalising this basic structure of society we call 'family' in our occidental horizon. The last point of our reflection will focus on the kind of tension in which the universal institution stands to 'modernity'.

7. FAMILY LAW EXPRESSED IN CULTURAL FORMS: THE FAMILY IN THE COURT TV SHOW

If it is true that an understanding of the living law in contrast to the law in the books also needs to include the presentational form of the media in our societies, then representations of the family in film and television, their obligations and resolutions of conflicts by way of the law must stand in the centre of a cultural sociology of family law.

One can imagine how useful it would be to compare migrant children in Dutch television or translations of Chinese family ideals into television or, as presented in a recent episode of the German television programme *Stromberg*, the transfer of family conflicts from Japan to the Japanese community of Düsseldorf clashing with less honour-oriented behavioural patterns in Germany. As exaggerated and caricatured as the representation may have been, such shows can nevertheless illustrate to what extent national and cultural identities are

---

29   C.A. Silva Dittborn, *Wir sind keine Fische dieses Ozeans. Eingliederungsprozesse von legalen, legalisierten und "illegalen" Migranten aus der Communidad Andina in Bonn*, Dissertation Bonn 2011.

30   E. Beck-Gernsheim, Ferngemeinschaften. Familien in einer sich globalisierenden Welt, in: G. Burkart (ed.), *Zukunft der Familie. Prognosen und Szenarien*, Leverkusen 2009, pp. 93–109.

represented by way of their specific family patterns.[31] Very often – as Nathalie Roebbel, another of my doctoral students, has shown in her study of Italian and Spanish family structures[32] – the myth of a family type has nothing to do with the reality of how these families actually live. On the other hand, as Patricia Pisters and Wim Staat sum up in their impressive collection *Shooting the Family*, family matters of all kinds, both reinforcements and radical reconfigurations of traditional family values, are increasingly constructed and reconfigured in a mediated form: 'the "reel family" (as in the "visual family shot") has become an important medium for intercultural affairs'.[33]

The 'family album', a wonderful methodological instrument for reading family structures, is completed by home movies and videos of a particularistic kind. There, we can find the pluralisation of family life and family forms, monoparental intergenerational relations, homosexual couples, up to affinities to friendship groups – the American series *Friends* undoubtedly portrays a substitute for family and some kind of blurring of the borders of the nuclear family model.

Against such tendencies to dissolve the concept of family into actor network concepts (Bruno Latour), assemblage (Michel Callon) or praxeological field concepts (Pierre Bourdieu), the law persists in a terminology that – as we saw during the conference on which this book is based – is able to adapt to new challenges. While it may very often not be at the forefront of cultural change, it not only identifies such shifts and lends them facticity, but also endows them with 'deontic power', as John Searle calls it.

8. THE EMERGENCE OF EUROPEAN NORMATIVITY REGARDING FAMILY

Even if cultural anthropologists and ethnologists are very critical of using an unreflected concept of family, that openly or tacitly identifies with the nuclear family, the success story of this social institution is simply fascinating.

'Utopia' denied the role of family; in Fourier's, Thomas Morus' and the Kibbutz projects, family acts as a particularistic counterpart to modernity, as Alois Hahn has shown.[34] The search for the 'modern family' looks like a contradiction in itself. Functional theories of the modern family always insisted on the corrective role of family towards the excesses of the mass and market

---

[31]   See as an example of family analysis in the US: L. SPIGEL, *Make Room for TV. Television and the Family Ideal in Postwar America*, Chicago/London 1992.

[32]   Cf. N. ROEBBEL, *Familie in Italien an der Schwelle zum 21. Jahrhundert*, Opladen 2006.

[33]   P. PISTERS/W. STAAT (eds.), *Shooting the Family. Transnational Media and InterculturalValues*, Amsterdam 2005.

[34]   Cf. A. HAHN, Familienutopien, in: G. BURKART (ed.), *Zukunft der Familie*, supra n. 30, pp. 299–310.

society: *emotionaler Spannungsausgleich* was the magic formula to give the family a value in the project of modernity! The family had to play the counterpart to the cold hands of the market. And when the theory of communicative action makes the diagnosis that modernity is characterised by a necessary tension between the 'life world' and the 'system's world', Habermas thinks about the role of family! And there is no doubt that in the semantic part of Tönnies' famous *Gemeinschaft und Gesellschaft*, the examples to demarcate the differences between those two social forms revolve around the vocabulary of the family. But whenever we characterise system worlds through family semantics, we end up in premodern *familism*, whether it be in politics, where it is known as nepotism, or in the market systems or in the art world. Axel Honneth's book *Das Recht der Freiheit* was criticised because in his re-launch of Hegel's philosophy of law he gave such a large room for the analysis of family.[35]

It is unbearable to read Auguste Comte's sociology of the family as a combination of the inferiority of women and the priority of the elder to the younger generation. He would have fallen completely out of historical favour had he not met Clothilde de Vaux, the adored figure of his later life, who urged him to convert from the most famous critique of the metaphysical and the theological age to proclaim positivism in the form of a new catechism in which the beautiful wife left by her unfaithful husband with two children who never followed his desire became the new saint of a religion of modernity! That is why her memory was celebrated in the conference brochure.

Herbert Spencer is no less crazy about family life. He, who never produced a family of his own, but projected himself into existing family structures, was not only a founder of British sociology, but also an inventor.[36] His famous chapter about 'Domestic Institutions' must be read in the light of this personal tragedy. Max Weber's family life was overshadowed by a complex affinity to his cousin Marianne who became his spouse. The late experience of an erotic life, if we must believe the biographers of Weber, starting with Martin Green's study about the Richthofen sisters and lately ending with Joachim Radkau's scandalous life story, was linked to a piano player from the chocolate dynasty Tobler and a distant relative of a certain red baron, namely the beautiful Else, whose sister was married to famous novelist David H. Lawrence. But scandals in the family did not hinder Weber from positing family in the process of rationalisation: the separation of household and enterprise (*'Haushalt und Betrieb'*) is a precondition of capitalism. This was one decisive moment in his doctoral dissertation on the *'Handelsgesellschaften im Mittelalter'*.[37] The 'house' and the household is Weber's

---

[35] A. HONNETH, *Das Recht der Freiheit*, Frankfurt 2011, pp. 277–317.
[36] His ideal of the caring wife healing the husband laid down in a hospital bed, is visualised in W. GEPHART, *Gründerväter. Soziologische Bilder mit Deutungen von Alois Hahn, Wolf Lepenies, Richard Münch u.a.*, Opladen 1998.
[37] M. WEBER, *Zur Geschichte der Handelsgesellschaften im Mittelalter. Nach südeuropäischen Quellen*, Tübingen 2008 (1889).

starting point, although he is concerned with the economic unity it represents rather than the emotive qualities of family life so much cherished in the code of Romantic love and varied in the British code of companionship (of which Spencer's phantasm is one example).

Do we dispose of a European source of normativity, of bindingness, of obligatory rules that are so to say sacred, as the French Declaration of Human Rights once demanded and the catholic interpretation of Article 6 of the German Basic Law tried to presume, whereas the Article 12 of the MRK stipulates in a laconic way the right to marry and found a family, whatever 'family' may mean?

What is 'European' in our discussion? The free choice of life partners, the non-discrimination of homosexual orientations, the equality of the sexes, the prohibition of genderism, some equity in property rights, age limits as an entry barrier to legitimate marriage. 'Nowhere' does otherness seems so evident as in the deeply rooted convictions of the conscience collective that shapes our memory and our projects for the future. A comparative cultural sociology of family and family-like structures would have to use the juristic discourse about the best laws to guarantee a mediation between the necessity to raise the biological *Mängelwesen* by a protective institution that does not suffocate the individual aspirations of its members, delivering the locus for solidarity and life chances, protecting against the inbuilt ambiguity of communal terror and destitution and the freedom to distance oneself from the highly emotionalised sphere of family relations.

All this sounds like 'European universalism'. Why should it not bridge the so-called unbridgeable gap between different legal cultures? But awareness of difference and the right to difference within commonness seems a strong point in the self-conception of Europe that from the beginning has been conceived as a *Rechtsgemeinschaft*, a legal community.